Secret Dialogues

Pitt Latin American Series

Billie R. DeWalt,

General Editor

Reid Andrews,

Catherine Conaghan,

and

Jorge I. Domínguez,

Associate Editors

Kenneth P. Serbin

Secret Dialogues

Church-State Relations, Torture, and Social Justice

in Authoritarian Brazil

University of Pittsburgh Press

Published by the University of Pittsburgh Press, Pittsburgh, Pa. 15261

LIBRARY OF CONGRESS CATALOGING-IN-PUBLICATION DATA
Serbin, Kenneth P.
  Secret dialogues : church-state relations, torture, and social justice in authori-
tarian Brazil /
Kenneth P. Serbin.
    p. cm. — (Pitt latin american series)
  Includes bibliographical references and index.
    ISBN 0-8229-4123-6 (alk. paper) — ISBN 0-8229-5726-4 (pbk. : alk. paper)
    1. Comisión Bipartite—History.   2. Catholic Church—Brazil—Political
activity—History—20th century.   3. Church and state—Catholic Church—
History—20th century.   4. Church and state—Brazil—History—20th century.
5. Brazil—Politics and government—1964–1985.   I. Title.   II. Series.
BX1466.2 .S48 2000
981.06'3—dc21   00-009649

Photo credits: Arquivo Nacional (cover and figures 4, 5, 9, 11–13, 15, 17, 19, 21–23, 25,
31, 32), CAALL (14), Maria Aparecida de Jesus da Silva family (29), FGV/CPDOC–
Arquivo Antônio Carlos Muricy (1, 3, 6–8, 10, 16, 26), FGV/CPDOC–Arquivo Haroldo
Pereira (2), Leme family (33), Terry Vincent McIntyre (30), Vice-Admiral Roberval
Pizzaro Marques (20), Evangelina Ribeiro family (27), O São Paula (34, 35), Kenneth P.
Serbin (18, 24), Virote family (28).

On the cover and title page: Cadets from the Brazilian Naval Academy (Escola Naval)
parading on the Avenida Presidente Vargas, Rio de Janeiro, Independence Day, 1968.
The Igreja de Candelária (Candelária Church) stands in the background.

For my parents and for Regina

Where does social justice end and subversion begin?
— *Dom Avelar Brandão Vilela, primate of Brazil*

Contents

Preface

This is the story of Brazil's Bipartite Commission, an effort by
Roman Catholic bishops and generals to overcome Church-state conflict during the military dictatorship of 1964–1985. The Bipartite and
other, related dialogues took place in secrecy, in the shadows of a
government that maintained a facade of democracy while cracking
down on opponents with the help of troops, spies, and torturers. The
Bipartite met from 1970 to 1974—during the period known in Brazil
as the *anos de chumbo*, the "leaden years" of the worst repression (see,
for example, the excellent collection of military interviews in
D'Araujo, Soares, and Castro 1994a). The history of the Bipartite provides a new understanding of how ecclesiastical-military relations
developed while the Roman Catholic Church acquired its famed role
as the "voice of the voiceless" against the inequities and atrocities of
the dictatorship. It is a story of ideological debate, accusation and
counteraccusation, and political compromise involving the competition between Brazil's two leading institutions in their bids to influence society. The story is also about the politics of human rights,
including the struggle over proof and denial of the existence of torture. Underlying the story is the tension between power and faith.
Out of these pages emerges the age-old question: when and how does
one talk with an adversary?

Starting with the Russian Revolution in 1917, and especially after
1945, the world was rent by the struggle between Communism and
capitalism, East and West. In the 1960s and 1970s, the cold war
caused intense political polarization throughout Latin America,
leading to the formation of yet another (and perhaps not the last)
wave of authoritarian states. This polarization had enormous impact
on institutions and ideology. In Brazil the armed forces viewed them-

selves as defending traditional Western Christian civilization against subversion, while sectors of the Church attempted to redefine the Christian mission by experimenting with new emphases on peace, development, and social justice. These differences produced deep conflict between the Church and the military.

This book is written as the world adapts to the post–cold war order. Polarization is gone, and with it the simple and attractive division between "left" and "right" that suffused thinking on Latin America (Fagen 1995). After five hundred years of their country's history Brazilians today are engaged in a struggle to strengthen democracy and the ideals of full citizenship and human rights for all, a process that has bred much interest in the country's authoritarian past. In December 1995 the government began officially recognizing the victims of the dictatorship and compensating their families. The writing of the history of the military regime has also begun. Archives are opened, once forbidden stories told, new interpretations offered. This book is part of the process of reassessment. Keeping in sight the major political, social, and religious themes of the era, the book explores the hidden dimension of dialogue and conciliation—the back channels of contact always reserved for the powerful. No matter how strong the temptation, history must not be seen in a Manichaean way but as conflicts among individuals whose personalities and attitudes have been sculpted by numerous historical factors.

The story of the Bipartite stirs memories and controversies, challenges assumptions, and reveals secrets. In Brazil, it will undoubtedly spark debate within both the armed forces and the Church, on both the left and the right, and among scholars. I have approached the Bipartite as a professional historian, but also as one who cares deeply about Brazil, its people, and its institutions. It is my hope that this book will contribute to a greater understanding of one of Brazil's most difficult periods and its legacy for Brazilians today.

Perhaps contrary to the academic canon, I have tried to write in a style accessible to a wide audience. I owe the inspiration for this goal to the late John Hersey, a masterful teacher and friend whose course at Yale on nonfiction writing taught me that historians should strive to portray people in all their simplicity and complexity. I also thank Dennis Macura and Phyllis Williams for teaching the basics of the craft of writing, and Richard W. Fox for introducing me to the passion of history. Paul Bass was another source of inspiration.

This book is possible only because of the work of previous scholars of the Brazilian Church and military regime. Three in particular have deeply influenced my work, unselfishly provided encouragement and guidance, and opened doors in

Brazil since I first began studying the Church in 1986: Thomas C. Bruneau, Scott Mainwaring, and Ralph Della Cava. I especially thank Ralph for countless hours of discussion about the Church, invaluable assistance in Brazil, and (most important) friendship. Tom furnished excellent commentary on the entire manuscript, as did Brian Loveman, Anthony Pereira, Carol Drogus, and Meg Crahan. Peter Beattie read chapters 2 and 10; the latter was also read by Dain Borges, Emerson Giumbelli, and João Roberto Martins Filho.

In Brazil I received generous and precious assistance from political journalist Elio Gaspari, an immense, perceptive, and no-nonsense repository of information on the history of the military regime. Elio suggested avenues of research and also read the manuscript. Celso Castro first pointed out to me the existence of important documentation on the Bipartite and helped in many other ways. Others who facilitated my work were Father Alberto Antoniazzi, Father Virgílio Leite Uchôa, Father Celso Pedro da Silva, Father Marcelo Azevedo, S.J., Riolando Azzi, General Mário Orlando Ribeiro Sampaio, João Roberto Martins Filho, Marcelo Ridenti, Cecília Coimbra, João Luiz Peçanha, Marco Aurélio Vannucchi Leme de Mattos, Aldo Vannucchi, Egle Maria Vannucchi Leme, José de Oliveira Leme, Gonzaga Souza, Terry Vincent and Zezé McIntyre, Alexandre Oliveira de Almeida, Célia Costa, Luiz Alberto Gómez de Souza, Lúcia Ribeiro, Aloysio de Oliveira Martins Filho and Rosângela Mello, Henrique Samet, Sátiro Nunes, Adriano and Arlete Diogo, Amelinha Teles, Magali Godoy, Pierre Sanchis and the members of the former Grupo de Estudo do Catolicismo of the Instituto de Estudos da Religião, Miguel Carter, and Alexandre Brandão Martins Ferreira. Of great assistance were the staffs of the Centro de Pesquisa e Documentação da História Contemporânea do Brasil, the Arquivo Público do Estado do Rio de Janeiro, the Arquivo do Estado de São Paulo, the Arquivo Nacional, the Diocese of Barra do Piraí–Volta Redonda, the Biblioteca Cardeal Câmara of the Archdiocese of São Sebastião do Rio de Janeiro, the Arquivo Edgard Leuenroth, the Central de Documentação e Informação Científica "Prof. Casemiro dos Reis Filho," the Instituto Nacional de Pastoral, the Centro Alceu Amoroso Lima para a Liberdade, and the Centro de Documentación y Archivo para la Defensa de los Derechos Humanos. Father Charles Antoine and Margarita Durán provided assistance in Paraguay. In the United States valuable assistance and support came from Timothy Power, David Dixon, Jeffrey Lesser, Michael Weis, Nancy Stimson, Steve Elliott, Marshall Buelna, Julie Edson, and Joe McGowan. I also thank Eric Van Young, Paul Drake, Steven Topik, Peter Evans, Michael Monteón, Joe Foweraker, and Aralia López González for intellectual guidance and support over the years. Loris Zanatta provided copies of important documents from the Archive of the Argentine Embassy to the Holy See. James Green furnished papers from the Arquivo do Itamaraty.

In addition, I wish to thank the many individuals in the Roman Catholic Church of Brazil, retired members of the Brazilian armed forces, and other Brazilian citizens who agreed to be interviewed. I extend my gratitude to those organizations that have provided funding for this research: the North-South Center at the University of Miami and the Department of History, the Office of the Dean of Arts and Sciences, and the TransBorder Institute of the University of San Diego. At Miami, Ambassador Ambler Moss and Robin Rosenberg provided the opportunity to begin this research; and in San Diego, Patrick Drinan, James Gump, Lisa Hoffman, Iris Engstrand, and Dan Wolf enabled me to continue it. I also thank Cambridge University Press for permission to reprint as chapter 10 most of my article "The Anatomy of a Death: Repression, Human Rights and the Case of Alexandre Vannucchi Leme in Authoritarian Brazil," *Journal of Latin American Studies* 30 (1998), 1–33. At the University of Pittsburgh Press special encouragement came from Eileen Kiley, Niels Aaboe, and Mark Jacobs helped smooth the path to publication. Many thanks also go to Pippa Letsky for a fine job of copy-editing.

Additional helpful comments on the work came from Maria Celina D'Araujo, Gláucio Soares, Antonio Carlos Quicoli, Michael Fleet, Manuel Vásquez, Michael LaRosa, José Casanova, Maria Aparecida de Aquino, Maria de Lourdes Monaco Janotti, Alexander Wilde, Louis Warren, Elaine Elliott, Jeff Ravine, Hector Aguirre, Elizabeth Bailey, James Black, Kevin Bratsch, Orousha Digius, James Gentry, James Gonzales, Steve Lawrence, Doug Raidt, Signe Salminen, Lucinda Snyder, Jeanne Tannone, Phillip Trotter, Jim Westlund, Dulce Chaves Pandolfi, Lúcia Lippi de Oliveira, Delaine Alvares, Janaina Teles, Luiz Lima Vailati, Sidney Oliveira Pires Júnior, Eduardo Yoshimori Ochi, and Regiane Augusto.

Most of all, I wish to thank those closest to me who have supported my work during this project and over the years—Stephen Downing, David Chappell, Stephen Prothero, Donald Gastwirth, John Glick, Maryse Bacellar *(minha mãe brasileira)*, Roberto Grimes, Mário Teodoro de Barros, Lourdes Alves Barros, Rogério Alves de Barros, Ricardo Alves de Barros; along with my parents, Paul and Carol Serbin; my sister Donna and her family; and above all, my wife Regina Barros Serbin, for tolerance, patience, and unending love.

All translations of documents from the original Portuguese into English are the author's. All variant spellings of certain Portuguese names (for example, Vannucchi/Vannuchi, Candido/Cândido, Castello/Castelo) are correct.

Glossary and Key to Abbreviations

Abertura—the political opening started under the administration of President Ernesto Geisel (1974–1979) and continued under President João Baptista de Oliveira Figueiredo (1979–1985). It resulted in the return to civilian rule.

ACB—Ação Católica Brasileira (Brazilian Catholic Action). A movement for the Catholic laity (nonclergy) first organized in the 1930s and politically significant in the 1950s and 1960s.

ACM—Arquivo Antônio Carlos (da Silva) Muricy

ADBPVR—Arquivo da Diocese de Barra do Piraí–Volta Redonda (Archive of the Diocese of Barra do Piraí–Volta Redonda)

ADESG—Associação dos Diplomados da Escola Superior de Guerra (National War College Alumni Association)

AEAASS—Archivo de la Embajada de la República Argentina ante la Santa Sede (Archive of the Argentine Embassy to the Holy See)

AEL—Arquivo Edgard Leuenroth

AESP—Arquivo do Estado de São Paulo (Archive of the State of São Paulo)

AI-1—Institutional Act No. 1

AI-5—Institutional Act No. 5. Issued on December 13, 1968, the fifth and most harsh in a series of dictatorial decrees by the military regime. It closed the Congress, eliminated civil liberties and freedom of the press, and gave the military carte blanche to squash the opposition.

AIB—Ação Integralista Brasileira (Brazilian Integralist Action). A quasi-fascist organization favored by conservative officers and churchmen in the 1930s.

ALN—Ação Libertadora Nacional (National Liberating Action). The most threatening urban guerrilla organization of the late 1960s and early 1970s. It was headed by Carlos Marighella, who was assassinated in November 1969. Members of the Dominican order collaborated with the ALN.

Glossary and Key to Abbreviations

APERJ—Arquivo Público do Estado do Rio de Janeiro (Public Archive of the State of Rio de Janeiro)

BEMFAM—Sociedade de Bem-Estar Familiar do Brasil (Brazilian Society for Family Welfare). Against the Church's wishes, it set up family planning clinics and distributed birth control devices.

BMFA—Branca de Mello Franco Alves Collection

BNM—Brasil: Nunca Mais (Brazil Never Again). A project sponsored by the archdiocese of São Paulo that collected military court records documenting the practice of torture. *Brasil: nunca mais* became a best-seller in 1985. The archive is an important source for scholars of the military regime.

CAALL—Centro Alceu Amoroso Lima para a Liberdade (Alceu Amoroso Lima Center for Liberty)

CDADDH—Centro de Documentación y Archivo para la Defensa de los Derechos Humanos (Documentation Center and Archive for the Defense of Human Rights)

CEBs—Comunidades Eclesiais de Base (Basic Ecclesial Communities). One of the most important innovations of the Popular Church of the 1970s and 1980s.

CEDIC—Central de Documentação e Informação Científica "Prof. Casemiro dos Reis Filho"

CELAM—Conselho Episcopal Latino-americano (Council of Latin American Bishops). Its second general conference at Medellín, Colombia, in 1968 resulted in a radical document calling for social justice in Latin America.

CENIMAR—Centro de Informações da Marinha (Navy Information Center). A secret and effective military intelligence unit. Political prisoners were tortured there.

CIE—Centro de Informações do Exército (Army Information Center). An important military intelligence unit charged with fighting the guerrillas in the Amazon and elsewhere.

CISA—Centro de Informações e Segurança da Aeronáutica (Air Force Information and Security Center). An important military intelligence unit. Political prisoners were tortured there.

CJP-BR—Pontifícia Comissão Justiça e Paz–Seção Brasileira (Pontifical Peace and Justice Commission–Brazilian Section)

CJP-SP—Comissão Justiça e Paz da Arquidiocese de São Paulo (Peace and Justice Commission of the Archdiocese of São Paulo)

CM—*Comunicado Mensal*. A monthly publication that reported on CNBB activities and published key documents of the organization.

CNBB—Conferência Nacional dos Bispos do Brasil (National Conference of the Bishops of Brazil). A national organization of Brazil's bishops that met regularly to discuss religious, social, and political issues. It became the voice of the Brazilian Church in the 1970s.

xiv

Concordat—an agreement between the Vatican and a national state that grants the Church certain privileges, often in return for political support

Conscientização—political "consciousness-raising," one of the main goals of the CEBs and the Popular Church

CPDOC—Centro de Pesquisa e Documentação de História Contemporânea do Brasil (Center for Research and Documentation in Brazilian Contemporary History). Important repository of oral history interviews and archives of Brazil's political elite.

CPT—Comissão Pastoral da Terra (Pastoral Land Commission). One of the most important innovations of the Popular Church of the 1970s, it sought to protect and assist small landholders in the São Félix region, the Amazon, and elsewhere.

DEOPS-SP—Departamento Estadual de Ordem Política e Social, São Paulo (State Department of Political and Social Order). An important police unit that combated the revolutionary movements of the late 1960s and early 1970s.

Desaparecido—an individual who disappeared as a result of the repressive forces' operations against the opposition

Descompressão—decompression of political tensions (see also distensão)

Distensão—the *descompressão* (decompression) or lessening of political tensions in the mid-1970s that eventually led to *abertura* (political opening).

DNS—Doctrine of National Security

DOI-CODI—Destacamento de Operações de Informações and the Centro de Operações de Defesa Interna (Detachment for Information Operations and Internal Defense Operations Center). The DOI-CODI was the popular term for the interrogation and torture centers run by the Army. In reality, abuses took place only at the DOI; the CODI constituted a meeting of intelligence officials.

DOPS—Departamento de Ordem Política e Social

DOPS-GB—Departamento de Ordem Política e Social da Guanabara (Department of Political and Social Order in Guanabara state. Guanabara was the political denomination for the city of Rio de Janeiro from 1960 to 1975).

EMBRATUR—Empresa Brasileira de Turismo (Brazilian Federal Tourist Agency)

ESG—Escola Superior de Guerra (National War College). A study center that educated both military officers and civilians in the Doctrine of National Security. It furnished the military regime with ideological justification.

FEB—Força Expedicionária Brasileira (Brazilian Expeditionary Force). Brazilian force that fought beside U.S. troops in Italy during World War II. Its leaders established close ties with the U.S. military and later became part of the conspiracy against President João Goulart in 1964.

FGV—Fundação Getúlio Vargas (Getúlio Vargas Foundation)

1st AIB—First Armored Infantry Battalion

Glossary and Key to Abbreviations

IBRADES—Instituto Brasileiro de Desenvolvimento (Brazilian Development Institute). A Jesuit study center that specialized in grassroots education. Attacked by the security forces in 1970.

INP—Instituto Nacional de Pastoral (National Pastoral Institute)

IPES—Instituto de Pesquisas e Estudos Sociais (Institute for Research and Social Studies). One of the organizations that conspired to overthrow President João Goulart in 1964.

ISEB—Instituto Superior de Estudos Brasileiros (Advanced Institute for Brazilian Studies). A nationalistic think tank at the Ministry of Education in the mid-1950s and early 1960s. Closed by the military regime because of alleged ties to Communism.

JB—Jornal do Brasil. An important newspaper in Rio de Janeiro.

Jesuits—a highly prestigious male religious order of the Catholic Church with special allegiance to the pope and known for its intellectual and educational activities. Very prominent in twentieth-century Brazil.

JOC—Juventude Operária Católica (Catholic Youth Workers). A progressive Catholic Action movement criticized by the conservative clergy and attacked by the military regime.

JUC—Juventude Universitária Católica (Catholic University Youth). A progressive Catholic Action movement closed by the bishops and attacked by the military.

LSN—Lei de Segurança Nacional (National Security Law)

MDB—Movimento Democrático Brasileiro (Brazilian Democratic Movement). The opposition party from 1965 to 1979.

MEB—Movimento de Educação de Base (Basic Education Movement). Employed grassroots education techniques among the poor. Attacked by the military regime.

MOLIPO—Movimento de Libertação Popular (Movement for Popular Liberation). A violent revolutionary organization destroyed by the military in the early 1970s.

Moral concordat—the informal, unwritten political agreement between the Brazilian state and the Catholic Church that functioned between 1930 and 1970.

MPL—Movimento Popular de Libertação (Popular Liberation Movement). A Christian-Marxist revolutionary organization repressed by the military in the early 1970s.

OBAN—Operação Bandeirantes (Bandeirantes Operation). A repressive organization started in São Paulo in 1969. It was replaced by the DOI-CODI the following year but to this day many Brazilians still refer to the unit as OBAN.

OESP—O Estado de São Paulo. An important newspaper in São Paulo.

PCB—Partido Comunista Brasileiro (Brazilian Communist Party). In the 1960s thousands of militants left the party, which was opposed to violent action against the military regime, to join revolutionary movements such as the ALN.

Popular Church—a wing of the Brazilian Catholic Church that emphasized the struggle for social justice and human rights and peaceful opposition to the military regime

PUC-RJ—Pontifícia Universidade Católica do Rio de Janeiro (Pontifical Catholic University of Rio de Janeiro). One of Brazil's most traditional institutions of higher education.

PUC-SP—Pontifícia Universidade Católica de São Paulo (Pontifical Catholic University of São Paulo)

REB—Revista Eclesiástica Brasileira

S2—internal security section of a unit of the Brazilian Army

SAR—Serviço de Assistência Rural (Rural Assistance Service)

SEDOC—Serviço de Documentação

SNI—Serviço Nacional de Informações (National Information Service). A government intelligence agency opened by the military regime in 1964. In each military government, its head was one of the most powerful men in the president's cabinet.

Te Deum—a thanksgiving service

UDN—União Democrática Nacional (National Democratic Union). A conservative political party in the period from 1945 to 1965.

UNE—União Nacional dos Estudantes (National Union of Students)

USP—Universidade de São Paulo (University of São Paulo). Brazil's first university and a center of student and revolutionary upheaval in the late 1960s and early 1970s.

Vatican II—the Second Vatican Council (1962–1965) brought together the world's Catholic bishops in a series of meetings to rethink the life and constitution of the Church. It advocated the most sweeping reforms in the history of the Church.

Timeline of Important Events

March 31–April 1, 1964. Led by General Muricy, Army troops invade Rio de Janeiro to depose President João Goulart.

April 15, 1964. Castello Branco becomes president.

March 1966. General Muricy and Dom Hélder end their thirty-year friendship.

March 15, 1967. Costa e Silva becomes president.

November 1967. Dom Waldyr enters into conflict with 1st AIB after soldiers enter his home and detain priests and others.

1968. Medellín document.

March 1968. Student Edson Luís shot by a policeman in Rio de Janeiro. Protests in major cities.

December 13, 1968. Military hard-liners force President Costa e Silva to issue AI-5.

May 1969. Right-wing terrorists murder Father Henrique Pereira Neto, an assistant to Dom Hélder Câmara.

July 1969. Operação Bandeirantes created in São Paulo to hunt down subversives.

August 1969. Costa e Silva suffers a stroke and is replaced by a military junta.

September 4, 1969. Kidnapping of U.S. ambassador by revolutionaries.

October 30, 1969. Médici is sworn in as Costa e Silva's replacement.

November 4, 1969. Death of ALN leader Carlos Marighella and imprisonment of Dominicans.

August–October 1970. Security forces attack JOC, invade IBRADES, and detain Dom Aloísio, the CNBB secretary general.

November 3, 1970. First Bipartite meeting. Candido Mendes proposes "decompression" in Church-state relations and outlines possibilities for collaboration.

Timeline of Important Events

January 1972. Murder by torture of four soldiers at 1st AIB in Barra Mansa.

August 1972. Bipartite resolves Church-state crisis over commemoration of independence sesquicentennial.

1972–1973. Military and police repression in São Félix do Araguaia. Arrest of Dom Pedro Casaldáliga and pastoral agents.

1973. CNBB commemorates twenty-five years since U.N. Universal Declaration of Human Rights.

January 1973. Barra Mansa torturers found guilty.

March 16–17, 1973. Alexandre Vannucchi Leme tortured to death in the São Paulo DOI-CODI.

March 30, 1973. Three thousand people attend a memorial mass for Alexandre Vannucchi Leme at the cathedral in downtown São Paulo.

May–August 1973. Bishops protest death of Alexandre Vannucchi Leme at Bipartite.

August 1973. Dom Fernando Gomes tells Bipartite that civilians are not yet ready to rule.

October 1973. Médici orders closing of Rádio 9 de Julho.

March 15, 1974. Ernesto Geisel takes office and begins distensão.

August 26, 1974. Last Bipartite meeting.

October 1975. Death of Vladimir Herzog.

1976. Murder of Father Burnier and kidnapping of Dom Adriano Hypólito.

March 15, 1979. Figueiredo becomes president.

March 15, 1985. Brazil returns to civilian rule after twenty-one years of military dictatorship.

Secret Dialogues

Chapter 1

Introduction

The Brazilian Catholic Church's opposition to military rule (1964–1985) and its defense of the oppressed have distinguished it among the world's religious organizations. The critical years were the early 1970s, the era of Brazil's impressive economic "miracle" but also of violent political repression and increased exploitation of people and resources. Brazil's cold war national security state tightly controlled politics, suspended civil liberties and freedom of the press, and tortured and killed members of the opposition, including Catholic activists. The worst Church-state clash in Brazilian history began. Scores of idealistic priests, nuns, bishops, and lay militants suffered abuses by the security forces. Seven clerics were killed. The Church built a highly public and political profile by denouncing human rights abuses and economic injustice. It criticized the regime in masses, processions, broadsides, statements to the press, and official pronouncements. The bishops' prophetic condemnations were a watershed, for throughout Latin America the institutional Church had historically guaranteed its privileges and influence by generally supporting the status quo.[1] The Conferência Nacional dos Bispos do Brasil (CNBB; National Conference of the Bishops of Brazil) became a powerful "voice of the voiceless" by speaking for the opposition and defending the victims of torture. To fight socioeconomic oppression the CNBB worked with activists to create new grassroots religious communities and programs for the poor that together became known as the Popular Church or the People's Church. The grist of liberation theology, these innovations gave rise to the "preferential option for the poor" adopted by Latin American Catholicism in the 1970s and 1980s. As one analyst has noted, through its moral legitimacy and strengthening of civil society the Brazilian Church greatly influenced the political liberalization that led to the military's exit from power in 1985.[2]

This book presents a different view. It reaffirms the Church's important role, but it also questions certain assumptions, explores new dimensions of Church-state relations, and rethinks the history of the military regime during its bloodiest period. The biggest assumption, implicit in practically all discussions of the authoritarian era, is that the Church and the armed forces only fought and had little or no dialogue or attempts at cooperation. Writing during the regime or shortly thereafter, authors studied the dialectic of authoritarianism and opposition but did not examine the interstices of state-opposition relations. They also showed a clear bias toward the opposition. In short, they had little incentive to consider dialogue.[3]

This assumption is wrong, however. At the peak of the repression, just as the Popular Church first emerged, an important group of bishops and military leaders held in secret a systematic series of meetings known as the Comissão Bipartite (Bipartite Commission). The Bipartite reduced tensions, allowing Church and state to coexist during the worst moment of their long and complex relationship.

The Bipartite began in late 1970 after the bishops received blunt confirmation that Church-state conflict involved not just Catholic radicals but the institution as a whole. In September and October 1970, security agents invaded an important Catholic study center and Church houses in Rio de Janeiro in the kind of sweep against grassroots militants that had become routine after 1964. Once again priests and activists were jailed and tortured. Visceral anti-Communists, most bishops had welcomed the coup, and many looked askance at Catholic radicals, ignoring or doubting their stories of torture. During this raid the security men mistreated several important fathers, including the provincial head of the Jesuit order and the president of Rio's Catholic university. They detained one of the country's leading bishops, Dom Aloísio Lorscheider, the CNBB secretary general. The trend against the Church was now unmistakable. The bishops, including the country's five cardinals, protested the violence and arbitrariness of the regime. The incident also stirred condemnation from Catholics abroad, including Pope Paul VI.

Within weeks of the raid a group of bishops began to meet with a team of officers headed by General Antônio Carlos da Silva Muricy. Although political considerations and the climate of repression kept the talks secret and as informal as possible, they were serious and regular. The Bipartite met more than two dozen times, starting in November 1970 under President Emílio Garrastazu Médici (1969–1974) and ending in August 1974 during the term of President Ernesto Geisel (1974–1979).

A mechanism such as the Bipartite was unnecessary under the first military president, Humberto de Alencar Castello Branco (1964–1967), because the bishops generally supported the regime and took their complaints directly to the president, a loyal and practicing Catholic (Piletti and Praxedes 1997:319). Civil liberties, freedom of the press, and political debate still existed. Under President Artur da Costa e Silva (1967–1969) the regime hardened and attacks on the opposition and the Church intensified, leading to more formal Church-state dialogue and eventually the Bipartite under Médici. Geisel abolished the commission because he wanted to avoid legitimating the more contentious CNBB leadership, which participated at the Bipartite. Moreover, the bishops welcomed Geisel's plan for political liberalization and looked forward to a more open dialogue.

Key representatives of both sides took part at the Bipartite. General Muricy was the Army chief of staff and had helped stage the military takeover of 1964. He was a devout Catholic. He organized and ran the Bipartite with Médici's approval. Muricy's team included a general, a vice admiral, and officials from the Serviço Nacional de Informações (SNI; National Information Service), a Brazilian version of a domestic CIA-cum-FBI mainly concerned with internal subversion, and from the Centro de Informações do Exército (CIE; Army Information Center), an intelligence unit that played a major role in defeating the armed left. Thus the bishops faced men from the very agencies that led the repression. Muricy's team also included proregime civilians. The most notable was Tarcísio Meirelles Padilha, a Catholic philosopher, member of the Federal Education Council, and secretary of the Associação dos Diplomados da Escola Superior de Guerra (ADESG; National War College Alumni Association), of which Muricy was president. The military's nerve center, the Escola Superior de Guerra (ESG) helped hatch the coup and through its anti-Communist doctrine of national security provided the regime with ideological justification.[4]

The Church's delegation included the most influential bishops from across the political spectrum. Some had strong ties to the military, but others—such as Dom Aloísio and his cousin Dom Ivo Lorscheiter, a highly vocal critic of the regime—held moderate and even progressive positions. In fact, the increasingly progressive CNBB leaders were the most important Church intermediaries at the Bipartite. Another key figure was Candido Antonio José Francisco Mendes de Almeida, known simply as Candido Mendes. He was a prominent intellectual and layman, the CNBB's assistant for social affairs, and the secretary general of the Pontifícia Comissão Justiça e Paz–Seção Brasileira (CJP-BR; Pontifical Peace and Justice Commission–Brazilian Section). Muricy, Padilha, and Candido Mendes were the architects of the Bipartite.

Goals, Outcomes, and Meanings of Dialogue

In considering the Church-state relationship, most works on the period concentrate on historical rupture. Reinterpreting the Church's role, this book demonstrates that continuity also played a central part.

The Bipartite aimed to salvage the close ties nurtured between Church and state in the previous half-century. Church-state strife was a frequent theme in nineteenth- and twentieth-century Latin America, but in Brazil the Church overcame anticlericalism among the armed forces and the elite to build the continent's largest and one of its most sophisticated ecclesiastical and charitable infrastructures. By the 1930s the so-called Catholic Restoration had gained the Church practical reestablishment as an official religion. During the era of Brazilian presidential politics dominated by the populist Getúlio Vargas (1930–1945, 1951–1954) and his successors Juscelino Kubitschek (1955–1961) and João Goulart (1961–1964), Church and state collaborated and offered mutual political support. This unwritten agreement lasted into the early years of the military regime. Referring to the formal agreements, or concordats, that the Church signed with some countries, one bishop described the Brazilian pact as a "moral concordat."[5] After 1964 the military regime focused on subversion, however, and the Church increasingly emphasized social justice. Christian activism and the national security state clashed. To restore harmony, the Bipartite sought to resolve the ambiguity between subversion and the struggle for social justice. It debated three major, overlapping themes: development, settling Church-state conflict, and violations of human rights. The last point became the most crucial and produced vehement discussion.

At the first meetings the bishops and the military hoped to renew cooperation in the field of socioeconomic development. Both the Church and the armed forces already had a substantial history of promoting development. Each side also had significant traditions of nationalism. Despite the regime's technocratic approach, the bishops believed that the Church's new social doctrine should serve as a framework for national development. The discussions included debates over ideology and democracy. Cooperation became impossible, however, because the military attacked the radical Catholics' implementation of the social doctrine as subversive. In other words, Catholic radicalism criticized the new socioeconomic order imposed by the armed forces and supported revolutionaries' efforts to overthrow that order. The attempt to collaborate was nevertheless meaningful, because it revealed continuity in the motives and intentions of both the military and the bishops. As churchmen and officers had so often maintained close ties in the past, so did they seek to preserve that relationship during the conflict-filled 1970s. Even Dom Hélder Câmara—a key founder of the Popular Church and a pariah of the regime—sought Church-state collaboration (Piletti and Praxedes 1997:353–54).[6] The Bipartite addressed some of the Church's institutional interests as Brazil's semi-official religion. And only Catholics participated in the religious delegation, even though the Church was striving to build ecumenical relations with members of minority Protestant religions who became its allies against the repression.[7] In effect, the bishops had proposed a modernized version of the moral concordat. The Church would retain its leading political role, only now in the name of social justice rather than purely in institutional and religious interests.

In its second, more pragmatic phase the commission focused on settling specific Church-state conflicts. In 1972, for instance, the Bipartite defused a dispute over Brazil's 150th Independence Day Celebration that threatened to create a public clash. Avoiding conflict prevented a deeper rift that neither side wanted. This result was significant for the regime. The military feared the clergy's influence among the people and needed the bishops' (and the pope's) approval in order to legitimate authoritarian rule. More important, the generals were extremely sensitive about maintaining a positive image abroad. The bishops and the Vatican criticized the government, but they did not sever relations with it. In addition, the officers at the Bipartite made a case for the government's achievements and warned the bishops about the armed revolutionary threat. The bishops received few concessions, but dialogue saved the Church from even harsher reprisal and benefited it in other ways as well (as discussed below).

Understanding a Paradox: Compromise and Public Versus Private Positions

The revelation of the Bipartite points out the need to reinterpret the bishops' modus operandi. With General Muricy and the officers pressuring them to tone down their criticisms and to curb the activist clergy, the bishops took great care to avoid the appearance of supporting alleged subversion and even worked to deter it. Publicly, through its famous pronouncements, the CNBB radicalized the bishops' opposition, but privately, the leadership temporized in order to avoid confrontation. These bishops were able, flexible politicians working to safeguard their institution and its traditional influence in Brazilian society. Opposition was not absolute; it was susceptible to negotiation. The Bipartite was a valuable reminder that leaders often form two faces: an idealist one for the public and a pragmatic one for Realpolitik.

The public/private dichotomy placed the bishops in a paradox. How could they compromise their public voice on certain political issues but stubbornly adhere to it on human rights? How could they seek collaboration and still criticize the regime's violence? Why enter talks that promised much for the generals but endangered the Church's moral standing? Why dialogue with the enemy? Resolving the paradox clarifies the bishops' motives and teases out the complexities and ambiguities of the Church-military conflict.

In hindsight, dialogue with a violent, insensitive military government seems incomprehensible, even lamentable. But let us return in history. The Bipartite began before the worst moments of Médici's term. In late 1970 the repression was severe, but nobody could foretell how terrible it would become or how long it would last. And it did become worse. Dialogue appeared as a new prospect for ending Church-state tension. As religious men, the bishops believed in hope. At first they were naive about the government's stated desire for Church-state collaboration, which seemed plausible in light of previously harmonious relations. Initially they were also naive about the repression, which they believed could be reduced through cooperation.

Then, as ideological and political differences remained unresolved, the Bipartite's primary focus shifted to human rights. This shift coincided with the strengthening of the Church's public, moral opposition. Thus the Church simultaneously criticized the regime and attempted to preserve the political influence it had enjoyed. The moral concordat became moral opposition.

Dialogue was useful. In a century of radically polarized political systems and ideologies it has allowed enemies to coexist and the weak to survive. Dialogue proved especially effective at the height of the cold war in the 1960s and 1970s. The United States and the Soviet Union agreed to live in "peaceful coexistence" while negotiating an end to the Cuban missile crisis, arms controls, a ban on atmospheric nuclear testing, and détente. Not just a "balance of terror" but also "mutual understanding" kept the United States and the Soviets from war (Craig and Loewenheim 1994:4). In the early 1970s, dialogue temporarily halted the Vietnam War, defused crises in the troubled Middle East, and opened relations between Communist China and the West. Dialogue could be a messy and risky process. Frequently it left behind losers and victims. It was often secret, as Machiavellian masters of back-channel diplomacy such as Henry Kissinger regularly illustrated.[8] Secret talks also took place in the late 1970s in the return to democracy in Peru and the Dominican Republic.[9] In a world of hatred, violence, and human shortcomings, dialogue was often the best in an imperfect set of options.

The Catholic Church dialogued with governments of all kinds. Although the modern era sharply reduced its overt political influence, it remained a major force in world diplomacy. The Church is a multinational institution par excellence with embassies around the globe. It has adjusted its approach according to the historical, political, and religious circumstances of each country, including the strength of the opposition, the degree of state repression, notions of patriotism, the previous record of Church-state relations, and the balance of forces within the Church.[10] The level of competition from other religions is also an important factor. As a result, the Church has had a mixed record with respect to authoritarianism and repression.[11]

For instance, as one scholar has observed, Pope Pius XI (1922–1939) "negotiated with all types of governments to attain as many concessions as possible for the church." Under him the Church signed concordats with the totalitarian regimes of Italy and Germany and thereby undercut early opposition to fascism, although in 1937 the pope denounced Nazi crimes against the Church. European episcopates responded differently to fascism and the Nazi persecution of the Jews. The Vatican, the official Church headquarters in Rome, remained silent on the Holocaust, but it did undertake many efforts to save Jews.[12] The Mexican Church fought that country's anticlerical revolutionary regime for nearly two decades before arriving at an understanding that barred the clergy from public life but allowed it to remain involved in society.[13] A network of informal Church-state ties and collaboration underlay this arrangement (Reich 1995). Pius XI supported the fascist strongman Francisco Franco in the Spanish Civil War (1936–1939), and the Church had a highly privileged role as an institutional and ideological pillar of the Franco regime (1939–1975) before shifting to a more democratic stance at the end. In pre-1964 Brazil, the Church had considerable political influence, but it was also used by leaders, as Vargas demonstrated during the dictatorial phase known as the Estado Novo (1937–1945) with his manipulation of the Church and the "Jewish Question" (Lesser 1995, esp. ch. 5). Later in the Philippines the Church played an important part in the overthrow of dictator Ferdinand Marcos.

The tendency to dialogue intensified after the Second Vatican Council (Vatican II, 1962–1965), which initiated Catholic relations with other religions and even dialogue with Marxism, the anathema of traditional Catholicism. Pope Paul VI (1963–1978) instituted a period of *Ostpolitik* in which the Church negotiated with Eastern European Communist countries to safeguard religious freedom. In Poland, a highly autonomous Church undergirded the Solidarity union movement against Communism in the late 1970s and early 1980s. Back-channel understandings and secret meetings and missives were an essential part of Pope John Paul II's involvement in this drama and the subsequent downfall of the Soviet empire (Bernstein and Politi 1996).

By the mid-1970s most of Latin America had fallen under the control of authoritarian regimes that frequently attacked the Church. The Church's new emphasis on human rights passed through the filter of particular national circumstances. As a result, it took positions on dictatorship that ranged from opposition to outright collaboration with the repressive forces. In Chile, the Church's experience somewhat paralleled the Brazilian bishops' public resistance to authoritarianism. During the government of socialist President Salvador Allende (1970–1973), the Chilean bishops followed the Church's usual strategy in difficult political situations: it stressed moderation and reconciliation while defending ecclesiastical prestige. After General Augusto Pinochet overthrew Allende, the bishops first backed him and did little to protest repression. They quickly became critical, however, as the security forces continued to kill and "disappear" large numbers of people. Cardinal Raúl Silva Henríquez set up a Vicariate of Solidarity to defend human rights and to aid the poor. This program intertwined religious, humanitarian, and political motives to provide one of the most incisive examples of moral opposition to authoritarian rule in Latin America.[14] The Church helped topple Paraguayan dictator Alfredo Stroessner (Carter 1991) and Nicaraguan despot Anastasio Somoza, and Archbishop Oscar Arnulfo Romero and some priests preached the right of insurrection against the militaristic government of El Salvador. Romero was assassinated in March 1980.

A striking contrast came in Argentina, where the most conservative bishops openly supported the armed forces' "dirty war" against the opposition. Thousands died or disappeared, including some opposition priests and bishops. Perquisites for the clergy, doctrinaire conservatism, and close ties between chaplains and soldiers in the military vicariate led to this extreme position (Mignone 1990). Those bishops who opposed the repression lodged their protests in private—apparently with few results (Klaiber 1997:136–37). Factions within the Church usually opposed the majority's decision to support or to oppose a regime, and at times deep splits formed. In Nicaragua, for instance, the People's Church collaborated openly with the revolutionary Sandinista government whereas conservatives harshly criticized it (Kirk 1992; Stein 1999). The Church also helped to bring about peace between governments and guerrillas, for example, in El Salvador in 1991 and 1992 and after the Zapatista rebellion in Chiapas, Mexico, in 1994.

The repression and political polarization in Brazil made contact appear unlikely between the military and the Church's moderates and progressives, but the

Bipartite demonstrated that, once again, the Church chose dialogue to protect its secular interests and to promote its spiritual and moral values. These different priorities were not always incompatible. The bishops aimed to preserve the Church's historic influence, but the theological innovation of Vatican II and the onslaught of authoritarianism in Latin America also made human rights a vital institutional interest. Moreover, the Church was striving to redefine its purpose in Brazilian society. Different aspects of its role could be defended in different ways.

The broader historical mosaic of Catholicism in Brazil reveals the ongoing primacy of institutional concerns and the Church's adaptability to the changing sociopolitical climate. As civilian rule returned, the Church partially withdrew from public politics as parties and other groups became the new voice of social justice. Catholic radicalism lost appeal because of the fall of Communism and criticisms by Pope John Paul II. Growing competition from other religions began to undermine the Church's quasi-official status. These changes led the bishops to focus on more traditional goals such as building their flocks and reviving orthodox spirituality.[15] Continuity with the past brought the Church's international character and long-term institutional religious interests into sharp relief. Seen in isolation, the Bipartite made little sense. In historical perspective it was quite logical.

Influence Through Dialogue

An important circumstance of the Bipartite was the immense asymmetry of power between the generals and the bishops. The military monopolized force, severely curtailed freedoms, and tortured and killed its opponents. It used its power to manipulate the bishops. The Church was nonviolent. Yet the bishops were not helpless. The Brazilian Church was institutionally strong, with some 250 bishops by the 1970s. They often disagreed among themselves, but the leadership of the CNBB, one of the world's first and best-organized episcopal conferences, spoke out confidently on national issues as a single voice for the bishops. The Church also had social prestige, international status, and the leadership of the pope, whom the military respected. Within the Church the bishops, and especially the participants at the Bipartite, held substantial power. Some sectors of the Church organized peaceful resistance to the regime.

The bishops astutely acknowledged their disadvantage. Trying to persuade the military was better than ignoring it, however. Dialogue provided the bishops with the possibility of moral and political leverage.[16] The Bipartite enabled them to attempt to influence the generals without public delegitimation of the regime, which was one of the government's worst fears. Refusing dialogue would have fur-

9

ther increased tensions and sharply reduced the possibilities of mutual understanding and protection of human rights.[17]

Dialogue further enabled the Church to deal more effectively with its opponent by giving the bishops a deeper appreciation for the military's internal politics and an understanding of which factions were open to dialogue. The extremists on both sides—zealous Catholic progressives and key officers close to Médici—criticized the Bipartite.[18] But the Church and the Army were not monoliths. Each had groups that wanted to end the Church-state strife. General Muricy and Candido Mendes formed the necessary bridge.

Human Rights

The third phase of the Bipartite dealt with abuses of human rights, which became the most compelling reason for the bishops' participation. Public posturing followed by compromise might serve for some issues, but defense of human rights was an important commitment of the post–Vatican II Church and, in the Brazilian context, one on which it had to radicalize quickly. Torture was authoritarianism incarnate, and the regime practiced it widely. Human rights therefore demanded a consistent and straightforward message. They became a central point of contention.

At the Bipartite, the bishops reinforced their public outcry against abuses. Under the leadership of Candido Mendes and Dom Ivo they pressed the officers to explain the jailings, disappearances, and violations committed by the security forces against a variety of victims, including peasants, clergymen, and members of the left. General Muricy and his team usually sustained the government's lies or denials of wrongdoing. (Publicly the regime refused to admit the existence of political prisoners and torture.) Thus there is little evidence that the Bipartite stopped abuses in the short run. The Church's public campaign also had little immediate success. Under Médici the military allowed the security forces to investigate, capture, and torture victims without restriction. Only after President Geisel's decision to carry out a political liberalization—the so-called *abertura*—did the regime rein in torturers.

Nevertheless, the Bipartite allowed the bishops to speak their minds freely on human rights. They contested and even disproved military denial of abuses. The bishops had no influence over torturers, but through the Bipartite they transmitted a forceful message to the torturers' superiors. After Dom Waldyr Calheiros de Novaes denounced the death and disappearance of soldiers at the Barra Mansa barracks in January 1972, the Bipartite helped spur the military's *only* public admission and prosecution of torture. The bishops' efforts were especially crucial because repression and censorship muffled public forms of protest. A year later, when protest by the public and attorneys against the death of popular Catholic university student Alexandre Vannucchi Leme failed to provoke an inquiry, the Bipartite once again became the ultimate forum for Church complaints to the military leadership. The bishops cumulatively built a case against the repression. They criticized censorship of Catholic publications and media. Behind closed doors, the Bipartite demonstrated a grudging necessity of the armed forces to discuss human rights. It prompted the military's tacit and explicit admission of abuses, helping the Church to gain the moral high ground. Some areas were open to negotiation, but human rights were not.

Publicity about torture soiled Brazil's image of economic progress and set off a diplomatic battle in Europe. The generals pressured the bishops at the Bipartite and in other contexts to stanch the flow of bad news about the regime. The diplomatic struggle generated a series of other private dialogues between military and Catholic leaders. It also sparked debate within the Church over the effectiveness of public versus private denunciation of atrocities. These dialogues played an important part in the story of the commission.

This phase of the Bipartite shed light on the origins of the politics of human rights in Brazil. The commission's activities provided a measure of military tolerance of human rights violations and the Church's use of them as a political lever. The bishops chose their battles carefully and fought them wisely. The Bipartite helped the Church build a commitment to human rights, which became a cornerstone of the later campaign for democracy. It also reflected some of the difficulties of the human rights movement in Brazil.

Progressives and Conservatives

The presence of bishops of different political stripes at the Bipartite destroys the prevailing notion that only conservatives dialogued with the military. Likewise, the Bipartite undermines the idea that only progressives defended human rights and opponents of the regime. Much has been written about the archdiocese of São Paulo, where Cardinal Paulo Evaristo Arns spearheaded the most important Church opposition movement. He exercised the prophetic approach to human rights and opposition. A more balanced view of the Brazilian Church, however, should include a closer look at the goals and outcomes of the conservative wing, which used more discreet tactics.

The most interesting case is Dom Eugênio de Araújo Sales, the archbishop primate of Brazil (1968–1971), the cardinal of Rio de Janeiro as of 1971, and a key member of the Bipartite. Dom Eugênio is usually remembered as a conservative with close ties to the military and as an enemy of the Popular Church. In a landmark work on the Brazilian Church, political scientist Thomas Bruneau states that Dom Eugênio became "overly compromised" with the elite (Bruneau 1974b:173). Indeed, no bishop had more respect from the martial leadership. In two important books on the Church and politics, former congressman Márcio Moreira Alves describes Dom Eugênio as an "authoritarian opportunist" and the "principal promoter of the alliance between the Church and the military government."[19] Yet this interpretation is incorrect. Dom Eugênio criticized human rights abuses, aided many political prisoners, and labored to protect the Church's interests. He was able to play this role and to bridge the gap between Church and state precisely because he had prestige in the barracks. This trust further allowed him to point out the errors of the regime, albeit usually behind the scenes. Dom Eugênio favored dialogue but not "alliance." His work requires a remapping of the Church's human rights movement to include Rio de Janeiro as an important center. It also suggests greater attention to personal and historical factors that shaped the bishops' politics. Most important, it points out the interpretative limits of the categories "progressive" and "conservative."

By joining the Bipartite, the progressives continued to work within the historical framework of Church-state cooperation. Although they opposed militarism, favored a more just socioeconomic system, and in theory rejected ties to the elite, they recognized the Church's need for influence and power. Thus the Bipartite reinforces the interpretation that the Popular Church was less a proposal for liberating the people than a way for guaranteeing the bishops' authority in Brazilian society (Romano 1979).[20]

Rethinking the Military in the Médici Years

As some scholars have noted, if the armed forces "won the war against the leftist revolutionary organizations, they were defeated in the struggle over the historical memory of the period." Discussion of the Médici era has remained taboo in the armed forces because of the need to protect esprit de corps. Normally written by the victors, history this time was forged by the vanquished.[21] With the gradual end of censorship under Geisel and the 1979 political amnesty that brought home exiles, a plethora of prose works and other media presented a version of events told by ex-guerrillas and victims of the regime.[22] The publication of *Brasil: nunca mais* was perhaps the most bitter pill for the armed forces. Issued as Brazil returned to

civilian rule in 1985, this best-selling book documented the horrors of torture during the Médici years, using military court files spirited off and copied by Church
lawyers.[23] More recently some officers have provided their own accounts, but military writings on the period remain few.[24]

The Bipartite is an important chapter in the historical narrative of the Médici
era, the bloodiest yet least studied of the military periods.[25] Long out of vogue in the
historical profession and largely absent from Latin American studies, interpretive
narrative helps define a particular period by portraying the convergence of individuals, incidents, and trends.[26] Intangibles made a difference in this story. The
emotional climate of secret dialogue and the nuances of personal relations and
small social networks played a role in mediating the dictatorship that is frequently
overlooked. The Bipartite involves political and diplomatic history as well as the
stories of the security forces, the soldiery, and the victims of the repression and
their families. It is also about the military leadership and the nature of the Médici
government.

The Bipartite invites reevaluation of the regime. It revealed that the Médici government was more varied in its approach to the Church than was previously
thought. On the one hand, the Médici administration was truculent, with the hard-
line leadership encouraging repression of the Church's new ideas and pastoral programs. On the other hand, as veteran journalist Carlos Castello Branco wrote,
Médici was always interested in a political dialogue (cited in Skidmore 1988:105).
Médici allowed the anti-hard-liners to try persuasion. General Muricy represented
an intellectualized military subculture that respected the Church for political, religious, and patriotic reasons and wanted conciliation with it. His creation of the
Bipartite suggests that the "soft-line" followers of Castello Branco had more influence on policy than they are given credit for.[27] Thus the Bipartite highlights an
important nuance in military attitudes and strategies. It provides a more subtle
view of the Médici years, emphasizes historical specificity, and cautions against
monolithic interpretations.[28] The Bipartite paralleled the earliest attempts at
descompressão, or *distensão* (decompression), the strategy of political liberalization
and lessening of tensions that was a forerunner to the *abertura* (political opening)
begun by Geisel and implemented under General João Baptista de Oliveira
Figueiredo, the last military president (1979–1985).[29] The Bipartite did not cause
Geisel's distensão, but it did decompress Church-state tensions.

Another unexamined area of modern Brazilian politics is Church-military relations. Studies of the Church focus on its relationship to the state. Normally a part
of the state, after 1964 the military dominated it.[30] But like the Church the armed

services are a special kind of institution with their own peculiar hierarchy, methods of recruitment and training, and history. These institutions have much in common, not least of which is their goal to influence the populace. Comparison of the two institutions helps explain post-1964 conflict. One example was disagreement over patriotism. This was a particularly complex issue given the national composition of the armed forces and the transnational makeup of the Church. Writings on Brazil, however, rarely discuss the shared experiences of soldiers and priests, outside conflict. General Muricy's experiences and the Bipartite demonstrated close contact between cross and sword.

In many works military leaders appear as distant, strident figures involved only in repression. Early on, the generals purposefully cultivated a somber, austere, even morbid image. They wished to strike a contrast with the populist presidents, seen as corrupt, willing to rub elbows with the people for the smallest political advantage. The generals' attitude reinforced the climate of fear, creating a chasm between the regime and the populace. Médici tried to soften this image by appearing as a simple man who enjoyed soccer, the national craze intensified by Brazil's victory in the 1970 World Cup competition. Figueiredo also used this strategy (Fico 1997, ch. 2). But the overemphasis on severity survives.

Understanding the regime requires a more multifaceted, historical, and dispassionate view of the military institution. The dictatorship was brutal, but factionalism and internal disagreements over policy and practices necessitate a less monochromatic picture of martial rule and a more careful look at the historical evolution of civil-military relations.[31] The Brazilian military had long political experience and deemed itself a force for democracy, though in a restricted form. The overthrow of President Goulart fully contradicted this image, but not the history of earlier interventions carried out to correct what many officers—and civilians—saw as the politicians' inability to run the country. After 1964 the leadership did not want to be seen as dictators or torturers but as true practitioners of democracy protecting Brazil from totalitarian Communism. Unlike perpetual strongmen such as Pinochet or Stroessner, the Brazilian generals rotated the presidency, held regular elections, and used propaganda to maintain a facade of democracy. The Brazilian armed forces were a large and sophisticated organization that worked hard to put a positive twist on authoritarianism. Some wanted to turn the country back to the civilians as quickly as possible. It is easy to demonize the military, but to do so makes for simplistic history. The examples of the deeply faithful General Muricy and of Colonel Mário Orlando Ribeiro Sampaio (who investigated a group of murderous torturers before joining the Bipartite) put a human face on the officer corps.[32]

The Bipartite and Elite Political Culture

Searching for a middle ground was difficult and politically risky for the Church, which sought to minister to all social groups.[33] The intense ideological polarization of the cold war heightened Church-regime tensions throughout Latin America, creating a logic of war versus a logic of politics (Loveman 1999:184–85). National security, militarism, and traditional Catholicism resonated with anti-Communist authoritarianism. Although the Church had long strived for a third way between capitalism and Communism, revolution, social activism, and the Popular Church found affinity with anti-Americanism and the Soviet bloc's support for the Third World.[34] In Brazil the bishops walked a tightrope between social activism and the fight against subversion. They also ran the risk of being seen as either too conciliatory with or too critical of the government (Drosdoff 1986:126).

The middle ground between Church and regime was the singularly Brazilian approach of the Bipartite. It was a precious example of the Church's famous but largely undocumented ability to wield influence behind the scenes with other members of the modern Brazilian elite. Many books on Latin America focus on the elite, but rarely do secret conversations come out so explicitly as in the story of the Bipartite.

Elite political culture was part of the wider reality beneath the history of the commission. Brazil is historically a society that emphasized not strong public institutions, but family, paternalism, and personal ties.[35] The elite had power, wealth, advanced education, and status. Its ranks included the so-called functional elites, from such professional categories as the bureaucracy, the bar, the clergy, and the military. In twentieth-century Brazil, elite origins diversified, leading to competition among different groups for control of the central state. At the same time, the state took on greater importance in the coordination of elite action (Conniff and McCann 1989a; Conniff 1989).

The Bipartite embodied several traits of this political culture. One of the most prominent was elite conciliation designed to prevent social and political reform and to keep the masses out of conflict. Historically, masses have had little involvement in politics and elections, and political parties and social movements have been relatively unimportant. Key decisions were not discussed by the people but were negotiated among the various factions of the ruling class.[36] Before and after the military regime, Brazilian politics remained highly authoritarian and hierarchical (Hagopian 1996). The form of government, whether despotic or democratic, was less important than the creation of clienteles by those in power (McDonough

1981:xxxiii–xxxiv, 241). Although it involved some grassroots political activity and constitutional provisions, the unwritten moral concordat between Church and state was basically a form of elite conciliation, an understanding among influential men.

The military shattered the compact of Brazil's elite by seizing power, creating open conflict among different sectors, and obstructing compromise. On one side stood the generals, rich businessmen, and technocrats; on the other side, opposition politicians, the Church, and the leaders of urban labor. More than any other group, including the opposition party Movimento Democrático Brasileiro (MDB; Brazilian Democratic Movement), the bishops contested the armed forces' participation in politics and government, in part because the military leadership and the technocrats tried to reduce the Church's own traditional political status. The military violated the rules of interelite relations and even went so far as to change them. This was unacceptable to the bishops. Normally at the fringe of civilian affairs, the Church and the military squared off against each other (McDonough 1981).[37] The Bipartite attempted to restore Church-state dialogue and set new rules for it. It was a variety of what political scientists have termed "elite settlement," whereby representatives of elite factions use secret negotiations to break through an impasse (Burton, Gunther, and Higley 1992:16–17).[38] For example, the commission established the right of the bishops to complain about the regime in private. Any member of the Brazilian elite would have normally claimed such a right. At the Bipartite it led to harsh debate over socioeconomic reform and torture.[39]

The Bipartite was also a gentlemanly affair involving highly accomplished, politically experienced members of an intimate elite. A rugged soldier, General Muricy was also a well-read intellectual who listened to classical music in his off hours. In 1969 he finished third in the internal Army campaign for president. Muricy had a deep religious faith and held the bishops in high esteem. A prolific writer, Professor Padilha was emerging as one of the world's most respected Catholic philosophers. His father was a governor; his deceased brother had been a prominent newspaperman. Padilha was Muricy's godson and had been a contemporary of Candido Mendes at a prestigious private Jesuit school. Candido Mendes was the great-grandson of an illustrious senator who defended bishops persecuted by the state. As a result, Candido Mendes inherited a title of papal nobility. He was imbued with great self-confidence and privilege tempered by noblesse oblige and a profound Christian conviction in favor of social justice. He was also a brilliant and extremely well-connected academic, lawyer, and politician. Years later both Candido Mendes and Padilha became members of the Brazilian Academy of

Letters, a society of so-called immortal literati. Considered by some to be stuffy and irrelevant, the academy beautifully mirrors the self-image of the Brazilian ruling class by electing members from across the professional and political spectrum and holding elaborate induction ceremonies. Bipartite member Dom Lucas Moreira Neves also became a member of the Academy of Letters.[40] He and the other bishops shared many of the advantages and characteristics of the Brazilian elite. Most had spent years studying in Europe and were sophisticated, cosmopolitan men familiar with the corridors of power at the Vatican and in Brazil. Two had attained the status of cardinal—a step just below that of pope—and three more would do so before the Bipartite ended. They were pastors but also veteran politicians.[41]

As Lieutenant Colonel Roberto Pacífico Barbosa of the SNI put it, the Bipartite was a sui generis Brazilian solution to the Church-state crisis.[42] It prized dialogue over conflict—a dialogue made possible by the participants' social status. Church and state spoke, but so did the intelligent general, the astute bishop, the well-connected philosopher, and the principled aristocrat. They gathered confident that they could smooth over their difficulties through secret conversations and the common bond of their Christian faith and Brazilian cordiality, a trademark of successful Brazilian politicians (Conniff 1989:37).[43] The Bipartite was also a unique system for dealing with human rights violations.

Opening Archives, Shaping History

The revelation of the Bipartite has its own history. For two decades, only a few Church and military insiders and a handful of journalists knew of its existence. It is mentioned only briefly in a few published sources.[44] The first detailed accounts of the commission became public in 1992 and 1993, when General Muricy unsealed his papers and the transcript of a fifty-eight-hour interview given in 1981. Both are housed at the Centro de Pesquisa e Documentação de História Contemporânea do Brasil (CPDOC) of the Fundação Getúlio Vargas (FGV) in Rio de Janeiro. Muricy's archive contains hundreds of pages of formerly classified Bipartite documents. It is one of the few archives from the military regime to be opened.

General Muricy shaped the history of the Bipartite in three ways. First, he participated in it. Second, he selected documents for his archive. As a leading military figure concerned with personal and national security he always took great care with his papers. In his 1981 interview the general stated that throughout his career he "tore up many things." He also wrote few letters, instead preferring personal contact (Muricy 1993:339, 408, 458). Therefore, the exceptional contents of the archive indicate the themes that Muricy thought most important for his own history and for the history of the regime, for example, the large number of items on the Church. The archive has only about half of the Bipartite minutes, however. Muricy "preferred not to keep" the others (Muricy 1993:661). The missing papers are most likely buried in the archives of the security forces, as yet unopened to researchers.[45] Nevertheless, sufficient minutes remain for piecing together the history of the commission.[46] The archive also holds correspondence between General Muricy and the bishops; records of smaller, less formal meetings of Bipartite members; intelligence files on priests and lay activists accused of subversion; the military's political evaluation of the bishops; and confidential intelligence evaluations of the gatherings. Finally, General Muricy decided when to release his interview and papers. In 1981, although the abertura had begun, Brazil was still firmly planted in authoritarianism, evidenced by the infamous RioCentro bomb explosion in which two terrorist officers tried to disrupt a prodemocracy rally. Only when the passions of the era had begun to dissipate somewhat did Muricy feel it was time to reveal his materials (Muricy interview 2).[47]

In their content and style the documents often reveal the voices of soldiers and intelligence officers. Given the lack of martial writings on the history of the regime, the records provide valuable access to the military's thinking on conflict with the Church. From the regime's standpoint the Church required courting—but also investigation and even manipulation in the drive for national security.

Two recently opened collections of military and police documentation offer new insights into regime surveillance and repression of the Church. These are the massive archives of the former political police of Rio de Janeiro and São Paulo—respectively, the Departamento de Ordem Política e Social da Guanabara (DOPS-GB; Department of Political and Social Order)[48] and the Departamento Estadual de Ordem Política e Social (DEOPS-SP; State Department of Political and Social Order).[49] After the government closed these two agencies in the early 1980s, their papers went to the Polícia Federal, the national investigative police, also a repressive force. Democratic consolidation after 1985 brought the sensitive documents to local-level historical archives. The papers were opened for research in the mid-1990s. These developments exemplified how the political process has affected the writing of history. The collections are especially important because they contain papers from the military security services, whose archives remain closed. For instance, they include interrogation transcripts and other documentation from the infamous torture centers known as DOI-CODI, the Destacamento de Operações de

```
                    ┌─────────────┐
                    │  SECRETO    │
                    └─────────────┘
RELATÓRIO ESPECIAL DO GRUPO BIPARTITE, SOBRE PROBLEMAS SURGIDOS    NA
ÁREA IGREJA X GOVERNO, REFERENTES À PARTICIPAÇÃO DO CLERO NAS COMEMO-
RAÇÕES DO SESQUICENTENÁRIO DA INDEPENDÊNCIA DO BRASIL.

DATA: AGOSTO/SETEMBRO DE 1972
LOCAL: RIO (GB)
PESSOAL PARTICIPANTE:

    Grupo religioso:

    - D. ALOISIO LORSCHEIDER (Pres.CNBB)
    - D. IVO LORSCHEITER (Sec.G.CNBB)
    - D. AVELAR BRANDÃO (Vice-Pres. CNBB)
    - D. EUGÊNIO SALES (Cardeal-Arceb. RIO DE JANEIRO)
    - D. PAULO EVARISTO ARNS (Arcebispo de S.PAULO)
    - Prof. CÂNDIDO MENDES (Assessor da CNBB)
    - D. HUMBERTO MOZONI (Núncio Apostólico)

    Grupo ligado à Situação:

    - Gen. Ex. R1 ANTONIO CARLOS DA SILVA MURICY (Ch. Grupo)
    - Prof. TARCISIO M. PADILHA (Membro Corpo Perm. ESG)
    - Ten. Cel. Ex. ROBERTO PACÍFICO BARBOSA (Assessor ARJ/SNI - Rela
                                                          tor)
    - Maj. LEONE DA SILVEIRA LEE (CIE/Gab. Min. Ex.)

SUMÁRIO GERAL

1 - DADOS RECEBIDOS PELO GRUPO DA SITUAÇÃO SOBRE PROBLEMAS NA ÁREA I-
    GREJA X GOVERNO.

    a - Impasse sobre o TE DEUM em S. PAULO, de 3 para 7 Set.
    b - Informe sobre reedição do livro "O CLERO E A INDEPENDÊNCIA",
        com possíveis Notas críticas ao Governo.
    c - Informe sobre edição de "O SÃO PAULO", de 3 Set, com críticas
        ao Governo.
    d - Informe de elaboração pelos bispos de Documento dogmático-pas
        toral, com conotações políticas de ataque ao Governo.
    e - Difusão do Folheto "CELEBRAÇÕES LITÚRGICAS", com notícias am
        bíguas de conotação esquerdista.
    f - VI Congresso Nacional dos Serra-Clubes, com presença de bis-
        pos e difusão de Documento crítico.

2 - PROVIDÊNCIAS GERAIS TOMADAS PELO GRUPO DA SITUAÇÃO.

    a - Ligações com membros do Grupo Religioso.

        1) Com o Prof. CÂNDIDO MENDES (Assessor CNBB).
        2) Com D. EUGÊNIO SALES (Cardeal-Arceb. do RIO DE JANEIRO).
        3) Com D. HUMBERTO MOZONI (Núncio Apostólico).

    b - Reunião informal de membros do Grupo da Situação com o Grupo
        Religioso.

                    ┌─────────────┐
                    │  SECRETO    │
                    └─────────────┘
```

General Muricy's archive contains about half of the secret military reports on the Bipartite meetings. The document shown here is the first page of the report from the Aug. 31, 1972 emergency meeting, which was called in an attempt to resolve the Church-military dispute over the commemoration of Brazil's independence sesquicentennial. The report lists the names of the bishops and regime representatives who attended the meeting and provides a detailed account of the conversations.

Informações and the Centro de Operações de Defesa Interna (Detachment for Information Operations and Internal Defense Operations Center).[50]

Numerous authors have chronicled the public aspects of Church-state clash. The DOPS and DEOPS documentation reveals in detail for the first time the internal process of how the regime's agents spied on, evaluated, and planned strategy against the Church. While most works focus on the Church's public rhetoric against the regime, the creation of a heretofore unstudied underground Church resistance is also examined here. Other primary sources make possible a new understanding of the Médici era, Church-state conflict, and the Bipartite—such as the Brasil: Nunca Mais collection of military tribunal proceedings against alleged subversives; the so-called Archive of Terror of Paraguayan dictator Alfredo Stroessner's Asunción-based police; the National Security Archive in Washington, D.C.; and Church-related collections such as the Central de Documentação e Informação Científica "Prof. Casemiro dos Reis Filho" (CEDIC), the Centro Alceu Amoroso Lima para a Liberdade (CAALL), the Archive of the Argentine Embassy to the Holy See, the archive of the diocese of Barra do Piraí–Volta Redonda (ADBPVR), the Jean Marc van der Weid Collection, the papers of Catholic activist Branca de Mello Franco Alves, the library of the Instituto Nacional de Pastoral (INP), the Arquivo Ana Lagôa, and the Arquiro do Itamaraty.[51] Besides written sources, this book employs interviews with sixty-four individuals, including retired generals, members of the intelligence community, bishops, priests, former revolutionaries, victims of the repression and their relatives, human rights activists, and others.

As the authoritarian era fades, the appearance of other primary sources will lead to greater understanding of the period. This process is essential in a postauthoritarian society where most people heard only the military's version of events or remained oblivious to them because of censorship. Political opening produces a documentary opening, which in turn illuminates the past. The degree to which researchers gain access to the highly sensitive, still hidden papers of the military security forces will be an important measure of the commitment to building a lasting democracy in Brazil. The Church also has a wealth of unreleased documentation that can further explain the history of the military regime.

The next three chapters lay the groundwork for understanding Church-military relations and the Bipartite. Chapter 2 charts the history of the Church and the Army in modern Brazil and analyzes how these two key institutions came to clash after 1964. Chapter 3 describes General Muricy's military career and devotion to Catholicism; chapter 4 explores the initial phases of Church-state conflict by examining his ties to key bishops, the diplomatic struggle over torture, and the debate within the Catholic leadership over the best method for denouncing regime abuses.

Chapters 5 through 10 analyze the history of the commission. Chapter 5 describes its founding and modus operandi. Chapter 6 presents the opening debates, in which the two sides attempted to define the boundaries of social justice and subversion. Chapter 7 examines key episodes of conflict resolution and consideration of the Church's institutional needs. Chapter 8 discusses the struggle over human rights violations and censorship. Chapters 9 and 10 provide detailed studies of two cases in which the Bipartite played a key role: the deaths by torture of the Barra Mansa soldiers and of Leme. Chapter 11 provides an epilogue to the Bipartite and discusses its significance.

A few words of clarification are necessary concerning the terms "social justice" and "subversion." Each term embraces a broad range of activities and interpretations that vary according to circumstances and perspective. Here "social justice" generally signifies the attempt by the Church to bring about a more equal society, in which human and democratic rights would be respected. For some Catholics "social justice" meant adhering to the measured teachings of the popes, whereas for others the term implied much more, including the implantation of socialism. Clearly some aspects of the struggle for "social justice" were indeed "subversion" in the sense that they threatened to upset or transform the social status quo. "Subversion" had an even more diffuse definition than "social justice." It could refer specifically to revolutionary or political actions prohibited by the regime—for example, kidnapping, bank robberies, and the creation of armed opposition movements. But during the Médici years it became the military's catchall phrase for anything that smelled of leftism, that threatened the political status quo or implied criticism of the regime—for example, peasant organizations, student unions, and protest songs. Subversion was alleged as if a crime, or imputed to individuals as if a violation of a larger moral, religious, and political code and system—the social order as defined by the regime. As one author has written, subversion was the regime's enemy, but also its justification for existence (Huggins 1998:197). Subversion here and in subsequent chapters is discussed from the military's perspective: a "subversive" was someone thought to be so by the regime. While chapter 10 analyzes in depth a particular case of alleged subversion, it is impossible here to examine in such detail the many other cases referred to. The relevant fact is that the military and the security forces used the notion of subversion to level accusations against their enemies. The Church questioned the notion but often also the veracity of the alleged acts. The very ambiguity of these terms led the bishops and the officers to debate them at the Bipartite.

Chapter 2 **The Church and the Army**

Modernization and the Dual Revolution

This chapter explains why and how the cross and the sword clashed after 1964.[1] The first section traces their histories from the start of the First Republic (1889–1930) to the eve of the military government. The second section demonstrates the rapid deterioration in their relations after 1964 because of a dual revolution in which the Church embraced social justice and human rights and the military attacked subversion. The third section reveals new dimensions of the resulting struggle: the regime's mechanism for controlling the Church and the Catholic opposition's organization of a peaceful resistance. It also explores the meanings of subversion for the military and the security forces.

In this period Brazil struggled to throw off four centuries of dominance by monarchy and the powerful landed elite to become a modern nation. The country remained steeped in tradition nevertheless, experiencing the stresses of economic development, rapid and massive urbanization, intermittent attempts at democracy, and slow, unsure steps toward social reform. In seeking to influence this process, the Church and the Army coexisted in a dialectical relationship of collaboration and competition. Each endeavored to act as the high priest of a Brazilian national ideology defined according to the values of religious tradition, patriotism, and social order. The Church preached the notion of an "intrinsically Christian Brazil," whereas the military emphasized an ethic of "order and progress" rooted in nineteenth-century Positivism, a philosophy that advocated the replacement of religion with belief in scientific explanation (Sanchis 1980).

These two pillars of Brazilian society had much in common. They were modern Brazil's only nationally dispersed elite institutions

(McCann 1989:47–48). They shared an emphasis on hierarchy, obedience, and discipline. Both were dominated by males.[2] Neither tied itself to a single political current. Historically, each contributed to national integration. During the first decades of the independent empire (1822–1889), the military helped hold together Brazil's varied and often rebellious provinces. As Portugal's partner in colonization, the Church helped impose European cultural dominance. It implanted Catholicism, pacified and indoctrinated the natives and African slaves, educated the elite, and prescribed Western models of the family and sexuality. In the nineteenth and twentieth centuries a number of clergymen spurred the development of nationalism.

Church and Army also diverged in many ways. The former stressed spirituality and peace, the latter trained for war. The Church was a transnational organization with multiple allegiances—to Brazil, the homelands of its numerous foreign clergymen, and the Vatican. The Army was a strictly national institution, though it was deeply influenced by the German, French, and U.S. armed forces.

The Military Academy and the Catholic seminaries highlighted how two very different cultures emerged in the Army and the Church in the twentieth century. Candidates to the priesthood prepared for celibacy, the instruction of Catholic orthodoxy, and devotion to the transcendent. They dwelled in a place of books, crosses, cassocks, and saints. They congregated before the altar and sang hymns. The Virgin Mary was their protectress. Isolated from the world and its purported evils, seminarians prepared to minister to their flocks as representatives of God. They were to imitate Christ and prepare for a life of the mass, spirituality, and morals. Cadets learned to become leaders of a different kind. Bellies to the ground, bodies hardened, subject to harsh hazing and the rituals of martial life, they drilled for battle. Their world was one of military manuals, guns, uniforms, heroic warriors. Salutes and the barking of orders filled their days. They were judged by standards of physical courage and manliness. The cadets' isolation made them different from the rest of the populace, but they had far more frequent contact with the public, including women, than the seminarians (Castro 1990). In sum, ecclesiastical and military training turned out men with contrasting visions of society. The differences did not preclude cooperation, but they often hindered understanding.

The Quest for Modernization

As Brazil began to modernize in the mid–nineteenth century the Church and the Army each responded to internal crises by seeking to reorganize and to increase their influence in society. As part of the emerging middle sectors, officers entered politics in order to improve their social status. They decried government neglect of the Army and the incompetence of civilian politicians. In 1889, the Army overthrew Emperor Dom Pedro II and set up Brazil's first military dictatorship (1889–1894). The increasingly interventionist armed forces took over the emperor's former role as a "moderating power" in civilian political crises. The military sought to create respect for authority. Sometimes it went to extremes, as in the bloody massacre of thousands at Canudos in 1897. "Order and progress"—not republican democracy—became the motto of the new Brazilian flag. The Army came to see itself as the *povo fardado* (the people in uniform), a justification for later incursions into politics (Carvalho 1987:48–52; Stepan 1971:43–44, 99).

During the First Republic, the Army struggled to maintain unity and to redefine its purpose and mechanisms of social control. Reforms in officer training aimed to strengthen institutional cohesiveness and discipline. French advisors convinced the leadership of the relationship between internal security, national defense, and the economy—the inspiration for the national security rationale of the 1950s and beyond. In the 1920s, young nationalistic officers, discontented with corruption and political favoritism, rebelled against the powerful rural oligarchy and their government allies. These *tenentes* (lieutenants) backed the liberal revolution that brought Vargas to power in 1930. Opposing factions emerged within this group, however. They helped define the struggle between the Brazilian left and the conservative proponents of the Doctrine of National Security (DNS) in the 1950s and 1960s.

The Church struggled to overcome chronic weakness caused by a jealous monarchy's restrictions on the clergy—for example, the expulsion of the powerful Jesuit order in 1759. From 1872 to 1875, Church and state clashed over the so-called Religious Question. Senator Cândido Mendes, the great-grandfather of Bipartite founder Candido Mendes, defended Dom Vital Maria Gonçalves de Oliveira and Dom Antônio de Macedo Costa, two bishops jailed for ignoring a government order allowing Masons to remain members of the important Catholic confraternities. The Church and the armed forces began the republican era in conflict. The Positivist-inspired military regime separated Church from state and ended Catholic privileges.

During the First Republic, freedom from government control allowed the Church to rebuild under the direction of the Vatican. The Catholic restoration spawned an ideology of neo-Christendom, which advocated a religious monopoly and a major political role for the Church. Under the leadership of Dom Sebastião Leme da Silveira Cintra, the archbishop of Olinda and Recife (1916–1921) and later

Rio de Janeiro (1930–1942), the Church recovered its privileges, and leaders acknowledged it as a bulwark of social stability. With Vargas, Church and state established an informal pact of cooperation, or moral concordat (Beozzo 1986:275, 287–89, 293–98). This was an extraordinary achievement in comparison with the cases of such countries as Mexico, Chile, Cuba, and France, where the church failed to reenter the public domain after being forced out. It included state subsidies for Catholic social works. This aid renewed the Church's historical role as a social arm of the state but also created financial dependence (Serbin 1995). The moral concordat thrived under President Eurico Gaspar Dutra (1946–1951), the second Vargas government (1951–1954), and the terms of Juscelino Kubitschek (1956–1961), Jânio Quadros (1961), and João Goulart (1961–1964).

The Church's new prominence led to vast improvement in its relations with the armed forces. As Positivism waned in the 1920s, the number of officers seeking baptism increased, and the Church cooperated with the military on the draft (Carvalho 1982). In 1923, Pope Pius XI issued a papal blessing for the Irmandade da Santa Cruz dos Militares (Military Confraternity of the Holy Cross) and granted it prestigious affiliation with a basilica in Rome (*Irmandade* 1981; *Relatório* 1952). Banned under the First Republic, military chaplaincies were revived in the 1930s. During this period the military cultivated new respect for the Church hierarchy. For instance, the military hailed Dom Leme as a "soldier of our country," after he arranged for the peaceful departure of deposed President Washington Luís Pereira de Sousa in the Revolution of 1930 ("Dom Sebastião Leme" 1930:26).

Political trends in the 1930s reinforced the Church-military relationship. A failed Communist revolt in 1935 caused a deep rift in the armed forces and heightened fear of Communism on the right and in the Church. The quasi-fascist Ação Integralista Brasileira (AIB; Brazilian Integralist Action) now gained influence. AIB adopted a heavily corporatist political philosophy combined with Catholicism, and it included many priests. Father Hélder Câmara, for instance, belonged to its supreme council. AIB also had a strong following in the military. But Vargas was interested more in holding power than in specific ideologies. After establishing the dictatorial Estado Novo with the military, he abolished AIB and all other political organizations. The Church, however, retained its privileges.

During World War II the Church sent military chaplains to minister to the Força Expedicionária Brasileira (FEB; Brazilian Expeditionary Force), which fought alongside U.S. forces in Italy. These priests built a strong relationship with the FEBianos.[3] One popular father, the Franciscan Frei Orlando, died in Italy and became patron of Brazil's military chaplains (Palhares 1969).

The "pious 1950s" marked the pinnacle of the neo-Christendom model and harmonious Church-state and Church-military relations.[4] For instance, the Thirty-Sixth International Eucharistic Congress, held in Rio in 1955, promoted the Catholic faith, anti-Communism, Brazilian tourism, and economic progress. More than a million people attended. Cardinal Jaime de Barros Câmara (Dom Leme's successor) and his auxiliary, Dom Hélder, united the efforts of the federal government, the business community, laborers, and the armed forces, which provided generous logistical and material support.[5]

Paragons of the moral concordat, Dom Jaime and Dom Hélder maintained close ties to the military. As a child, Dom Jaime first wanted to enter the military. A number of his relatives were officers. His uncle and godfather was Marshal João Xavier da Câmara, a Positivist who nevertheless believed that "a priest serves our country just as well as a soldier" (Calliari 1996:32). His older half-brother became a colonel. As archbishop, Dom Jaime was vicar of the armed forces and supported the military chaplaincies. He traveled on Brazilian Air Force planes, met regularly with high officials, and frequently celebrated special masses for the military, including the

Dom Leme (seated at left) escorting deposed president Washington Luís to safety during the Revolution of 1930. The cardinal's leadership brought the Church to new prominence in Brazilian life and inaugurated the era of the moral concordat.

Anti-Communism strengthened Church-Army ties during the cold war. Using a jeep as an altar, a priest says an open-air mass for soldiers and their families in Cachoeira do Sul, Rio Grande do Sul, April 1947.

annual memorial services for soldiers killed in the 1935 Communist uprising. (After 1964 these commemorations served as a warning against the dangers of leftist revolution.) When Dom Jaime died in 1970, the Air Force flew his body to Rio de Janeiro for burial (Calliari 1996). Dom Hélder was especially popular with the elite. He became an advisor to President Kubitschek. His prestige extended to the armed services, where he preached to soldiers. Officers donated to his charitable fund, the Banco da Providência (Caramuru interview).

The Church and the Armed Forces, 1955–1974: The Dual Revolution

In the 1950s, however, the Church and the armed forces also began to plant seeds of disagreement. Both worked to modernize again by developing new ideologies in response to new challenges. The political polarization of the 1960s deepened these differences. Ideological and historical shifts unleashed a dual revolution in Brazil. These were not social revolutions, but institutional, political, and religious. They had a deep impact on both the military and the Church and for two decades largely shaped national life. On the one hand the armed forces overthrew President Goulart to avert what it believed would be the communization of Brazil. The armed forces referred to this action as the Revolution of 1964. They quickly expanded their fight against Communism to include all opponents of the Brazilian status quo (as defined by the regime). On the other hand most of the bishops instinctively supported the coup as an anti-Communist measure. As polarization led to violence and the military deepened its control of the country, however, the Church carried out a religious revolution in which it stressed social justice and assimilated the efforts of a new generation of Catholic radicals. Over the next ten years, the Church and the military engaged in the worst conflict in their history.

The Military

The military revolution began after World War II. The integration of U.S. and Brazilian militaries was unparalleled in Latin America and led Brazil to believe it had a special relationship with the United States. Sweetened with aid packages, these ties led the FEBianos to join the West in the cold war.

In 1949 the Army established the National War College, the ESG, modeled on the U.S. National War College, which became a bastion of anti-Communism and the advocate of free trade. The Army also formulated a new Doctrine of National Security (DNS), which reflected the experience of total war in Europe and the fear of internal threats to security from the cold war. DNS focused on the political and psychological dangers of leftism and asserted the interdependence of security and economic development. The ESG, which also had civilian graduates, expanded the armed forces' role in politics and supplied the leadership of the military regime. In the analysis of historian Carlos Fico, the ESG and the DNS reflected the Brazilian elite's traditional authoritarian view of the Brazilian people as morally degenerate and lazy and therefore incapable of self-government (Fico 1997). Like the Positivists and the *tenentes,* the ESG program hoped to reform the nation in a military mold (McCann 1989:75). Ultimately, the DNS helped resurrect Brazil's centuries-old aim to become a world power and cast the armed services as defenders of Western Christian civilization against Communism (Fico 1997:85–86).

The ESG competed for political influence with the CNBB, the Brazilian Communist Party (PCB), and the Instituto Superior de Estudos Brasileiros (ISEB; Advanced Institute for Brazilian Studies). The ISEB was a nationalistic think tank formed within the Ministry of Education in 1954. Members such as Candido Mendes espoused the Vargas and Kubitschek models of nationalist developmentalism and political and cultural independence. The CNBB and the Church essentially represented a "third way" reformist strategy that rejected extreme leftism but also criticized capitalism.

The ESG officers played an important role in political events between 1954 and 1964. They opposed Vargas, who ended his second presidency (1951–1954) by committing suicide after the military pressured him to resign. Some tried to block Vargas's political heir Juscelino Kubitschek from inauguration to the presidency in 1956, only to be foiled by a preemptive coup staged by moderates. (The ESG candidate, General Juarez Távora, had lost the election.) In 1961 the conservative officers nearly prevented Vice President João Goulart, another Vargas heir, from assuming the top office after President Quadros, elected in 1960, suddenly resigned. Anti-Communism became the justification for these military interventions.

The Cuban Revolution, the failed Bay of Pigs invasion, and the Cuban missile crisis raised the stakes of the cold war and made Latin America a crucial center of operations. As revolutionary warfare erupted around the globe, Brazil joined the U.S. and other Latin American militaries in preparing counterinsurgency operations. Conservative officers opposed the populist Goulart because of his ties to Vargas, unions, Communists, and other groups demanding profound social reform. As he turned left, Goulart angered conservatives and the United States. Anti-Communism reached a frenzy. ESG officers, businessmen, and opposition politicians conspired to overthrow Goulart, and half a million people, including conservative Catholics, marched in protest against the government in the streets of São Paulo.

The *golpe*, or coup, that came on March 31, 1964, inaugurated an era of violent McCarthyism in Brazil and Latin America. Golpes ensued elsewhere until virtually all the region fell under anti-Communist military rule in the 1970s. These regimes shared a common belief in national development, anti-Marxism, and disdain for politicians and traditional liberal democracy (Loveman 1999:187–88).

The military revealed plans for long-term occupation of the Palácio do Planalto, the presidential offices in Brasília. A helpless Brazilian Congress voted in as president General Humberto de Alencar Castello Branco, a FEBiano, ESG member, and coup leader. The military swiftly purged the armed forces and the political system of thousands of leftists, labor leaders, opposition politicians, officers, priests, and Catholic militants. Many were tortured. In 1965, the military replaced the three major political parties with two official ones and made certain elections indirect. In 1967, it issued a new constitution. Manipulation of elections and the political system continued to the end of the regime.

Intelligence-gathering and repression were top priorities of the dictatorship. In 1964 chief ESG ideologue Colonel Golbery do Couto e Silva, a FEBiano, founded the

SNI. The SNI spied widely on Brazilians and worked with other agencies to combat subversion. Its power became so immense that Golbery later lamented he had created "a monster" (D'Araujo, Soares, and Castro 1994a:14). However, the feared CIE, the Centro de Informações da Marinha (CENIMAR; Navy Information Center), and the Centro de Informações e Segurança da Aeronáutica (CISA; Air Force Information and Security Center) carried out the actual repressive operations and became powerful components of the intelligence community. Through the CIE, for example, the Army Ministry commanded the DOI-CODI interrogation centers. The intelligence community formed "a state within the state" (Stepan 1988:27).[6] In 1967 Castello Branco issued the Lei de Segurança Nacional (LSN; National Security Law), which made national security a civic duty. These measures established the basic repressive policies of the regime until the abertura gained momentum at the end of Geisel's term.

In the early years, the generals spoke of redemocratization, but the prospects lessened as conflict between the regime and the opposition worsened and as intra-military factionalism developed. A fundamental division became clear between the so-called Castellistas (the moderate soft-line group of Castello Branco), and the Costistas (the more radical hard-liners, followers of General Artur da Costa e Silva). The Castellistas demonstrated a greater outward commitment to democracy and constitutional procedure, and saw military intervention as only a temporary solution to political crises. They wanted a quick return to civilian rule. The Castellistas included Golbery, Ernesto Geisel, Muricy, and a host of other generals who had studied at the ESG. Because of their more intellectual orientation they became known as the Sorbonne Group. They were also largely pro-American. The hard-liners foiled Castello Branco's plans to redemocratize, forced the regime to become more authoritarian, and pushed successfully for the election of Costa e Silva, who took office in 1967. The hard-liners had strength among the colonels and tended to be more nationalistic than the Castellistas. They emphasized repression of the opposition and the Church and were more distrustful of civilian politicians. They generally opposed a quick return to civilian rule and in the 1970s fought for the permanence of the military in power. They committed terrorist acts in an attempt to push the regime further to the right. Costa e Silva, who himself announced intentions to humanize the Revolution, increasingly lost control of the hard-liners, who forced him to deepen martial rule yet further.

Although the soft-line/hard-line categorization is helpful for understanding the regime, other subfactions developed based on the personal leadership and ideological tendencies of particular generals. In the late 1960s and early 1970s all factions rallied around Costa e Silva and Médici in the fight against the guerrillas. Whether any of them were actually democratic is highly doubtful, because they had supported the overthrow of the freely elected Goulart.

The year 1968 was critical. Around the world cold war paranoia, student protest against the establishment, and cultural experimentalism reached their height. In Brazil labor strikes and student protests against the regime and its pro-American policies led to a renewed crackdown on the opposition. The cascade of events began in March 1968 when a policeman killed a student, Edson Luís de Lima Souto, sparking street battles between soldiers and students in Rio de Janeiro and nationwide protests. In June, one hundred thousand people filed through the streets of Rio in the largest demonstration against the regime since the coup. Both right-wing terrorists and leftist revolutionaries had become active in Brazil in the early 1960s,[7] but the increasingly polarized domestic and international political climate intensified the radical left's violent efforts to overthrow the government. It appeared as if the military were losing control.

The situation worsened after congressman Márcio Moreira Alves denounced the repression and asked Brazilian women to deny themselves to men in uniform. The hard-liners staged a "coup within a coup" against Costa e Silva, forcing him to issue Ato Institucional No. 5 (AI-5; Institutional Act No. 5). Broadcast repeatedly on December 13, 1968, AI-5 closed Congress, eliminated civil liberties and freedom of the press, and gave the military carte blanche to squash the opposition. Hundreds were arrested. One visiting foreign political scientist observed that AI-5 provided the Brazilian armed forces with more powers than Mussolini had held in fascist Italy (Trindade 1994:136).

National politics became the domain of the armed forces. Along with growing competition among diverse factions, this immense responsibility threatened to shatter military unity. An intense competition for Costa e Silva's post ensued after he suffered a stroke in August 1969. The compromise choice was General Médici, the commander of the Third Army in Rio Grande do Sul, former SNI head, and for many the best bet to keep peace within the military.[8] Although Médici finished his term uncontested for power, many at first wondered whether his political weakness and inexperience would permit him to survive. Such was the assessment of a secret seven-hundred-page study prepared for Henry Kissinger in late 1969. A team of U.S. diplomatic, military, and national security officials interviewed members of the Brazilian elite and commented on the country's political and socioeconomic conditions.[9] The threat of social instability was especially dangerous.

Brazil had begun a small-scale civil war.[10] The spiral of guerrilla warfare and repression made the Médici era the most violent of the regime. In the cities the guerrillas hoped to spark a popular uprising. In emulation of the Chinese and Cuban Revolutions, they also tried to open a rural front in the vast Amazon region. They stockpiled arms, robbed banks, exploded bombs, kidnapped diplomats, and attacked military installations. The most spectacular operation was the September 1969 abduction of U.S. ambassador Burke Elbrick. To obtain his release the military agreed to broadcast the guerrillas' revolutionary manifesto and to fly fifteen political prisoners to safety in Mexico City on September 7, 1969, Independence Day.

In response Médici allowed the military, the police, and special antiguerrilla units to work freely. They fiercely counterattacked, spying on leftists, infiltrating their ranks, and raiding hideouts. With thousands of victims, the use of torture to extract information was clearly a policy of the military regime (Nassif 1995). The "dirty war" against subversives resulted in 138 disappearances and 184 deaths (Comissão de Familiares 1996:9–18). These numbers paled beside the statistics of the regime in Argentina, where estimates put the number of *desaparecidos* at 10,000 or more, or in Guatemala, where a decades-long war between guerrillas and the government took as many as 200,000 lives. The figures become even less significant in light of Brazil's population, the largest in the region. Even so, Brazil's security forces created an effective climate of fear by systematically intimidating the populace. At a moment's notice troops and agents could round up thousands of people. Torturers used a horrifying array of techniques on prisoners: beatings, starvation, suffocation, near drowning, electric shocks to the genitals, rape, exposure to snakes and cockroaches, psychological abuse, and the infamous "parrot's perch," a metal bar from which a bound individual was hung, then shocked and beaten. The São Paulo archdiocesan report *Brasil: nunca mais* later documented the abuses in detail.[11] By 1971 the military had largely liquidated the urban guerrilla threat; the Amazon fighters went down between 1973 and early 1975. As a result, the government was able to relax the repression, but shocking incidents still kept alive the fear of repression throughout the Geisel years.

One of Médici's most potent weapons was a brilliant, subtle propaganda campaign carried out by his special assistant for public relations, Colonel Octávio Costa, with the assistance of psychologists, sociologists, journalists, and publicity agencies. Costa's work advanced the techniques of modern political advertising in Brazil. His films and television spots conspicuously lacked personal reference to the generals and deflected attention from the dirty war by avoiding mention of the guerrilla movement. Costa's campaign stole the opposition's thunder. His puns turned the revolutionary left's favorite slogans into catchy phrases expressing the

Regime propagandist Colonel Octávio Costa lauded the "miracle" while ignoring the guerrillas.

government's concern for the people. For instance, "down with the dictatorship" became "down with the dictatorship of prices" (on Costa and publicity, see Fico 1997). The regime skillfully used religious symbols and language to demonstrate its adherence to Catholic culture—for example, by incorporating statements from papal encyclicals in descriptions of government programs (Comblin 1979). Borrowing Christian themes, Colonel Costa's "spiritualized" propaganda often spoke of love, peace, social harmony, solidarity, participation, and "nonviolence."[12] Não-Violência was the name of an opposition group founded by Dom Hélder.

On the economic front, the regime worked to correct what it saw as the errors

Playing the role of politician, General Médici visits the Transamazon Highway in October 1971. It became one of the symbols of his administration's drive to enhance Brazil's greatness.

and profligacy of Vargas and his successors. Conservative technocrats figured prominently in government strategy. Castello Branco's pro–United States advisors moved to cut the high inflation rate, stabilize the economy, and attract foreign investment. These policies laid the basis for the high growth rates of the so-called economic miracle of the late 1960s and early 1970s, when annual growth topped 10 percent. During this period the government invested heavily in infrastructural projects such as dams and the Transamazon Highway and provided fiscal incentives for loggers and ranchers to exploit the rain forest. In São Paulo heavy industry boomed. In the 1970s the generals also made Brazil a major arms exporter. The social price of economic success was the repression of the workers, with the regime prohibiting strikes and intervening in an already paternalistic labor system inherited from Vargas. Wages showed little if any improvement (Alves 1985:74–79, 151–53).[13] Yet Médici was popular. Although the poor owned less and less of the total wealth, jobs were plentiful. Economic euphoria affected all sectors of the population as Brazil grew from forty-third-largest economy in the West in 1964 to the eighth-largest in 1980.[14]

The Church

The Church's revolution also began after World War II. Rapid socioeconomic change, the threat of Communism, the growth of Protestantism and Afro-Brazilian religions, and the assimilation of European theological and philosophical innovations provided impetus for change within the Church. Priests, bishops, and lay workers adhered to a new economic nationalism and preached social transformation. For instance, in the late 1940s bishops began demanding reform of the highly inequitable system of landholding, which they saw as the cause of burgeoning migration to the urban slums. Many Catholics also questioned the neo-Christendom model of the Church.

A key innovation was the creation in 1952 of the CNBB, one of the world's first episcopal conferences and one of the foundations of Brazilian Catholic progressivism. Dom Hélder, other bishops from his native Northeast, and a small group of priests and lay volunteers dominated the CNBB during his tenure as secretary general (1952–1964). The CNBB served as an advocate for the Brazilian Church at the national and international levels, sponsored biannual (and later annual) assemblies, and addressed numerous Church problems, including the need to establish national pastoral and political strategies. Most important, it advocated economic nationalism as the way to social progress (Bernal 1989). Dom Hélder also helped found the Conselho Episcopal Latino-Americano (CELAM; Council of Latin

35

American Bishops). At the second general assembly of CELAM at Medellín, Colombia, in 1968 the bishops forged a statement calling for social justice and condemning Latin American underdevelopment and violence. This statement launched liberation theology and the Popular Church in the continent.

A strong Catholic left emerged in Brazil in the early 1960s. The leading group was Ação Católica Brasileira (ACB; Brazilian Catholic Action), which became heavily influenced by economic nationalism. Counseled by priests, in the late 1950s young ACB militants joined the labor movement. Many worked in the Church's Movimento de Educação de Base (MEB; Basic Education Movement). Like other literacy programs of the era, MEB stressed *conscientização,* the political "consciousness-raising" of the downtrodden. The most radical ACB groups were the Juventude Operária Católica (JOC; Catholic Youth Workers) and the Juventude Universitária Católica (JUC; Catholic University Youth). They were further galvanized by the Cuban Revolution into advocating anti-imperialist socialism.

Change in the international Church legitimated innovations in Brazil and spurred others. Meeting in Rome from 1962 to 1965, the Second Vatican Council (Vatican II) gathered more than two thousand bishops and hundreds of theologians from around the globe. They reformulated doctrine and structures in an attempt to move Catholicism out of its post–World War II malaise and toward relevancy in the rapidly changing modern world. Vatican II was clearly the most wide-ranging reform in the history of the Church. It approved such novelties as worker-priests, the mass in the vernacular (instead of the traditional Latin), and greater emphasis on the laity as the "people of God," a trend shared by ACB. Vatican II stressed dialogue within the institution and with other faiths and philosophies. Although dominated by Europeans, Vatican II assimilated many ideas from Latin America, thanks to the behind-the-scenes lobbying of Dom Hélder and Dom Manuel Larraín of Chile. In turn, the council's emphasis on social justice and human rights impelled Latin American theologians, clergymen, and sisters to delve into work with the impoverished majority.

Human rights were an especially new idea for the Church. The Church had hesitated in adopting human rights because of their close association with liberalism, an enemy of Catholicism in the nineteenth century. In his 1963 encyclical *Pacem in Terris,* Pope John XXIII, who had convoked Vatican II, made the United Nations' 1948 Universal Declaration of Human Rights part of the official teaching of the Church (Lowden 1996:13).

Vatican II created great expectations but also great uncertainty in the Church. After so much change, what did it now mean to be Catholic? Priests embodied the crisis of identity. They were suddenly expected to leap from a sixteenth- to a twentieth-century mentality, but Vatican II had done little to clarify their role. Surveys and scrutiny by sociologists did little to help. Some clergymen bared their souls before psychoanalysts. Others sought relevance by living among the poor and resisting the dictatorship. Many awaited the development of a more democratic Church and an end to obligatory celibacy. But dialogue had limits, and the Vatican refused to budge on these last two points. As a result, tens of thousands of clergymen left the ministry. In Brazil alone almost two thousand of the country's thirteen thousand fathers quit their positions in the late 1960s and 1970s. The Church lost some of its best minds. For the bishops it was a painful situation that undercut their ability to command their clergy, tend their flocks, and show a secure face to the military.[15]

In the midst of Vatican II, the coup provided a political litmus test for the Church. Brazil's political polarization highlighted two opposing camps. On the right stood religious and social conservatives, who decried the dangers of change. On the left were ACB militants, radical priests, and the CNBB leadership, which had supported Goulart's social reforms. The two sides clashed when thirty-three of the leading bishops assembled at a special meeting in late May 1964 to write a declaration on the Revolution. The conservatives praised the coup and condemned Communism. A previously unstudied draft of the progressives' statement showed that originally they pushed for a condemnation of the "martyrdom" of Catholics targeted by the repression. The draft criticized the military for claiming the right to distinguish between Christianity and Marxism and for lacking respect for even the pope. If the regime refused dialogue, the progressives were prepared to jettison the moral concordat in order to preserve the "purity" of the Church's testimony.[16] Had this document been published, it would have overshadowed even the episcopal statements of the 1970s that harshly criticized the regime but did not call for a break with the state.

The two sides compromised. The result was a confusing, self-contradictory pronouncement that profusely thanked the armed forces for saving Brazil from Communism as it also pleaded for an end to attacks on Church activists and for protection from "the abuses of liberal capitalism" (Lima 1979:147–49). This was an odd and surrealistic restatement of the traditional Catholic "third way" between Communism and capitalism. More significant, in the words of priest-journalist Charles Antoine, the bishops showed "an extraordinary agility in the art of compromise, even at the risk of opening the way to injustice." Indeed, the declaration served as an important vote of confidence for the new regime.[17]

37

Some bishops took a neutral position by advocating a wait-and-see approach. This last group included progressives such as Dom Hélder, who held out hope that social reform could move ahead under the new government. Although he did not win their full confidence, Dom Hélder remained cordial with the military leaders and initially refrained from criticizing them in public.[18]

Indeed, until the early 1970s most bishops maintained a cautious but hopeful attitude toward the regime and largely remained silent as Catholic radicals were arrested and tortured. The bishops themselves dissolved JUC in 1968, and JOC was brutally hounded by the security forces, leaving ACB a shell of its former self. Many bishops even doubted that abuses existed.[19] Political considerations caused the Church to hold back on its criticism of torture. In 1969, for instance, Father Amaury Castanho, the editor of the archdiocesan newspaper *O São Paulo*, prepared an editorial against torture but was ordered by Cardinal Agnelo Rossi, the archbishop of São Paulo, not to print it.[20]

The repression aggravated tensions between Catholic ultraconservatives and progressives, but on the whole it caused the Church to close ranks to defend itself and other victims of the regime. In the late 1960s, some bishops started to denounce torture and violence as well as the government's highly inegalitarian economic policies. Soon the Church became the "voice of the voiceless," practically the only institution able to contest the dictatorship.[21] As power in the CNBB shifted to the progressives, former ACB members and other militants undertook grassroots political and religious activism. The emerging Popular Church implemented a series of politically important innovations such as the Comunidades Eclesiais de Base (CEBs; Basic Ecclesial Communities) and organizations to promote the redistribution of land, the rights of Amerindians, and the independent labor movement. The Popular Church's theoretical blueprint was liberation theology, which emphasized social transformation as salvation.

Repression and Church Resistance, 1969–1974

The military increasingly viewed the Church as a nest of subversion, especially the radical sectors that opposed the government. Military suspicions started as early as 1960, when General Castello Branco warned Dom Hélder that the Church was "abandoning its religious functions and exaggerating its involvement in the affairs of the state" (Viana Filho 1976:530–31). The attacks on the Church were the worst since the expulsion of the Jesuits two centuries earlier. Looking for subversive literature, in 1967 soldiers invaded the home of Dom Waldyr Calheiros de Novaes, the bishop of the important steel town of Volta Redonda. Bishops and clergy from around Brazil voiced their indignation, which exacerbated tensions with the generals. General José Horácio da Cunha Garcia's bulletin to his troops described the progressives as "bacteria" infecting Brazilian society. "Let us not forget that priests have much more contact than we do with the people, especially poor people," he warned. "Even though they are Catholic, these individuals have betrayed the Revolution. Today they are working for the opposition, not the one in Congress and the press, but the one that wanted to Communize Brazil in 1964."[22]

During the Médici years the security agencies focused intensively on the Church. In Recife the authorities constantly harassed Dom Hélder for his progressive statements. In 1969, his assistant Father Henrique Pereira Neto was murdered by a right-wing group. Once decorated by the armed forces, Dom Hélder tried to recover the medals he had given to friends because he needed them as a potential passport to safety in case of imprisonment (Bandeira 1994:81). In May 1970, he denounced torture at a large public meeting in Paris. This and other pronouncements led the infuriated generals to consider him a traitor. The government unleashed a major smear campaign against Dom Hélder and schemed successfully to deny him the Nobel Peace Prize. It then barred his name from the media. Many moderates and even conservatives were affected by the repression. For instance, the DOI-CODI in Belo Horizonte tortured to death a nephew of Dom Jaime suspected of involvement in the kidnapping of the Swiss ambassador.[23]

The regime's biggest triumph was the assassination of Carlos Marighella, the founder of Ação Libertadora Nacional (ALN; National Liberating Action), the most important of the urban guerrilla groups. Hundreds of people belonged to ALN, one of the two groups that had abducted the U.S. ambassador. Led by the infamous torturer Sérgio Paranhos Fleury, in November 1969 the São Paulo political police ambushed and killed Marighella. To catch him, the police first captured and tortured Dominican friars who collaborated with the ALN. The government widely publicized this affair to discredit the progressive clergy and to pressure the Church against criticizing the regime. After a military trial the government imprisoned three of the Dominicans.[24]

A partial Church tally between 1968 and 1978 documented more than a hundred arrests of priests, seven deaths, and numerous cases of torture, expulsion of foreigners, invasion of buildings, threats, indictments, abductions, infiltration by government agents, censorship, prohibition of masses and meetings, and forgeries and falsifications of documents and publications. Thirty bishops were victims of the repression. Priests faced charges stemming from their sermons, antigovernment protests, alleged membership in subversive organizations, the harboring of fugitives, defense of human rights, grassroots pastoral work, and other activities.[25] In addition, the Church suffered constant verbal attacks from regime officials ranging from complaints about political activity to accusations of sexual immorality. "Communist" was one of the most frequent adjectives.

Intelligence-gathering by the DOPS facilitated the repression. These state-level political police were organized early in the century and played a major role in the Estado Novo repression and the surveillance of Communists in the 1940s and 1950s. Early in the cold war, the DOPS already detected supposed Communist infiltration in JOC and other religious organizations.[26] After 1964 they worked closely with the military, federal, and local services. Organizations such as the DOI-CODI were created because the DOPS were insufficient for handling guerrilla warfare (with the exception of Fleury's brutal São Paulo department). The DOPS nevertheless aided the repression. The DOPS-GB Information Division in Rio de Janeiro, for instance, collected and shared information on subversion. It employed sixty people just to manage and analyze its vast files. The DOPS-GB also legally controlled the foreign travel of all citizens, ran security checks on candidates for important government jobs, and provided individuals with certificates of a correct ideological record for prospective employers. During the Médici years, the DOPS-GB issued as many as five thousand of these certificates per month. In addition, the DOPS-GB had units for gathering evidence and arresting and interrogating suspects, at times in collaboration with military agencies (Maurano interview).[27]

The DOPS-GB carried out extensive surveillance on the Church in the search for the slightest hint of subversive activity. It seized personal papers, studied newspapers and Church publications, worked to learn the content of Church meetings, listened to preachers, read parish flyers, and tracked the movement of clergy and bishops.[28] The DOPS-GB kept an extensive file on Dom Paulo Evaristo Arns, the archbishop of São Paulo and Dom Hélder's successor as Brazil's most important human rights leader. It noted, for instance, that Dom Paulo visited prisoners, spoke to the press about torture, and maintained contacts with the left. "He is a new Dom Hélder Câmara who is trying to project himself," one report stated.[29] A detailed DOPS-GB profile of Dom Hélder revealed the workings of the regime's smear campaign against him. Probably written with the help of Church insiders, it praised his abilities but accused him of disloyalty to the Church and friends, the use of poverty for political ends, and the misappropriation of Church funds. Dated in 1969, the report appeared a year later in *O Estado de São Paulo,* a daily newspaper that participated in the attacks on the archbishop.[30] There were also files on bishops who were seen as friends of the military such as Dom Eugênio de Araújo Sales, Dom Jaime's successor as archbishop of Rio de Janeiro.[31] The DOPS agents paid attention to a wide variety of Church groups, themes, and activities, including Catholic Action, alleged subversion in Catholic schools and seminaries, bishops' meetings in Rome, and publications that denounced the regime. DOPS-GB further noted that priests and lay activists used their "cover" as Catholics to hide militants fleeing from the authorities. The Church's international status allowed both native and foreign fathers "to circulate freely throughout national territory, using their priestly vestments as passports."[32] The CNBB was also closely watched.[33]

DOPS in Rio and elsewhere also collaborated with the infamous DOI-CODI units. Both soldiers and police officers filled the ranks of the DOI-CODI, which routinely used torture in its interrogations. The DOPS-GB Information Division received DOI-CODI interrogation reports of an investigation into an international opposition movement involving clergymen and other individuals linked to the Church. At least one of the suspects was tortured.[34]

In mid-1971, DOPS-GB contemplated a full-blown national investigation of the progressive Church, including its foreign contacts. The SNI had already requested a nationwide investigation of ACB in 1966,[35] and in 1969 a similar proposal came from the First Army, which investigated "subversive activities in the Catholic Church" in Minas Gerais and Rio de Janeiro. The colonel in charge wanted the Second, Third, and Fourth Armies to follow suit.[36] The DOPS-GB agents recognized, however, that the inevitable international repercussions of a national operation made it politically delicate. The decision, they stated, lay with President Médici.[37] The investigation did not take place, although in March 1974 President Geisel requested an intelligence overview of the Church and subversion. It was prepared by CISA (Costa 1979). And in 1977 Dom Ivo revealed that the security forces were investigating Church finances and the ideological background of each bishop and priest ("Lorscheiter, Ivo," forthcoming). The Figueiredo administration also investigated Church finances (Evilásio de Jesus interview). In reality, the already widespread repression against the Church and the charges leveled against priests and lay activists in military tribunals made a larger inquiry unnecessary during the Médici years. Nevertheless, the Rio agents continued to supply Brazil's intelligence network with reports on the progressive clergy.

DOPS-GB analyses revealed that the profound suspicions about the Church flowed not only from anti-Communist extremism, but from a sense of betrayal concerning the clergy's abandonment of traditional Catholicism and, therefore, traditional Brazilian symbols and social structures. Like many military officers, conser-

vative civilians, and right-wing journalists, the police had difficulty comprehend-
ing—or outright rejected—the Church's new emphasis on social justice and other
innovations. Church and state were drifting apart not only politically but also in
terms of their cosmologies, which they had shared for centuries (Serbin 1993b, ch.
8). For instance, in the 1960s many priests began wearing black wooden rings as a
sign of a simpler Church and a commitment to the poor. A military investigation of
Dom Waldyr accused him of not using the proper ring of gold and precious stones
and preferring to be called simply "father."[38] A DOPS-GB report noted that Father
Francisco Rocha Guimarães "never wore a cassock." Even worse, he had given a sermon at the chapel of the Army's Copacabana Fort "using words that affronted the
elite" and consumer society.[39]

Other reports demonstrated concern about post–Vatican II questioning of
religious structures and practices. "The climate of disobedience to the pope and
the teachings of the Church is the result of Communist influence and infiltration, which introduced Christians to a certain spirit of disrespect towards authority and hierarchy," stated one. Another defined innovative priests as "visibly
Communist, revolutionary, without hierarchical distinctions, hardly using tem-
ples." They worked to raise the people's consciousness and to create CEBs. A
1972 CIE evaluation concluded that Dom Paulo's decision to allow a new version of
the mass at São Paulo's traditional Consolação church would make it look like a
"brothel."[40]

One perceptive DOPS-GB report attributed Church-regime conflict to the crisis
in Catholicism. It viewed the clergy's oppositional politics as a conscious choice for
shoring up a flagging institution. Brutally honest, the report also invited criticism
of the regime with respect to military strategy toward the Church. Before 1964,
priests had opposed Communists and even competed with them in the union
movement, it stated. Now, however, priests allied with Communism. "Could it be
that Communist propaganda is so efficient that it was able to Communize the clergy? Or have we been incapable of keeping on our side our most traditional and natural allies in the struggle against Communism?" For two decades the Church had
suffered a crisis of faith. "So the Vatican began to carry out a true war to stabilize
the faith and conquer new members. To do so it resorted to arms that only recently would have been inadmissable." The Church changed the mass, clergymen's
clothing, and its music in order to attract youths "in the same way that the missionary of the colonial period used the Tupi-Guarani language to catechize the
natives." The military's big mistake was its failure to emulate the clergy's efforts to
move closer to the people. For instance, the regime had failed to explain immedi-

ately the need for repression; it too needed to "raise the consciousness" of the people for its own political ends. "Hence there was the impression that the government stood on one side and the people on the other," allowing the Communists to score a public relations victory and to attract the clergy to their cause. Without winning over the people, repression would have no effect, the report concluded.[41]

The regime attempted to counteract the progressive Church in other ways. One was to discredit radical priests. After the August 1970 arrest of JOC Latin America coordinator Father Agostinho Pretto, security agents smeared his reputation by occupying his home in a Rio favela for several months. They claimed to be searching for a clandestine radio unit used for contacting revolutionary leader Carlos Lamarca, a hated Army deserter. They also planted arms in the home at night and removed them in sight of favela residents during the day (Pretto interview).

Another stategy used against the Church was to give greater leeway to competing religions such as Umbanda and Protestant Pentecostalism, which had been gaining adherents in the Army and the general population. Repressed during the Estado Novo and combated by the Church in the 1950s, the nationalistic, syncretistic Umbanda grew rapidly after World War II and by 1964 had drawn in 4 percent of the officer corps. During the regime its popularity increased. The military not only allowed Umbanda to operate freely but recognized its holidays, counted its members in the census, and moved its tens of thousands of religious centers from police to civil jurisdiction. In the Amazon region, the Pentecostals received open support from Jarbas Passarinho, a military governor and then Minister of Education, while the Presbyterian Church throughout Brazil heavily supported the regime.[42]

Some in the military tried to stir further animosity against the progressive clergy by raising charges of sexual immorality. A number of bishops were characterized as women chasers (Soares, D'Araujo, and Castro 1995:204). To denigrate his image, the intelligence services circulated pictures of Dom Ivo sitting with a woman in a movie house. Others were accused of homosexuality, which was detested and rooted out in witch-hunt fashion within the armed forces (Octávio Costa interview 3). Army intelligence, for example, noted that one monk who supported the opposition was rumored to be a pederast.[43] In sum, the meanings of subversion varied according to the specific objectives of repressive actions and also the background and degree of sophistication of the security agents.

The Church countered the military with a three-pronged effort. First, the bishops' promotion of human rights and denunciations of regime atrocities stimulated opposition and created a public relations disaster for the generals outside Brazil.

The bishops reacted in large part because of pressure from the clergy and the Catholic grassroots. Second, the Church worked for social and ideological changes that contested the military's development strategy. These types of opposition were mainly political. A third and little known aspect sought to build an active, though entirely peaceful resistance movement.

Resistance took a number of forms. Progressive bishops, priests, and militants schemed to avoid repression directed against themselves and others by developing specific tactics for evading surveillance and aggression. Priests, bishops, and nuns hid fugitive revolutionaries and other individuals sought by the security forces. Some fled the country with Church help. Father Pretto harbored refugees in the Catholic schools where children of the elite studied. To mislead the police he placed a sign at one school entrance reading "silence—retreat."[44] In Belo Horizonte, to avoid interception of their mail, one group of priests used a social center for housemaids as an address. Confessionals served as drops for messages about political prisoners. One of these notes led Father Luiz Viegas de Carvalho to inform a soldier that his guerrilla son was wounded. The priest then helped the son escape (Luiz Viegas interview 2). While in prison Father Nathanael de Moraes Campos informed his bishop about torture by way of messages placed in the bottom of a thermos brought by a visiting relative.[45] To avoid further torture, Father Mário Prigol faked a circulatory illness and pretended innocence before interrogators' questions (Prigol interview).

The Church built its own intelligence service. Priests received information from contacts at all levels of society. The Church learned of the October 1970 jailing of priests in Maranhão from prostitutes who reported to the local curia how they had heard soldiers bragging in a bordello about the torture of one of the men. On another occasion, prostitutes fearful of being dismissed as unserious had friends of Dom Hélder take them to the archbishop to warn him of an assassination plot.[46] Members of the armed forces also helped the clergy avoid repression. For example, in Recife Father Ernanne Pinheiro, a close assistant to Dom Hélder, met with officers at the local military base for study sessions on *Populorum Progressio*, Pope Paul VI's controversial 1968 statement on economic justice. One of the men was married to Father Ernanne's cousin. The officers told the priest of their opposition to torture and how they had saved some prisoners from abuse. One also helped Father Ernanne avoid the expulsion of a Church worker from Brazil. Soldiers who belonged to revolutionary organizations also informed the Church about political prisoners (Ernanne Pinheiro interview). Dom Waldyr received safety tips from General César Neves, a former parishioner (Dom Waldyr interview). Dom Paulo obtained information from military sources by way of a priest who ministered to officers. Dom Paulo's intelligence was so good he was able to confront commanders with lists of prisoners in the process of being tortured.[47]

The Church tuned into a large and creative network of informal communications that skirted censorship and other repressive measures. The Church in large part built this network. Brazilian telecommunications were highly unreliable, and television had only recently debuted as a form of mass communication. Thus, local churches still served in their traditional role as sources of information. Members of the clergy and CEBs acted as messengers with news about the bishops' documents and human rights.[48] Bulletins and flyers of a flourishing underground press passed from hand to hand among the faithful (Della Cava and Montero 1991:39–42, 216–19; Lopes 1994:133). Dom Paulo had news posted on the doors of Church buildings. As a security measure, however, clergy and militants avoided carrying written material. Brazil and the Church had returned to an "oral civilization" (Luiz Viegas interview 2).

A small group of progressive clergymen and activists worked to organize resistance into an attempt to topple the regime. Alceu Amoroso Lima, modern Brazil's greatest Catholic intellectual, encouraged the bishops to pursue this objective (see chapter 4). Although the Church succored the violent left and shared many of its political and social objectives, this particular movement was strictly nonviolent. During the Médici years, its members held a series of clandestine meetings in which they discussed how to strengthen the Church's position and demoralize the government. The members sought to account for political prisoners and missing persons, to pressure public officials about human rights abuses, and to provide opposition politicians with concrete information about the repression.[49] The group also established ties to Protestant pastors, labor leaders, and the grassroots movements. The participants in this campaign followed strict security measures similar to those used by the armed revolutionaries (Pretto interview). To support their work, priests slipped into neighboring countries to pick up funds. One key underwriter was Earl Smith, a retired, unsuspicious-looking North American Methodist pastor based in Uruguay who obtained money from the United States. Dom Hélder also donated funds received from foreign sources.[50]

Another initiative took place in São Paulo. Every two weeks Dom Paulo convened leading opposition intellectuals such as economist Paul Singer and sociologist Fernando Henrique Cardoso (president of Brazil, 1995–present) for the "grupo dos loucos" (the crazy group). Undertaking the seemingly impossible task of discussing Brazil's future during the heavy repression, the group sought strategies for redemocratization and solutions to the country's socioeconomic ills. The group survived until 1976 (Luiz Viegas interview 2; Dom Paulo interview). Cooperation between the Church and a research institute founded by Cardoso led to the publication in 1975 of a report demonstrating the deep inequalities of the military's economic model.[51] These interrelated initiatives helped establish the Church's leadership during the abertura.

Conclusion

After both 1889 and 1964, the Church and the armed forces entered into conflict resulting from each one's quest to shape the nation's development through its own institutional modernization. In both instances the military tried to exclude the Church from the public sphere, but each time the clergy resisted by exerting political influence. In the first case the Church recovered its power and proceeded to become a staunch ally of the armed forces in the struggle against Communism. The post-1964 conflict was particularly surprising because of the rapidity and the profundity of the rift that opened between cross and sword after a period of close cooperation.

In the mid–twentieth century the Church and military had entered a marriage of convenience founded more on cultural identity and anti-Communism than on religious conviction. At base, the histories and outlooks of the two institutions were very different. The military's outward profession of Catholicism hid the fact that neither institution really understood the internal life and motives of the other. Church influence on the military was based on mutual admiration for hierarchy, discipline, and tradition—not on a profound teaching of Christian values. The Church was likewise unprepared to comprehend security matters beyond a reflex action against Communism.

When the Church abandoned much of its tradition in a new but painful attempt to modernize, the military's one-dimensional emphasis on security prevented the officer corps from understanding the process of religious change. For the regime, "subversion" could mean anything that threatened not only the regime's political foundations but also social, ecclesiastical, and moral traditions. Catholicism for the military leadership was not an evolving idea, as Vatican II had made it, but an unmovable anchor of patriotism and stability. The generals saw no contradiction between national security ideology and Christian beliefs. DNS defended Western Christian civilization and therefore reserved an important role for the Church. The military reminded the clergy that in joining the fight against Communism it was battling the archenemy of Christianity. The national security state promised privilege and prestige to the Church if it continued its traditional support for the status quo. Alliance with the national security state was a tempting possibility (Comblin 1979, chs. 5, 6). But the armed services viewed the clergy's new engagement with the people as a threat to the class structure and to the military's own social and political prominence. As their relationship deteriorated, the two sides found it increasingly difficult to see eye to eye on questions of social justice and subversion.

Chapter 3 **The Making of a Devout *Golpista***

The Brazilian generals' defense of Western Christian civilization is often attributed to geopolitical concerns with little or no discussion of the religious background of the armed forces. General Muricy's biography exemplifies Catholicism's significance for the military, helps explain the genesis of Church-state conflict, and provides a more nuanced view of religious-military strife. A soldier to the bone, Muricy was also a devout man who displayed great loyalty to the Church. He embodied a patriotism that sought material progress and international political prominence for Brazil, but also the preservation of the traditional religious and cultural values embedded in the country's Catholic heritage. National security was a military matter, but also a religious one. This chapter describes General Muricy's martial and religious evolution.

The story of how Brazil's military and bishops clashed and conciliated can be traced through General Muricy's intimate contact with the Church leadership in the 1960s. He was both friend and enemy to bishops, particularly while he was in the Brazilian Northeast, an impoverished, drought-stricken region that many feared would explode in revolution as Cuba had done in 1958. In the late 1950s and early 1960s it was also the heart of Catholic progressivism. Muricy served there three times in the years just before and after the coup. This experience provided him with an intimate understanding of the Church's changing outlook and its relationship to security concerns. He also clamped down on the Catholic left, which he believed had moved too close to Communism. Muricy ultimately broke with his friend Dom Hélder Câmara, Brazil's leading proponent of progressive Catholicism.

The Good Catholic Soldier

General Muricy was a deeply religious man. He represented a generation of soldiers that collaborated closely with the Church to defend the social order and Brazil's Catholic tradition. As a result, over the years Muricy cultivated numerous contacts in the Church.

Muricy's early religious formation was uneven and mixed. Brazilian women more often than men have exercised religious influence in the private space of the home, and such was the case for Muricy. His mother attended mass; his father, despite growing up in a traditional Catholic environment, had become a Mason and distanced himself from the Church. Further maternal religious reinforcement came from the nuns who ran the first school Muricy frequented as a toddler. He later entered a Protestant school run by North Americans who used the Bible as a basic classroom text. In general, though ecumenical dialogue was still more than half a century away, the ethnic diversity of Muricy's home state of Paraná created a climate of religious tolerance (Muricy 1993:6–8). Another possible influence came from his older half-brother José Cândido de Andrade Muricy, who studied in the seminary at São Paulo and then at the Colégio São Bento, a prestigious school for the elite run by the Benedictine order in Rio de Janeiro.[1]

Muricy definitively adopted Catholicism as an adult in the 1920s, when the Church's campaign for neo-Christendom was in full swing. He remained faithful to the Church throughout his life. He practiced the conservative, Tridentine Catholicism of the elite, regularly going to mass, confession, and Holy Communion and maintaining close ties to the clergy.

In the 1930s Captain Muricy and his first wife, Ondina Pires de Albuquerque da Silva, struck up a friendship with Father Hélder Câmara that would last for three decades. A schoolteacher, Ondina had been a childhood acquaintance of Virgínia Côrtes de Lacerda, one in a group of young laywomen who worked as aides to Father Hélder.[2] José Muricy also knew Father Hélder through membership in the Centro Dom Vital, a conservative, dynamic, and influential Catholic think tank founded in Rio in the 1920s. Ondina became Father Hélder's assistant when the priest went to work in Rio's municipal education department. Muricy and Father Hélder rode the streetcar together to their respective jobs at the General Staff College and the Catholic Ursuline college (Muricy 1993:137).

An example of the Muricys' religious devotion was their scrupulous adherence to the pre–Vatican II Catholic teaching that reserved sexual activity strictly to procreation, not pleasure. When a difficult first pregnancy caused the couple to avoid

General Muricy (third from right) and Dona Virgínia Ramos da Silva Muricy meet Pope Paul VI (in white) at the Vatican, June 1972. Brazil's military leadership held the pontiff in deep reverence for political reasons but also out of religious conviction.

further children, they stopped receiving Communion because they knew they were going against the Church. Years later, when Ondina's health deteriorated because of a heart condition, she wanted to receive Communion. She explained the couple's predicament to Father Hélder. "Your case is just," the priest told Ondina, absolving her of her sins and allowing the Muricys to resume participation in the Eucharist. As Ondina neared death in 1954 after seven years of illness, then Bishop Hélder remained close to the family by serving as her personal confessor and paying frequent visits to her bedside.[3] Muricy's second wife, Virgínia, helped her husband establish ties to the Church in her native Recife in the late 1950s and 1960s.

Muricy gave one of the clearest statements of his beliefs while commanding the barracks at Cruz Alta, Rio Grande do Sul, in 1961. When the new bishop of the diocese of the area, Dom Luiz Victor Sartori, made his first pastoral visit to the town during the May festival of its patroness Our Lady of Fátima, Muricy was chosen to welcome him. New to the town and the bishop, Muricy introduced himself as a "steadfast Catholic" who knew the "importance of an experienced spiritual guide" in the figure of the bishop. He spoke of the deep bond between religious and military life and their common Christian goals: "As paradoxical as it may appear, the life of the priest and the soldier have much in common. . . . In the life of the priest, as in the life of the soldier, we also have the great opportunity to come to know profoundly our neighbor, to feel him, and, principally, to love him." Muricy also spoke against Communism. He asked the bishop to counsel Brazilians in a world in which the "clash between the material and the spiritual becomes greater and greater." Like many Catholics, he viewed the Church as a bulwark against Communism. Even the Church recognized that Marx was a good economist, but he had erred by forgetting that humans were "more spirit than material." Marxist doctrine "depersonalized" individuals and made them servants of the state. In Brazil, Communism had insidiously made its way into Catholic circles, "producing deviations that the Church must avoid." Some Catholics now thought it possible to "humanize Communism, that is, to humanize what by definition cannot be humanized." The Church provided the true way of life through the social teachings of the popes. The bishop was a key figure for setting straight these "ex-Catholics." But the Church in Brazil had a big job ahead. Most Catholics did not practice their religion. Catechism had to be not just a onetime event but a lifelong process. Active members of the Church needed to learn how to comprehend the Brazilian people.[4]

This speech revealed a remarkable appreciation for the political, social, and religious strengths—and weaknesses—of Brazilian Catholicism. It also highlighted the seriousness of the armed forces' intellectual elite. Muricy's anti-Communism had profound roots in Catholicism. But his beliefs did not blind him to the Church's need to improve through innovation. He was not a knee-jerk anti-Communist, but an individual who had carefully thought through his positions over a lifetime of military and religious experience.

A *Troupier* Exposed to Politics

Muricy was a disciplined *troupier* who relished action and the chance to command (Farias 1994). He did not hesitate to make major decisions on the spot, usually speaking his mind before subordinates and superiors alike. Muricy displayed a ruggedness and an uncanny survival instinct that allowed him to work effectively throughout his career and to live into his nineties. At the age of forty-three in 1949, for instance, Lieutenant Colonel Muricy felt pains in his chest and immediately suspected a heart attack. His doctor confirmed the self-diagnosis. Muricy recovered, went on to become a general, and served twenty-one more years in the military (Muricy 1993:203–04). While serving as Army chief of staff, Muricy vowed with his bodyguards to fight to the death if, as intelligence sources were warning, guerrillas tried to kidnap him.[5]

His stamina is even more remarkable in light of an incident that took place in 1979. Then seventy-three, Muricy was sleeping with his wife when four burglars invaded their home in Santa Teresa, a historic hillside neighborhood in downtown Rio de Janeiro. Reacting as a young soldier might during wartime, Muricy awoke immediately and lunged at one of the intruders as he entered the bedroom. Another of the prowlers shot Muricy, the bullet lodging near the heart. The general not only reached the emergency room alive but lived many more years with the irremovable bullet in his chest.[6]

Recognized for his field skills, Muricy led with patience and composure. He was a student of people. His long experience as an instructor and personnel officer afforded him ample opportunity to observe individuals carefully. Together with his postings in various regions of Brazil, these jobs made Muricy one of the best-known officers in the Army. He also showed deep concern for intellectual matters. He read constantly, and in the 1950s he joined the elite ESG staff. This background led him to show considerable restraint during crises and to calm the volatile tempers of younger soldiers.

An early model of military involvement in politics came from his father's experience. Lieutenant Colonel José Cândido da Silva Muricy took part in the conspiracy that overthrew Emperor Dom Pedro II and installed the Republic in 1889.[7] The younger Muricy was not born until seventeen years later, but he grew up with the legacy of his father's involvement. In 1917, at the age of ten, he enrolled in military prep school in Rio de Janeiro. In 1923 Muricy entered the Military Academy, from which he graduated two years later as an Army artilleryman, which had also been the elder Muricy's service branch.[8] Artillerymen saw themselves as an elite group within the Army because of their scientific training in heavy arms (Castro 1990:120, 134).

While in the academy, Muricy sympathized with the young officers who revolted against the government in 1922. Like the *tenentes*, Muricy wanted to see Brazil modernize politically and economically by ending the monopoly on power held by the landed oligarchy. In the Revolution of 1930, Lieutenant Muricy identified with the Vargas forces, though he had little choice but to obey the progovernment generals who controlled the Army in Rio de Janeiro.

During the decisive and divisive 1930s, Muricy avoided the extremes of Communism and Integralismo. He tended instead toward democracy and concentrated on Army unity—a constant theme throughout his career. He quickly distanced himself from the Communists, whose inroads into the armed forces threatened unity. After the 1930 conflict and a revolt in São Paulo in 1932, men from opposing sides immediately reconciled. However, after the 1935 Communist rebellion profound ideological differences prevented a return to harmony. Muricy felt for the first time the hatred of conspirators toward victors. He later defined this period as the root of the tensions that led to the coup of 1964. The events of 1935 survived as a powerful symbol of ideological struggle for Brazil's armed forces, which annually commemorated their victory over the Communists.

Muricy also declined to enter the Integralistas. He believed he already supported their ideals as a soldier defending country, family, and religion. Moreover, he saw a contradiction between democracy and the antiliberal current of Integralismo. Yet Muricy was also not a complete proponent of democracy. He supported the Estado Novo dictatorship because of its opposition to Communism. At any rate, he viewed the Integralistas as less dangerous than the Communists and maintained contact with them over the years. Among these early right-wing friends was Raimundo Padilha, who became a leader of the progovernment party after 1964 and whose son was Tarcísio Padilha, a founder of the Bipartite.

The ESG: Defining Security and Breeding "Political" Officers

During World War II, Major Muricy established ties with the group of officers who would define and implement the DNS in the 1950s and 1960s. While teaching at the General Staff College, Muricy met Captain Golbery do Couto e Silva, the emerging master of Brazilian security policy. In 1944 Muricy, Golbery, and numerous other officers traveled to the United States for a training course at the U.S. Army Command and General Staff College at Fort Leavenworth, Kansas. There they prepared for battle in the FEB. Muricy did not go to the front. Instead, his orders took him back to the Brazilian General Staff College, where he worked intensively to prepare other men for war (Muricy 1993:132, 173–83, 193). During this period Muricy also worked closely with FEB leader and future *golpista* Castello Branco.

After the war, Muricy was promoted to lieutenant colonel and worked as head of personnel on the staff of War Minister Canrobert Pereira da Costa, an outspoken anti-Communist who aspired to succeed General Eurico Gaspar Dutra as president of Brazil in 1950. As War Minister during the Estado Novo, Dutra had participated in the deposition of Vargas following the opposition's cries for redemocratization in 1945. When Vargas was elected again in 1950, however, General Canrobert protected Muricy from political reprisal by sending him off to the ESG to take its course in national security. Muricy simultaneously received an appointment to the school's permanent staff. In 1952 he was made a full colonel.

Muricy stood in the thick of the ESG's intense intellectual life as a teacher, thinker, and organizer. From 1951 to 1953, he and the other staff members worked feverishly to move the DNS from its embryonic state to a full-blown, systematic corpus of ideas for guiding Brazil's future. Muricy coordinated the school's work methods, often relying on his experience at Leavenworth and his readings of the North American educational philosopher John Dewey. He moderated the frequent debates between officers arguing over competing concepts of security. Muricy's particular area of expertise became Communist revolutionary warfare. The bibliography on this subject was nonexistent in Brazil, leading the colonel to spend long nights reading sources in English. Over time he accumulated documentation measuring six meters on the shelves (Muricy 1993:229, 234–35, 242–43, 247, 255–56).

About this time the ESG became a nest of political machination against Vargas and then Kubitschek. In 1954, for instance, Muricy and other ESG officials endorsed an anti-Vargas memorandum that complained of political corruption, government neglect of the Army's needs, and the dangers of leftist infiltration in the military. Muricy's position marked him as a "political" officer in some Army circles. One fellow officer called him a *golpista*, a coup-plotter (Muricy 1993:296–98). Although Muricy abhorred politics as being divisive for the military, the facts validated his colleagues' fears. In 1955 he and other ESG officials joined the conspiracy to block the inauguration of president-elect Kubitschek and vice president–elect Goulart.

Muricy's political activities in the 1950s kept him from promotion to general during the Kubitschek years and led to an informal but golden exile as head of the Brazilian Military Commission at the Brazilian embassy in Washington, D.C., from 1956 to 1958. Although this bureaucratic job sidetracked Muricy's military career, it brought him an excellent salary—approximately $24,000 per year—payable in U.S. currency.[9] The respite in the United States capital further helped the middle-aged colonel put his personal life in order after a period of depression following the death of his wife Ondina in 1954. While in Washington he married Virgínia Ramos da Silva, an ESG librarian.

Plotting and Leading the Coup

At the end of the Kubitschek administration, Muricy was finally promoted to general and sent to Rio Grande do Sul—the home state of Vargas, Vice President Goulart, and the vitriolic populist Leonel Brizola, who was the state's governor from 1959 to 1962. Brothers-in-law Goulart and Brizola led Vargas's Partido Trabalhista Brasileiro (Brazilian Labor Party) until the coup forced them into exile. Brazil's system of ticket-splitting elections allowed Goulart to be reelected to the vice presidency in 1960, while Quadros, of the opposition União Democrática Nacional (UDN; National Democratic Union) became president. Muricy personally received orders from Army Minister Odylio Denys to keep pro-Brizola forces in check. The charismatic populist was carrying Rio Grande do Sul politics to the left by expropriating foreign companies and carrying out other radical measures. Muricy's job included ridding the Army of Communist infiltrators and fighting Brizola's military allies should they revolt against the central government. One of Muricy's tasks was to stop a transit strike supported by Brizola (Muricy 1993: 360–70).

When Quadros unexpectedly resigned in August 1961 after less than seven months in office, Muricy sided with the Army faction outside Rio Grande do Sul that wanted to block Goulart's succession to the presidency. Vargas's men had power again, angering the conservative military and stirring fears of Communism. Brizola armed the populace and threatened to fight, persuading Rio Grande do Sul's Army contingent to support Goulart. Muricy broke with his commanding general, fled the state with his family, and prepared to fight as Brazil came to the brink of civil war. In the end, however, calmer heads prevailed, and Goulart was allowed to assume the presidency under a compromise instituting a parliamentary system of government that reduced the powers of the chief executive (Muricy 1993:360–70). Dom Vicente Scherer, the cardinal-archbishop of Porto Alegre, thanked Muricy for helping to "convince the authorities and the people of the seriousness of the Communist danger."[10]

Stationed in the Northeast, in 1963 Muricy became embroiled in an incident with Brizola, now a congressman, that gained national attention. Both men were in Natal as Muricy dined with United States ambassador Lincoln Gordon and other dignitaries. Speaking on a national radio broadcast, Brizola called Muricy a "gorilla" and a *golpista* for his actions in 1961. Muricy had to restrain the many angry officers who wanted to punish the congressman. He then delivered speeches warning of the advance of leftist subversion.[11]

The golpista *General Muricy (third from left) in command of the Destacamento Tiradentes, which swept into Rio de Janeiro the morning of April 1, 1964, putting an end to the government of President João Goulart. To the far left is Walter Pires de Carvalho e Albuquerque, future Minister of the Army under President Figueiredo.*

As an early conspirator against Goulart, Muricy used his large network of contacts to work for military unity during the coup. He sounded out other officers with respect to a takeover and served as a liaison between Army conspirators and Golbery, who retired when Goulart became president. He also reported to Castello Branco that Goulart was planning his own coup (Dulles 1978:314–15). On March 13, 1964 Goulart held a large rally in downtown Rio that convened Brizola, radical Pernambuco Governor Miguel Arraes, and an array of left-wing, union, and grassroots groups who supported Goulart's call for basic reforms in Brazilian society. The demonstration firmed the conspirators' resolve to act and convinced many undecided officers to join them. Hinting at a later hard-line reaction against the left, a group of lower-echelon officers wanted to disrupt the rally by starting a fire. Muricy put a stop to their plans. Later, Muricy used his prestige to keep peace between factions headed by General Castello Branco and General Artur da Costa e Silva, allies against Goulart but rivals for the presidency. Costa e Silva became Castello Branco's Army Minister.[12]

Muricy was the only general who actually led troops into action during the bloodless coup of March 31, 1964. Leaving his post in Rio de Janeiro, he rushed to Minas Gerais to take charge of the Destacamento Tiradentes, a detachment named for the executed national hero who opposed Portuguese rule during the colonial era. Muricy led his troops on a march from the hills of Minas down onto the lowlands of Rio on the morning of April 1. In his characteristic manner, Muricy blustered loyalist soldiers into joining his column.[13] His military support disintegrating, Goulart fled Rio to Brasília and then quickly left the country by way of Rio Grande do Sul. A new era in Brazilian history had begun, and Muricy stood among its leaders.

Stopping Subversion and Torture in the Northeast

Muricy had been stationed in the Northeast for two years following his return from Washington in 1958. He commanded the reserve officers training program in Recife, his second wife's hometown. Virgínia had attended an exclusive Catholic school in Recife and headed a young women's Catholic Action group before the radicalization of the late 1950s. The Muricys mixed with Recife's active lay elite, became friends with priests, and frequented discussion circles for Catholic couples. These groups often examined the crying social issues of the Northeast. To prepare for these discussions Muricy studied the Church's social doctrine. On several occasions the circles heard pedagogue Paulo Freire, whose grassroots literacy method profoundly influenced progressive Catholicism. At times Freire and the conservative general debated their different approaches.[14] In the Northeast the general also met Dom Avelar Brandão Vilela, the bishop of Teresina and future Bipartite member, and Dom José Távora, the progressive bishop of Aracaju and former collaborator of Dom Hélder in Rio.

The Northeast—and Recife in particular—vibrated with radical politics and religion. In the countryside Francisco Julião organized the Ligas Camponesas (Peasant Leagues) to fight the centuries' old monopoly of the large landowners. Scenting Communism, priests competed with the leagues by organizing more moderate unions. In 1962 Arraes, the radical populist mayor of Recife, became the leader of the left in the Northeast after winning the governorship of the state of Pernambuco. A defender of the poor, Arraes had Freire set up a statewide literacy program. Through Freire's *conscientização*, or consciousness-raising, Arraes and other leftists hoped to enfranchise the mass of illiterates prohibited by law from voting. Freire's endeavor exemplified how Brazilian Catholics radicalized as they became disillusioned with the nationalist developmentalism of the 1950s (Callado 1964). Poverty and political agitation in the Northeast led the U.S. government to attempt to control events in the region in the hopes of avoiding another, even larger Cuba.

General Muricy worked to educate fellow soldiers and the populace about the dangers of Communist revolutionary warfare. In the early 1960s most Brazilians, officers included, had no notion of this concept.[15] First outlined by Lenin in 1917 and refined by other Communist leaders, the theory of revolutionary warfare proposed the seizure of power through propaganda, infiltration, and guerrilla action. In a private speech to officers after the Brizola incident in May 1963, Muricy declared that "revolutionary warfare is already spreading through Brazil" and had to be combated. "The struggle against revolutionary warfare is the duty of the military as well as [of the] civilians," Muricy stated. He urged political and social reforms to eliminate the "internal contradictions" that allowed Communists to act. The people, especially political leaders and the press, needed to cooperate with the armed forces. Muricy provided an eerily accurate scenario for the Brazil of the late 1960s: "The moment in which the armed struggle begins, or when it is imminent, a new situation appears. A state of siege is imposed and the entire military machine, with the support of the civilian population, must act with energy. It is necessary to impose limitations on individual rights."[16] Muricy kept the Brizola controversy alive by repeating the speech in public. He also sent a copy to Dom Carlos Coelho, the archbishop of Recife, and Dom Luiz Sartori, the bishop of Santa Maria.

Muricy soon took measures against subversion. A new posting took him to Natal, the capital of the state of Rio Grande do Norte, in early 1963. From there he traveled frequently to nearby Recife, where the political storm was worsening. Muricy admitted the need for social change in the region. This sentiment led him first to try persuasion with radicals rather than heavy-handed measures. He admonished his Catholic friends, who were shifting from theoretical discussion to political action, to beware of allying with the Communists. In private meetings he advised Freire and Germano de Vasconcellos Coelho to keep Catholics in control of the Popular Culture Movement in Recife, where Communists were increasingly active in the program.[17] At the request of Dom Carlos, the general and his wife tried to convince Father Almery Bezerra to stop writing radical newspaper articles. Bezerra had a strong following among Catholic students and went into exile immediately after the coup. When Peasant League leader Joel Câmara invaded a private ranch, Muricy brought the student in for a face-to-face meeting. On another occasion Muricy argued with Dom José Lamartine Soares, the auxiliary bishop of Recife, over the archdiocese's broadcast of a Communist rally in support of Arraes. "I am not a bishop, and you are," Muricy told Dom Lamartine. "But I have the impression that my Catholicism is better than yours, because I think that if the Church does not support Communism it should not be helping to install Communism" (Muricy 1993:588). But Muricy also resorted to harsher tactics. His men seized a controversial booklet written by acquaintances of the general for Arraes's city literacy program. Muricy also organized a group of students to counter leftist graffiti by scribbling their own slogans on walls in the early morning hours (Muricy 1993:420–28).

Muricy encountered less agitation in Natal, partly because of the firm anti-Communism of Dom Eugênio Sales, the archdiocese's apostolic administrator. In 1949 Father Sales had created the Serviço de Assistência Rural (SAR; Rural Assistance Service). SAR's roots lay in the clergy's attempt to alleviate the negative impact of the large influx of U.S. troops during the war, when Natal was a major link to the African theater. The priests soon realized that rural social inequalities fed urban blight. SAR battled poverty by teaching better farming techniques and providing drought relief. Moreover, as Natal's auxiliary bishop after 1954, Dom Eugênio exposed the so-called drought industry that was sapping relief funds from the poor. This action made him enemies among the corrupt politicians. In 1961, SAR started Brazil's first radio schools and the first Catholic rural unions, which grew to fifty thousand members at SAR's apogee in 1963. SAR's programs served as models for the MEB and the Pernambuco clergy's anti-Julião unions. Given the history of conservatism in the Northeast, SAR was quite progressive and drew international attention (Camargo 1971). After the coup Dom Eugênio was tabbed a Communist, a charge he was able to avoid with the help of General Muricy (Dom Eugênio interview).[18]

Indeed, Muricy later observed that he saw little difference in the methods of the SAR unions and Julião's Peasant Leagues. Nevertheless, SAR was a centrist, pointedly anti-Communist program. For this, General Muricy greatly admired Dom Eugênio. He also supported Dom Eugênio's efforts to stop Communist infiltration of Catholic student groups. As a result, the two men established enduring ties. In addition, SAR member Father Nivaldo Monte (later archbishop of Natal) became confessor and friend to the Muricys (Muricy 1993:422, 437–440).

In September 1963, Muricy was transferred to Rio de Janeiro, where he conspired against Goulart, but shortly after the coup he returned to the Northeast. The

Northeast bore the brunt of the postcoup repression. As one observer noted, Recife became a "city covered by a hood of fear." Headless bodies of peasant leaders lay on the road from Recife to João Pessoa, and others were burned in furnaces. Subversives were rounded up and tortured.[19] Muricy helped crush the left by dismantling radical organizations such as the Peasant Leagues and threatening militant students and clergy with reprisals.[20] The drive against subversion eventually exploded into conflict with the Church. Virgínia Muricy was now considered a spy sent to infiltrate Catholic Action (Virgínia Ramos da Silva Muricy interview), and the general was shocked to learn that his Catholic acquaintances now opposed the Revolution. He extricated one couple from jail (Muricy 1993:551), but he also ordered the arrest of Father Paulo Meneses, a JOC militant linked to Father Bezerra. Meneses was set free by request of Dom Hélder and then went into exile in Portugal.[21]

Yet Muricy did not participate in the postcoup atrocities. On the contrary, his primary mission was to stop them. President Castello Branco was embarrassed by the "excesses" in the Northeast. He called on his trusted colleague, General Muricy, to carry out the delicate, highly unusual, and practically secret mission of curbing Army mistreatment of the opposition. Muricy carried out this task while serving under Fourth Army commander General Joaquim Justino Alves Bastos. Muricy used his prestige in the region to curtail the abuses.[22] He and his wife personally obtained the release of some one hundred political prisoners. Dom Hélder sent the families of a number of detainees to the general's residence to seek help.[23] The abuses further prompted an official investigation by General Ernesto Geisel, the chief of the presidential military staff. Muricy escorted his friend and superior through the prisons to show that conditions had improved, though journalist Márcio Moreira Alves described the visit as a whitewash for the regime.[24]

Muricy's actions made him an important and widely known figure in the region. In 1966 he made a bid for the governorship of Pernambuco with the support of local military officers and the Catholic right.[25] Muricy and other generals hoped to use their military status to forward personal political ambitions. Castello Branco, however, opposed military participation in local elections and cut short Muricy's candidacy (Dulles 1980:328–33). This was one of the lowest points of Muricy's career.

It was during this last stint in the Northeast that Muricy severed ties with Dom Hélder. In the early 1960s, Dom Hélder's prestige among the Brazilian elite crumbled as he criticized capitalism in the midst of nationalist developmentalism's failure to sustain the economy and resolve social problems. Archconservatives labeled

General Muricy (center) counted among his friends the top military leaders of his day, including General Humberto de Alcenar Castello Branco, the first president of the military regime (to Muricy's left). In white is Admiral Clóvis de Oliveira.

Dom Hélder a Communist. Shortly after the coup, troops invaded his quarters in search of deposed Governor Arraes's sister, to whom Dom Hélder had given refuge (Page 1972:214–15).[26]

Army officers in Recife wanted to break with the archbishop, but Muricy held them at bay and maintained cordial relations with his friend. The two worked to avoid Church-military conflict. But Muricy also began to differ with Dom Hélder over the arrest of Catholic militants and some of the bishop's public statements (Piletti and Praxedes 1997:327).

In 1966 their friendship came to an abrupt halt. On March 31, 1966, the second anniversary of the coup, the two men clashed. The military leadership, including Muricy, pressured Dom Hélder to offer a thanksgiving mass for the troops.

General Muricy broke thirty years of friendship with Dom Hélder Câmara because of the contro-versial bishop's refusal to sanctify the military regime.

However, Dom Hélder's friends and followers persuaded him against holding the mass. As a question of conscience the archbishop formally refused the invitation; he considered the event to be related to the gubernatorial campaign and therefore mainly political, not religious. (Pope Paul VI supported this decision.) Muricy was stunned. By sheer coincidence, a bomb planted by leftists exploded outside the home of Fourth Army commander General Setúbal Portugal, whom Muricy had gone to meet. Another went off at a post office. In all there were nine explosions in Recife on March 31. In a scheduled television appearance to commemorate the Revolution General Muricy denounced what were the first terrorist attacks against the regime. He finished by criticizing Dom Hélder's refusal to celebrate mass. Although Dom Hélder had nothing to do with the explosions, Muricy had linked terrorism with the archbishop's moral protest.[27]

Tensions between Dom Hélder and the military worsened in the following months. With the approval of General Portugal the commander of the Tenth Região Militar in Fortaleza, General Itiberê Gouveia do Amaral, circulated a pamphlet attacking Dom Hélder. The incident created a political crisis for Castello Branco. General Muricy arranged a meeting between the president and the archbishop that temporarily reduced tensions (Dulles 1980:298). After unsuccessfully lobbying the Vatican to have the archbishop removed to Rome, the president replaced General Portugal with an officer friendly to Dom Hélder, General Rafael de Souza Aguiar (Piletti and Praxedes 1997:340–41; Schneider 1971:235–36).

The falling out with Dom Hélder was one reason for Castello Branco's decision to make Muricy a four-star general in late 1966 and thus remove him from Recife to Rio (Piletti and Praxedes 1997:340–41). The president passed over a number of other generals considered more eligible for promotion and named Muricy chief of Army personnel. General Muricy now stood in the uppermost echelon of the armed forces and was poised to take part in events of national importance.[28]

Chapter 4 **Prelude to the Bipartite**

Dialogue, Torture, and Diplomacy, 1968–1970

eneral Muricy steadily rose in the military government. Although a Castellista, he also had ties to General Costa e Silva, who became Brazil's second military president in March 1967. Muricy had served under Costa e Silva in the Fourth Army in 1962, and the two collaborated against Goulart. This connection and Muricy's wide contacts in the Army were helpful. In April 1969, Costa e Silva elevated Muricy to Army chief of staff, one of the top positions in Brazil's armed forces. Muricy commanded all other generals, tapped into a broad network of military intelligence, and even overshadowed General Aurélio de Lyra Tavares, the Minister of the Army.[1] Though not a hard-liner, Muricy clearly supported vigorous action against the revolutionary left[2] and believed that to suppress subversion democracy should be restricted.[3]

The crisis of Costa e Silva's rule gave Muricy a chance at the presidency. When the president was forced from office by a stroke in August 1969, Muricy and other members of the high command of the armed forces denied the right of succession to the civilian vice president, Pedro Aleixo, who had argued against the harsh AI-5. The Ministers of the Army, Navy, and Air Force formed a temporary junta. When Costa e Silva failed to improve, Muricy and other top officers chose another president. In the internal military election, Muricy finished third behind Médici and General Orlando Geisel. Muricy personally informed Costa e Silva of the results. Médici kept Muricy as Army chief of staff until November 1970, when he assumed control of the Bipartite.

By this time torture had become a major political issue and the

General Muricy (center) and President Artur da Costa e Silva (glass in hand), Brasília, August 1967, at a meeting of the Army high command. Muricy belonged to the inner military circle that governed Brazil after 1964 and was a candidate for president after Costa e Silva's stroke in 1969.

object of intense diplomatic maneuvering in Rome. Faced with increased aggression against the clergy, in 1968 and early 1969 the CNBB began to take a critical stance toward the state, denouncing AI-5, human rights violations, and the inequality produced by the regime's economic policies. A chilling in relations—though never a break—took place between the Vatican and the Brazilian government.

General Muricy and Dom Eugênio were central figures in the attempt to pull Brazil out of the moral and political morass of violence and ideological conflict. Anti-Communism sealed their friendship, but the repression troubled it. Focusing on the Muricy-Sales dialogue, this chapter reveals how Dom Eugênio worked with Muricy to improve Brazil's image, but also how frank a critic he became of the regime's arbitrariness. The chapter also studies internal Church debate about how best to denounce torture. These dialogues were both background and basis for the Bipartite.

Hard-line Repression and the Muricy-Sales Dialogue

In public Dom Eugênio contrasted with his CNBB colleagues by taking a more discrete stance toward the regime. He preferred to deal through private channels in order to avoid antagonizing the government and therefore losing his ability to resolve conflict and seek redress for Church grievances.[4] Discretion and dialogue were policies also adopted by Dom Hélder for dealing with the repression during the early years of the regime (Piletti and Praxedes 1997:329). A patriot who believed in maintaining stable Church-military relations, Dom Eugênio had gained the respect of the armed services for his anti-Communism, but also for his circumspection and emphasis on obedience to authority. Since their days together in Natal, General Muricy had tracked Dom Eugênio's rising star. In late 1966, he invited Dom Eugênio to study at the ESG, a "dream" the bishop had to decline because of his duties as apostolic administrator of the archdiocese of Salvador.[5] Dom Eugênio suggested Father Afonso Gregory as a participant, and the future bishop enrolled in the program.

Yet Dom Eugênio was no supporter of the regime. Although anti-Communist, he did not stand with the right-wing traditionalist sector of Brazilian Catholicism that applauded the coup. Dom Eugênio was committed to reforming Brazilian society. He helped set the foundation for progressive Catholicism in Brazil, although he eschewed its radical elements and relied less on the grass roots and more on the upper and middle classes in working for social change.[6] Moreover, as apostolic administrator of Natal in 1964, he was one of the few bishops in a state capital to prohibit a public religious celebration of the Revolution. After the coup, he stated that his position was one of "neutrality and expectation." Yet Dom Eugênio was perturbed by the attacks on priests and the lack of respect for human rights. For example, in April 1964 he and Dom Hélder met privately with President Castello Branco to complain about the violence of the repression against the left.[7]

By the time of AI-5, Dom Eugênio had become a national figure. Pope Paul VI had named him archbishop of Salvador, Bahia, and primate of Brazil. In April 1969 (the same month Muricy became Army chief of staff), the pope made Dom Eugênio a cardinal. He thus became one of the most powerful men in the history of the Brazilian Church. The responsibility was enormous. His constituency was no longer a small diocese in the Northeast (Natal), but Bahia, the historical seat of Catholicism in Brazil. And because he was a cardinal, his influence extended to national and international issues. He carried the burden of power—which meant dealing with

Dom Eugênio de Araújo Sales (left) and Dom Avelar Brandão Vilela waiting for a flight to Rome from the Galeão International Airport, Rio de Janeiro, 1969. Transatlantic diplomacy became crucial in maintaining the delicate relationships among generals, bishops, and the Vatican.

the dictators and playing the role of politician and diplomat. As a frequent visitor to the pope, he spoke not only for the Church, but also for Brazil.

Although he had close contact with individuals in the government, Dom Eugênio continued to maintain a certain distance from the regime. Two months before AI-5, for instance, Cardinal Agnelo Rossi, Dom Paulo's predecessor as archbishop of São Paulo, publicly refused to accept a medal from the government, provoking an angry response in hard-line military circles.[8] Following suit, Dom Eugênio refused the same award and practically humiliated the general who had offered it. As one of his reasons the archbishop cited worsening Church-state relations. Dom Eugênio also personally admonished President Costa e Silva against the use of *cassação* (suspension of an individual's political rights), which was frequently applied by the regime against its enemies.[9] After the promulgation of AI-5, Dom Eugênio denied a request from the military to say mass in celebration of the new order (Gaspari 1997b).

In his private communications, Dom Eugênio criticized the generals. On Christmas Day 1968, weeks before the CNBB's public protest, he composed a critical letter about AI-5 to General Muricy. Dom Eugênio began by stating his desire for a long, personal conversation, "as is our custom." Unable to leave Salvador, however, he asked Antônio Carlos Magalhães, the mayor of Salvador and soon one of Brazil's most powerful politicians, to deliver the confidential missive during a trip to Rio. The tone of the letter echoed their long friendship, but it also expressed the concerns of a pastor toward a fellow Christian as Brazilian society was torn asunder.[10] "I have been profoundly preoccupied with the direction of the country, before the last act and after," Dom Eugênio wrote. Relations between the Church and the government were "dark," even after Dom Eugênio's two meetings with the pope and the CNBB's creation of a commission to seek dialogue. The Church-state relationship had become sensitive because of "problems of conceptualization, for example: what is subversion? What is *conscientização?* Do we or do we not have the duty to denounce injustices?" The government could at least promote "authentic reforms" in the civilian sphere, the only way "to reconcile the Revolution with the people," Dom Eugênio stated, adding that the government's agrarian reform program had degenerated into just "one more task force."

Finally, Dom Eugênio revealed his keen concern about the effects of AI-5. "It is a grave matter when one man has to depend on the will of another without appeal," the archbishop wrote. "If everybody were like you, I could temporarily remain calm. The reality, however, is different, and there is no deadline for returning to normality. How can this situation be resolved? I don't see how," Dom Eugênio wrote. He urged Muricy to prevent the regime from using AI-5 to alter the Supreme Court, which had shown itself to be uncooperative with the military by releasing student prisoners just before the act was declared. (His plea went in vain: the next month the government removed three members of the body and cut its powers.) "Muricy, write me, tell me something so that I can see things more clearly," Dom Eugênio closed. "There is much suffering."

General Muricy replied on December 27.[11] "We are not interested in pursuing adversaries but in building a better Brazil, principally for the least advantaged," he wrote. "We continue as Christians and humans and lift up our prayers to God so that He might help us not to err." He then gave a detailed justification of AI-5. First of all, in an extraordinary admission, Muricy stated that the government's own failure to implement reforms had allowed the opposition to exploit the political situa-

tion. But the general quickly shifted blame to the opposition. He supported suppression of subversive movements, "now better structured and acting particularly
on the minds of people, whether youths in the schools or adults in various areas,
including the Church."

The government had tried to work for democracy and had even studied the possibility of an amnesty for political prisoners and a return to direct elections. But in
the antimilitary speech that had prompted the declaration of AI-5, congressman
Márcio Moreira Alves had threatened a key basis of the regime: all Brazilians' legal
responsibility to protect national security. "From that moment we were certain that
all of our work since 1964 would be lost if we did not make a drastic decision,"
Muricy wrote. "Although unwillingly, we acted. We acted to save a weak Brazilian
democracy, although, paradoxically, the government had to arm itself with extraordinary powers." The general added that, after examining his conscience, he had no
regrets. "The remedy was bitter, but it was necessary."

Muricy proceeded to assess Church-state relations. "The Church and the armed
forces are the basic pillars on which democracy in Brazil sits," Muricy wrote,
adding, however, that the archbishop was well aware of ongoing "attempts to
involve the Church in conflict." The Catholic left worried the regime "tremendous-
ly." Priests involved with students and workers penned documents so subversive
that they made Miguel Arraes's precoup literacy pamphlet sound like "the work of
beginners." The fathers preached violence, Marxism, and socialism as solutions to
Brazil's problems. According to the general, one clergyman declared that "the
Church will have to move towards a Communo-Christian accord just as an
Aristotelian-Thomistic accord was once made." Another text titled "A History of
the Brazilian Proletariat" advocated struggle against the government. The government showed the subversive documents to the cardinals of Rio and São Paulo, and
Muricy further raised the matter with Dom Aloísio and Dom Avelar.

The general proposed to Dom Eugênio that they try to end this "calamitous situation. . . . From what I have personally seen, I can imagine your anguish and, even
more so, that of the pope. It is my judgment, however, that this question must be
resolved principally by the Church itself. It is the most affected."

After this exchange Muricy continued his dialogue with Dom Eugênio in a
mutual effort to reduce Church-state conflict. Even as the two men congratulated
each other on their respective promotions to Army chief of staff and cardinal, however, the repression drove cross and sword further apart. On April 7, 1969, Dom
Eugênio wrote the general to complain of the arrest of Tibor Sulik, accused of subversion in his work as the president of JOC's international branch, which was

linked to the Vatican. Sulik also belonged to the CJP-BR, the Brazilian Section of the Pontifical Peace and Justice Commission, and had attended the historic Medellín bishops' meeting in 1968. His jailing created great "uneasiness" and made it "profoundly more difficult to do anything on my part" for Church-state understanding, Dom Eugênio wrote.[12] Under pressure from Dom Eugênio and the papal nuncio Sebastiano Baggio, the government released Sulik after ten days in prison.

Such incidents soiled Brazil's international image. Like the Brazilian elite of the past, the generals were deeply embarrassed by negative publicity and feared judgment by European countries (Fico 1997:45–47; Huggins 1998:175). Once received cordially, in Europe Brazilians were now labeled "torturers."[13] This perception completely contradicted the notion of social progress wrought by the economic miracle. The government vehemently denied the existence of torture and political prisoners. It described negative reports as part of a foreign campaign to denigrate Brazil.

The Diplomatic Struggle in Rome

In Rome the Brazilian government and its Church critics competed for the approval of Pope Paul VI and of the Vatican Secretariat of State, which coordinated the Church's diplomatic relations. The pope's opinion was a key variable in the construction of Brazil's image.

The Vatican walked a delicate line. On the one hand, it condemned human rights violations and defended the clergy and the bishops, including the increasingly critical CNBB. The official Vatican newspaper *L'Osservatore Romano* published CNBB documents that criticized the regime, and Vatican Radio broadcast a message of solidarity to the victims of abuses in Brazil. An official at the Secretariat of State affirmed that the pope had "irrefutable proof" of torture.[14] Although the regime eagerly cultivated the Catholic tradition of the Brazilian people and armed forces, the Vatican rebuffed attempts to manipulate the Church. For instance, the government attempted to convince Paul VI to visit Brazil in 1970 for the inauguration of the new national cathedral built in Brasília with government funds. Irritated by a false leak to the press by President Costa e Silva's wife, Iolanda, that the pontiff would make the trip, substitute secretary of state Dom Giovanni Benelli, who had worked in the Rio nunciature in the early 1960s, commented privately (and sarcastically) that "the Brazilians will have to find another 'parish priest' for the consecration of their cathedral."[15]

On the other hand, however, Brazil and the Vatican maintained normal relations. Although noting the existence of social inequality, Paul VI recognized the country's efforts to develop.[16] In condemning torture, the pope did not make direct public reference to Brazil. The Vatican also denounced the terrorism of the revolutionary left and refused to associate itself with guerrilla movements. For instance, the Vatican showed little concern for the Dominicans imprisoned for collaborating with revolutionary leader Carlos Marighella.[17] In early 1970, after the pope's embarrassing denunciation of torture, José Jobim, Brazil's ambassador to the Holy See, began missing Vatican diplomatic ceremonies and social functions. Yet in 1971 the Secretariat of State informed Jobim that it opposed the campaign against Brazil's image. Paul VI made it clear that, whereas the Church had a moral and doctrinal duty to denounce injustice, it should not make political judgements.[18]

The diplomatic struggle also generated debate among Brazil's Catholic leaders over the best method for stopping the atrocities. Moderates and conservatives tended toward the Vatican line of persuasion and conciliation, whereas progressives and radicals favored public denunciation. There was also conflict between the bishops, who were more apt to try discussion, and some lay leaders and the progressive grass roots, who favored stronger condemnations and opposition to the government. A key example was the case of Cardinal Agnelo Rossi.

Notwithstanding his refusal of a military medal, Dom Agnelo stood out as an opponent of the campaign against Brazil's image. He expressed this position in a meeting with Paul VI.[19] In late 1970, his promotion to Prefect of the Sacred Congregation for the Evangelization of Peoples, a major Vatican post, was surrounded by controversy. The progressive grass roots had pressured for Dom Agnelo's removal, because they believed he was conservative and showed a "benevolent attitude" toward the military, as some European papers reported. Other reports asserted the opposite: that Dom Agnelo opposed the governor of the state of São Paulo and supported subversion (an implausible interpretation). The pope and other high-level churchmen vigorously denied these assertions as pure speculation by the press, and they emphasized Rossi's capabilities for his new assignment. The incident occupied the attention of the press and Rome's diplomats for months.[20] It was a fine illustration of how the hierarchy's public voice could override the clamor of internal dissent. More important, it illustrated how human rights, Church-state relations, and conflict over religious renovation revolved around the explosive question of torture.

Voices from Brazil

The examples of three leading defenders of human rights personify the diplomatic maneuvers in Rome. The first was Dom Hélder. While serving as de facto

Vatican secretary of state in the 1950s, the future Paul VI had encouraged Dom Hélder's restructuring of the Brazilian Church. Dom Hélder now had privileged access to the pope.[21] Both the government and the opposition tried to court Dom Hélder to support their respective political causes. In 1965, for instance, Brazil's ambassador to the Vatican, Henrique de Souza Gomes, politely warned the archbishop that Brazilian exiles in Paris were hoping to exploit his name. When Dom Hélder proved ever less cooperative with the regime, rumors emerged about diplomatic pressures to have him removed from Recife (Piletti and Praxedes 1997:328, 339). In the words of one diplomat, Dom Hélder's strict obedience to the Church built him a "reserve of benevolence" that allowed him to speak freely about the situation in Brazil.[22]

Silenced in his own country, he became the leading critic of the regime abroad. To stop Dom Hélder, Justice Minister Alfredo Buzaid proposed to President Médici that the government revoke the archbishop's special passport. Foreign Minister Mário Gibson Barboza, a moderate, vetoed the measure as being illegal, however. He argued that it would backfire and actually strengthen Dom Hélder's position. As a rule, he told Médici, it was best to allow the bishops to act freely so as not to create martyrs.[23] This was sound advice, but it obviously went unheeded as the regime and its allies continued to attack the Church. In another episode, Dom Hélder's opponents alleged that his frequent trips were backed financially by Communists, allegations that the government probably investigated.[24]

Using a more subtle approach, Ambassador Jobim spoke with Dom Hélder about improving Church-state relations. Jobim concluded that Dom Hélder was open to dialogue, but that the ongoing Church-military tensions and pressure from grassroots radicals on the bishops discouraged it.[25] Despite the goodwill he found in the Vatican, Dom Hélder encountered resistance there also. Because of the complaints of bishops who disagreed with his statements, he received instructions from the secretariat of state to ask these bishops' permission before speaking in their dioceses. The secretariat, however, denied that it had required prior approval of Dom Hélder's speeches. In addition, in 1971 one observer of the Vatican reported that Paul VI had warned Dom Hélder to concentrate on his own diocese.[26]

Another source of information on the repression was Branca de Mello Franco Alves, the mother of the exiled congressman Márcio Moreira Alves. A Brazilian Catholic Action leader, in mid-1968 Branca Alves was named to the Pontifical Council for the Laity, a new, experimental organization created in the wake of Vatican II to increase the voice of the faithful in international Church affairs. (The council later became a permanent commission.) Her appointment and subsequent advocacy represented an important advance for Latin Americans and for women, two groups that had little representation in the mainly European and male Vatican bureaucracy.[27] Believing that the council should extend its work to questions of peace and justice, Branca Alves used her position to denounce the repression in Brazil.[28] In Rio in May 1970, for instance, she hosted the council's secretary, Monsignor Marcel Uylenbroeck, who met with important members of the Catholic left and filed a confidential report on the "fascist tendency" of the regime, including torture and the prohibition of citizen participation.[29] After the heavy attacks on JOC in August and September, she proposed to the council that a personal representative of the Holy Father be sent to Brazil as a form of pressure on the regime.[30]

Branca Alves met opposition in the government and the Church. Shortly after the promulgation of AI-5, she had difficulty in obtaining a passport for a trip to speak to the council on the Brazilian Church.[31] Later, in March 1970, she wrote Cardinal Jean Villot, the Vatican secretary of state, to complain that papal nuncio Dom Umberto Mozzoni had blocked her attempt to send sensitive dossiers to Rome in the Church's diplomatic pouch in order to skirt military security. According to Branca Alves, Mozzoni did not want the government to learn that such information had reached the Vatican with his help.[32]

Mozzoni had come to Brazil from Argentina in mid-1969 to replace Dom Sebastiano Baggio. Dom Baggio defended Dom Hélder and encouraged other clergymen to hide suspected subversives from the police, leading the military to consider him practically persona non grata.[33] The more cautious Mozzoni was opposed by a large number of progressive Brazilian bishops, but the Vatican viewed him as the best choice for the challenging Brazil post, made even more difficult by the civil strife. He spoke good Portuguese, was an able negotiator, and had long experience in Latin America.[34] He later took part in the Bipartite.

The third example was Alceu Amoroso Lima, modern Brazil's leading Catholic intellectual. Known as Alceu, he played a multifaceted role in Brazilian life. Alceu led the Centro Dom Vital, acted as a Church-state intermediary, nurtured Brazilian higher education, and authored numerous important books and articles. He deeply influenced several generations of Catholic activists and intellectuals across the political spectrum. Like Dom Hélder, Alceu had embraced Integralismo and the Estado Novo in the 1930s, but moved left in the 1940s and 1950s, inspiring Catholic Action to liberalize along the lines of the new progressive Catholic philosophy emerging in Europe. Dom Hélder was the father of the Popular Church, and Alceu its grandfather.[35] Alceu opposed the coup and fearlessly criticized the censorship and torture perpetrated by the military regime. In May 1964, for instance, he denounced as "cultural terrorism" the arrest and exile of major intellectuals. Thereafter he continued to write his weekly newspaper column, which often criticized the regime. His immense prestige put him above censorship and arrest.[36]

In mid-1969 Alceu wrote a long confidential letter to Dom Aloísio Lorscheider asserting that the Church should work to end the dictatorship, "not by violent or revolutionary means, but through the legal transformation of current institutions." The military's obsessive anti-Communism had divided Brazil into "the good and the bad," Alceu wrote. "Nazi" elements in the government wanted the "total extinction" of all political movements, including the Church and the traditional political class. They "ruptured our traditional history of compromise and amnesty" by repressing the opposition. "The greatest danger is that they are anesthetizing Brazil" and converting Brazilian cordiality and the willingness to forgive political opponents "into lack of character, into an opportunistic malleability."[37]

Alceu worked through a new Vatican board to denounce torture and the dictatorship. Paul VI appointed him to the Pontifical Peace and Justice Commission in 1967. Composed of representatives of different nationalities and ideological perspectives, this commission focused on Vatican II's goals of the defense of human rights and the advancement of socioeconomic development. The Pontifical Peace and Justice Commission led to the founding of national commissions around the

Dom Sebastiano Baggio (in photo at left) and Dom Umberto Mozzoni represented two different styles for dealing with the military regime. Baggio angered the generals for his defense of Dom Hélder and alleged subversives. Dom Mozzoni, Baggio's replacement, worked persistently to smooth over Church-state difficulties.

Catholic intellectual Alceu Amoroso Lima opposed the military regime and argued for strong public denunciation of human rights violations.

world, including the very important Brazilian branch and its local offshoots. As a new structure, the pontifical commission sidestepped the traditional channels of diplomacy of the Vatican secretariat of state, giving a greater voice to the laity and rapidly bringing human rights issues to the attention of the press.[38] Through Alceu's efforts the commission became a source of negative publicity on the regime.[39]

Stopping Torture: Quiet Protest or Exaggerated Publicity?

Both Alceu and Branca Alves urged public condemnation of the regime on the torture issue. In 1970 they debated the Church's position with Dom Eugênio and also Cardinal Vicente Scherer, the archbishop of Porto Alegre. A June 1970 letter from Dom Eugênio to Branca Alves reveals the issues at hand:

> I believe that you were mistaken in saying that after God only I could help solve the problem of torture. I do not consider myself to be so powerful. If it were up to me, there would be no torture or terrorism or even struggle against the government as it is done here in Brazil. But there would be, in Christian harmony, an effort to resolve our problems in favor of greater progress for our country. I will continue to take a position, before God, against torture, arrests, incidents of kidnapping [and] a certain ideological orientation that is not ratified by the Gospel. I also continue to be firmly against . . . the deformation of public opinion about our country. The facts may be true, but they are presented untruthfully abroad.[40]

Dom Eugênio clearly rejected Marxist class struggle and the revolutionary left, and in a polarized world it was easy for people to see him as "promilitary." Alceu received a similar letter from Dom Vicente after sending the cardinal a report on torture. Dom Vicente undoubtedly opposed torture and heard testimony of abuses while visiting political prisoners at the Tiradentes Prison in São Paulo. However, Dom Vicente condemned "what is being done in Europe, that is, the disclosure of news that in Brazil torture is an official institution and practiced openly everywhere."[41] Dom Vicente did not know, or purposefully ignored, that this description was not far from the truth: the regime had indeed made torture its unspoken policy and used it widely, albeit secretly.

In a September 1970 letter to Dom Eugênio, Alceu rebutted the bishops' arguments and explained the public campaign against the government. "To appeal to the authorities to confirm torture is to knock on doors that will never open," he wrote. Alceu reasoned that only public attacks—even exaggerations—could break through the horrible code of fear and intimidation that ruled torturers, their victims, and witnesses. Victims rarely confirmed their suffering publicly for fear of repeating the experience. Witnesses such as doctors and nurses denied their testimony for fear of losing their jobs or of being tortured. The torturers were kept unidentified.

> Everything occurs in the most complete anonymity precisely so that no judicial proof can ever be invoked. The silence, the denials, the impossibility to obtain proof are what make torture even more gloomy. Therefore, it is a thousand times better to have exaggerated denunciations than for us to keep a silence that might be confused with complicity.

Dom Hélder, Alceu added, suffered persecution precisely because he had made the "terrible choice between silence and denunciation." Alceu concluded that without ample publicity about the treatment of prisoners and the guarantee of habeas corpus (suspended by AI-5), "we will live the drama of attacks and denials" and "reciprocal exaggerations."[42]

The anti-torture campaign was carried out by human rights groups, journalists, Church leaders, and Brazilian exiles who gave detailed accounts of the atrocities in Brazil. These reports appeared in the foreign media and became grist for political and legal action against the Brazilian government.[43] Headlines about Brazil in the United States, for example, frequently mentioned torture (Drosdoff 1986:86–87). Because of censorship, such outside reports were often the only public source concerning abuses in Brazil. The opposition tried to magnify the atrocities in order to undermine the regime, whereas the government almost always downplayed them. Muricy, bishops such as Dom Eugênio and Dom Vicente, and supporters of the regime accurately pointed out that the foreign reports gave a distorted view of Brazilian reality. But Alceu and the human rights activists also accurately demonstrated to the world how torture destroyed Brazilian democracy.

Dom Eugênio's anti-Communism and position as a top Church leader led him to prefer the safeguarding of Brazil's image, though without abandoning defense of human rights. His and Alceu's contrasting positions highlighted the competing ideas about patriotism within the Church as it developed a new corpus of social teachings and tended to split into the so-called conservative and progressive factions. As Dom Eugênio rose in the Church hierarchy, he had to distance himself from his earlier, controversial work as a Church union organizer in the Northeast (Tibor Sulik interview 2). Dom Eugênio's embrace of hierarchy, order, and discipline further informed his attitude. Nevertheless, his position, prudence, and prestige before the armed forces made him a potential intermediary between the Church and the generals.[44]

Indeed, Dom Eugênio believed in preserving the traditional Church-state relationship as a means of resolving disagreements. Especially in a dictatorship, he reasoned, confidential channels worked best, while open protest could only serve to irritate those in power. On this point he differed sharply with Dom Paulo and Dom Hélder, who by 1970 had abandoned discretion to denounce torture. Thus, by his own account, Dom Eugênio purposely cultivated a double image, "sacrificing" one in favor of the other: *publicly* he appeared by his silence to favor the repression, but *privately* he worked against the mistreatment of alleged subversives.

Dom Eugênio did not come to this decision easily. He consulted Heráclito Sobral Pinto, the highly respected conservative Catholic jurist who had defended PCB leader Luís Carlos Prestes during the Estado Novo and vocally opposed the 1964 regime. Sobral Pinto urged Dom Eugênio to continue working quietly in order to protect victims of the repression. Dom Eugênio's double image convinced military intelligence that he acted in an "ambiguous way, supporting the government and the CNBB." Regardless, no less a figure than Alceu recognized Dom Eugênio's contribution to human rights. In his September 1970 letter, Alceu thanked the archbishop for contacting the authorities in an effort to free prisoners and stop police abuse.[45]

Muricy and Sales: Remaking Brazil's Image

Dom Eugênio and General Muricy both worked to improve Brazil's image. In Brazil, Muricy used his power and the media to expose and interpret the dangers of leftist influence among students, who supplied the guerrillas with a large number of recruits. In his view the breakdown of traditional values among students swayed by radical idols and ideas typified the psychological effects of revolutionary warfare and threatened national security. Chief of Staff Muricy ordered three studies of political prisoners ("terrorists," in his words) held in jails across Brazil. Carried out by military specialists assisted by professional psychologists, these studies employed a battery of questions and tests and sought to define the social and psychological profiles of subversives. Muricy revealed the outcome of this research to the press in 1970, and in a widely publicized speech to the Association of Brazilian Educators in 1971. In the process he made the important revelation that some five hundred individuals accused of subversion were in prison. The majority were high school and university students. Very impressionable, they had entered revolutionary movements influenced by radical infiltrators, professors, members of the opposite sex, and their own idealism. Muricy's diagnosis of their involvement echoed the concerns of conservatives and government authorities in other Western countries struggling to deal with student unrest and the "generation gap" of the late 1960s and 1970s. Subversives were attacking Brazilian morals, religion, and the family structure, Muricy stated. "Promiscuity" and "lack of hygiene" reigned at the famous 1968 student gathering in Ibiúna, Brazil's attempted political Woodstock.[46] One congressman praised Muricy's studies and recommended "occupational psychotherapy" for young, middle-class individuals susceptible to the revolutionary call.[47] At the Bipartite, Muricy told the bishops that drug abuse was another cause of student radicalism[48] (although in reality the revolutionary left strictly rejected drug usage).

A number of the tested prisoners stated that abuses occurred in connection with these ostensibly voluntary psychological examinations. They received guarantees that the test results would not be revealed. During questioning, some were asked about their reactions to torture. Those who refused to cooperate were intimidated with the threat of further torture. Given the many violations of human rights that occurred in Brazilian prisons at the time, the prisoners' affirmations are credible, though it is unclear whether General Muricy knew of these abuses.[49]

General Muricy also worked on the international front. For instance, in 1972 he published a long article in a German military journal praising Brazil's Army and its stance against Communism. The article argued that foreign journalists who "do not understand Brazil" falsely distorted the country's image. Communists and "bad Brazilians" betrayed their homeland by presenting to Europeans and North Americans a picture of a completely militaristic and antidemocratic regime that promoted only "genocide, torture, and the restriction of human rights." On the contrary, Muricy wrote, Brazil was a nation in evolution with a "strong people," a growing economy, and an army that recruited its soldiers from all sectors of society. Furthermore, the Revolution of 1964 was "bloodless"; Brazil spent relatively little per capita on its armed forces; and most military members of the government were not active duty officers, but retired. "By the year 2000 this country should have an effectively developed, democratic, and sovereign society that assures the economic, social, and political viability of Brazil as a great power," Muricy concluded.[50]

Dom Eugênio cooperated with Muricy. After a visit to Pope Paul VI, Dom Eugênio reported to the general in early May 1970 that he had tried to "neutralize" the foreign media's reportage of a "great religious persecution." The cardinal gave positive interviews to the European press and met with Ambassador Jobim and Brazil's envoys to Belgium and Italy. In a letter to Muricy, Dom Eugênio relayed a message from the pope to the Brazilian government denying that information damaging to Church-state relations had come from the nunciature in Rio.[51]

Dom Eugênio also made it starkly clear, however, that he knew of abuses and that the government could redeem itself only by stopping them. "I maintained many contacts, trying to reestablish the truth," Dom Eugênio wrote. "Unfortunately, I believe that this will only be possible on a definitive basis with the suppression of torture and greater knowledge of that very situation." In fact, Dom Eugênio had already proposed to Muricy a "private investigation" that, presumably under the auspices of the Pontifical Peace and Justice Commission in Rome or even of the pontiff himself, could shed light on this "situation" of torture. While in Rome, Dom Eugênio did not pursue the matter because Muricy had not given the "green light."

The archbishop further noted the "very bad impression" left by the regime's publication of prosecution documents in the case of the thirty-two priests in Belo Horizonte who were accused of violating national security for their protests of the death of student Edson Luís. "If it hadn't been published by someone in the Army, I would have supposed that it was the work of subversives wanting to augment the friction between the government and the Church," Dom Eugênio wrote. He also complained to Muricy about the regime's decision to obstruct the entrance of foreign missionaries into Brazil.[52]

Immediately after Dom Eugênio's private warnings about torture, the bishops increased their public denunciations. Dom Eugênio had assisted greatly in this process by prompting Candido Mendes to investigate and verify the existence of abuses. Candido Mendes accepted only those complaints for which the victim and two witnesses were willing to sign an affidavit. Despite the rigorous and risky requirements, Candido Mendes documented thirteen cases in Rio alone. He took note of dozens of other reports made by the parents, friends, and lawyers of political prisoners. At the CNBB's Eleventh General Assembly in Brasília, Candido Mendes presented his information to the bishops. The episcopate as a whole faced hard proof of atrocities.[53] The evidence was crucial in convincing the bishops to become more critical of the regime. They issued a sharp condemnation of violence, torture, and the wrongs of the military justice system.[54] In Paris on May 26, 1970 Dom Hélder brought further bad publicity with his aforementioned speech denouncing torture.

Nevertheless, during another trip to Rome in June 1970, Dom Eugênio continued his "discrete but intense" work to "remake the true face of Brazil." In a July letter informing Muricy of these efforts, the cardinal requested information from the general to help refute potential criticism of Brazil in an upcoming meeting of the Peace and Justice Commission. Dom Eugênio's fears were based on documents cir-

Dom Eugênio de Araújo Sales (right), the archbishop of Salvador and primate of Brazil, established a solid friendship with President Médici (left) but rejected the regime's excessive anti-Communism and its use of torture.

culating in Brazil that presumably criticized the human rights situation. To assist the cardinal, General Muricy turned to Army intelligence. The file he received from the CIE brings the cardinal's concerns into focus. It contained a rundown of accusations of subversion against five professors from the Instituto Brasileiro de Desenvolvimento (IBRADES; Brazilian Development Institute), the Jesuit study center where Dom Aloísio was detained months later. Among the five was Father Meneses, who had been arrested six years earlier by order of General Muricy. The suspects had links to grassroots organizations, the student movement, Marxist university professors, and Paulo Freire. A note from an Army Ministry official assured General Muricy that the documentation would give Dom Eugênio "abundant resources to rebut the accusations of our detractors." Ably used, the information would "lend great service to Brazil, particularly if we consider the opposing attitude of our other known 'prelate.'" This was a clear reference to Dom Hélder.[55]

Dom Eugênio closed by thanking General Muricy for helping to establish a connection with President Médici. While serving as papal legate to the Eighth National Eucharistic Congress in Brasília at the end of May 1970, Dom Eugênio had been received by the president with honors appropriate for a chief of state. Médici also met with the top bishops of the CNBB, who declared that "the Catholic Church will continue collaborating with the government, openly and faithfully, in all that is concerned with the welfare of the Brazilian people." The ceremonious attention to the episcopate softened the impact of the CNBB's statement against torture. Indeed, government officials were optimistic that Dom Eugênio's encounter with Médici had signaled greater Church-state understanding. "I believe that we have established a solid friendship," Dom Eugênio said in his letter to Muricy. "Upon returning from Rome, I wrote him [Médici] and sent a confidential, private message from the Holy Father."[56]

Conclusion

Shaped by torture and Church-state conflict, the struggle over Brazil's image was a central part of the larger conflict between the Médici government and the opposition. Dom Eugênio and Vatican officials sought a balance between the Church's duty to preach social justice and the need to maintain friendly relations with the largest Catholic nation on earth. In the world of diplomacy, perception was often more important than the actual facts of torture. Factors such as patriotism, the institutional needs of the Church, and ecclesiastical politics filtered how torture was to be interpreted. As one Italian priest familiar with Brazil noted, its bishops spoke with one voice in Brazil and with another when outside the country.[57]

Dom Eugênio embodied the tensions and contradictions of the era. As a pastor he reserved the right to criticize the regime's abuses and inadequacies, but as a politician he worked with General Muricy in an attempt to patch over Church-military differences. Their efforts helped to keep Church-state relations in Brazil civil and prevented a worsening in relations with the Vatican, whose word carried great weight with the regime and the average Brazilian. As one observer in Rome noted in October 1971, the key diplomatic gestures of Dom Eugênio and others overrode the reports of the Peace and Justice Commission and made the Vatican's opinion of the military regime more favorable.[58] However, episcopal diplomacy would become more difficult as conflict increasingly involved the hierarchy. This became shockingly evident after the invasion of IBRADES and the arrest of Dom Aloísio Lorscheider in October 1970.

Chapter 5

Dialogue in the Shadows

The Creation and Function of the Bipartite

From 1970 to 1974, the Bipartite met regularly in an attempt to avoid worse Church-state conflict. By most accounts the dialogue produced a no-holds-barred exchange of ideas, accusations, and counteraccusations between the bishops and the officers. By channeling conflict into talk, the Bipartite reduced Church-state tensions. At the same time the discussions highlighted each side's stubborn adherence to its basic positions. This chapter sets the stage for the next five chapters' examination of the debates by providing crucial background on the Bipartite's creation and operation. The chapter discusses the events and trends that shaped the formation of the commission; the struggle between General Muricy and other regime officials over its continuing; the individuals and institutions involved in its foundation and the importance of elite political culture in this process; its structure, membership, and procedures; and the role of secrecy and intelligence-gathering in its activities.

The Bipartite provided for a formal dialogue that was as informal as possible. General Muricy was the ideal choice to oversee this urgent yet often ambiguous task. He represented the core of the Revolution and held immense power within the Army. On the verge of mandatory retirement, he was about to lose his ability to issue formal orders, but his prestige would preserve his influence. At the Bipartite he represented the government—but to what extent? The answer was purposely left in the penumbra of the regime. Coupled with cold war suspicion, the uncertainty led some wary individuals in both the Church and the military to see the Bipartite as an opportunity not only for dialogue but also for intelligence and political purposes.

The Tripartite Encounters and Other Attempts at Dialogue

Dialogue in and of itself was not the novelty of the Bipartite. Dialogue was part of the Church's historical political repertoire. In the years immediately following Vatican II, the importance of dialogue increased, and it seemed quite logical for the bishops to talk with the military regime. From 1964 to 1970, traditional forms of negotiation and cooperation had continued. In fact, through the early Médici years both sides went to great length to project an aura of good relations (Alves 1979:201), and the bishops continually spoke of the need for collaboration and dialogue (Bernal 1989:142–51).[1] In late 1967 and early 1968, for instance, Dom Avelar worked for the creation of a high-level Church-state commission to study the causes of civil-religious conflict. The bishop met with high government officials, including Costa e Silva. However, the government rejected the plan as military hard-liners argued for controls over the clergy and even over the bishops.[2] Nevertheless, Dom Avelar's idea planted the seed for the Bipartite. In early 1970 Ambassador Jobim proposed that the Ministry of Foreign Relations establish an assistant for ecclesiastical affairs as a channel of communication with the bishops at the national level. Later that year Cardinal Baggio, the former nuncio, asserted in an interview in Italy that the Brazilian Church and state "know that they cannot do without each other in the search for the common goal of the country's development."[3]

Only weeks after the decree of AI-5, businessmen, military officers, and clergymen held a series of informal meetings aimed at reducing Church-state strife. Underwritten by entrepreneurs, the so-called Tripartite Encounters looked to build mutual understanding and reduce tensions among the three sectors. A representative of each sector presented its history, goals, methods of recruitment and operation, social contributions, and political difficulties.[4] The Tripartite lapsed, but after the attack on IBRADES, Colonel Octávio Costa suggested it be resurrected to give the Church "a more correct picture" of the Communist threat to Brazil. The Tripartite reflected the unsuccessful attempt by the regime to graft the Church onto the new military-technocratic establishment, which increasingly viewed the clergy as unnecessary for organizing the most modern sectors of Brazilian society.[5]

At about this time, the progressive Dom Hélder expressed a similar desire for Church-state cooperation. At first neutral about the coup, he subsequently became the frequent target of conservative Catholics and military hard-liners. He nevertheless maintained contact with several officers and continued to hold considerable goodwill toward the regime. He counseled some of his followers to end their "antimilitary prejudices." Incredibly, he was also at first neutral about AI-5. He even believed it could help in the "combat against corruption" and the accomplishment of social reform. Dom Hélder proposed that dialogue with key military officials could contribute to "development and peace" as well as "national security" and "social order."[6] As some observers noted, Dom Hélder "emphasized that he would rather work with the government than against it."[7]

Turning Points Toward the Bipartite: The JOC and IBRADES Incidents

The attacks on the Catholic Youth Workers (JOC) and the Jesuit study center (IBRADES) in the second half of 1970 precipitated the Bipartite. These incidents highlighted the arbitrariness of regime violence and the resultant damage to Church-state relations. In September and October 1970, agents jailed and tortured numerous militants and priests in a sweep against JOC, a progressive group intensely involved with the poor and working class. In Rio, JOC priests and lay militants were particularly active at the Morro de São Carlos, a favela near downtown. The JOC national headquarters were located there, and across the street stood a residence of nuns that was also invaded by the police. Father Agostinho Pretto and other JOC priests had developed a close relationship with the São Carlos community, some of whose members were temporarily detained during the sweep.[8] In the process of this operation, agents from the Rio DOPS and the First Army invaded IBRADES, which trained Jocistas and other grassroots activists and served as a CNBB think tank. The agents roughed up several important Jesuits, including Father Pedro Belisário Velloso Rebello, the provincial head of the Jesuit order, and Father Ormindo Viveiros de Castro, the president of the Pontifícia Universidade Católica do Rio de Janeiro (PUC-RJ; Pontifical Catholic University of Rio de Janeiro). The soldiers also ransacked the fathers' private rooms in search of subversive writings, including those of the center's director, Father Fernando Bastos de Ávila, an intellectual who earlier was considered by the generals to head the Ministry of Education and was seen by some in the regime as a strong anti-Communist, an "anti–Dom Hélder."[9] Father Ávila later protested angrily to the commander of the attack. The officer responded, "I don't have diplomats to do this work. I have soldiers" (Father Ávila interview).

Worst of all for Church-state relations, the security men detained the CNBB's secretary general, Dom Aloísio, and held him incommunicado for more than four hours. Dom Aloísio was an unthreatening moderate who did not belong to the group of outspoken bishops persecuted by the military as a radical fringe element.

In fact, the incident caused him to miss a meeting with Alfredo Buzaid, Médici's archconservative Minister of Justice.

The protests against the attacks on JOC and IBRADES unified the Church in its denunciation of human rights violations and authoritarian rule.[10] The country's five mostly conservative cardinals protested in a letter to Médici deploring the "deterioration" of Church-state ties. Dom Aloísio's detention was "unprecedented in the republican history of Brazil," they stated. The CNBB leadership also denounced the raid. It criticized Communism but defended the Church's social policies and declared that "the terrorism of subversion must not be met with the terrorism of repression."[11] Because of press censorship, however, few people in Brazil learned of the JOC arrests or of the detention of Dom Aloísio.

Protest overseas was more important and produced a near diplomatic disaster for the regime. In Europe thousands of Jocistas demonstrated in the streets; they jammed the telephone lines and inundated the mailboxes of Brazil's embassies with protests (Alves 1979:205). In Rome, Vatican Radio and the official newspaper *L'Osservatore Romano* joined the chorus of criticism against the repression, and the paper published the CNBB's statement. Pope Paul VI declared his support for the Brazilian Church and condemned the use of torture. These reactions further tainted Brazil's image as a violator of human rights and angered the hypersensitive generals. Although President Médici was reportedly irritated by his subordinates' actions in the IBRADES episode, he attributed the country's worsening image to "bad Brazilians."[12]

From September through November 1970, the bishops used their prestige to the hilt in trying to locate the imprisoned clergymen and lay militants, but they became increasingly frustrated as officials at all levels gave them the runaround. Priests, bishops, cardinals—even Dom Jaime, the conservative cardinal and a great friend of the military—met with colonels, generals, and Justice Minister Buzaid but received little or only contradictory information about the prisoners and no indication as to when they would be released. Dom Alberto Trevisan, a highly respected former military chaplain with excellent contacts in the armed forces and the SNI, also made no progress.[13] With great effort they learned that the JOC arrests had been carried out by DOPS officers on orders from the First Army,[14] and that the investigation took place at the feared DOI-CODI, one of Rio's torture centers.[15] On October 1, 1970, Dom Jaime spoke of a "war against the Church." The next day he met with General Médici in the Laranjeiras Palace, the presidential residence in Rio. The meeting came at the suggestion of Dom Lucas Moreira Neves, who, as CNBB national secretary for lay affairs, was responsible for the work and welfare of the beleaguered JOC. He accompanied Dom Jaime. Médici listened politely, took notes, but agreed only to correspond with Dom Lucas.[16] "Twenty-one days after the first arrests and despite our efforts, searches, and long waits in antechambers, we still do not have the least indication as to who ordered the arrests, for what motives, or where the detainees are located," Dom Lucas wrote to Médici the same day, adding that, once again, Brazil appeared to the world as a place of "true persecution of the Church."[17] The records indicate that Médici did not respond. The cardinals' protest of Dom Aloísio's detention was also unsuccessful.

The bishops continued their private contacts with government officials in the attempt to aid the Jocistas and to calm the growing Church-state crisis. Dom Aloísio met with Justice Minister Buzaid twice, leading the proregime newspaper *O Estado de São Paulo* to deny the existence of a crisis. Foreshadowing the Bipartite, the paper reported that the government would "examine all problems that might make the relationship more difficult, including the study of individual cases." Immediately thereafter Dom Eugênio, Dom Vicente, and twenty other bishops allowed Júlio de Rosen, a special envoy from President Médici, to sit in on their deliberations before they penned the CNBB Central Commission's stern mid-October protest of the IBRADES assault.[18] The bishops believed all hopes for understanding had been exhausted, however.[19] Finally, President Médici authorized Dom Vicente, accompanied by officers, to visit the priests jailed at DOI-CODI, but not the lay militants. The bishops nearly refused this meager concession.[20] By mid-November human rights lawyer Heleno Fragoso had still not received permission to visit his clients, leading him to bring suit in the military courts against First Army commander General Sizeno Sarmento for violation of the regime's own rules on political prisoners.[21] The priests were finally released on November 22 and the lay militants thereafter.

After the Jocistas' release, the bishops met privately with Father Pretto and others to hear their personal accounts of torture at DOI-CODI. Dom Vicente Scherer asked Father Pretto if he would repeat his story on television. The priest consented, but only if the cardinal agreed to appear with him.[22] The broadcast did not take place; nor would the military have permitted it.

As the Jocistas concluded in an internal report, the naked truth was that the bishops had no power of persuasion with a military bent on stamping out the slightest hint of subversion. Fearful of being associated with the revolutionaries, naively confident of the religious sentiment of the generals, and accustomed to social privilege, the bishops had taken years to understand the violent nature of the regime, which the Jocistas and other grassroots militants had known all too well from the horrors of the jails. The bishops came to this realization only after the detention of Dom Aloísio "directly wounded" the bishops, forcing them "to take up a position of defense." This defense, however, failed to extend beyond the Church to "all men who find themselves in the same situation and with the same ideals." Moreover, the episcopate showed little interest in the JOC movement, which many bishops viewed with suspicion. After all that had happened, the hierarchy still hoped for "conciliation" with the government.[23]

Yet the JOC and IBRADES incidents marked a turning point, precisely because they exposed the cardinals and other top bishops directly to the repression and deepened their distrust of the government. The military misled the bishops in exactly the same way it did the relatives of jailed, disappeared, and dead political opponents: bouncing the clergy up and down the martial hierarchy and from one installation to another in a fruitless, weeks-long search for the prisoners. Meanwhile, Médici and top generals could wash their hands of the affair by claiming ignorance of their subordinates' actions. The message was finally sinking in that a significant part of the military no longer respected the Church.

Neither bishops nor generals could explain away such an incident as just a mere misunderstanding to be pinned on subversives or smoothed over with polite letters or a tête-à-tête. More systematic conflict resolution was needed. "The time has come for us to sit down at the table for an earnest dialogue," declared Dom Avelar Brandão Vilela, soon to become Brazil's archbishop primate. "In order to solve all of our problems we need to know frankly what is interfering in our relations, or else conflicts could multiply indefinitely."[24]

The Birth of the Bipartite

The Bipartite was a fresh start. It differed substantially from previous efforts at dialogue in several ways: duration, secrecy, the novelty of including intelligence officers, its overall systematic nature, and intensity of debate on themes of vital interest to both sides. Several key figures contributed to the commission's foundation, in addition to the link between General Muricy and Dom Eugênio.[25] The most important were Tarcísio Meirelles Padilha and Candido Mendes. These members of the carioca Catholic elite had sharp ideological disagreements but shared a concern for the welfare of the clergy and Church-state relations.

Padilha's father was a powerful archconservative. Like Justice Minister Buzaid, the elder Padilha had been a prominent Integralista in the 1930s. Whereas former Integralistas such as Dom Hélder moved left, in the 1960s strident conservative

From left to right: Tarcísio Padilha, General Arnaldo José Calderari, Muricy, and Guanabara governor Chagas Freitas at Muricy's induction as ADESG president, January 1971. Padilha helped start the Bipartite by introducing Muricy to Candido Mendes.

remnants of this group entered strongly anti-Communist, right-wing Catholic organizations, where they worked to undermine the progressives (see Antoine 1980). They shared the conservative military's fear of social upheaval. In 1964 Raimundo Padilha joined the conspiracy against João Goulart and then served as the progovernment party's majority leader in the Chamber of Deputies. From 1971 to 1975, he governed the state of Rio de Janeiro. Following a strong CNBB denunciation of torture and other forms of terror in early 1970, Raimundo Padilha joined the chorus of regime supporters who denied the existence of political prisoners and claimed the existence of an international conspiracy to defame Brazil (Della Cava 1985:140).

Tarcísio Padilha shared this outlook, yet he also subtly distinguished himself from the archconservatives and military hard-liners. On the one hand, he clearly established himself as an apologist for the regime. He had graduated from the ESG in 1969 and become a member of its teaching staff. He also served in the government as a member of the Federal Education Council and as president of the Special Commission for Moral Education and Civics. In a book finished just weeks before the start of the Bipartite, he excoriated the left, attacked "subversive" literature and university professors, defined Brazilian revolutionaries as "terrorists," and doubted the existence of torture. He also criticized the "participation of priests in subversive movements" and the "theology of violence" (Padilha 1971:195–210). On the other hand, Padilha was an intellectual interested in interpreting Brazilian reality, fostering the country's socioeconomic development, and creating a political opening. By this time he had already gained international recognition as one of Brazil's leading Catholic philosophers and educators. He pushed for a greater emphasis on the humanities at ESG and, risking reprisal, criticized the philosophical materialism of the regime's development strategy as well as its exaggerated stress on security and technocracy. As a Catholic he also viewed with great concern the Positivist ideas that he believed still influenced military action. A firm believer in the need for strong institutions, the younger Padilha feared that the growing friction between Church and state would lead to an outright rupture of Brazil's two most important and best-organized institutions. He believed it was his duty to help avoid such a rupture and thus prevent further social unrest.[26] Padilha saw the Church as a "political force" that should work toward the social betterment of Brazilians, albeit without interfering with the government. Yet Padilha also perceived the Church as divided over the question of social activism (Padilha 1975:85, 89–90).

Candido Mendes's broad background eminently qualified him to bridge the gap between clergy and military. He rose to importance in the Brazilian Church as the descendant of the nineteenth-century senator whose wife and sons received a papal title of nobility for the senator's devotion to the Church, including the defense of bishops against the Empire. Candido Mendes inherited this title, though he never used it.[27] But Candido Mendes was an intellectual, educator, public official, and leader in his own right. At the age of fifteen he wrote a biography of his great-grandfather (Almeida 1943). He first became involved in politics while studying law and philosophy at the PUC-RJ. In 1948 he became the secretary general of the highly active and politicized União Nacional dos Estudantes (UNE; National Union of

Students). He also joined the JUC, a group that radicalized in the 1960s before being repressed by both the Church hierarchy and the regime. In the 1950s he helped organize the ISEB, a nationalistic think tank within the Ministry of Education, which advised the government on questions of development. As an advisor to President Quadros, Candido Mendes established ties with General Golbery, the leading ESG ideologue, secretary of Quadros's National Security Council, and eventual founder of the SNI. In 1965, he organized a private meeting at his home between Robert Kennedy and leading Brazilian intellectuals to discuss human rights violations in Brazil. In the mid-1960s he was also a visiting professor at Harvard, at Columbia, and at the University of California, Los Angeles. In the United States, he spoke out on the political situation in Brazil. In the Church Candido Mendes worked as an assistant to Dom Hélder, helping him prepare for Vatican II. Candido Mendes's experience brought him to the CNBB undersecretaryship for social affairs in 1969, the leadership of the CJP-BR, and finally to membership on the Pontifical Peace and Justice Commission in Rome. In 1971 he also acted as an advisor to the synod of bishops held in Rome to discuss the theme "Justice in the World."[28] Candido Mendes was also the brother of Father Luciano Mendes de Almeida, an intelligent and politically able Jesuit who became a bishop in 1976, the CNBB's secretary general in 1979, and its president in 1987.

Candido Mendes stood on the left. He advocated nationalist developmentalism (Almeida 1959, 1963, 1973 et al.), believed that the United States hindered this, and urged intellectuals to take the lead in producing Latin American progress (Almeida 1972). He also embraced Catholic progressivism. His 1966 book on the Catholic left, *Memento dos vivos* (Memento of the living), was criticized by elements of the military and conservative Catholics (Almeida 1966a). Candido Mendes came under investigation on several occasions because of his ties to ISEB (abolished by the regime), progressive clergymen, and opposition intellectuals and politicians. In 1968 the DOPS-GB identified him as a member of the "Intellectual Command" of the student movement.[29] In 1972 he wrote a perceptive essay that recognized the regime's economic achievements but also its narrow-mindedness and inability to escape "the trap of its own logic" of repression (Almeida 1977:103).

Nevertheless, Candido Mendes's prestige, connections, and elite status allowed him to work largely unhindered and to travel in opposing political circles. While orchestrating the Bipartite, he became one of the principal proponents of descompressão (decompression), or political liberalization. Descompressão led to abertura in the Geisel and Figueiredo administrations. Candido Mendes worked to promote it at the highest levels of the government, and he emphasized the importance of giving the opposition a role in the process (Almeida 1977:103–04). At his behest, in 1972 the chief of Médici's civilian presidential staff, João Leitão de Abreu, began internal discussions about liberalization. Candido Mendes used his friendship with José Guilherme Merquior, one of Brazil's greatest political philosophers and an aide to Leitão de Abreu, to establish contact with this "viceroy" for political matters. In 1973 Candido Mendes convinced Leitão de Abreu to discuss liberalization with Harvard University political scientist Samuel Huntington, a specialist on Third World military politics. Huntington also met with Finance Minister Antônio Delfim Netto. The conversations stirred debate about decompression in the government and the opposition, and for a while Leitão de Abreu pushed the notion of a civilian (potentially himself) as successor to Médici in order to "demilitarize" the regime.[30] These discussions carried on as president-designate General Ernesto Geisel prepared his own plans for liberalization.

Padilha's ties to Candido Mendes and Muricy made him a go-between in the formation of the Bipartite. Padilha and Candido Mendes had known each other since the mid-1940s, when they studied at the Colégio Santo Inácio, the prestigious Jesuit school that educated many members of the twentieth-century carioca elite. They continued together in the philosophy program at the PUC-RJ. A former classmate of Muricy's first son, Padilha had strong links to the general. The two had known each other since 1944, and Muricy served as a *padrinho*, or godfather, at Padilha's marriage (Padilha interview 1). Padilha's membership in the Centro Dom Vital, gave him access to Rio's ecclesiastical hierarchy. Thus he became an important collaborator of Dom Eugênio after the cardinal's transfer to Rio in 1971 (Candido Mendes interview 1).

The detention of Dom Aloísio prompted the formation of the Bipartite. Padilha took Candido Mendes and IBRADES director Father Ávila to meet Muricy. To "straighten out" the situation the general called in the security agent who had led the attack.[31] Meeting with Dom Aloísio in mid-October, Muricy promised a solution to the crisis, although the priests and pastoral agents still remained incommunicado. At about this time the CNBB agreed to participate in the commission.[32] As Candido Mendes proposed to Muricy, the idea of holding periodic encounters could help to resolve Church-state difficulties "in a more efficient manner" (Muricy 1993:660).

On November 3, 1970, the first meeting of the Bipartite Commission took place at the Jesuit fathers' retreat house in the Gávea district of Rio de Janeiro. Organized by General Muricy and Candido Mendes, it brought together military officers and

Brazil's most important ecclesiastics in the hopes of reducing Church-state tensions. Dom Vicente Scherer, cardinal-archbishop of Porto Alegre and president of the CNBB, headed the Church delegation, referred to by the military as the Grupo Religioso. He was joined by Candido Mendes, Dom Eugênio, Dom Aloísio, and Dom Avelar, Dom Eugênio's eventual successor as archbishop-primate. Muricy brought representatives of key military, ideological, and political sectors of the regime: General Adolpho João de Paula Couto, head of the psychological warfare section in the office of the Army chief of staff; Colonel Omar Diógenes de Carvalho, chief of the Rio office of the SNI; Padilha; and Dantas Barreto, assistant to Justice Minister Buzaid and a participant in the ESG program. The military called its own contingent the Grupo da Situação (the group in power), a name later changed to Grupo Leigo (lay group).

Candido Mendes and Dom Eugênio called for a descompressão in Church-state relations. Both sides readily agreed on the need to improve Church-state dialogue and collaboration. "Church-government relations should be centralized at the highest level," Padilha asserted. This dialogue should be "permanent," Dom Aloísio added.[33]

The only discordant note came from Barreto, who reacted strongly to Candido Mendes's proposal for cooperation in the field of economic development. Barreto stated that the suggestion ignored the separation of Church and state in Brazil. Church-state frictions had resulted from "undue incursions by men of the Church into the *temporal domain*," which Barreto considered the exclusive concern of the state.[34] Barreto nearly shipwrecked the Bipartite by repeating his assertions even more vehemently at the second meeting.[35] It would be his last, for he was clearly out of tune with General Muricy's goal of dialogue and conciliation. Nevertheless, his position echoed the hard-liners: the clergy should remain in the sacristy and leave Brazil's material progress to the government.

Despite Barreto's outburst the Bipartite started auspiciously. The two sides agreed to debate national security, the Church's social doctrine, and development policy. In the first of its many postmeeting analyses (to which the bishops did not have access), the Grupo da Situação struck an optimistic chord. "The most important elements of the Catholic hierarchy were present at the meeting and showed themselves to be very open to dialogue," the conclusions began. The Grupo da Situação formed a list of proposals to be studied by Médici and his advisors. The first and most important advocated continuation of the meetings. It also suggested contact between bishops and security and intelligence agents at the regional level. The Situação further recommended the naming of a special presidential assistant from either the SNI or the National Security Council to study "the problem of the clergy and establish contacts with them when necessary."[36]

Power Struggle over the Bipartite: Defining Representation

A political conciliator who delegated responsibility to others, President Médici had initially approved Muricy's Bipartite in the hopes of garnering Church support.[37] However, after the first meeting the commission met resistance in the Planalto as questions emerged about its objectives and proposals. Both the head of the military presidential staff, General João Baptista de Oliveira Figueiredo, and SNI chief General Carlos Alberto Fontoura opposed the Bipartite. These were two of the most powerful men of the authoritarian era. Figueiredo became head of the SNI under President Ernesto Geisel and ultimately succeeded him in 1979. Under Médici, Fontoura controlled the most important of the intelligence services. Together with Leitão de Abreu, Figueiredo and Fontoura met regularly with Médici and wielded great influence over the internal politics of the regime. General Muricy, on the other hand, was leaving the government. He began mandatory retirement on November 25, 1970, and in December he relinquished his post as Army chief of staff.[38] He ultimately saved the commission, but the terms imposed by Médici and his advisors kept its status as unofficial and ambiguous as possible in order to avoid making concessions to the Church. This situation reflected the tensions between hard-liners and moderates over how to deal with the opposition and the bishops in particular.

In December Bipartite member General Paula Couto met with Figueiredo to defend the Bipartite. Paula Couto learned that Figueiredo and Fontoura considered the Bipartite incapable of bringing positive results for the regime. In his report to the Grupo da Situação, Paula Couto noted that both men "naturally influenced" Médici against the Bipartite. Moreover, Médici saw Dantas Barreto's fulminating speech to be the "only valid" words of the first meeting. Clearly the president favored a tough stance toward the Church. He rejected the proposal to extend the Bipartite to the regional level. In Figueiredo's eyes such additional contact could "officialize" government positions with respect to the Church—exactly the opposite of the effect desired by Médici. The Bipartite, Figueiredo added, should not represent the government. For the same reason Médici rejected the request for a presidential specialist on the clergy, although he permitted the SNI to serve as a government-Bipartite link by allowing a representative to continue at the meetings. Paula Couto concluded:

President Médici ascending the ramp of the Palácio do Planalto on his first day in office, October 31, 1969, with three of the most powerful men in his government: from left to right, SNI chief General Carlos Alberto Fontoura, chief of civilian presidential staff João de Leitão Abreu, Médici, and chief of military presidential staff General João Baptista de Oliveira Figueiredo. Fontoura and Figueiredo opposed the Bipartite, whereas Leitão de Abreu explored a formula for liberalization along with Candido Mendes.

> The general impression that I got is that the President has not made a firm decision on the problem as a whole and thinks that the matter must be better studied. At least this is the impression clearly transmitted to me by General Figueiredo. . . . I tried to explain that these meetings are the last chance to give the Catholic hierarchy the knowledge necessary for understanding the connection between revolutionary warfare and the corresponding need for SECURITY. . . . so that they finally comprehend that certain actions of certain priests and bishops, which the hierarchy judges to be carried out in obedience to the recommendations of Medellín, are in reality subversive acts.

With Figueiredo's assent, Paula Couto urged General Muricy to meet immediately with Médici "to define well the purpose of the encounters."[39]

Muricy retained considerable influence. He was a friend and staunch supporter of the president. Not only had Muricy helped navigate the armed forces through the difficult transition from Costa e Silva to Médici in 1969; he had been the first officer to support Médici publicly for the presidency. In addition, Muricy had maintained a close friendship with Army Minister Orlando Geisel since the two met at the Military Academy in 1923. Like Muricy and Ernesto Geisel, Orlando also had ties to Golbery.[40] Orlando Geisel was more powerful than either Figueiredo or Fontoura (D'Araujo and Castro 1997:220–21). Upon leaving the Army, Muricy kept a high political profile by giving newspaper interviews and winning a nearly unanimous election to a two-year term of the presidency of the ADESG (ESG alumni association), a flagging organization that he aimed to resuscitate.[41]

Muricy met twice with Médici.[42] He explained the goals of the Bipartite but also added that he needed "credentials." Médici approved the commission's continuing, and on his directive Muricy came to an agreement with the previously skeptical Fontoura (Muricy 1993:660). Muricy had prevailed. With Médici's blessing he acted on Bipartite matters as if still a commander, ordering high-level active duty officers in the names of Army Minister Geisel and the president himself. An exchange with General Milton Tavares, the extremist hard-liner who headed the CIE, makes the point:

> Muricy: Miltinho, do this.—
> Tavares: But General Muricy—
> Muricy: Your commander [Geisel] told you to do it, and you are going to. Don't ask about the problem, you're going to do it.[43]

Muricy met again with Médici after the second Bipartite meeting in January 1971.[44]

Yet despite Muricy's connections it was never quite clear as to where the Grupo da Situação fit into the nebulous web of the Médici administration nor to what extent it represented the president. As Paula Couto's report stated, Médici and his top men wanted it this way. The regime aimed to control the clergy through the bishops, but without losing its grip on Brazilian society. Thus while it hoped to improve Church-state relations, the Médici administration did not want any formal agreement or ties with the Grupo Religioso or with the CNBB. Dantas Barreto's point rang clear: the Church could expect no privileges.

The recollections of those who knew of the Bipartite attest to its importance for dialogue but also its ambiguous status. On the side of the government, for instance, General Fontoura believed that Muricy represented Médici. But Fontoura also recalled that no formal link existed between the commission and the administration. Professor Padilha asserted that Muricy had the full backing of Médici. He emphasized that the commission's goal was to create dialogue as an alternative to the hard-liners' opposition to the Church. Candido Mendes's assessment was different but not inconsistent. In Mendes's view, Muricy's efforts exemplified how the old guard of generals sought to reduce the excesses of the younger hard-liners, yet Muricy's effectiveness was reduced because he had lost power upon retirement and therefore was not an "insider" in the Médici government. Likewise Dom Eugênio stressed Muricy's opposition to human rights abuses but affirmed that intraregime struggles caused doubts as to who really controlled the government.

General Muricy, of course, believed he had Médici's support, but even he seemed unsure as to what he stood for at the Bipartite. "I was nobody's representative," Muricy stated in his 1981 interview. "I presided over a commission that wanted to settle the problems with the Church. The bishops were also nobody. The CNBB came to discuss problems with somebody who wanted to help. Officially there is no record of anything."[45] This mixture of retrospectives also partially explains the Bipartite's secrecy.

The Men and Methods of the Bipartite

In all, the Bipartite met twenty-four times during the Médici administration and the first months of Ernesto Geisel's presidency. Each encounter had a predetermined agenda. Many lasted an entire day. Additional special meetings also took place, as did many informal contacts between elements of the two parties. The parleys with the nuncio, one-to-one meetings, and luncheons connected with the commission revealed that it was but an extended network of negotiation. The many types of contact illustrated how conciliation worked in the Brazilian elite, between the Church and the armed forces, and between the Brazilian state and the Vatican's representatives. Table 1 below lists the dates, locales, and topics of the principal meetings according to the reports available in General Muricy's papers.

The discussions focused on conflict resolution in three broad areas. First, the initial meetings in late 1970 and early 1971 aimed at lessening the ideological discord that had developed between Church and state since 1964. While the military declared national security the duty of every Brazilian, the Church stressed a new social doctrine based on the conclusions of Vatican II and the work of Catholic progressives such as Dom Hélder. The goal was mutual understanding. Second, the commission adopted the Grupo da Situação's suggestion that the final half of each encounter focus on the solution of specific cases of Church-state friction. As the repression and the regime's political intransigence deepened, this aspect came to

Table 1. Bipartite Meetings and Related Gatherings, Rio de Janeiro

No.	Date	Locale	Description/Key Issues
1	Nov. 3, 1970	Jesuits' Gávea retreat house	Discussion of Medellín document and need for "permanent dialogue" between Church and state.
2	Jan. 9, 1971	Colégio Sagrado Coração de Jesus	Discussion of Medellín document and Communist revolutionary warfare.
—	April 3, 1971	Hotel Excelsior	Government-Church luncheon including General Muricy, João Paulo dos Reis Veloso (Minister of Planning), Antônio Dias Leite (Minister of Mines and Energy), Chagas Freitas (governor, state of Guanabara, and ally of Army Minister Geisel), Mons. Joseph Grémillion (secretary general, Pontifical Justice and Peace Commission), Dom Umberto Mozzoni (apostolic nuncio), Dom Eugênio, Dom Aloísio, Dom Ivo. Discussion of social and economic problems, national security, torture, Church-state relations.
—	April 5, 1971	Office of General Muricy	Preparatory meeting of Grupo da Situação for third Bipartite.
3	April 28, 1971	Jesuits' Gávea retreat house	Discussion of national security, Church social doctrine, priests accused of subversion.
4	July 1, 1971	Jesuits' Gávea retreat house	Discussion of Medellín document, positions of the Pontifical Peace and Justice Commission (Rome), human rights, alleged subversion in the Church, social inequality.
5	Aug. 24, 1971	Sumaré (archbishop's retreat house)	Documentation incomplete. On agenda: subversion, Church in the Amazon, national development.
6-14	1971-1972	—	No documentation available.
?	Late Jan. 1972	—	No documentation available. Discussion of death of soldiers from torture in Barra Mansa.
?	July 28, 1972	—	No documentation available.
?	Aug. 31, 1972	CNBB headquarters (Villa Venturoza, Bairro da Glória)	Special informal meeting to defuse potentially subversive activities by clergy during independence sesquicentenary.
15	April 25, 1973	Official residence of Vice Admiral Roberval, commandant of the Marines, Ilha das Cobras	Discussion of CNBB pronouncement on twenty-fifth anniversary of U.N. Universal Declaration of Human Rights.
16	May 30, 1973	CNBB headquarters	Discussion of subversion, human rights, bishops' statements.
17	July 25, 1973	CNBB headquarters	Discussion of subversion in the Church, human rights.

(table 1 continued)

No.	Date	Locale	Description/Key Issues
18	Aug. 3, 1973	CNBB headquarters	Special meeting to discuss pastoral letter by Dom Fernando Gomes criticizing the government.
19	Aug. 29, 1973	CNBB headquarters	Discussion of military pressure against bishops, human rights, Church's religious competitors.
20	Sept. 26, 1973	CNBB headquarters	Discussion of military pressure against bishops, censorship, human rights.
21	Nov. 5, 1973	CNBB headquarters	Discussion of Church criticisms of regime, censorship, human rights.
22	March 24, 1974	CNBB headquarters	Discussion of alleged subversion in the Church, human rights, Church's institutional interests.
—	May 29, 1974	Office of General Muricy	Preparatory meeting of Grupo da Situação for twenty-third Bipartite.
23	May 29, 1974	CNBB headquarters	Discussion of alleged subversion in the Church, human rights, censorship, Church's institutional interests.
—	Aug. 26, 1974	Office of General Muricy	Preparatory meeting of Grupo da Situação for twenty-fourth Bipartite. Discussion of upcoming CNBB election.
24	Aug. 26, 1974	CNBB headquarters	Discussion of human rights, Church's institutional interests.

Sources: FGV/CPDOC/ACM; Dom Waldyr interview (Jan. 1972 meeting).

overshadow, though not to eliminate, the initial concerns. It is significant that, as a way of maintaining its traditional position in Brazilian society, the Grupo Religioso used the framework of conflict resolution to advance the Church's doctrinal and institutional interests. Third, over time the bishops increasingly sought to use the Bipartite as a way to protest human rights abuses. Indeed, as the impetus to resolve ideological discord waned, this issue became dominant.

By the twenty-first meeting in November 1973, a certain dissatisfaction set in on both sides. The bishops wanted greater responsiveness from the Grupo da Situação on human rights. In Dom Aloísio's words, the Bipartite needed to be more "objective." Likewise, the Situação believed that the Bipartite failed to provide adequate solutions to the military's problems with the clergy. In Padilha's estimation the commission had drifted away from cooperation and the original "study of principles" toward "an examination of quibbles [*problemas casuísticos*]." The two groups agreed that the Bipartite was valuable but that it was also time to review their work critically. In the next three meetings, they continued to address important issues,

Most of the secret Bipartite meetings took place at CNBB headquarters at the Villa Venturoza in the Glória district near downtown Rio de Janeiro.

including the Church's desire to collaborate with the incoming administration of Ernesto Geisel. Geisel, however, wanted to deal with the Church through the traditional hierarchy rather than through the CNBB and ultimately abolished the Bipartite.[46]

The dialogue was a curious amalgam of hard-nosed, often heated debate and the cordiality and elite conciliation that traditionally marked Brazilian political and social life. Harsh disagreement was at times followed by reconciliation over a meal (Pacífico interview). Whereas, after 1964, the military viewed the clergy with increasing anger and disdain, General Muricy brought to the Bipartite a long experience of devotion to traditional Catholicism and reverence for the bishops. Bishops such as Dom Avelar displayed similar esteem for the prestige and authority of the armed forces. Such mutual respect was essential for any successful dialogue.

The Bipartite's participants also shared the social and economic benefits of membership in Brazil's elite. Although since the 1930s Brazil had been evolving into a more dynamic society with new avenues of upward social mobility, people of this level maintained many of the characteristics of the traditional Brazilian elite that are still apparent even today. They typically did no manual work, had several servants in the home, and shared a sense of family and hereditary status as the determinants of their position and success. They stood apart from the masses and identified strongly with European or North American ideas and culture. They also valued social stability.[47] Moreover, the participants at the Bipartite were all male, mainly light-skinned, and educated far beyond the Brazilian norm.

Neither side hesitated to attack the other's positions, however. Directly facing their opponents, the bishops often repeated their public criticisms of the regime. Dom Ivo Lorscheiter in particular was outspoken. When General Muricy protested Dom Ivo's complaints about economic inequality under Médici, the bishop responded that the people had "increasingly less" while the government tried to impose a climate of "naive euphoria." Economist Moacyr Gomes de Almeida, a participant in the ESG program, asserted that salaries were rising. He argued that naïveté and euphoria were necessary for mobilizing the populace in favor of development.[48] For its part the Grupo da Situação frequently warned the bishops about subversive priests. Although openness generally prevailed, the Situação sought additional, behind-the-scenes discussion with those members of the Grupo Religioso it considered most trustworthy (see below). In effect, the Bipartite constituted a new set of rules for elite dialogue in an authoritarian setting. The bishops could criticize freely, but only as long as they did so in private.[49] In addition, Gomes de Almeida's unconcern about euphoria reflected the simultaneously assertive and apologetic nature of the authoritarian regime's own public statements.

Table 2 describes the makeup of the Grupo Religioso. It is significant that not only bishops with ties to the military such as Dom Eugênio and Dom Vicente participated in the Bipartite. (In fact, Dom Vicente attended only the first two meetings.) The moderately progressive Dom Aloísio attended more than any other member of the group. In 1971 he defeated Dom Vicente for the presidency of the CNBB. As president of the CNBB until 1979, Dom Aloísio supported the organization's increasingly activist agenda. His outspoken cousin Dom Ivo was another regular. The two were from Rio Grande do Sul, one of the most important centers of Catholic progressivism. Dom Ivo had begun his episcopal career as an auxiliary bishop to Dom Vicente in Porto Alegre but increasingly affirmed his independence to become one of the most respected leaders of the Brazilian episcopate. Dom Paulo attended the Bipartite twice. On other occasions his archdiocese was represented by Dom Lucas. Other important bishops and even the papal nuncio joined the talks. One of the regulars was Dom Avelar, the CNBB vice president who would attempt to unseat Dom Aloísio from the presidency in the 1974 election. The ideological mix of the Grupo Religioso reflected the episcopal solidarity achieved in the face of the military threat by a Church otherwise split over how it should change in the post–Vatican II era. The CNBB embodied that unity and spoke out on national issues. This important representative role helps to explain the apparent contradiction between the moderate and the progressive CNBB leaders' skepticism toward the regime and their dominance of the Bipartite. Of course, specific issues such as institutional interests and human rights also drew the bishops to the commission.

Unity, however, did not produce uniform opinion about the Bipartite. Even though they opposed the regime, some priests welcomed the talks as a ray of hope at a moment when all possibility of dialogue had appeared doomed. In the evaluation of this group, Muricy was open-minded and intelligent and had a vision of society that went beyond the barracks (Aldo Vannucchi interview). Bishops, priests, and pastoral agents of the radical Catholic left criticized the Bipartite because they opposed contact with the enemy on principle and thought it counterproductive (Marina Bandeira interview). Dom Pedro Casaldáliga and his priests belonged to this group. Constantly assailed by the security forces, they feared that the Bipartite allowed hypocritical generals to provide an image of dialogue among leaders while ordering repression at the grass roots. They also mistrusted the more conservative members of the Grupo Religioso (Dom Pedro Casaldáliga interview). Other progressive priests believed that Muricy was little more than a "puppet" or "doorman" of the Médici administration (Luiz Viegas interview 1). The Jocistas also expressed deep skepticism about dialogue.

Within the Grupo Religioso itself the degree of commitment to the Bipartite varied. For example, Dom Ivo disagreed with the existence of the commission and became irritated with Candido Mendes's repeated invitations to take part. Dom Ivo had no faith whatsoever in the military. During the Médici years, people came to the CNBB on almost a daily basis to denounce torture or to seek help in finding missing loved ones. In fact, Dom Ivo believed that Candido Mendes compromised the Church's positions during the encounters.[50]

Candido Mendes's prestige and persistence kept the dialogue alive. As a member of the elite, he could be audacious, unconventional, even quixotic. He was fully dedicated to serving the Church and seemed to believe that he had a historic role to play in improving its relations with the state. And he envisioned a society in which

Table 2. The Grupo Religioso, in Order of Frequency of Appearance

Name	Positions
Dom Aloísio Lorscheider	Secretary general, CNBB, 1968–1971; CNBB president, 1971–1979; named archbishop of Fortaleza, 1973; appointed cardinal, 1976.
Candido Antonio José Francisco Mendes de Almeida (Candido Mendes)	Secretary general, CJP-BR; Latin American representative, Pontifical Justice and Peace Commission (Rome); subsecretary general for social action, CNBB. Attorney, political scientist, educator.
Dom José Ivo Lorscheiter	Secretary general, CNBB, 1971–1979.
Dom Avelar Brandão Vilela	Named archbishop of Salvador and primate of Brazil upon Dom Eugênio's transfer to Rio in 1971; vice president, CNBB; president, CELAM; appointed cardinal, 1973.
Dom Lucas Moreira Neves	Auxiliary bishop, São Paulo; headed archdiocesan and CNBB commissions on communications; represented archdiocese of São Paulo at Bipartite; appointed cardinal, 1988.
Dom Eugênio de Araújo Sales	Archbishop of Salvador and primate of Brazil, 1968–1971; named cardinal, 1969; transferred to Rio, 1971.
Dom Alfredo Vicente Scherer	Cardinal-archbishop of Porto Alegre; president, CNBB, 1970–1971, after Dom Agnelo Rossi's transfer to Rome.
Dom Fernando Gomes dos Santos	Archbishop of Goiânia; a leading progressive and critic of military regime.
Dom Paulo Evaristo Arns	Named archbishop of São Paulo in 1970 after Dom Agnelo Rossi's transfer to Rome; named cardinal, 1973; one of Brazil's most influential bishops.
Dom Alberto Gaudêncio Ramos	Archbishop of Belém; member of the CNBB's national Episcopal Pastoral Commission.
Dom Gilberto Pereira Lopes	Bishop, Ipameri, Goiás; substitute for Dom Lucas at Bipartite.
Dom Umberto Mozzoni	Papal nuncio.

Sources: FGV/CPDOC/ACM; CNBB 1984.

Church and military worked together for social and economic progress.[51] This objective explained the highly academic character of the Bipartite's early stages. Working with ESG graduates and intellectually oriented members of the armed forces, Candido Mendes hoped to arrive at a formula for cooperation. In short, Candido Mendes was the glue of the Bipartite.

Differences among the bishops also affected the Bipartite. One example was the clash between Dom Ivo and Dom Eugênio. Dom Eugênio was a "prince" of the Church. The armed forces respected him more than any other bishop, and they admired him for his emphasis on punctuality, discipline, and his sense of duty and hierarchy. He had long experience in dealing with officers. In addition, he knew how to create social distance from others at the appropriate moment. In effect,

Dom Eugênio could behave like a general. At the Bipartite he helped maintain the necessary level of ceremony, but he also knew when to laugh in order to relieve tensions. His prestige with the regime grew as his contacts with the pope multiplied. From the armed forces' standpoint his most important attribute was his distinction between human rights abuses and incidents of repression of revolutionary warfare. He made this distinction in such a way as to uphold the Church's opposition to violations without compromising its credibility.[52]

A man of forceful temperament, Dom Ivo was also military-like and jealous of authority. The towering bishop from Rio Grande do Sul had a Prussian character and a physical appearance that made him a "Geisel in a cassock" (Octávio Costa interview 1)—like the Army Minister, highly driven and determined to impose his will. Yet his progressive ideas did not sit well with either Dom Eugênio or the military. After the Bipartite Dom Ivo enthusiastically welcomed the move of CNBB headquarters to Brasília as a way of distancing himself and the organization from Dom Eugênio (Virgílio Rosa Netto interview). Attentive to internal Church politics, the Grupo da Situação noted "personal disagreements" between the two men.[53] It is ironic that Dom Ivo became one of the most assiduous members of the Grupo Religioso, participating out of a sense of duty to the Church (Virgílio Rosa Netto interview). Dom Eugênio actually quit the Bipartite in anger at the regime (see the next chapter).

Table 3 describes the Grupo da Situação and its links to the ESG. General Muricy had two decades of ties to the school and General Golbery. Indeed, at the third Bipartite meeting in April 1971, Golbery presented an ADESG study on the Church's social doctrine and state policies.[54] Padilha was both an ESG graduate and a professor. In the early 1970s, he and Muricy ran the ADESG, which had hundreds of members. This period marked the apex of ESG's influence in Brazil. Other members of the Situação also had links to the ESG. The Navy was represented, but the absence of Air Force representation was striking. The Army dominated the regime and had plenty of individuals linked to the Church to man the Bipartite.[55]

The makeup of the Grupo da Situação displayed the purposeful ambiguity of the commission. Whereas the Church sent its top leaders to the Bipartite, table 3 illustrates that the government did not. The bishops could be expected to negotiate with General Muricy and Vice Admiral Roberval Pizarro Marques but certainly not with the colonels and majors who worked as assistants. Yet these mid-level officers played an important role. They came from the SNI, the CIE, the office of the Army chief of staff, and the Army Ministry. Some were specialists in psychological warfare.

Dom Ivo Lorscheiter (standing), his cousin Dom Aloísio (middle), and Dom Lucas Moreira Neves, three leading participants in the Bipartite. Dom Ivo was the most outspoken member of the Church delegation.

General Muricy called upon the intelligence operatives to verify the Church's allegations of human rights abuses. These organizations, especially the CIE, played a major role in combating guerrillas and other subversives. Thus the bishops faced men from the very agencies that were accused of human rights violations and other misdeeds. Some of these agents supplied information that was used by the Situação to attack the Church's positions. They also provided analyses of the Bipartite and the bishops. Their positions in the intelligence network and upper echelon of the military bureaucracy underlined their importance. At least three—Pacífico, Lee, and Sampaio—later received promotion to general. Sampaio had been a member

Table 3. The Grupo da Situação, in Order of Frequency of Appearance

Name	Positions
General Antônio Carlos da Silva *Muricy*	Four-star Army general, retired; president, ADESG; appointed to head Bipartite by Médici.
Tarcísio Meirelles Padilha	Member, Federal Education Council; secretary, ADESG; ESG graduate (1969) and professor; member, Centro Dom Vital. Philosopher, university professor. Personal friend of General Muricy.
Lieutenant Colonel Roberto *Pacífico* Barbosa	Secretary of Bipartite; assistant, SNI Guanabara office. Later headed Belo Horizonte and Rio SNI offices. Finished career as three-star general.
Colonel Mário Orlando Ribeiro *Sampaio*	SNI. Conducted the Army's investigation of Barra Mansa deaths. Later commanded the CIE. Ultimately became four-star general.
Major Leone da Silveira *Lee*	CIE; on staff of Army Minister Orlando Geisel. Later promoted to general and commanded East Command (former First Army) in Rio de Janeiro. Attained three-star status.
Vice Admiral *Roberval* Pizarro Marques	Commander, Fuzileiros Navais (Marine Corps). ESG graduate (1966).
General Adolpho João de *Paula* Couto	Divisional general; fourth subchief (psychological warfare), office of Army chief of staff. Finished career with four stars.
Dantas Barreto	Assistant to Justice Minister Alfredo Buzaid; ESG participant.
Colonel *Omar* Diógenes de Carvalho	Chief, SNI Guanabara office.
Lieutenant Colonel Sérgio Mário *Pasquali*	Adjutant fourth subchief (psychological warfare), office of Army chief of staff.
Major Carlos de Souza *Schéliga*	Adjutant fifth secretary (public relations), office of Army chief of staff.
Major José Carlos *Duarte*	Assistant to General Paula Couto.
Moacyr Gomes de Almeida	Economist; participant in ESG program.

Sources: FGV/CPDOC/ACM; Muricy 1993; interviews.
(The military name of each officer is in italics.)

of the SNI since its founding in 1964. Before joining the Bipartite, he helped combat torture in the Army by investigating the officers accused of murdering soldiers at the Barra Mansa barracks (see chapter 8). As a general he headed the CIE in the mid-1980s and ultimately earned four stars.

An Operation of War: Secrecy, Intelligence, and Politics

The Bipartite was an instrument of political strategy for the regime. Intelligence was crucial in this process. Years later, General Muricy vehemently denied that the Bipartite's goal was to collect information for the government. Its motives were "pure" (Muricy interview 2). Yet the general's own documentation confirms the use of the intelligence services in the attempt to influence the bishops. It also demonstrates how the Situação worked behind the scenes to strengthen the government's position vis-à-vis the Church.

The bishops learned to harbor no illusions about the aims of the military, which viewed the Brazilian clergy as highly susceptible to leftist influence. General Muricy brought this attitude to the Bipartite from his work against subversion in the Northeast. During the Médici years, violence, intrigue, censorship, and denunciations of torture abounded. The Brazilian clergy knew that the security forces kept an eye on the Church. As one priest remembered it, the Bipartite became "an operation of war" (Virgílio Rosa Netto interview).

Secrecy

Secrecy was one of the principle factors that allowed the Situação to exploit the Bipartite for political purposes. But how concealed were the meetings? And why did the bishops agree to secrecy? Private high-level contact was not a novelty. Figures such as Muricy, Candido Mendes, and Tarcísio Padilha belonged to a small, interconnected ruling class magnified in importance by the fact that still only a minority of the citizenry (because of a literacy requirement) had qualified to vote in the last free presidential election in 1960. The dictatorship eliminated most political participation and freedom of expression and elevated the importance of negotiation through informal private channels. The Bipartite conveniently institutionalized Church-state contact.

Neither group wanted leaks. The Bipartite required secrecy to protect its status as a forum for resolution of Church-state disputes. The press was censored, but the regime's control over it was not absolute. As a practical matter, confidentiality allowed bishops and officers to trade information and accusations about the delicate matters of human rights abuses and subversion without causing public scandal or providing a pretext for the armed opposition to retaliate.[56] Likewise, the Grupo da Situação needed to respond to the bishops' charges of atrocities without raising the ire of hard-liners. For their part, the bishops accepted secrecy as a way of facilitating contact with the military on human rights questions (Candido Mendes interview 1). Secrecy also helped the bishops shield themselves from the skepticism about dialogue among the grass-roots clergy and lay activists targeted by the repressive forces. In addition, the hierarchy did not want to be publicly tinged with allegations of subversion made by the regime and right-wing groups.

Few people knew of the Bipartite. The Situação jealously guarded its secrecy, allowing only the highest military officials and their assistants access to reports of the meetings (Muricy interview 1). Even within the Planalto, there was little discussion of the commission (Octávio Costa interview 1). Foreign Minister Barboza, for instance, did not know about the Bipartite. Nor did the Rio DOPS intelligence unit (Mário Gibson Barboza interview; Maurano interview). Occasionally the military permitted small, discrete notes about the commission to appear in the press (Marina Bandeira interview). After the IBRADES raid, for instance, *Jornal do Brasil* political columnist Carlos Castello Branco briefly alluded to the formation of a commission but did not report on the first meeting. A Church news bulletin also made oblique references to a "solution" to Church-state conflict, as did Dom Avelar in a statement to the press.[57] At the September 1973 Bipartite meeting, General Muricy underscored the preoccupation with secrecy when he sharply criticized Dom Fernando Gomes, the archbishop of Goiânia, for giving a Church press bulletin substantial details on the commission. The mainstream press received this bulletin and occasionally printed material from it, and on this occasion the Buenos Aires daily *La Nación* used Dom Fernando's comments to write a large article revealing the existence of the Bipartite. The military postmortem on the session noted that Dom Fernando's slip jeopardized the commission's survival. Major Lee once again reminded the Grupo Religioso of the secrecy requirement after his name appeared in a publication issued by Dom Pedro.[58]

In the Church a "grapevine" of contacts extended from the Bipartite to Catholic human rights workers and some families of victims who sought the bishops' assistance.[59] Papal nuncio Dom Mozzoni took part in the Bipartite and reported on it to Paul VI (Muricy interview 1). Other bishops perhaps mentioned the commission's efforts in their periodic *ad limina* visits with the pope.[60] To show that Church-state dialogue was working, the Grupo da Situação wanted the bishops to apprise their fellow prelates of the proceedings. Few people learned of the actual content of the talks, however. The tight-lipped prelates told little to their assistants or to other priests. To the military's dismay, they also spread little word of the Bipartite to their colleagues.[61] They discussed the substance of the talks only in the small closed sessions of high-level CNBB councils (Marina Bandeira interview; Candido Mendes interview 1). Only in late 1976, two years after the Bipartite ended, did Dom Ivo officially reveal the Bipartite to the Brazilian press in a brief statement (Prandini, Petrucci, and Dale 1986–1987:5:15–16). Thereafter the hierarchy gave no further details, as illustrated by Dom Paulo Evaristo Arns's reticence when questioned by journalists (Arns 1978:127).

Intelligence: Seeking Political Advantage

The Situação gathered, disseminated, and used information in a number of ways. A central concern was the actual meetings. They were an excellent opportunity for observing the bishops closely and learning their ideas. In fact, both sides hoped that such contact would lead to better relations. The officers kept detailed minutes and wrote assessments of the meetings and the bishops. General Muricy reviewed and approved these reports (Pacífico interview). Then they went to the intelligence community, including the CIE (and therefore the Army Ministry too) and different offices within the office of the Army chief of staff.[62] They also went to SNI chief General Fontoura, who reported on the Bipartite to Médici (Pacífico interview). In addition, the Situação held preliminary meetings to plan strategies for dealing with the Grupo Religioso. Early on, Professor Padilha pointed out the need for "political tactics" to achieve the Situação's goals.[63]

The Grupo Religioso worked at a distinct disadvantage in the context of a powerful and repressive authoritarian system. The bishops never saw the Situação's reports. Nor did they have the resources, time, or intentions to match the military's specialization of tasks and thoroughness of preparation and review. For the bishops, the Bipartite was one among many pastoral duties on a crowded schedule.[64]

Audio recordings were another tool of the Situação. At the second Bipartite meeting, Colonel Omar Diógenes de Carvalho of the SNI played a tape of a former Communist who had entered the seminary as part of a purported plot to infiltrate the Church. Dom Eugênio responded by explaining that the bishops shared the government's concerns about Communism. He cited the example of a suspicious student who had been expelled from the seminary in Salvador and added that in turn the Church had managed to infiltrate the Communists.[65]

While Watergate and CIA scandals came to light in the United States, the Situação secretly taped the bishops during the two meetings held at the official residence of Vice Admiral Roberval. The Marine Corps leader later asserted that he requested authorization for the taping from General Muricy for historical purposes. The location of the recordings is now a mystery. Both Muricy and Roberval denied ulterior motives for the taping.[66] However, if they had fallen into the hands of the regime's evidence forgers the tapes could have become material for distorted attacks on the Church in the media. These kinds of attacks had already occurred.

Another tactic of the Situação was to present the bishops with documents that demonstrated what the military considered subversive activities among the clergy

Bipartite member Vice Admiral Roberval Pizarro Marques was a staunch traditional Catholic like General Muricy. He secretly taped the bishops during the two Bipartite meetings held at his residence.

and pastoral agents. The largest sample was captured during the security forces' attack on the prelacy of São Félix do Araguaia, where Dom Pedro Casaldáliga and his assistants aided squatters, rural migrants, and Amerindians in their struggles against large landowners allied with the government. Dom Pedro's work irritated the military, making the Church-state conflict in São Félix one of the most serious of the authoritarian era. The speedy transfer of the São Félix documents to the Bipartite illustrates the Situação's excellent access to intelligence. Muricy had Major Leone da Silveira Lee of the CIE read "compromising" passages.[67] (The CIE was waging war against guerrillas in the neighboring state of Pará.) In fact, the minutes of the Bipartite suggest that the bishops had no access to these documents. Thus the Situação held the power of both evidence and interpretation.

Evaluation of the bishops and their positions formed another facet of the Situação's intelligence efforts. In preparation for debate at the Bipartite, the officers carefully analyzed the controversial pronouncements of the CNBB, regional episcopal groups, and individual bishops. Church publications and the press were also checked for criticisms of the regime.

Other documents of the Bipartite reveal military impressions of the bishops based on particular incidents, personality traits, and ideological tendencies. Dom Fernando Gomes was "a profoundly vain personality" who became "aggressive toward the regime" because he felt discredited by the public authorities in Goiânia. Dom Paulo was seen as malleable and influenced by the left, an inexperienced pastor nevertheless working to improve his abilities. Dom Eugênio inspired the highest respect from the military for his emphasis on hierarchy, whereas Dom Ivo was disliked for being too political and outspoken. Dom Lucas was similarly distrusted for his complaints against censorship. The Situação first perceived Candido Mendes as being the most dedicated to dialogue but lost faith in him as he pressed for resolution of human rights cases. Implicit in these observations were the military's own institutional preconceptions about the priestly vocation and the Church's efforts at renovation.[68]

The military's knowledge of the Grupo Religioso and the CNBB increased with the help of a bishop who acted as informant. As early as 1968, some priests suspected that individuals within the bishops' conference were feeding information to the SNI (Pinheiro 1994:114). During the Médici era, Dom Luciano José Cabral Duarte, the archbishop of Aracaju, did so for the Situação. Dom Luciano was known for his efforts at articulating the conservative opposition to progressive Catholicism. He gained notoriety in 1979 when a Mexican newspaper published the text of a letter to him from Colombian bishop Alfonso López Trujillo. The missive urged Dom Luciano to "prepare your airplane bombers" for the important CELAM meeting at Puebla (Lernoux 1982:435). In the early 1970s, Dom Luciano sat on the CNBB's important Pastoral Episcopal Commission and thus had regular access to the decision-making process of the country's leading bishops. He informed Professor Padilha about internal Church politics, progressive bishops, a key 1972 meeting of the CNBB's Representative Commission, and the 1974 CNBB elections. General Paula Couto also met with Dom Vicente Scherer to obtain information about the 1973 CNBB assembly.[69] Dom Eugênio was seen as another reliable contact outside the Bipartite.

Ultimately, the goal of intelligence was to gain political advantage over the Grupo Religioso and the Church. The Situação pushed for the bishops to rein in activist priests and to tone down and even retract their criticisms of the regime. The Situação was particularly interested in seeing a more conservative slate of bishops replace Dom Aloísio and Dom Ivo as leaders of the CNBB. After the regime shut down the archdiocese of São Paulo's radio station in 1973, the Situação tried to have it reopened as a way of swinging support within the CNBB to the conservatives. Dom Luciano worked on organizing the conservative slate and kept the Situação informed of its progress.[70] However, the Situação was unsuccessful, as Dom Aloísio and Dom Ivo won election to second terms.

Conclusion

Close Church-state relations were the rule in Brazil for at least four decades before the coup of 1964, and they continued throughout the military era. The general historical impression of the Médici years is one of an inflexible, heavy-handed authoritarianism toward all sectors of society, but the existence of the Bipartite Commission demonstrates that, long before the political liberalization of the Geisel presidency, bishops and officers engaged in discussing their differences and seeking points of mutual understanding.[71] Although the Bipartite was not a cause of the post-1973 liberalization, it clearly served as an example of political decompression between two of the most important political actors of the authoritarian era.

The creation of the Bipartite reveals how different visions of Church-military relations existed within the regime. Some technocrats and hard-liners no longer saw the Church as a central institution necessary for Brazil's progress. General Muricy represented more moderate and traditional forces that desired to preserve the Church's loyalty and its historical influence as a stabilizing force. From this current emerged the proposal for dialogue, conflict resolution, and even continued collaboration.

Because of the repression, the dialogue became the most institutionalized in the history of Church-state relations in modern Brazil. The meetings were regular, had established agendas, and included a fixed core of participants. These men belonged to the elite and shared the Catholic faith. The meetings lasted four years. Both sides obviously saw an interest in maintaining contact. Also quickened by the repression, the rise of the CNBB as the voice of a unified episcopate reinforced the formality and importance of the Bipartite. In Dom Aloísio and Dom Ivo, the CNBB sent to the Bipartite two key leaders of the leftward shift of the Church.

Indeed, the Bipartite was created precisely as the CNBB was becoming a major opponent of the military government. The Bipartite was an exercise in dialogue but also a school for the two sides to learn in greater detail about each other's ideas and tactics. In this respect, the Bipartite was especially valuable for the Church. General Muricy faded from the political scene after the Bipartite, but Dom Ivo, Dom Aloísio, and other members of the Grupo Religioso were moving into their prime. The continued production of pastoral statements, the fight against torture and censorship, and the struggle for the return to democracy were hard political battles. The Bipartite provided experience and momentum for winning them.

Yet the Bipartite was not a summit. General Muricy had Médici's nod to run the commission, but its secret and purposefully ambiguous status allowed the regime to remain noncommittal toward the Church and to attempt to use the Bipartite for political gain. The Médici administration was perhaps more flexible than it has been given credit for, but the logic of the authoritarian system ultimately made its differences with the Church irreconcilable. The bishops were not to be completely trusted. In late 1970, however, both bishops and officers held out hope that these differences could be overcome.

Chapter 6 **Social Justice or Subversion?**

This chapter examines the Bipartite debates concerning ideology and the alleged subversion committed by clergymen. It covers the first four meetings in 1970 and 1971, the period in which the commission established its basic agenda, and helps to explain how the Church and the military viewed each other and attempted to build mutual understanding. At the first meeting on November 3, 1970, Dom Avelar laid out the central question of Brazil's Church-military conflict: "Where does social justice end and subversion begin?" The Church had become entangled in this question as the armed forces tightened the national security net and took control of the country's economy and political system. The question was implicit in the dialectic between social activism and repression that had existed since 1964. In 1967 the Church explicitly asked for a definition of subversion. At the Bipartite the bishops repeated this request. They wanted to clarify the Church-regime relationship by seeking sharper definitions of subversion and other polemical themes such as capitalism, socialism, nationalism, and political participation.[1]

The discussions revolved around the radical statement on social justice issued by CELAM at its second general assembly at Medellín, Colombia, in 1968. In particular the bishops and officers concentrated on socioeconomic development. The cold war and Third World economic nationalism had exacerbated the controversies over this theme. In Brazil the clergy and the armed forces struggled for the right to define it. Through the Bipartite, the bishops attempted to affirm their right to propose and implement Catholic notions of development. The commission aimed to preserve Church-state collaboration in this key area of national interest. The Bipartite also sought to resolve disputes arising from the repression of priests and activists, and it succeeded in reducing tensions, although it also had limits.

Setting the Agenda: Church-State Collaboration in Development

Meeting privately, General Muricy and Candido Mendes decided that the latter would coordinate the first Bipartite encounter. Candido Mendes focused on structuring an effective Church-state dialogue. He set the tenor by distributing copies of the Medellín statement to the Grupo da Situação. He then read two papers that interpreted the important CELAM document and Church-state relations in light of the Brazilian crisis. The CJP-BR's secretary general believed that cross and sword should collaborate for the benefit of Brazil. So emphatic was Candido Mendes that Dantas Barreto accused him of ignoring "the separation of Church and state in Brazil." No "concordat" between the two existed, Dantas Barreto added. Yet the Bipartite clearly worked within the framework of the moral concordat that had been operative since the 1930s. The Bipartite sought to renew that relationship. Candido Mendes defined the commission as a "search for paradigms," as "a system of exchange and consultation" in favor of social and economic development. He hoped to synthesize Catholic social doctrine with the Médici government's plan for national progress.[2]

The episcopal delegates at Medellín had produced the region's most radical Church document to date. It resulted from a convocation by Pope Paul VI to implement Vatican II's ecclesial liberalization in Latin America. It also formed part of a strategy to preempt violent revolution in the region by offering the laity a greater role in the Church and by bringing radical elements under its wing.[3] The document was a new version of the Church's third way between Communism and capitalism, the latest in a long line of statements on social justice dating from the late nineteenth century. "Latin American underdevelopment . . . is an unjust situation which promotes tensions that conspire against peace," the bishops declared. They expanded the notion of sin to include "institutionalized violence," a powerful concept given the oppressive political and social structures of Latin American countries. They praised the work of peaceful "revolutionaries," encouraged a "consciousness-raising evangelization," and called upon Christians to become engaged in the transformation of society (CELAM 1985). The document became the Magna Carta of Latin American progressive Catholicism, fostering the development of liberation theology, the so-called preferential option for the poor, and the CEBs. The Medellín statement also exacerbated divisions in the Church. It spurred conservatives to begin a campaign against liberation theology and involved the clergy in social activism. The Brazilian bishops took a leadership role at Medellín. Among the key envoys were Dom Hélder, generally credited (along with Chilean bishop Dom Manuel Larraín) with pushing CELAM to the left; Dom Avelar, the CELAM president; Dom Aloísio; and Dom Eugênio, who headed the conference's Commission of Peace and Justice and wrote the document's section on social justice.[4]

Candido Mendes staunchly supported Medellín. Titled "Fundamental Principles of Development in the Medellín Document," his first exposition offered a critique of Latin American society based on both nationalist-developmentalism and the Medellín document's embrace of dependency theory, which had come into vogue on the left as an explanation for underdevelopment. He proposed equality in the international economic order, the decentralization of Latin American political systems, the formation of labor unions, and national autonomy as a mechanism for integrating all individuals into the development process.[5]

Candido Mendes's second paper outlined the major task facing the Bipartite: how to avoid a collision between Church and state. It was titled "Perspectives for Dialogue Between Church and State with a View Toward Development." This exposition was more creative than the first. In it he not only analyzed Brazilian reality but also advocated a "Christian vision of development." Candido Mendes emphasized that Catholic social thought and pastoral strategy had entered a new, more "concrete" phase, in which the Church would actively struggle for development guided by the concepts of social science. The regime had its own development plan, but it employed an imposed rationality and repression. The two sides needed to study carefully each other's ideology and efforts for development. In the government's approach what was the tradeoff between "sacrifice" and real benefits for the people? A comparison of values could help answer this question. Moreover, dialogue had to be ongoing in order to avoid reliance on "slogans," "stereotypes," and the "obsolescence" of old ideas.[6]

Candido Mendes was optimistic that the Church and the military could agree on a common vision. His deepest worry was conflict resulting from each side's different "strategy" and "timing" in the quest for development. Rather than compete, Church and state needed to join forces. Here again dialogue was of key importance.[7] This proposal was the most audacious to be put forth at the Bipartite. In hindsight and in light of the existing literature on Brazilian Catholicism, the idea of Church-state unity at a time of growing conflict appears illogical and counterproductive. And cooperation on socioeconomic progress seemed unrealistic.

The Church-state relationship was about more than the question of political

The great-grandson of the prominent Catholic senator who defended Brazil's bishops in the 1870s, Candido Mendes believed that the Church and the military regime could cooperate to bring about Brazil's socioeconomic development.

support, however. A series of factors made Candido Mendes's proposal plausible: the Brazilian tradition of elite conciliation, past Church-state dialogue and collaboration on development, the Church's self-image as a moral beacon, a certain naïveté of the bishops, the regime's need for religious legitimation, General Muricy's devotion to the Church, the desire by both sides to reduce conflict, and the hope for redemocratization. A political scientist who subscribed to the theoretical framework of power elites, Candido Mendes believed that the military regime could widen its political base and join nationalist ideology and technocratic planning to produce a new phase of development (Martins Filho 1995:108–10). Latin America's new military regimes were above all highly patriotic and embraced one form or another of developmental nationalism (Loveman 1999:188). The Church too was patriotic. Candido Mendes's background and personality were two more key factors. In an authoritarian regime only a figure like Candido Mendes—a cordial aristocrat and internationally prestigious intellectual with the self-confidence and ability to make contacts and plant his ideas across the political spectrum—could formulate such a proposal and be taken seriously. In sum, the idea of joining forces was truly extraordinary—and understandable.

Candido Mendes outlined how cooperation could evolve. Church and state needed to avoid tensions arising from the social distortions that had appeared in Brazilian development. Social and political change had failed to keep pace with the country's impressive economic performance under the military. Did this "synchronic alteration" of objectives imply a crisis in the development paradigm adopted by most poor countries? Or did it mean that new forms of political participation and social mobility had to be found to replace those of the old model? The solution lay in understanding the government's long-term development goals in the light of Medellín (and Pope Paul VI's *Populorum Progressio*). Catholic social activism could remove the social distortions of development, while effective Church-state cooperation could make Brazil the first living example of the new Church teachings.[8]

The Grupo da Situação gave Candido Mendes's ideas a mixed review. The officers and their civilian collaborators all agreed that Church and state shared the goal of Brazil's development, but not the means to reach it. General Muricy stated that some in the Church lacked patience and knowledge about the government's development program and therefore did not understand the regime's actions. Moreover, the Church's social doctrine was "very theoretical" and failed to account for the difficulties encountered by the government. Professor Padilha attacked Candido Mendes's understanding of national security as "outdated." Political and social progress was already lagging behind economic development when the military assumed power, Padilha argued. The harshest criticism came from Ministry of Justice official Dantas Barreto, who believed that the juridical separation of Church and state in Brazil precluded the bishops from interfering in the "temporal domain." He stated that the Church should instead concentrate on preaching strictly spiritual themes to the people.[9]

The Military Response: Medellín as Subversion

While Candido Mendes and the bishops emphasized social justice through economic development and political participation, the military tried to steer the debate toward its main concern: subversion of the political and socioeconomic order established by the armed forces. The officers hoped to reestablish the two institutions' compatibility in outlook. Despite the Church's anti-Communist stance, however, the officers believed that the Church had little understanding of revolutionary warfare and the methods used by the left to co-opt susceptible groups such as students and the clergy. In the officers' view the bishops naively failed to consider these dangers while carrying out their new social doctrine.[10]

The military's concerns were underlined at the first Bipartite meeting by General Paula Couto of the psychological warfare division of the office of the Army chief of staff. In Paula Couto's interpretation, the West had embarked upon a "neo-capitalism" that was incorporating the Church's new social teachings. The Church's lack of knowledge about economic realities, however, allowed it to be manipulated by the international Communist movement. Paula Couto stated that the challenge for the Brazilian regime was to avoid allowing democracy to commit "suicide" with too many liberties but also not to "disfigure it" with too much "containment" of subversion. "The Church and the government are on the same line," Paula Couto concluded. "The difference is that the Church lacks information about the enemy."[11]

At the second Bipartite meeting, in January 1971, General Paula Couto presented a study titled "Revolutionary Warfare and the Church in Light of the Medellín Documents." It was a more elaborate response to Candido Mendes's explication of Medellín. "The Catholic hierarchy is ignorant of . . . the Communist revolutionary process known as Revolutionary Warfare, just as the rest of the civilian elites are ignorant of it," Paula Couto's exposition began. Using insidious and subtle tactics, the international Communist movement "exploits altruistic and humanitarian sentiments and awakens consciences to apparently noble causes." He further cautioned the bishops to proceed carefully with the Church's new idea of studying Marxism, an "undesirable ideology" that easily influenced the "inattentive and the unprepared."[12]

The core of Paula Couto's criticisms concerned the Medellín document's use of concepts similar to those of revolutionary warfare. Thus Medellín could provide "precious aid" to the Communist cause. Citing the warnings of the conservative Dom Vicente Scherer, Paula Couto explained that many Church documents subscribed to the Marxist strategy of fomenting class struggle. If the Church did not address this danger, friction with the state would continue, for the government would no longer be able to distinguish between real Communists and subversive priests who thought that they were simply following Catholic social doctrine. The bishops needed to explain more clearly the "constructive" meaning of their teachings in order to avoid confusion between "Church and subversion."[13]

Paula Couto proceeded to critique the Medellín document. He first cited "nationalism," an especially "passionate" example of a number of "intermediate ideologies" used by the Communists to infiltrate the Church and other groups. Nationalism was "the greatest source of revolutionary energy of our time," Paula Couto stated. Medellín played on this sentiment by decrying Latin America's "dependent" status as a producer of primary goods for the First World. By condemning "the international imperialism of money," Medellín attacked the United States without recognizing that country's leadership of the "Western and Christian world" as exemplified by its actions in Vietnam. Latin America's struggle for "liberation" echoed Josef Stalin's own guidelines for the Communist movement by highlighting the contradictions between rich and poor nations and ultimately causing them to reject the United States and to move in the direction of Moscow.[14] In effect, Paula Couto had associated the Church's nascent liberation theology with Communism. This kind of analysis hinted at the conservative critique of liberation theology soon to emerge in Latin America.

Paula Couto shifted from international to domestic tensions. The Communists aimed to "demoralize" democratic Third World regimes from within by exaggerating their social inequalities. The Church strengthened the Communists' hand by failing to admit that "neocapitalism" had evolved beyond the laissez-faire economies of the nineteenth century to become a socially responsible system. The authors of post–Vatican II Church documents errantly condemned capitalism and its internal contradictions without seeking to distinguish themselves from the Communists. The Medellín manifesto, for example, failed to couch its call for structural change in democratic terms. In addition, Paula Couto stated, the bishops advocated the formation of unions and youth groups without realizing that such organizations were prime targets of the Communists. Medellín spoke out against the "bourgeois civilization" that emphasized "eroticism" and "hedonism," but not the real causes of social decay—radicals such as the popular philosopher Herbert Marcuse. The Medellín document was "excellent" for promoting class hatred, Paula Couto continued. The bishops had abandoned their search for a "third position" between capitalism and Communism. Paula Couto appealed to Paul VI's opening statement at Medellín, in which the pope criticized unjust economic systems but also ruled out violence and anarchy, obvious Communist tactics that were repressed by the regime.[15]

Paula Couto further criticized the Medellín document's use of Communist "jargon" such as "oppression," "imperialism," and "bourgeoisie." Medellín encouraged the formation of "grass-roots organizations" (a reference to the CEBs) based on the repressed Catholic Action movements. He also assailed the statement for making "violence a noble ideal, a glorious heroism" through "sympathetic references" to the idealism of revolutionaries.[16] To support Paula Couto's arguments, Colonel Omar of the SNI played for the bishops the tape recording of a former seminarian that allegedly proved Communist infiltration in the Church (see chapter 5).

While asserting a basic harmony between the government's and the Church's concerns, Dom Eugênio found inconsistencies in the general's words. Legitimate nationalism, the cardinal noted, was actually rooted in Brazil's armed forces, although he agreed that the Communists tried to use it to separate Brazil from the United States. The Medellín document was like the Gospel: both could be used in revolutionary warfare. But by intervening in several areas of the economy the regime itself had abandoned the theory of free enterprise and adopted elements of socialism. Dom Eugênio also downplayed the importance of anti-Communism for Brazil. He maintained that for discussing the problem of subversion "not in favor of Communism" was a better term than "anti-Communism." Excessive emphasis on the "Communist bugaboo" diverted attention from social reform.[17]

Paula Couto and Muricy objected to these statements. Paula Couto asserted that no socialists were in the government. Muricy added that intervention and planning were simply "a modern solution" to national economic problems. Paula Couto reminded the bishops that social reform was already part of regime strategy for combating revolutionary warfare.[18] Dom Avelar admitted that Medellín contained "equivocal terms" because "we live in a society in transformation that speaks an ambiguous language." By the same token, Paula Couto's exposition also lacked clarity. Given the context of the times, Medellín was a moderate statement. It rejected violence and invited all groups to join together in solving Latin America's problems.[19]

Candido Mendes offered the most incisive commentary. He (correctly) foresaw an aggravation of the conflict between the ideology of Medellín and the policies of the regime. He then posed three interrelated questions. First, was Brazil's leadership not too rigid in its premises? Had the idea of revolutionary warfare not become "sclerotic"? And, in echo of Dom Eugênio, had this concept not received "excessive emphasis" within military strategy? The Grupo da Situação did not think so. Paula Couto explained that he had based his talk on a scenario of "orthodox and complete" revolutionary warfare. Some of its "insidious and subtle" techniques had succeeded in Brazil; thanks to the government's action, others had not. He cited the example of Chile, where socialist Salvador Allende had won election to the presidency peacefully. Allende had been able to use the psychological and political tools of revolutionary warfare because the Chilean government had failed to keep "vigilance." General Muricy added that national security policy demanded the

121

defeat of all antagonistic forces. Professor Padilha also disagreed with Candido Mendes. Development and security were tied together, he stated. Revolutionary warfare in Brazil was a "reality" that had to be "combated."[20]

Religion and Politics

Dantas Barreto tried to radicalize the debate by shifting attention from Medellín and subversion to the theory of Church-state relations. He was aggressive. He first attacked Candido Mendes's document as "abstruse and obscure," "biased," and "most inappropriate" for meeting the goal of Church-regime cooperation. Citing papal encyclicals, Barreto attempted to prove that the bishops could only speak about the social sphere, not act in it. It was not the Church's duty "to promote the temporal well-being," Barreto stated. "Religion and politics are distinct spheres." Moreover, Barreto affirmed that although poverty was "unmerited," it was not "unjust," for the government was working to eliminate it. (He distributed copies of the Médici administration's *Metas e Bases para a Ação de Governo* [Goals and bases for government action], an ambitious outline of industrial development, national integration, and social progress.) He described Catholic activists as fanatics who had lost their faith. "They give the impression that they possess the key to progress and the secret, the exact formula for development, and that governments do not use this formula because of conservative egoism and imperialistic malice," Barreto stated. "The truth is that they want to use the Church to cover themselves with immunity in order to preach, protect, or commit illegal and subversive acts and do not shy away from violence, assault, terrorism, and kidnapping." He offered the example of Chile, where radical priests collaborated with the Allende regime.[21]

The bishops reacted "violently" to these remarks, according to the military's secret report on the meeting. Dom Eugênio termed them "profoundly unfortunate." The cardinal expressed complete support for Candido Mendes's document. Because Barreto had defined the Church's and the state's respective areas of competence a priori, Dom Eugênio suggested that the Bipartite come to a halt. General Muricy tried to calm the air by stating that Barreto's exposition was "personal" and did "not reflect the thinking" of the officers. But Dom Avelar joined Dom Eugênio in questioning the usefulness of the commission. Barreto's way of thinking was "rigid," "polemical," and "professorial." The Church had not interfered in state affairs, Dom Avelar added. The Church was undergoing an official "process of renovation" commanded by the pope, and all had to accept it, including the mistakes committed. Professor Padilha made another effort at conciliation. "It is difficult to dissociate the religious man from the citizen," he stated. "A perspective of Christian anguish is what led Dr. Dantas to such a vehement position."[22]

This exchange revealed the cleavages within the regime about how to deal with the Church. Whereas Muricy, Padilha, and most of the Grupo da Situação stressed dialogue, Barreto's position resonated with that of the hard-liners and technocrats who believed that the clergy should exercise a traditionally spiritual function. Barreto had the backing of both Médici and Justice Minister Buzaid.[23] He acted as an important political voice as the commission established parameters of debate and possibilities for mutual understanding. Having left a bad impression on other members of the Bipartite, he dropped out, but not before putting the bishops on notice that the regime would not tolerate their interference. Meanwhile, in vigorously defending Candido Mendes the bishops displayed a united front.

The Attempt to Deflate Medellín

Revolutionary warfare remained a stumbling block as the two groups continued to search for ways to link the theology of Medellín with the developmental goals of the regime. The minutes of the April 1971 gathering are missing from General Muricy's papers. Notations on the military's premeeting planning session, however, reveal that the Grupo da Situação carefully prepared rebuttals to the Grupo Religioso's previous arguments. In a draft of meeting strategy, General Paula Couto emphasized the need to refute Dom Eugênio's belief that the stress on anti-Communism was harming Brazil. "A true democrat has to be an 'anti-Communist,' and not just 'not in favor of Communism,'" he wrote. "If there were no aggression, democracy could be less hostile, as Dom Eugênio wants. It is not democracy that wants to conquer the Communist countries, but the opposite is definitely true." Furthermore, Paula Couto wanted to clarify such controversial terms as "capitalism," "neocapitalism," "socialism," "security," and "participation." He specifically cited Candido Mendes's statement that "nationalism is the political conscience of development." Another example was Dom Avelar's observation about the unclear distinction between social justice and subversion.[24]

In addition, the Grupo da Situação outlined a critique of Candido Mendes's papers on Medellín and Church-state cooperation. According to this analysis, the Church's "participation in the education and *conscientização* of the people" was "dangerous" because the Communists ran "an identical movement exploiting themes similar to those of the Church, that is, . . . 'internal contradictions.'" The Situação questioned Candido Mendes's use of such terms as "urgent transformations," which sounded revolutionary.[25] The report dismissed Candido Mendes's defense of traditional civil liberties. The Brazilian government had surpassed the "classical political system" to become a "social democracy," in which some individual rights had to be restricted. Furthermore, Candido Mendes's proposal that the Church help form "a national political conscience" was an "invasion" of the government's responsibilities. The Church's new pastoral activism and its decision to denounce injustice were turning the institution into a transnational "political party" that might clash with the national interest. Church and state now competed over questions of development. "If two organisms of an intrinsically political nature, composed of different persons but of the same ideology, cannot reach perfect agreement over a development program, what can be said when competition occurs between the competent political organ and another of a completely different nature, as is the case of the Church?"[26] Despite this rather pessimistic evaluation, the document echoed Candido Mendes's hopes for improved Church-regime relations. In retrospect such a task seemed futile, but the whole reasoning behind the Bipartite was that the clergy and the military could and indeed should collaborate.

Another Situação study presented at the April 1971 meeting outlined the possibilities. It was written by an ADESG team headed by General Golbery do Couto e Silva, the grand theoretician of Brazilian DNS, founder of the SNI, and political acquaintance of both General Muricy and Candido Mendes. Persona non grata in the hard-line Costa e Silva and Médici administrations, Golbery remained active in the private sector as president of Dow Chemical. He returned to the government as the chief of the presidential civilian staff in the Geisel administration and became a leading architect of the abertura. The other members of the ADESG team were Judge José Murta Ribeiro, economist José Garrido Tôrres, Ambassador Geraldo Eulálio do Nascimento e Silva, and Jesuit Father Francisco Leme Lopes, a supporter of the coup.[27]

Titled "Church Social Doctrine and Brazilian Government Policy," the Golbery document attempted to discover whether the causes of Church-state conflict were rooted in doctrinal differences or other factors. Comparing Pope Paul VI's *Populorum Progressio* with the pronouncements of the Médici government, the team concluded that harmony existed on questions of development, population control, agrarian reform, health care, wage policy, disarmament, and numerous other areas. Like the other documents analyzed here, this study made no reference to actual examples of subversion or to regime atrocities. Yet it concluded that Church-regime tensions originated not at the leadership level but among the lower tiers of the clergy and the armed forces.[28] This analysis was generally true for the period before 1968, but the two hierarchies clearly began to clash thereafter. Moreover, the Golbery study was superficial because it spoke only of intentions, not results. Thus it was not so much a description of Church-state relations as a plea for continued dialogue.

The question still facing the Bipartite was how to stop Medellín from inspiring subversion. This was a tricky matter because, despite all of their debate, the two sides never resolved, at least in a theoretical sense, Dom Avelar's conundrum about social justice and subversion. The Grupo da Situação tried to convince the bishops to issue a supplementary, antisubversive interpretation of Medellín in the name of the CNBB and to distribute it to all of Brazil's thousands of parishes. The Golbery team had observed that the Church's documents were often vaguely worded to appeal to its large multinational membership. According to the military's wishes, the Medellín supplement would speak specifically about Brazil and reflect the "perfect compatibility" between Church and state expressed in the Golbery study.[29] Such a statement would discourage and delegitimate the actions of the radical clergy.

Dom Eugênio only partially obliged the Situação. At the July 1971 Bipartite meeting, he gave a positive commentary on Medellín. In contrast with Candido Mendes's presentations, Dom Eugênio did not distribute copies of this "personal analysis." The Medellín statement was not an official document of the Church, but it was recognized by the pope, the cardinal stated. It was also not a "social document" but a religious one. It was valid for all Latin American countries. Medellín should be interpreted as a whole, Dom Eugênio cautioned, and not according to a few faulty, isolated phrases. He admitted that some elements outside the Church had "distorted" the document, but it diverged sharply from Marxism. Moreover, only bishops—and not priests—could interpret it. Dom Eugênio told the officers that Medellín was "original" and one of the "best things the Church has ever done." It sparked a "healthy dynamism" in the institution.[30]

But Dom Eugênio also tried to allay the Situação's fears about Medellín's potentially subversive phrases. He gave the officers copies of a secret Church report that summarized a meeting of presidents of episcopal social action commissions from ten Latin American countries. The meeting had taken place in Bahia in April 1971. This extraordinary document revealed how CELAM centrists were reacting to conservative criticisms of Medellín by quietly trying to control its impact within the Church. This action preceded the well-known 1972 CELAM election in which conservative Colombian bishop Dom Alfonso López Trujillo won the CELAM presidency and campaigned to roll back Medellín. In effect, the bishops at Bahia were quietly trying to achieve for all of Latin America what the Grupo da Situação wanted the CNBB to do for Brazil. They echoed the Medellín conclusions' criticisms of dependency, underdevelopment, and human rights violations. Yet they also sought to moderate the progressive clergy and the radical goals of Medellín by advocating a more traditional pastoral approach. First, they criticized pastoral workers who concentrated on social issues at the expense of religious salvation. Second, they advocated a top-down approach for shaping social change in Latin America. The best groups for achieving this goal were elites: university students, businessmen, politicians, military officers, and leaders of organizations for the rural and urban poor. Third, and most important, they called on fellow bishops to act firmly against Marxist "infiltration" in the Church.[31]

"Correcting" the Subversive Clergy

The two sides also discussed the practical ramifications of the conflict over social justice and subversion. In particular, they tried to reduce tensions by seeking a mechanism to resolve the cases of priests accused of subversion. The bishops and the military alike saw the need for the Church to rein in some of the activist clergy, although for different reasons. The Grupo da Situação identified these men as opponents of the regime. The bishops looked to protect priests and activists and to remove stumbling blocks to dialogue with the generals.

The bishops and the generals agreed that a major cause of Church-state friction was lack of control over their respective rank and file. Although they had different styles, both the Church and the armed forces relied on hierarchy, discipline, and obedience. The Church was especially vulnerable on these points because of the crisis of the clergy sparked by post–Vatican II liberalization. Many priests rejected authority and discipline, including obligatory celibacy. Hundreds left the ministry. Lack of control made the Church appear weak and disorganized. The renovation of the Church was "an official process, commanded by the pope," Dom Avelar told the officers. "There are, unfortunately, errors."[32] By leading the institution to renew itself and to eliminate support for the political status quo, the clerical crises' damage to authority further reduced the bishops' ability to negotiate with the regime. One influential progressive Church bulletin described base-hierarchy harmony as "fundamental" for a successful dialogue. "Without this, new *crises* will occur, slowly leading to deeper conflicts and ruptures."[33]

The military faced a similar challenge in the turbulent early 1960s when many soldiers and sailors went so far as to mutiny in favor of the left's call for basic social reforms. After the hard-liners took power with AI-5, it was the turn of the right-wing security forces to veer out of control. President Médici privately expressed frustration to Dom Eugênio about his inability to command effectively against the abuses occurring at lower levels of the armed forces (Dom Eugênio interview). One of the worst cases occurred in the barracks at Barra Mansa, where officers tortured and killed their own soldiers.

Bishops and officers identified with each other's plights. For Church-state decompression to work, the bishops needed a "prior understanding" with the regime about measures against the clergy or at the very least a subsequent explanation of the motives. Such communication would strengthen authority.[34]

At its first meeting the Bipartite worked to build this linkage. According to the military's minutes, Professor Padilha observed that the government's security structure was varied and complex, making it difficult to solve "local problems" and therefore necessitating the centralization of Church-state contact.[35] The Situação's postmeeting report recommended greater communication between the CNBB and the "key elements" of the government's information and security services. It further suggested the establishment of Church-government dialogue at the regional level and the selection of a special presidential assistant for Church affairs.[36] The bishops, the Situação later noted, wanted to "take responsibility for controlling priests whose actions might be considered harmful to the government." As Dom Aloísio had stated, "The Church would like to be informed with respect to the activity of its members concerning security, with the idea of fostering the necessary corrections."[37]

This kind of discussion with the bishops was a political hot potato inside the regime. In 1964 the Church and President Castello Branco had first tried to set up a clearinghouse for cases against the clergy. After meeting with a delegation of bishops, Castello Branco telegraphed the entire episcopate with the suggestion to contact the Ministry of Justice about priests in trouble with the authorities. Castello Branco offered this measure as an olive branch to the Church, which suffered heavily in the first months of the dictatorship.[38] It evidently had little effect, for priests, lay activists, and even bishops continued as targets of the security forces. Many in the military were either ignorant of the agreement or simply chose to disregard it. The poor transition of administration from Castello Branco to Costa e Silva further weakened compliance (Bruneau 1974b:195, inc. n. 54).

President Médici vetoed the presidential assistant and the regional talks but permitted officers from the SNI, CIE, and the office of the Army chief of staff to continue at the Bipartite (see chapter 5). Dantas Barreto revealed, however, at the January 1971 Bipartite meeting that Médici had approved Justice Minister Buzaid's suggestion of the "possibility" of providing the CNBB with information on the cases against priests "in order to help the government resolve them." The Situação's secret conclusions even advocated turning over allegedly subversive priests "into the custody of the bishops."[39] The Church had provided precedent for such a solution. For example, in 1964 Dom Geraldo Proença de Sigaud, the ultraconservative archbishop of Diamantina, kept a radical priest under arrest in the archiepiscopal residence (Serbin 1993b:420–21; Alves 1979:271–74). The police turned other arrested churchmen over to their bishops (Della Cava 1985:73). In 1972 Dom Eugênio tried to shield a priest from arrest by holding him in Church quarters (see below). At the Bipartite, Dom Ivo pressed for the creation of an "arrangement" permitting greater exchange of information, but SNI chief Fontoura, following Médici's wish to avoid official military contact with the bishops, restricted contact to civilian channels such as the Justice Ministry and the Federal Police.[40] Fontoura thus vetoed the Situação's hopes for a direct CNBB-intelligence community link.

The Bipartite itself became the crucible for mediating cases. Both sides accepted the proposal of Lieutenant Colonel Sérgio Mário Pasquali of the office of the Army chief of staff that the commission divide its meetings into two parts: first, discussion of "doctrinal matters" and, second, "concrete, practical cases" of Church-regime conflict.[41] One example was Dom Eugênio's effort to defuse the activities of militant laity and clergymen in Rio de Janeiro upon his assumption of the archdiocese in early 1971. At the April Bipartite meeting General Muricy raised the case of Father José Sainz Artola, the vicar of the favela Brás de Pina in Rio de Janeiro. Artola had earlier gone to jail for resisting a government plan to move his parishioners to a distant public housing project. Artola was released, but in October 1970, he was arrested again after allegedly joining a group of men to destroy a government office in protest of a new tax for favela improvements. Dom Eugênio, Alceu Amoroso Lima, and opposition leaders defended the priest against accusations of Marxism and subversion. Artola went free in January 1971 pending judgment.[42] General Muricy complained about the priest's "undignified" behavior, and the cardinal promised to transfer him to another parish.[43] Artola was later convicted but excused from his sentence.

At the same meeting, Dom Eugênio announced that he would reorganize IBRADES and JOC along religious lines. He asked the military not to interfere in this effort. General Muricy backed the initiative, but he also requested that the cardinal await "confirmation." Coming in the wake of the security forces' attacks on the two Church organizations and Muricy's intervention on their behalf, this exchange indicated that the general was negotiating support for Dom Eugênio's plan within the armed forces and possibly averting further action against Jocistas and IBRADES participants.[44] Such discussion highlighted the Bipartite as a forum for privileged communication and Church-regime negotiation.

Another case involved Father François Jentel, a French missionary who had worked with peasants in Mato Grosso since 1954. In 1972 a land development company tried to force out the villagers of Santa Terezinha, where Jentel worked. The dispute broke into armed conflict after the company manager destroyed a clinic the priest was building. Although he was not present during the worst clash, Father Jentel was arrested, convicted of violating the LSN, and sentenced to ten years in prison. Claiming that Jentel had distributed arms to the peasants, the members of the military tribunal termed him a "dangerous element" who fomented class struggle and conflict with the armed forces. A civilian judge dissented, stating that Jentel deserved not a prison sentence but a prize for displaying "solidarity" with the poor. During the proceedings Jentel's lawyer pointed out that "national security" was "a badly understood subject in this country." Dom Ivo, other bishops, and Catholics from throughout Brazil protested the verdict. Father Jentel was found innocent on appeal and immediately left the country for France. Jentel's bishop, the Spaniard Dom Pedro Casaldáliga, was also implicated in the incidents and was nearly expelled from Brazil.[45]

Unbeknownst to the public, the Bipartite helped smooth Father Jentel's exit from Brazil and orchestrated his eventual—though brief—return. Candido Mendes revealed that the CNBB discussed the matter intensively with General Golbery, President Geisel's chief of civilian staff, "in order to facilitate the actions and decisions of the government." To avert further difficulties, Jentel wrote Golbery and offered to leave the country. Fearing negative publicity, General Muricy complained that the priest had given an interview to *Le Monde* about his experience in Brazil. Dom Aloísio told the commission, however, that Father Jentel had promised to maintain "discretion," avoiding contact with the press and therefore any "undue exploitation" of the episode. Candido Mendes asked Muricy to have the government consider Jentel's return to Brazil. The general agreed to take up the matter, but only after the furor over the incident had died down. Seldom had the CNBB been "put to the test" as it had in negotiating Father Jentel's exit, Candido Mendes stated. In one of its secret reports on the Bipartite, the Grupo da Situação noted that Candido Mendes and the CNBB were profoundly interested in "cooperating with the government." If Father Jentel spoke out further about the episode, the

Situação could use his words as an "instrument . . . to force the Grupo Religioso to recognize its absolute lack of control over certain problems."[46] In December 1975 Father Jentel returned to Brazil, only to be expelled by order of Geisel.

Willingness to control the rank and file had limits. Using his contacts in the armed forces, Dom Eugênio prevented the imprisonment of lay activists and clergymen in Rio and elsewhere. Dom Eugênio had a virtual twenty-four-hour hot line to Lieutenant Colonel Pacífico of the Grupo da Situação, which allowed the cardinal to raise questions about Church-military problems anywhere in Brazil. Pacífico, for example, immediately contacted area commanders to obtain information on detained priests (Pacífico interview). In January 1972, however, the authorities violated the agreement that allowed the cardinal himself to handle cases of alleged subversion. The police had wanted to arrest Father João Daniel de Castro Filho on suspicion of subversive activities in the suburban parish of Oswaldo Cruz (Dom Eugênio interview). According to an underground opposition newspaper, a DOPS officer tortured a woman picked up on suspicion of distributing pamphlets for the priest. Dom Eugênio convinced the police to allow Father Daniel to remain in the archdiocesan residence as if on "retreat." Dom Eugênio later agreed to let him give a deposition at the DOPS. Instead of returning the father to Dom Eugênio's custody, however, the police held him incommunicado (Dom Eugênio interview).[47] Dom Eugênio tried but failed to reach Muricy and other top generals to register a complaint. In protest he quit the Bipartite (Dom Eugênio interview). A judge later released Father Daniel and related suspects, and the regime fired the police chief who had detained the priest (Dom Waldyr interview). Top officers also visited Dom Eugênio in an attempt to convince him to return to the Bipartite. Dom Eugênio refused. In his secret report on the episode, General Paula Couto wrote that the "main cause" of Dom Eugênio's irritation was not the arrest of Father Daniel, whose "faults" the cardinal recognized, but rather the "difficulties" he had experienced in contacting the authorities. Such lack of communication could undermine Dom Eugênio's "prestige" among his clergy, the general concluded.[48]

The Dominican Affair

The imprisonment of the Dominican friars for involvement with Marighella and the ALN inevitably hovered in the background of the discussions about allegedly subversive priests. Domestically the assassination of Marighella was a major victory for the regime. It marked the beginning of the end of the short life of the guerrilla movement in Brazil. But it also contributed greatly to damaging Brazil's foreign image. In the United States, for instance, *Look* magazine published an article on the affair titled "Brazil: Government by Torture." One of the Dominicans, Frei Tito de Alencar Lima, described in detail his horrible torture by the São Paulo DOI-CODI and his subsequent suicide attempt ("Brazil: Government by Torture" 1970). The incident put the bishops in the difficult and, for some, embarrassing position of having to defend men accused of aiding the most dangerous armed threat to the regime.

The crux of the matter for Church-state relations revolved around two Dominicans who were brutally tortured until they revealed the place and code for meeting with Marighella. Fleury and the DEOPS-SP then used the two men to lure Marighella into an ambush. The exact circumstances are in dispute to this day. Regardless, the regime and its allies tried to use the incident to undermine the progressive Church by demonstrating links between the clergy and armed revolutionaries. They even tried to involve Dom Hélder. The regime's version received heavy coverage in the press, and the police, the military court, and right-wing Catholic columnists attacked the accused Dominicans as virtual heretics who should be expelled from the Church. There is no doubt that the Dominican order in Brazil helped the ALN in a number of important ways—for example, by providing safe passage out of the country for hunted militants and by scanning a potential guerrilla front in the Amazon. But the regime failed to connect the Dominicans or, for that matter, any other clergyman or Church worker to violent acts. Nevertheless, a number of bishops did not defend the Dominicans. Dom Vicente Scherer, for example, believed they should be punished if convicted. In particular, Dom Vicente, Dom Agnelo Rossi, and Dom Lucas (who was himself a Dominican) appeared insensitive to the prisoners' plight even after learning of their torture. Dom Paulo, however, lent his support to the prisoners. Representatives of the Dominican order also came to Brazil from Rome to press for a resolution of the case and to demonstrate solidarity.[49]

The Bipartite discussed the Dominican affair only superficially. The bishops refused to accept the military's allegations that the Dominicans had collaborated with the police against Marighella. At this point the matter was dropped (Candido Mendes interview 3). There is not even the slightest allusion to it in General Muricy's papers. The two sides certainly had ample opportunity and reason to discuss the case further. The accused friars and other clergymen and seminarians involved in the episode in both São Paulo and Rio Grande do Sul were jailed in November 1969—a full year before the start of the Bipartite. The conviction of the three friars came less than two months before, and they did not go free until October 1973—a full year before the Bipartite's end. In the interim their lawyer,

131

Mário Simas, appealed the case, and they participated with other political prisoners in two hunger strikes. Meanwhile, Catholics abroad pressured the regime for better treatment of the prisoners. In August 1974, the final month of the Bipartite, Frei Tito, banished from Brazil, hanged himself in France.[50]

Why did the Grupo Religioso not try to help these clergymen? The outcome was already a fait accompli by the start of the Bipartite.[51] The dubious proceedings of the military investigation and trial violated even the regime's own norms. These political trials were used routinely against the opposition since 1964. Moreover, to seek the reversal of one of the government's major victories against the Church would be futile. The Dominican affair was another example of the limits of the Bipartite, and also of the unwillingness or inability of the bishops to push too hard against the regime. Dom Lucas, for instance, had refused a request by Simas that he testify at the Dominicans' trial that he had seen marks of torture on Frei Tito.[52] At the start of the Bipartite, the CNBB president was Dom Vicente, who showed the least sympathy for the Dominicans. Finally, the Vatican itself took little interest in the case (see chapter 4).

Conclusion

The Bipartite began with optimism about the prospects for Church-regime collaboration. As General Muricy stated, "the separation between the spiritual—the soul of Brazil—and the temporal was inadmissable." Church-state cooperation lay at the heart of Brazilian reality, and in late 1970 and early 1971 the bishops and the generals believed it would continue that way. The commission enabled the two sides to discuss their ideological differences. The Grupo da Situação was so confident that it even considered holding public meetings of churchmen and government officials "to inform public opinion of the true dimensions of reciprocal understanding between the Church and the Revolution."[53]

The moment was extraordinary. Brazil's ecclesiastical and military intelligentsia acted to conciliate their respective institutions. It is surprising that the Church's catalyst was not a bishop close to the military such as Dom Eugênio—though his role was important—but a leading member of the Catholic left, Candido Mendes. He and the progressive bishops of the CNBB debated ideas with the heralds of national security. The debate involved a high-level philosophical discussion over the meaning of social justice, pastoral activities, Church doctrine, papal encyclicals, and democracy. Muricy, Paula Couto, Golbery, and other members of the Situação demonstrated the seriousness with which the Army believed its role transcended the purely military and extended to social issues and politics. Both the military and the Church saw themselves in the vanguard of Brazilian development. Each had reaffirmed its membership in Brazil's political elite.

In the absence of a free press and an open political system, the bishops and officers had taken it upon themselves to create the terms of political debate and to wrestle over them. In the wake of the repression that had emasculated Brazilian politics, the Bipartite was a partial surrogate for the political system. Debates that could have taken place in the press, the Congress, and the streets were restricted to the inner room of Church-state relations.

The two group's analyses of Catholic pastoral innovation and the Brazilian political situation revealed serious disagreements over the means to socioeconomic progress. For decades the Church and the military had been working to establish models for Brazilian society. Both agreed in principle on the need for social justice as defined by the pope and the bishops. But the existence of widely different concepts of Catholicism reinforced the contrast between the two groups. The cold war mentality of national security required that all efforts at social justice first pass the litmus test of subversion. In the hyperpolarization of the era, the military viewed as its enemy anything that did not explicitly declare itself anti-Communist. It is ironic that the Medellín manifesto, a cornerstone of the Church's own alternative to violent change, fell into this category. Polarization blurred the distinctions between social justice and subversion. It led the military to equate the two, for, in a fundamentally unequal society such as Brazil's, even the slightest change could be interpreted as a threat to the social order.

Thus while the Bipartite sensitized each side to the other's outlook, it was only partially successful in establishing a middle ground between Church and military. Their goals were countervailing forces: the Church was for social justice, the regime against subversion. The bishops recognized the dangers of the latter, but refused to give up the tenets of Medellín. They advocated democracy by emphasizing the need for broader political participation in Brazilian society. The officers supported social justice, but only as it might fit into their anti-Communist agenda. Their notion of "social democracy" was authoritarian and intolerant of dissent. For the armed forces, social justice almost always became subversion. Moreover, the Grupo da Situação saw the Church as encroaching on the armed forces' prerogative as holder of state power and director of Brazilian development. Unable to solve the political and ideological puzzles, the Bipartite concentrated increasingly on settling specific conflicts among the lower echelons. Both sides of the Bipartite perhaps engaged in wishful thinking, however, when they defined Church-military difficulties as primarily a base-hierarchy issue. As Dom Eugênio pointed out to the officers, there were differences between military and religious discipline. Military order depended on strict authority, but because the Church was attempting to renovate its structures and stimulate more active lay participation, it required that its leadership dialogue with its base. In Dom Eugênio's words, this process rested "on patience and slow and continuous work." The differences sharpened greatly as the generals stressed national security and the bishops social justice. Indeed, the repression of the opposition continued even after General Muricy admitted to the bishops and the press that the government had defeated the most serious revolutionary threats.[54] Furthermore, the campaign against subversion had hit the Church leadership. The Bipartite's most serious challenges involved disputes between the two hierarchies in which the conflict between social justice and subversion continued to fester.

Chapter 7

The Cotton Between the Crystals

In his oral memoir General Muricy aptly summed up the Bipartite as a group that "served as cotton between crystals" (Muricy 1993:424). It helped Brazil's two most important institutions to coexist during some of the most tense and delicate moments of their historic relationship. This chapter revisits several examples of the commission's efforts at conflict resolution. First, it studies the dispute over commemoration of Brazil's independence sesquicentennial in 1972. The second example provides a study of the bishops' public/private dichotomy in the person of one of the country's leading progressives. In both instances, conflict revolved around institutional competition between the Church and the armed forces, notions of patriotism, and the Church's new grassroots social action. Third, the chapter examines the attempt by the bishops to use the Bipartite to salvage the Catholic privileges and status of the moral concordat. The underlying question is: how could the Church maintain its importance in Brazilian life in the context of an authoritarian system seeking rapid modernization of the country? As the discussion will demonstrate, the bishops compromised to safeguard institutional interests. The chapter concludes by considering their strategy as well as the effectiveness—and limits—of the Bipartite.

The 1972 Independence Celebrations: The Battle over Patriotism

The case of Brazil's 1972 sesquicentennial celebrations dramatized the commission's ability to defuse potentially explosive situations. As a national holiday, Independence Day (September 7) provided the Church and the military with the opportunity to leave their mark on the country. Soldiers marched in parades; priests and bishops prayed for the welfare of Brazil. Both institutions viewed themselves as forming the basis of Brazilian nationhood.

After 1964, Independence Day took on added significance as the generals and their opponents made it part of the battle over the hearts and minds of Brazilians.[1] In 1967, for instance, the regime temporarily closed the radio station of the northeastern archdiocese of São Luís do Maranhão after it broadcast a message doubting Brazil's independence in light of its deep poverty and exploitation by foreign countries. The following year, congressman Márcio Moreira Alves urged Brazilians to boycott Independence Day. This incident enraged the military and led to the declaration of AI-5. In Goiânia, students tried to disrupt the traditional Independence Day parade (Duarte 1998:136–37). In 1969, urban guerrillas embarrassed the regime by capturing U.S. ambassador Burke Elbrick just three days before the holiday. The government met the kidnappers' demands by broadcasting revolutionary statements and then flying ransomed political prisoners out of the country on September 7. The same year, subversives threatened to stop the ceremonies in São Paulo.[2] In 1980 the government expelled an Italian priest who protested against the regime by refusing to celebrate an Independence Day mass.

Both Church and state prepared to use the 1972 observances as a political platform. In January 1972, the CNBB announced the Church's intentions to collaborate in the official sesquicentennial program, and in April it revealed that the episcopate would prepare a special document for the occasion. The announcement generated press speculation about the political impact of the statement.[3] The year held additional meaning for the clergy because it marked the centenary of the start of the Religious Question, one of the most serious Church-state conflicts in Brazilian history. The archdiocese of Olinda and Recife commemorated the inauguration of Dom Vital, a protagonist of the 1870s crisis. His seat, ironically, was now occupied by Dom Hélder, the symbol of the new Church-state difficulties.[4] Meanwhile, President Médici declared on national television that the government would bring from Portugal the preserved remains of Dom Pedro I, Brazil's first emperor, for a tour of the country. In addition, General Antônio Jorge Corrêa, the official coordinator of the sesquicentennial, planned a major military presence for the weeklong celebrations. Carlos Fico describes the military's use of public commemorations as an attempt at "decorative citizenship" (1997:93). Celebrating its own fiftieth anniversary, the PCB termed Médici's plans a "propaganda maneuver."[5]

The CNBB had named Archbishop Dom Paulo Evaristo Arns to oversee the

Independence Day celebrations such as the 1967 parade in Rio drew large crowds and became instruments of the political struggle between the dictators and the opposition. A group of Brazilians (above) watch as soldiers carrying weapons display the nation's military force.

preparation of the Church's national sesquicentennial mass in São Paulo, where Dom Pedro I had proclaimed separation from Portugal in 1822. Dom Paulo cooperated with the state and the municipal authorities. In August, however, control of the event turned into a power struggle between the CNBB and the Army when they reached an impasse over dates and places. The regime had assumed that the Church would participate at a national thanksgiving service set for September 7, but the generals had not consulted the CNBB, which had chosen September 3 for the Te Deum. An editorial in the archdiocesan newspaper *O São Paulo* recognized that some might find the separation of ceremonies strange, but it explained that the CNBB wanted to avoid mixing religion with the "festive, profane, and even martial" aspects of the official commemoration. The earlier date would also permit the hundred bishops coming to São Paulo from throughout Brazil to return to their home dioceses in time for the September 7 masses.[6] Furthermore, Church and government disagreed over the site of the religious proceedings. Dom Paulo had obtained written permission from the mayor's office to hold the CNBB mass at the Ipiranga Monument, which commemorated Dom Pedro's declaration of independence on the banks of the Ipiranga River.[7] In August, General Corrêa overrode the city's decision. He claimed that remodeling of the site for the government ceremonies made it unusable before the seventh. When Dom Ivo tried to negotiate privately with Corrêa, the general insisted that the bishops switch the Te Deum to September 7 to comply with the official program.[8] According to the newspaper *O Estado de São Paulo*, the work at the Parque da Independência was done by late August. Meanwhile, Dom Agnelo Rossi and Nuncio Dom Umberto Mozzoni had met on August 22 with President Médici and agreed to a sesquicentennial Te Deum to be celebrated in Rome.[9]

The battle over scheduling reflected the growing differences between the Church and the military. In 1972, competing views of patriotism especially stood out. In a draft of its sesquicentennial statement, for example, the CNBB emphasized the Church's historical contributions to Brazilian national identity. Nowhere else in the modern world had the Church identified itself so closely with the history of a people, the document continued. It would be "impossible to eliminate the Church without essentially disfiguring the image of [Brazilian] nationality."[10]

In a newspaper article, Justice Minister Buzaid rebuked the bishops for their unpatriotic attitudes. "Those who should preserve the Christian traditions of the country opt for an anti-Christianity," he wrote. The bishops "no longer feel part of the Brazilian family and dedicate themselves to a utopia of celebrations that compete with the sesquicentenary, as if Brazil had two different and parallel histories."[11]

Tensions mounted when the Grupo da Situação learned that the Church's sesquicentennial document and other publications would contain language critical of the regime.[12] For months the left had already been exploiting the commemoration for political purposes, and it viewed the Church as an ally against the regime.[13] Also, Alceu Amoroso Lima called for amnesty for all political prisoners and a return to the rule of law.[14] The Situação feared the bishops' words might cause commotion in São Paulo.

Strong precedents for trouble existed. Under General Humberto de Souza Mello, a hard-liner who enthusiastically supported the notorious security forces, Brazil's largest city bore the brunt of the repression. On the opposing side, Dom Paulo was emerging as the nation's leading spokesman for human rights. At a regional meeting of bishops in June he led the way in drafting one of the most forceful Church protests against torture. The bishops called upon all Brazilians, including the government, to use the sesquicentenary as a moment for "a sincere examination of conscience." Army intelligence considered this document highly subversive.[15]

In late August 1972, Dom Paulo confirmed the military's fears. He announced that the September 3 document, to be titled "The Church and the Sesquicentenary of Brazil's Independence," would ask Brazilians to reflect on the true meaning of independence. In addition, he recalled that the First Republic had left the Church out of the official celebrations of the independence centennial in 1922. "The organizers appeared to have forgotten the contribution of the Church, especially the clergy, in the formation of the Brazilian fatherland," Dom Paulo stated, adding that in 1972 priests were once again misunderstood for their actions in favor of the country's development.[16] These remarks recalled the jailed Dominicans, who during their trial were compared to the many priests who had taken part in Brazil's independence struggle (Simas 1986:111–13).

Another example of the military's concerns was the Church document *Celebrações Litúrgicas* (Liturgical celebrations), a mass booklet specially produced for the sesquicentennial. The CNBB's National Liturgical Commission had officially approved *Celebrações* and was distributing it throughout Brazil for the September 3 mass. The CIE, CENIMAR, both the Rio and the São Paulo offices of the SNI, and General Muricy all reviewed the content after obtaining a copy from Dom Ivo. The armed forces concluded that *Celebrações* was "dangerous, ambiguous, and easily exploitable by subversive elements."[17]

Celebrações contained phrases from liberation theology that could easily be construed as inflammatory challenges to the regime. In one example, a reflection on the classic liberation text of Exodus lamented the exploitation of Brazil's workers. In the workers' mass, the priest asked God to liberate "your sons from all forms of slavery, ancient and modern." The text of a meditation for youth decried social inequities such as "unjust salaries" and "lack of hospital assistance in the interior" and further questioned the values echoed in the government's catchy publicity phrases. "Patriotism is not noise," the text stated. "It doesn't consist only of shouting, in believing oneself bigger than others, in waving flags. If it is genuine, it has a basis in reality and truth" (*Celebrações litúrgicas* 1972:14, 44–53).

A major crisis was in the making. Fearing the impact of *Celebrações* and other statements, members of the Situação protested to the Grupo Religioso and tried to learn more about the Church's intentions. In the final days of August 1972, Muricy met once with both Dom Eugênio and papal nuncio Dom Umberto Mozzoni and three times with Candido Mendes. The general told Candido Mendes the situation was "grave" and might lead to a suspension of the Bipartite. The two sides agreed to an emergency meeting of the Bipartite on August 31, 1972. The encounter took place just as the CNBB's key Comissão Representativa (Representative Commission), which spoke for all bishops, convened in Rio to draft the long-awaited sesquicentennial statement. Going to extremes to maintain secrecy, General Muricy stressed to Candido Mendes that the emergency Bipartite meeting would be "private" and "personal." Dom Aloísio, Dom Ivo, Dom Avelar, Dom Eugênio, Dom Paulo, and Dom Mozzoni represented the Church; General Muricy, Tarcísio Padilha, and an officer each from the SNI and the CIE appeared for the government.[18]

The atmosphere was tense. According to the military's secret notes, General Muricy stated that he was worried with "what might happen at the sesquicentennial commemorations and that it would be very serious and dangerous if there were a clash between the Church and the government." Dom Ivo complained that nobody from the government had ever contacted the Church about collaborating in the celebration. It was too late to change dates. Dom Eugênio agreed.[19]

As attention shifted to the more serious matter of the Church's publications, the initial posturing took a remarkable turn toward conciliation. Dom Ivo informed the commission that, although copies of *Celebrações* had reached every bishop in Brazil, he had requested that they be withheld from the people. Dom Eugênio then revealed what he had earlier told General Muricy in private: the archdioceses of Rio de Janeiro and São Paulo had each printed ninety thousand copies of *Celebrações* but had omitted the Bible commentaries considered most dangerous by the Situação. General Muricy then reviewed a list of other concerns, all addressed in a mollifying manner by the bishops. Dom Avelar, the CNBB vice president, disclosed that he had "personally controlled" the drafting of the episcopal sesquicentennial statement. According to the archbishop, the document was "clean" and "contains nothing that could provide cause for frictions." The prelate further agreed to provide a copy of the statement as soon as it was typed.[20] Thus on September 1, 1972, the Church announced publicly that its document was being substituted with a mere "message" from the CNBB. The conservative daily *O Estado de São Paulo* praised the CNBB's "prudence" in avoiding polemics.[21]

A look at the debates of the Representative Commission further highlights the seriousness of the sesquicentennial dispute. From August 29 to August 31, 1972, the clergymen had wrestled in private with the text of the Independence communiqué. Dom Ivo reminded his colleagues that the content was confidential. The Church's published minutes of the gathering do not mention the Bipartite, but the bishops were clearly concerned with frayed Church-state relations. Opinions ranged from saying nothing to publishing a strong commentary on Brazilian reality. All of the key Grupo Religioso members were there to express the caution advised by the Bipartite. However, Dom Ivo and others stressed that the faithful expected their bishops to speak out at this historic moment. The argument that carried sought to strike a balance between the document's political meaning and the Church's need to follow "supreme criteria," as Father Ávila put it.[22]

The bishops' discretion was a major achievement for the Situação. In mid-September, Dom Luciano José Cabral Duarte—the government's archconservative contact among the bishops—confided privileged information to Professor Padilha about the gathering of the Representative Commission. He stated that a number of bishops had wanted a formal condemnation of torture. Dom Luciano was opposed, arguing that it was tendentious and "incompatible" with an episcopal statement, especially for the sesquicentennial. If the CNBB were to denounce human rights abuses, the bishop stated, it should also call attention to the crimes committed daily in Brazil's cities. The Church had three alternatives. The first two—total indifference toward the government or direct confrontation—contradicted the institution's strategy for survival in even the most totalitarian of societies. The third and best alternative was collaboration. According to Dom Luciano, a number of bishops reacted strongly to this suggestion, but, he reasoned, cooperation was the long-standing policy of the CNBB and the historical tradition of the Brazilian Church. Why should it withhold its contribution just as Brazil was developing into a "great power"? "The government is not the incarnation of evil," he added, reminding his colleagues that the ancient Church had condemned the

Manichaean heresy of dividing the world into good and bad. Dom Luciano's motion carried, leading the bishops to describe the sesquicentennial as a time for defining the "extent and limits of collaboration." Dom Hélder's acceptance of the document, according to Dom Luciano, signified an additional "victory" for the Situação because it compromised the outspoken archbishop's earlier criticisms of the regime.[23]

Nevertheless, the Representative Commission still sought a formula for admonishing the regime on torture. Dom Luciano revealed to Padilha that the bishops designated a subcommittee to study whether the CNBB should publish a document elaborating on Dom Paulo's June statement. The subcommittee vote was three to two in favor. However, Dom Luciano convinced the subcommittee that the small majority did not justify a document. In the eyes of the Situação, yet another crisis had been avoided.[24] Dom Luciano's important role at the assembly of the Representative Commission is supported by the published minutes. They show that some of those present, including Dom Lucas, were concerned that the document's reference to Church-state collaboration would give the impression that the Church wanted a formal concordat with the state. The text was then modified to prevent this interpretation.[25]

The Situação's internal report on the emergency Bipartite conference spoke triumphantly. It had obtained the suspension of controversial passages in *Celebrações*, the moderation of the CNBB's Independence Day message, and copies of five Church documents *before* publication. The Bipartite had achieved the regime's goals of avoiding conflict and improving Church-state relations. After nearly two years of encounters, the positive results were "undeniable." Demonstrating the Situação's growing confidence, Professor Padilha even suggested that future episcopal statements be examined by the officers "not as a form of censorship" but to avoid new misunderstandings.[26] In effect, he wanted a military veto on the Church's actions.

The military postmortem further noted that the "moderating action" of Dom Eugênio and the nuncio had influenced Dom Paulo and helped create "an environment of calm" in São Paulo. According to Dom Paulo, it was only a rumor that the archdiocesan newspaper *O São Paulo* would attack the government in its September 3 edition, for he himself had reviewed it carefully. On September 2 he sent two copies to the Situação. Dom Paulo also assured General Muricy that a new edition of *O Clero e a Independência* (The clergy and Independence), published fifty years earlier by Archbishop Dom Duarte Leopoldo e Silva, did not contain suspected criticisms of the regime. Dom Paulo added that he expected the São Paulo commemorations to be peaceful. The Grupo da Situação was convinced that the archbishop truly desired better relations with the São Paulo military command. During the gathering, General Muricy had seized the opportunity to ask the archbishop about his relations with General Souza Mello. Dom Paulo responded that they were neither good nor bad, as he had yet to have contact with the officer despite three visits to Second Army headquarters. He maintained that "the problem was still one of communication." The Situação's report recommended that efforts be made to eliminate the "prejudice" between the two men. It was a crucial moment. Dom Paulo had now participated in two Bipartite meetings and had described them as "very useful." In the Situação's words, he was ready for "approximation" with the regime and "to be talked into joining the group of the moderate bishops." Dom Luciano confirmed the military's conclusions, asserting that Dom Paulo was a serious but "naive" man influenced by leftists who had begun to abandon him once he adopted "new" and presumably less radical attitudes."[27]

Yet the emergency parley also confirmed that other bishops were uncooperative. The military report singled out Dom Lucas and Dom Ivo as "not meriting full confidence."[28] The former oversaw the highly critical *O São Paulo*, while the latter was combative and publicly deprecated the regime's economic policies.

Following the meeting, Professor Padilha took Dom Ivo to task for asserting that Church and state were in "confrontation." Padilha gave a tendentious though instructive commentary on the hierarchy's outlook since 1964. The Church was criticizing the government "as if that were its principal mission, an attitude all the more strange if one observed in the recent past, immediately before the Revolution, the ostensive presence of high prelates of the Church at palace banquets." The brusque shift of the Church to the opposition was "illogical" in the context of Brazilian history, Padilha said. Moreover, the bishops' public declarations were unjustifiable in light of the Bipartite's existence. Nevertheless, Dom Luciano noted that even Dom Ivo had "improved" from his "initial intransigence."[29]

The resolution of the sesquicentennial crisis drove home yet another point for the Situação: that informal contacts between Bipartite members could bring as much success as the encounters themselves. The Situação's report observed that personal communication helped plan effective strategy because it allowed for greater frankness than the larger, more formal conferences, where rivalries, individual interpretations, and institutional concerns could impede candor. The Situação, of course, had to choose the right people. Dom Eugênio, Dom Mozzoni, and Candido Mendes had each used private conversations to settle differences.[30] Their efforts largely explained why the bishops made concessions during the emergency meeting.

Why, in the final analysis, did the bishops give in with respect to their publications? Did General Muricy's fear of an Independence Day clash suggest knowledge of an impending assault by the repressive forces should the Church choose to radicalize? The records do not say. Moreover, if he knew, General Muricy could not reveal such information without seriously compromising the regime. It was perhaps best to leave concern in that ambiguous region between veiled threat and friendly warning. Either way, the climate of terror in Brazil and especially São Paulo was sufficient to keep the two sides talking. Although they disagreed on many points, their common denominator was to avoid conflict. To do so the bishops tempered their public criticisms with private understandings.[31]

The Bipartite's orchestrations remained unknown to most Brazilians, and the week of independence celebrations took place without disturbance. Foreign journalists reported favorably on the events. On September 3, 1972, the CNBB held its national sesquicentennial mass in the Praça da Sé, the large plaza before the cathedral in downtown São Paulo. According to *O São Paulo*, between sixty and seventy thousand of the faithful attended, while people across Brazil went to other liturgies. Unlike the controversial texts of *Celebrações*, the biblical readings did not contain political connotations.[32] At the start of Independence week, President Médici had attended the Te Deum held at the National Congress in Brasília. On September 3 he went to São Paulo to watch a horse race but did not appear at the Praça da Sé. On the seventh he attended the official ceremonies, including a parade of heavy armament and eighteen thousand members of the military on the Avenida Paulista in the heart of the capital. The apparent calm was contradicted by the contrast in styles and symbols chosen by the clergy and the armed forces. Yet, in the words of Archbishop Dom Carlos Carmelo Vasconcelos Motta to General Corrêa, Church-state relations were "all okay."[33]

Dom Fernando Gomes: Defining Opposition

The participation of Dom Fernando Gomes dos Santos at the Bipartite illustrates how a bishop publicly opposed to the regime could act quite differently during dialogue with its representatives. At the invitation of the bishops, Dom Fernando took part in a special meeting of the Bipartite in August 1973 in an attempt to resolve tensions between him and the authorities in the archdiocese of Goiânia, the capital of the state of Goiás in the Center-West region of Brazil. Dom Fernando came to an understanding with the Grupo da Situação and, to its satisfaction, dampened his fiery rhetoric.

Dom Fernando had impeccable progressive credentials. He worked in his native Northeast, the Church's most reform-minded region in the 1940s and 1950s, until his promotion to the archbishopric of Goiânia in 1957. A supporter of Catholic Action, Dom Fernando belonged to the core group of socially conscious bishops who controlled the CNBB from its inception in 1952 until 1964. That year he lost the election for the CNBB presidency as the conservatives for the first time took power of the conference. Dom Fernando welcomed the coup (Duarte 1996, ch. 1), but he vehemently opposed the laudatory aspects of the CNBB's postcoup declaration. He continued to support basic social reform and defended Dom Hélder. In the words of Carlos Rodrigues Brandão, an acute observer of religious life in the Center-West, Goiânia became "one of the most courageous and persistent Catholic centers of active resistance to the military regime."[34] As for many, 1968 was a defining moment for Dom Fernando. In the aftermath of the death of student Edson Luís in Rio, officials in Goiânia harshly repressed student demonstrations, invaded the cathedral while youths met with the archbishop, and shot several people, killing one. Dom Fernando broke off all dialogue with local officials and sent an angry telegram to President Costa e Silva demanding an end to the "sacrilegious arrogance" of the authorities. In the 1970s Dom Fernando firmly backed neighboring colleagues in their disputes with the military. In 1975 he supported the formation of the Comissão Pastoral da Terra (CPT; Pastoral Land Commission) in Goiânia. The CPT was one of the most important pastoral innovations of the post–Vatican II era, and it clashed frequently with the dictatorship over agrarian reform.[35]

In 1973 Dom Fernando came into the sights of the Grupo da Situação. Marking the twenty-fifth anniversary of the U.N. Declaration of Human Rights, on May 6, 1973, the CNBB and regional groups of bishops published documents that once again focused international attention on Brazil. In their "Marginalization of the People," for instance, Dom Fernando and the other bishops of the Center-West declared capitalism the "worst evil." In one scholar's analysis, this and a similar pronouncement by the bishops of the Northeast "were probably the most radical statements ever issued by a group of bishops anywhere in the world" (Mainwaring 1986:93). The Grupo da Situação analyzed these documents carefully and debated them with the Grupo Religioso.[36]

Throughout this period, Dom Fernando acted as a political *padrinho* (godfather) to Dom Pedro Casaldáliga. Dom Fernando ordained his younger colleague bishop in 1971 and defended him against attacks from the right. In 1972 the two men joined other Center-West bishops in supporting the São Paulo bishops' declaration against torture.[37] They maintained close ties throughout the ensuing years of

Dom Pedro Casaldáliga was a frequent target of the regime for his work among the posseiros.

conflict, and Dom Fernando kept the junior bishop informed about the Bipartite talks (Dom Pedro Casaldáliga interview).

Dom Pedro was a major target of the repression. In the view of the generals he typified the radical Catholic duped into aiding the Communist movement. A Spanish missionary and poet, he had once been a religious conservative. In Brazil, he opposed the regime and became a prophetlike leader of the progressive Church. He called his first pastoral letter "The Church of the Amazon in Conflict with the Latifundium and Social Marginalization," a 120-page booklet describing the atrocities of the region. In the prelacy of São Félix do Araguaia, Mato Grosso, Dom Pedro and his pastoral agents defended Amerindians and *posseiros* (squatters with legitimate claims to land) from the Northeast and elsewhere who fought over land with the government, agribusiness firms, and ranchers. In many cases the posseiros had escaped from ranches that used forced labor. In 1976 Dom Pedro himself was nearly killed. In a case of mistaken identity the police murdered Jesuit Father João Bosco

Penido Burnier instead after he and Dom Pedro had protested the imprisonment and torture of people in São Félix. Dom Pedro also drew the ire of archconservative Catholics.[38]

In the early 1970s rural conflict increased in the Center-West, the Amazon, and the Northeast. A reign of terror set in at São Félix. In 1972 the Army staged antiguerrilla training exercises there and in surrounding villages.[39] This presence formed the southern flank of a secret jungle war by the CIE against guerrillas along the Araguaia River in the neighboring states of Pará and Goiás. Five thousand soldiers took part. The Army arrested and tortured many noncombatants, including a priest and a nun, and harassed Dom Estevão Cardoso Avelar, the bishop of Marabá. Only after several years of fighting in Pará did the Army defeat what was the best-organized guerrilla force of the authoritarian era.[40]

The regime suspected that other fighters were operating in São Félix. Indeed, the Church's consciousness-raising efforts strikingly resembled the political tactics of the guerrillas (Richopo 1987:74–75). The regime worked to soften military presence by setting up local health clinics. In June and July 1973, it sent hundreds more soldiers and policemen into the area in an attempt to neutralize the pastoral work of Dom Pedro and his followers. The assault paved the way for further aggression by *grileiros* (claim jumpers) and large firms moving in to dominate the area. The security forces abused peasants and Church militants, and they put Dom Pedro under house arrest after searching his home. The soldiers took eight prisoners to the barracks at Campo Grande, where all were tortured to force confessions about the Church's supposed ties to guerrillas. Dom Ivo, Dom Fernando, and the papal nuncio traveled to São Félix to review the situation along with government and military officials, but it was weeks later before the prisoners went free.[41]

The Grupo da Situação carefully monitored the situation in São Félix. At the July 23, 1973, Bipartite meeting it criticized Dom Pedro's ideas and actions. General Muricy accused priests and lay activists of "agitation" in São Félix. The Situação had obtained copies of dozens of pages of letters, legal papers, internal Church bulletins, petitions, the transcript of a tape of Dom Pedro's ordination of a radical priest, and other material seized by the police.[42] Muricy had Major Leone da Silveira Lee of the CIE read "compromising" passages from these documents in an attempt to discredit Dom Pedro and his pastoral agents.

According to the Situação, the documents proved that the Church in São Félix intended to mount a revolutionary counterattack on the government forces. Among other charges, the clergy had asserted the right to "excommunicate" squatters unwilling to cooperate with the prelacy's land strategy. Even worse, Muricy said, Dom Pedro had usurped the country's legislative powers by drafting a "Law of the Squatter." This document defined the rights and obligations of posseiros so as to assure possession of their lands. It reminded Muricy of the politicized literacy pamphlet he had repressed in the Northeast before the coup. Major Lee added that Dom Pedro was trying to incite the populace.[43] One "psalm" penned at São Félix read:

> Free me, O Lord,
> From the DOPS, from the OBAN and CODI, from the SNI.
> Free me from their councils of war,
> From the anger of their judges and their soldiers.
> You judge the great powers.
> You are the one who judges the ministers of justice and the supreme courts of justice.
> Defend me, O Lord, from false charges.
> Defend the exiled and the deported, those accused of espionage and sabotage.[44]

In the eyes of the Situação, Dom Pedro simply did not understand the nature of the regime. While the bishop protested the conviction of peasant sympathizer Father Jentel (see chapter 6), he ignored the verdicts of innocence in the cases of dozens of other priests.[45]

Although the seized papers clearly substantiated intensive Church efforts to organize and minister to the posseiros, they offered no actual evidence of violent subversion. However, Dom Avelar admitted that the notion of "excommunications" was "ridiculous." Dom Ivo agreed but also severely criticized the military for beating the priests and detaining the eight individuals, whom he classified as disappeared. Moreover, Dom Ivo had personally complained to federal officials about the situation in São Félix. "All the territory of Mato Grosso has been sold to various business groups, including foreigners," the bishop added, noting that Dom Pedro would not give up his "option" to defend the Amerindians and the posseiros.[46]

In late July 1973, Dom Fernando issued his own scathing attack against the government. Like Candido Mendes, he had long believed in the possibility of Church-regime collaboration. For Dom Fernando, the prime concern was not the type of regime, but the Church's right to guide Brazilian progress (Duarte 1996, ch. 1). However, the repression was eroding that hope. Circulated in Goiânia and to Brazil's bishops, Dom Fernando's pastoral letter baldly asserted that the regime based itself on the use of force, spying, control of the media, the cover-up of criminal activity, and the negation of such basic rights as habeas corpus. The administration valued people and religion only to the extent that they served its interests. The letter also demonstrated that although Dom Fernando was associated with leftist causes he outright rejected Communism. Citing papal encyclicals, Dom

Fernando affirmed that Communism was "intrinsically evil" because of its substitution of the party for divine revelation. However, in combating this threat the regime itself had adopted "Communist morals." This was an "arrogant but disguised Communism, with the aggravating factor of not using this name but projecting it on whoever does not make himself subservient." Thus the regime banished, tortured, and killed people who had never been Communists but who had refused to accept an "unethical and unreligious" system. Although the Church adhered to no party and accepted the regime as a "reality," it would continue to denounce these "excesses" and to fight for social justice through the *conscientização* of the poor.[47]

Another crisis was at hand. Despite his rhetoric, Dom Fernando was still seen as linked with the left. Right-wing congressman Clóvis Stenzel, the vice leader of the proregime party and a member of the Chamber of Deputies' National Security Commission, wrote a newspaper column casting Dom Fernando as another Dom Hélder trying to "Marxicize" the Church.[48] At the same July Bipartite meeting at which the São Félix incidents were debated, General Muricy called Dom Fernando's letter "a very violent document against the government." Major Lee added that he had warned Dom Fernando not to publish the document because of the "problems" it could cause. (Lee had surreptitiously obtained a draft of the letter in early June.) Worried about possible repercussions both in Brazil and abroad, General Muricy and other members of the Situação demanded that the Grupo Religioso prevent further distribution of the pastoral letter. The officers reminded the bishops that the CNBB had requested its members not to make individual statements. Candido Mendes and Dom Ivo agreed, and the former proposed a special meeting of the Bipartite to include Dom Fernando.[49]

Fearing his arrest, some of Dom Fernando's followers opposed his trip to Rio (Gomes 1982:240). Nevertheless, as the faithful held prayer vigils for his safety, Dom Fernando arrived at the Bipartite without incident. There he elaborated on his accusations. The regime had declared more than anybody that "God is Brazilian" and that "Our Lady had saved Brazil," yet it had reneged on its promise to carry out the basic social reforms proposed by the CNBB. If the Revolution had espoused the spirit of Vatican II, it could have made Brazil "the most vigorous nation in the world." Dom Fernando accused the Revolution of falling under the influence of the Masons. The struggle between the Church and freemasonry had become largely irrelevant by the 1920s, but Dom Fernando raised the specter of the Religious Question as a way of centering discussion on the regime's systematic violation of Church interests.[50]

In response, General Muricy stated that Dom Fernando had given an inaccurate picture of the administration by "generalizing" about certain incidents. His letter contained "poison" against the government. In fact, the Revolution was indeed working to solve Brazil's social problems. It had never stopped battling Communism. The restriction on habeas corpus existed only for subversives, Muricy reminded the bishops. He explained that "there have been some excesses among the enforcement echelons, but the government has acted energetically against the excesses. . . . Sometimes it becomes necessary to imprison elements in order to discover the 'network of collaborators.'" The administration ultimately wanted to provide "conditions of tranquillity for the government and for private businesses to think and to work." The subversives, however, upset the people's right to peace. Dom Fernando needed to see the Bipartite's efforts at "conciliatory solutions," Muricy said. Repeating one of the main requests of the Grupo da Situação, he urged the bishops to register their complaints directly with the authorities to avoid further political agitation. Finally, he asked Dom Fernando what he hoped to achieve by publishing the pastoral letter—to fight with the government, or to improve the lives of his flock?[51] General Muricy had conveniently reduced the issue of Church-state relations to one of politics versus religion. The Church should concentrate on the latter, quietly smoothing over its political differences with the regime as the two collaborated to solve the country's problems.

Dom Fernando temporized. He was happy to take part in the Bipartite, he said. Yes, he had generalized in the pastoral letter. But he was not accusing the government of any specific violations. The problem was not President Médici or his government; it was the regime's philosophy and the fact that some officials refused to take action against abuses. As for the regime's "Communism," he meant it in the "practical" sense of arrogating all power, not in a Marxist-Leninist sense. He spoke as a pastor, not an economist, sociologist, or even theologian. "A bishop is a kind of sandwich," Dom Fernando explained, adding that pressure from different groups shaped his attitudes.[52]

The archbishop retreated on several fronts. He read a prepared statement softening the assertions of the pastoral letter. The Church-state conflict had traumatized Brazil, yet the Bipartite could repair the damage, he said, underlining the need for continued dialogue and "respectful collaboration." He cited Christ's oft-quoted dictum to "give unto Caesar what is Caesar's, and give unto God what is God's." Church and state had interdependent values, but they were autonomous. General Muricy concurred with Dom Fernando's analysis.[53]

Dom Fernando temporized still further by emphasizing his anti-Communist

A leading progressive, Dom Fernando Gomes nevertheless told the Bipartite that the military should retain power because of civilians' inability to govern.

stance. He affirmed that before the coup no one had fought Communism in Goiás more than he himself. He had opposed Luís Carlos Prestes's visit to Goiânia and gone on radio to rebut the PCB leader's speech. Before the coup, a group of Communists and students had even performed a symbolic burial of the bishop. At the time of his 1968 break with the Goiás authorities he had suggested that the police arrest Communist agitators in Goiânia. Dom Fernando therefore rejected as illogical the allegations by military leaders of Communist infiltration in the Church. Nothing denigrated a bishop's dignity more than an accusation of Communism![54]

Most significant, the archbishop expressed *support* for the government. He asserted that the initial "rigor" of the regime was justified. He did not like a weak government. Moreover, though he disagreed with much of AI-5, Dom Fernando had obeyed the decree by refraining from public statements. For instance, he spoke in defense of political prisoners and the desaparecidos only when implored by their families, and then only within the walls of the cathedral. He had further avoided political involvement by refusing a request by MDB politicians to mediate between them and the governor of Goiás. Finally, Dom Fernando agreed with General

Muricy that for the time being the military should keep power, for the civilians were still not ready to run the country.[55]

The contrast between the pastoral letter and Dom Fernando's remarks at the Bipartite is striking. Stated publicly, Dom Fernando's words would have jeopardized his leadership in the progressive Church. Yet as a bishop he was bound to see the anti-Communist struggle as legitimate. In his view Brazil needed a strong government in order to become a more stable, just nation. On this score he agreed with the many Brazilian workers who believed that an authoritarian regime promoted their interests better than a democratic one (Cohen 1989:116). The difficulty resided in the harm done to Brazilians by the anti-Communist struggle. Rather than true reform, the regime had turned to violence. Dom Fernando had to reconcile the quest for social change with the drawbacks of a strong state. Publicly he attacked the government as being inconsistent with the Church's teachings on social justice, whereas privately he backed it as the only way to change Brazil. Dom Fernando was expressing the many voices of a bishop: patriot, anti-Communist, religious leader, politician. Circumstances determined which spoke most strongly at any particular moment.

The Situação believed that the Bipartite had again alleviated serious tensions. In the military's interpretation, Dom Fernando had accepted the critique of his pastoral letter. Although he refused to withdraw it, he agreed to publish a partial retraction—the more "judicious" statement read at the Bipartite.[56] Dom Fernando also stated that he found the meeting "useful" and "agreeable." The Situação concluded that he desired to live "in harmony with the government."[57] In addition, General Muricy arranged for the authorities in Goiás to apologize to Dom Fernando for past aggressions (Muricy 1993:662).

As in other cases, however, the military expressed skepticism about Dom Fernando's ability to comprehend its policies. The Grupo da Situação's final report stated that he did not understand Marxist-Leninism, subversion, or national security. The officers partially attributed the conflict with Dom Fernando to personal factors—namely, his inability to get along with the authorities in Goiânia. Thus, ending the discord required a plan of able "human relations" in which the archbishop could be brought back into dialogue with local officials.[58]

Salvaging the Moral Concordat

A central theme of the Bipartite was the attempt to preserve the moral concordat. Although the regime desired their political blessing, the bishops in turn sought to safeguard privileges traditionally considered crucial to the Church's welfare. Because of the political constraints and repression of the Médici years, efforts at cooperation often fell short. But history is not about results only; intentions count too. The attempts to salvage traditional Church-state ties thus bear investigation.

Political Restraint and Saving a Subsidy

The moral concordat provided the Church with financial assistance for its myriad of educational and social assistance works. After 1964, the state began to cut aid to seminaries, Catholic universities, and other initiatives such as the Basic Education Movement, but, interested in placating the bishops, the military leadership continued spending on other Church projects. For example, the government underwrote the building of the national cathedral in Brasília (Serbin 1995:162, 165).

In July 1971, Dom Aloísio and Dom Ivo used their Bipartite ties to save state support for one of the Church's most important schools, the Pontifício Colégio Pio Brasileiro. The Pio was inaugurated in 1934 as a residence and spiritual center for Brazilian seminarians studying at the Gregorian University in Rome. It prepared Brazil's ecclesiastical elite to occupy important posts as seminary professors and diocesan administrators. Several dozen Pio graduates rose to the episcopate. Dom Ivo, for instance, had lived there in the early 1950s while he was studying for his degree and then his doctorate in theology at the Gregorian. In the 1950s and 1960s, the Brazilian state gave the Pio hundreds of thousands of dollars (Serbin 1995:162). Dom Aloísio and Dom Ivo feared that Médici would veto the annual subsidy, even though it had already been approved by the Ministry of Foreign Affairs. Shortly after the fourth meeting of the Bipartite, they sought General Muricy's assistance.[59] A few days later, Dom Ivo sent the general a letter explaining the Pio's importance. "As the largest Catholic nation in the world, Brazil should also maintain this institute in Rome," Dom Ivo wrote.[60]

Since 1964, however, the Pio had become snarled in the same combination of ecclesial renewal and opposition politics that involved many Church militants. As the former rector of the highly politicized seminary at Viamão, Rio Grande do Sul, Dom Ivo knew well the difficulty of supervising young men in an atmosphere of antiregime student agitation and post–Vatican II deemphasis on discipline. The local political police invaded Viamão on several occasions to interrogate seminarians and to search for subversive literature (Serbin 1993b:392–93, 395, 405, 412, 417, 428–32), and the SNI collected information on the school (Fontoura interview). In Rome, Ambassador Jobim investigated but could not substantiate allegations that the Pio "lodged subversive elements on the way through Italy to the Soviet Union and Czechoslovakia." Nevertheless, Dom Ivo and Dom Aloísio admitted to General Muricy that, unbeknownst to some ecclesiastical authorities, the Pio operated as a "meeting point for elements that were criticizing the Brazilian government."[61] Moreover, the school was inviting progressive bishops as speakers (Gervásio Queiroga interview).

Dom Ivo and Dom Aloísio emphasized a "new orientation" for the Pio. The rector, for instance, had already rejected the application of a Dominican priest who had been denounced by the regime. Concerned about the youthful excesses of their students, the school's directors shifted admissions toward older, more mature candidates who would not abuse the "liberty" of studying abroad.[62]

The regime worked with the Church to change the Pio's image. Few other countries had a special residence in Rome for seminarians. Cardinals, bishops, ambassadors, and other leading Brazilians traditionally paid visits to the Colégio. It was a Brazilian showcase. During the height of the IBRADES crisis, Dom Agnelo Rossi thus decided that the Pio should house a Center for Brazilian Studies to combat the country's bad reputation for incidents of torture and attacks on the Church. He was shocked at the number of priests, sisters, and Brazilian youths in Rome "poisoned by distorted information about our country." Dom Agnelo called for all Brazilians to contribute documentation to the Center.[63] General Muricy solicited bibliography and other materials from military and civilian officials. The São Paulo state government, the Empresa Brasileira de Turismo (EMBRATUR; Brazilian Federal Tourist Agency), and the SNI sent Brazilian artisanry and government publications. In addition, Colonel Fernando Cerqueira Lima, a military attaché at the Brazilian embassy in Rome, requested additional shipments of "books of good ideological content." After its inauguration in November 1972, Brazilians and foreigners alike visited the center and purchased some of the new items.[64] Brazilian priests and seminarians, however, opposed the initiative because of Dom Agnelo's conservatism.[65]

The efforts of Muricy and the bishops were partially successful. The general's papers indicate that he pursued the matter of the subsidy with Médici, Foreign Minister Mário Gibson Barboza, or some other high administration official. In November 1971, Jesuit Father Frederico Laufer, the rector of the Pio, wrote General Muricy to thank him for obtaining "part of the sum appropriated in the budget" for 1970–1971. "We have the sincere desire to dedicate ourselves to the good of the Brazilian people in the way that the Church has worked for the nation since 1500." Nevertheless, with less government funding the Pio entered into a financial crisis, eventually forcing the episcopate to reconsider its decision not to accept donations from the faithful. By 1975 the government had completely cut off funding. Like the Brazilian Church as a whole, the Pio began seeking aid from the wealthy Catholic community of Germany.[66]

The most significant aspect was not the money, however, but the bishops' expectations. Despite the CNBB's growing criticism of the regime, they still sought the kinds of benefits routinely awarded at the height of the moral concordat. As a moral pillar of Brazilian society, the Church believed it had a right to such privileges no matter what its theological position. The bishops viewed the Bipartite as the channel for safeguarding such important institutional interests. The Pio moderated its stance, and in return the government maintained part of its public subsidy.

Anti-Communism, Population Control, and Divorce

The Bipartite touched on other matters crucial to the Church's religious identity and institutional interests. On some issues, the two sides easily agreed. One was anti-Communism. In the 1970s the Church allied with the left in the struggle for democracy, and liberation theologians and radical bishops embraced socialism as the solution to Brazil's socioeconomic ills. But as the case of Dom Fernando illustrates, even some progressives strongly opposed Communism. Indeed, at the final meeting of the Bipartite in August 1974, the Grupo Religioso wanted to know the motives for the Geisel government's decision to break with Taiwan and to reestablish ties with Communist China. General Muricy explained that China's enormous size and membership in the U.N. Security Council made diplomatic recognition inevitable. Brazil, however, would not accept China's ideology. China offered Brazil new markets, Tarcísio Padilha noted. This was "healthy pragmatism." Though not opposed to relations with China, Dom Avelar did not miss the irony. In a forum in which the Grupo da Situação had so often alleged Communist infiltration in the Church, he turned the tables: How did the new policy square with the regime's concern with Communist revolutionary warfare in Brazil? The only response that Padilha could muster was that Brazil remained vigilant against Communism.[67]

Noting Geisel's policy shift on China, the Grupo Religioso suggested that the government study the possibility of reopening diplomatic relations with Cuba. General Muricy's papers do not offer details of the discussion. At any rate, the military opposed such a move. Only in 1986, a year after the armed forces left power, did Brazil reestablish ties with Cuba.

Population control and the family were other critical topics. Here the Church used the Bipartite not to temporize its public positions, but to reinforce its role as Brazil's moral guardian. In the post–World War II era, papal pronouncements came to advocate family planning but still kept the prohibitions on abortion and artificial methods of contraception. Unexpectedly, in 1968 Paul VI braked the tendency toward a more liberal birth-control teaching by reaffirming the ban on artificial methods in his famous encyclical *Humanae Vitae*. As elsewhere, this document stirred negative reactions in Brazil, which was undergoing the dramatic impact of the sexual revolution and the introduction of the birth control pill. Castello Branco, Costa e Silva, and Médici publicly backed the Church's teachings, and Costa e Silva bestowed praise on the pontiff for condemning "anti-Christian methods." The Geisel administration kept in step by following CNBB recommendations for the first World Population Conference held in Bucharest in 1974. For Candido Mendes, who had attended part of the Bucharest conference, the position of Brazil and the Vatican were "most difficult . . . because international feminist movements have a tremendous opposition against the ideas of both." Nevertheless, more than ever, Brazil and the Church stood publicly together on the population issue.[68]

However, the official statements cloaked what was actually an ambiguous military policy about population growth. On the one hand, appealing for national security, the regime joined the left, the Church, and other groups in denouncing alleged international conspiracies to stop Brazil from populating its vast uninhabited territories. On the other hand, technocrats and some military leaders asserted that unbridled demographic growth actually created national insecurity because it outstripped job creation. In actuality the regime took a laissez-faire approach. In 1965, for example, it permitted a group of physicians to open the Sociedade de Bem-Estar Familiar do Brasil (BEMFAM; Brazilian Society for Family Welfare). BEMFAM started dozens of clinics throughout the country and distributed tens of thousands of birth-control devices. In 1971 BEMFAM obtained official nonprofit status, an important advantage for any social service organization operating in Brazil. BEMFAM received further permission to sign agreements with state governments. Meanwhile, commercialization of the pill spread during the Médici years, and the Geisel government angered the bishops by actually distributing it for free.[69]

Geisel was Brazil's first Protestant president to serve a full term. Nevertheless, like his predecessors, he sought good relations with the hierarchy. The president would accept the "disinterested collaboration" of "intermediate organizations." He would refuse their interference in affairs pertaining only to the government, however. He would admit no criticism or "insistent pressures" from those outside the public sphere.[70] Geisel's words both encouraged and restricted the moral concordat. Thus the Grupo da Situação concluded that the bishops might use the Bipartite to circumvent Geisel's constraints.[71]

As Geisel's government got under way in 1974, the Grupo Religioso proposed that Church and state conduct joint studies or collaborate in a number of areas: the environment, the energy crisis, Brazil's position with respect to Portuguese colonialism, basic education, the problem of the Amerindians, land conflicts, and the fight against drug abuse. Population control and BEMFAM stood out prominently among the bishops' concerns. The military interpreted the bishops' sudden desire for greater cooperation as a reaction to President Geisel's inaugural message.

They used the Bipartite to maintain the pressure against BEMFAM. At the August 1974 meeting, Dom Ivo pressed for continued state adherence to Church positions on population growth.[72] His statements echoed protests by the CNBB and smaller groups of bishops against BEMFAM. In May, for instance, Dom Eugênio defined the population problem as religious and ethical, but also as economic, political, and social. "What engenders misery is not the fertility of the miserable, but social iniquity," one of Dom Eugênio's assistants wrote in an official archdiocesan study criticizing BEMFAM's use of Church social doctrine to justify its activities. Besides, the study noted, Brazil did not fall into the category of countries with "uncontrolled growth," for the 1970 census had already indicated deceleration.[73] A month later, a group of sixteen progressive bishops asked the CNBB to help divert attention away from "moralizing" on the issue and onto its socioeconomic and political roots.[74] Above all the Church wanted families to be able to look out for the welfare of their children. Therefore, Dom Ivo asked whether the Brazilian government could deal with the specter raised at Bucharest of worldwide social collapse if growing populations could not be fed. Adopting the national security position, Colonel Mário Orlando Ribeiro Sampaio of the SNI seconded Dom Ivo's concerns. After the meeting, the Grupo da Situação noted that population themes provided a platform for Church-state cooperation.[75]

The bishops' opposition to the prodivorce movement in the Brazilian Congress provided another example of Church pressure. Since the 1930s the state had fulfilled the Church's requests to keep divorce out of Brazilian law. In 1960 and 1962, annulment laws failed to pass because of Church opposition, and in 1971, the Médici administration instructed the progovernment bloc in Congress to vote against a similar measure. Congress finally passed legislation in 1977, but it was a compromise, allowing a person to divorce only once. The Congress also rejected a proposal to hold a national plebiscite on divorce. In both instances the Church's influence played a major role (Ribeiro and Ribeiro 1994:101, 112, 119–20, 126–27). Throughout this period the hierarchy publicly opposed divorce. At the August 1974 Bipartite meeting, the bishops also pressured behind the scenes: Dom Ivo expressed dismay about the twenty-one divorce bills pending before the legislature, and General Muricy promised to relay the Church's concerns to the government and to request that Justice Minister Armando Falcão consult the CNBB about the issue.[76]

Protecting the Catholic Monopoly

The bishops also pushed for continued recognition of Catholicism as Brazil's semi-official religion. The Grupo da Situação readily agreed. In the post–Vatican II era the Church became committed to ecumenical relations with other religions, but no representatives of non-Catholic organizations took part at the Bipartite. After World War II, Protestant Pentecostal as well as spiritist religions (especially the Afro-Brazilian Umbanda) had increased in popularity. At the August 1973 meeting of the Bipartite, Dom Aloísio referred to the "proliferation" of these religions. General Muricy and the SNI's Colonel Sampaio pointed out that the spiritists had made substantial inroads into the armed forces. Tarcísio Padilha warned the bishops that the Church must not be surpassed by its competitors. In addition, a small schismatic church known as the Igreja Católica Brasileira (Brazilian Catholic Church) had also emerged. When Dom Ivo informed the Bipartite that the CNBB would meet to discuss the breakaway organization's "interference in the activities of the Apostolic Roman Catholic Church," General Muricy agreed with the need to react "against that false church."[77]

The disagreement over a new church building in Brasília illustrated the Church's efforts to retain its religious hegemony. In the final months of the Médici administration, Army Minister Orlando Geisel decreed that the military would build an ecumenical temple at which soldiers of all faiths could worship. An agnostic who showed little sympathy for the Church, Geisel did not consult the bishops on his decision. They immediately opposed the universal character of the temple. The hierarchy had already convinced the government to make the new national cathedral Catholic rather than ecumenical. Now, as Ernesto Geisel took the reins of power, Dom José Newton de Almeida Baptista Pereira, the archbishop of Brasília, spearheaded the effort to change the plans for the new temple.[78] His involvement added political overtones to the dispute, for in 1964 he had been accused of Communism and of defending João Goulart in a national radio broadcast on the day of the coup. Dom Newton complained to President Geisel that the proposed temple should be strictly Catholic. Other prelates echoed his sentiments at the March 1974 Bipartite meeting. Dom Aloísio, for instance, stated that the idea could lead people into thinking the inconceivable: that diverse religions could celebrate their faiths in a common ceremony. Furthermore, Dom Ivo feared that the administration of the temple would be ambiguously defined and therefore proposed that it come under the exclusive control of the Catholic Church.[79]

President Geisel ordered Army Minister Sylvio Frota to negotiate a solution with the Church. In the meantime, the Bipartite also determined that Major Lee of the CIE would contact Dom Newton. Lee was perhaps the Army's leading expert on the Church. He studied the different factions within the institution and familiarized himself with canon law. As a member of the CIE Lee worked in the Army minister's cabinet. He joined Colonel Octávio Costa—Médici's public relations director and Frota's intermediary with Dom Newton—in the difficult negotiations with the archbishop. For the two officers, the situation was especially sensitive because they had to find a solution agreeable not only to General Frota but also to former minister Orlando Geisel. Ultimately, the two sides struck a compromise. The Church could use only removable religious images in the ecumenical building. However, alongside this structure the military would construct a small chapel strictly for Catholic services. In addition, Dom Newton and the officers settled on a name for the complex that implied religious neutrality as opposed to sharing. Thus what began as a "temple" became a compound designated as the Oratório do Soldado (Soldier's oratory).[80] The outcome was an important symbolic victory for the Church and indicative of its power to negotiate through the Bipartite.

The Church further exercised its influence to gain crucial access to the airwaves. During the Médici years Dom Aloísio sought out Colonel Costa to request that the government cede the time for its public service television spots for advertisements of the CNBB's annual Lenten Campanha da Fraternidade (Fraternity campaign). The Campanha involved a religious theme as well as an important fund-raising component. The government obliged Dom Aloísio's requests.[81]

Defending Ecclesiastical Honor

The defense of Church interests included the preservation of ecclesiastical honor, an intangible yet highly important component of the moral concordat. Bishops were religious authorities but also public figures and leaders. The military attacks on them after 1964 raised doubts about their public prominence, not to mention the feelings of anger, bewilderment, and hurt that many must have experienced after years of respect and collaboration with the state and the military. The Bipartite focused on several such cases. The most telling involved Dom Avelar.

The archbishop primate was a consummate moderate with a curious mixture of aristocratic airs and popular appeal. A native of the northeastern state of Alagoas, he came from a family of sugar plantation owners. In the 1930s and 1940s, Father Avelar worked in prestigious jobs such as seminary professor and secretary of the bishopric of Aracaju, Sergipe. He was only thirty-four when the Holy See named him bishop of the interior town of Petrolina, Pernambuco, in 1946. Dom Avelar culled numerous honors reserved for the elite, for example, membership in the Academy of Letters of both the states of Bahia and Piauí (CNBB 1984:83–84). In the 1960s and 1970s, he had close ties to the military and even spoke at the ESG. Despite his patrician status, Dom Avelar showed concern for social issues and had a great following among the people. As a priest he set up an organization to aid domestic servants and became a leader of Catholic Action, and in Petrolina (1946–1955) and later Teresina (1955–1970) he worked among the inhabitants of the rugged backlands. Dom Avelar was known especially for his ability in sacred oratory. Before a crowd or on the radio he would begin speaking softly and then raise his voice in a dynamic way that captivated his listeners. This was a natural talent that the bishop shared with his brother Teotônio, a senator who left the progovernment party in 1979 to give blustering speeches against the regime for the prodemocracy movement. Dom Avelar's aristocratic manners and traditional rhetorical style caused progressive clerics to reject him. Yet in the Northeast, where publicly improvised poetry and music *(desafios)* frequently drew crowds of the poor, the people "adored" Dom Avelar for his oratory.[82] "I was always concerned with social justice and defended human rights," Dom Avelar said in 1973. "I am neither a petrified person stuck in one place nor a utopian dreamer. Therefore, those who are most progressive do not fully understand me, nor do the conservatives count me as one of theirs" (Prandini, Petrucci, and Dale 1986–1987 3:168).

On August 23, 1973, the governor of Pernambuco, Eraldo Gueiros Leite, announced that Dom Avelar, named cardinal in May, would receive the state's gold medal of merit. A week later, however, Gueiros suddenly canceled the award. Similarly, the city council of Salvador revoked plans to grant honorary citizenship to its archbishop because of "orders from above." Although the officials gave no reason, the withdrawal of Dom Avelar's honors clearly resulted from his public attempts to offer the regime moral guidance. In a magazine interview, for instance, he stated the need for justice in the government's Amazon development program. He also supported "Eu Ouvi os Clamores do Meu Povo" (I heard the cry of my people), the radical document on poverty issued by the northeastern bishops. The affront to Dom Avelar brought protest from opposition politicians. Dom Avelar himself demanded to know the federal government's role in the cancellations. High civilian and military officials, including the Grupo da Situação, denied responsibility; Army Minister Orlando Geisel and military presidential chief of staff Figueire-do ignored the cardinal's inquiry.[83]

The magnitude of his humiliation surfaced in Dom Avelar's private letters to General Muricy. He was especially anguished because his attempts at a balanced view of the political situation had drawn attacks. "I am beginning to convince myself that they want to characterize me in a way that does not correspond to my reality," the cardinal wrote in early September 1973, alluding to government officials and members of the information services. "I have become, from one moment to the next, a dangerous element." The bishops could no longer speak out, and if they did, they were misinterpreted, Dom Avelar further implied. General Muricy replied that he was stupefied by Governor Gueiros's action. His behind-the-scenes investigation had turned up no evidence of federal participation in Gueiros's decision, yet he promised to dig deeper into the matter. It did not end there. Dom Avelar wrote in another letter that although he had acted with "prudence" and "dignity," "the manner in which I was treated was rude and violent. . . . If I were not an experienced man, there would have been commotion in our religious circles." He complained that the government censors in Salvador blocked him from publishing his side of the story, while the city's commanding general avoided meeting with him. In yet another missive at the end of September, the archbishop wrote, "I have experienced a difficult test. I think I have done well. I tried to speak for myself, for the Church, and also for the government." Yet the regime had still failed to explain the offense. Although Dom Avelar's emotional "wound" had started to close, he feared further attacks on his honor. "I thus hope that my conduct towards the government is respected."[84]

The Bipartite's intervention in the affair eventually resulted in Salvador's reversal of its decision.[85] Ten months later Dom Avelar's wish was granted as the city made him an honorary citizen. Municipal and military authorities looked on as the archbishop received the title in a formal ceremony (Prandini, Petrucci, and Dale 1986–1987:4:30–31).

Conclusion

Through the Bipartite, the Situação obtained a substantial moderation of the bishops' criticisms, while the Church avoided the potential for further repression. In the process both sides held onto the hope—or the illusion—of preserving traditional Church-state collaboration. Did the bishops go too far in meeting the demands of General Muricy? Did they compromise their religious mission? Did they undercut grassroots work in favor of *conscientização* and human rights? On the one hand, the Bipartite gave the regime a window onto the thinking and decision-making process of the Catholic hierarchy, its most formidable opponent. Far more than the Situação, the Grupo Religioso revealed its intentions during the meetings. The Church's public posture mattered so much that it was first discussed in private. The Situação believed it was effectively modifying the bishops' attitudes and even controlling their behavior.

On the other hand, the military was perhaps overconfident in its evaluation of at least some of the bishops. This certainty was rooted in self-assurance or even wishful thinking about the Church-state conflict. Regardless, the Situação did not always have a clear picture of the bishops' ideological tendencies, and it underestimated their political abilities. In part these misreadings resulted from the basic cultural and institutional differences between clergyman and soldier. Dom Paulo is the best example. The Situação believed the archbishop was becoming more moderate. Yet less than a year after the sesquicentennial he risked a major confrontation with the military by holding a memorial mass for Alexandre Vannucchi Leme, a student who had been tortured to death at the DOI-CODI (see chapter 10). A similar conclusion can be applied to the case of Dom Fernando. He vilified the regime but also retreated when necessary. Thus in the interests of the institution, the bishops displayed an enormous capacity for what Brazilians popularly call *jogo de cintura*, or flexibility. As a result, participation in the Bipartite bought the Church time to shape its response to the regime while resolving its own internal conflicts. The bishops exercised strategic accommodation. At times flexibility meant criticizing the attitudes of the grassroots in the presence of the Grupo da Situação. However, the Grupo Religioso still defended the clergy's right to carry out its religious mission.

But the Bipartite was more than a battle of political strategies. It involved a process in which two institutions tried to map out areas of responsibility in a long-term regime of exception bent on modernizing the country. Dom Fernando's comments embodied a major challenge: how to temper the imperative for economic growth with social justice. Thus both within and beyond the Bipartite, Church and regime struggled over new definitions of patriotism in light of the competition between national security and religious liberation. In the broader historical context of rapid socioeconomic and political change, the Bipartite aimed to protect but also redefine and even limit the moral concordat.

The Bipartite might extinguish isolated or incipient confrontations, but once incidents gained national and even international prominence as decisive encounters between the regime and its opponents, its effectiveness was limited. The contrast between the cases of Dom Fernando and Dom Pedro is instructive. The Bipartite temporarily neutralized the former but had no effect on the latter. The land question was a larger structural issue that profoundly affected Brazilian society and generated widespread conflict, including Dom Pedro's decision to side with the posseiros. In effect, the land question was too big an issue for a secret commission to negotiate in the context of an authoritarian system. The "cotton" of the Bipartite was only partial protection.

Chapter 8   **The Struggle Against Human Rights Abuses and Censorship**

H
uman rights violations were a prime reason for the Bipartite. Concern about abuses stemmed from the commission's initial goal of alleviating conflict result-ing from the repression of Catholic activists. It grew into the main issue of the Grupo Religioso. This chapter focuses on the struggle for human rights in Rio de Janeiro and the commission's debates over human rights and censorship. Most analyses of the Brazilian Church correctly point to the arch-diocese of São Paulo as a leader in the struggle for human rights, but Rio also made a significant contribution.

Whereas the bishops took the defensive on subversion, they went on the offensive for human rights. From the Church's standpoint, frictions would diminish if the government freed unjustly accused individuals and stopped the mistreatment of prisoners. As radical priests and outspoken bishops were the Church's weak point, tor-turers and executioners were the regime's. Especially in the last two years of the Bipartite, Candido Mendes, Dom Ivo, and the other bishops insisted that the military explain the whereabouts of desa-parecidos and the circumstances of fatalities. General Muricy and the intelligence officers defended the version of events put forth by the regime. In this sense they showed less candor than the bishops, who were more willing to recognize the faults within their institu-tion. The bishops did not get the kind of concessions they them-selves had made. This is not surprising given the strength of the hard-liners and the repressive forces. Nevertheless, the Grupo Religioso relentlessly challenged the Situação on this issue.

The Bipartite's importance for human rights lies not so much in the release of prisoners as in its function as a voice of opposition. In contrast with the sometimes self-contradictory positions taken on political issues, the Church's private voice on human rights consistently reinforced what it said publicly. There could be no compromise. And when the regime muffled the Church's public statements, the Grupo Religioso kept pressure on the military behind the scenes until the Church could become more vocal in the Geisel years. The political culture facilitated this process: one sector of the elite privately pointed out the errors of another. Not until the Geisel administration did the public voice grow stronger and have an impact on politics, as evidenced by the key protests of Dom Paulo and his archdiocese in 1975 and thereafter. By then the regime had begun to use repression more selectively, not only because the security forces had effectively stifled opposition (Gorender 1998:232) but also because the Church had exposed the existence of torture. The Bipartite played a key part in making torture a political issue.

Torture was not unique or new to post-1964 Brazil. It had a long record in the history of civilizations, including presumably advanced ones. The British employed torture in Kenya, and the French used it in Algeria, for instance. The U.S. government quietly trained and heavily equipped the Brazilian military and police for combat against internal security threats. It also did nothing to stop torture and death squads; in fact, U.S. operatives collaborated with the repressive forces and supplied materials such as generators that Brazilian torturers used to apply electric shocks to their victims (Huggins 1998, Langguth 1978). Torture echoed powerfully from the Church's distant past. As the Brasil: Nunca Mais project recognized, the national security state's methods strongly resembled the inquisitorial techniques of the Middle Ages (Archdiocese of São Paulo 1985:281–90). Latin America's torturers had plenty of examples from their own societies' long history. Torture figured prominently in the slavocracies tolerated by the Church and the authorities for hundreds of years. In Brazil police routinely used torture against the lower classes long before 1964 and continued to do so after 1985.[1]

Top military leaders claimed that torture was not official policy and that it did not exist or only rarely occurred. Twice Médici issued to his cabinet explicit orders against torture: "Our people are dying and have a right to strike back with arms. This is a war in which you kill or are killed. But to arrest someone and submit him to torture is so cowardly and ignoble that I cannot find the right words for condemning such a sordid practice. I categorically prohibit torture in my administration."[2] The security forces either never received or conveniently ignored these orders, however, and torture became part of the regime's systematic witch hunt against the opposition. Except for one case (discussed in the next chapter), torture went unpunished during and after military rule.

In Brazil no institution, including the Church, had ever bothered to lift its voice against torture. It became an issue after 1964 for a number of reasons. Greater consciousness about human rights developed in the West after the atrocities of World War II. At Vatican II, the Church officially adopted the human rights cause. The Médici era was decisive in building a commitment to human rights in the Brazilian Church. Torture deeply affected the intelligentsia (including the media), the middle class, and the clergy for the first time in the country's history, although Vargas's authoritarian Estado Novo had employed it against Communists and other suspected regime enemies. In addition, torture took place in a highly polarized political climate, and the opposition used it to criticize the regime at home and abroad. The regime's minimalization of torture as an exceptional "excess" only increased moral indignation and the opposition's ability to capitalize on it.

The Battle for Human Rights in Rio de Janeiro

In the early 1970s the Grupo Religioso became part of a growing mosaic of Church and other domestic and foreign groups working to defend human rights in Brazil.[3] Three of the most important groups were located within blocks of each other in Rio de Janeiro—the CNBB headquarters; the curia of the archdiocese of Rio de Janeiro; and the CJP-BR, the Brazilian Section of the Pontifical Peace and Justice Commission. Because of these organizations' international prestige, Rio de Janeiro became a kind of human rights clearinghouse. Each organization had representatives at the Bipartite.

The CNBB

In the 1970s, the CNBB became the national voice of the Brazilian Church, issuing critical statements against human rights violations and socioeconomic inequality. Dom Aloísio and Dom Ivo provided the key leadership. Their discretionary power was enormous, for the CNBB usually operated not as a general assembly or representative subcommittee but as a small administrative unit directed by the president, secretary general, and a small number of aides. They received denunciations of abuses almost daily (Virgílio Rosa Netto interview). The CNBB headquarters stood as one of the most important contacts in the Church's underground network of information about human rights.[4]

The core of the CNBB's human rights work was the so-called Grupo Não-

Violência, inspired by Dom Hélder's preachings against violence. Because the regime prohibited all reportage on Dom Hélder, Church militants proposed Dom Paulo, the new archbishop of São Paulo, as the leader of the group. In early 1971, Dom Paulo, Dom Waldyr, and more than a dozen other bishops and Church insiders met at the archiepiscopal palace in São Paulo to ratify the decision. The embattled Dom Hélder also attended, passing on the mantle to Dom Paulo. The group established the Centro Informativo e Não Violência and an underground human rights bulletin. The Grupo Não-Violência met every year on the eve of the CNBB general assembly and grew to include sixty bishops. Representatives of Protestant churches also participated.[5]

The Curia of the Archdiocese: Dom Eugênio

Human rights work in the archdiocese of Rio de Janeiro stemmed from the discrete leadership of Dom Eugênio, whose influence extended into the CNBB and the CJP-BR. Dom Eugênio's attitude angered and puzzled people in the Church and the regime. On one hand, his diplomatic, more traditionally patriotic approach to Church-state relations and his attempt to "remake" Brazil's human rights image in Europe made Dom Eugênio unpopular with progressive Catholics. When he became cardinal-archbishop of Rio de Janeiro after the death of Dom Jaime de Barros Câmara in 1971, he fully assumed the role of "prince" of the Brazilian Church.[6] A large group of priests in Rio protested the appointment because they believed he was too conservative.[7] He further irritated progressives because he insisted on representing the institution at civic acts with military leaders. On the other hand, the CIE believed that Dom Eugênio acted "in an ambiguous way, . . . supporting the government and the CNBB" at the same time.[8] The cardinal sometimes showed outright hostility to security agents. In 1975, for instance, he blocked DOPS agents at the door of his residence and prohibited them from returning to ask questions about radical priests.[9] The noncommittal stance allowed Dom Eugênio to tap into different circles in his attempts to protect people.

During the Médici years, Dom Eugênio aided dozens of people, including priests who were imprisoned or threatened by the repressive forces (Ponte Neto interview; Pretto interview). The cardinal exercised the utmost care, refusing to act if he did not have all the facts. For instance, when a member of a progressive, anti-regime Catholic think tank was tortured, Dom Eugênio did not intervene because he lacked clear information. When he did act, however, he was efficacious.[10] In some cases he took individuals into his home or had them spend the night in the residences of archdiocesan employees. Dom Eugênio frequently used old, unsuspicious priests to help in these missions. In some cases the cardinal himself or a Church official personally escorted wanted subversives from the archdiocese to Rio's Galeão International Airport, where Dom Eugênio moved about without interference from security men.[11] In addition, Dom Eugênio often received requests for help from Dom Paulo to help free individuals from prison, despite the ideological differences of the two bishops.[12]

Dom Eugênio protested to Médici about the use of torture. Médici admitted that torture existed but blamed it on disobedience in the chain of command—a not uncommon way for the regime's leaders to explain abuses. Dom Eugênio understood Médici's difficulties, because, as he told the general, he too gave "orders that are not complied with in my diocese." Yet, while the cardinal sought to maintain dialogue with Médici, at no moment did he allow it to serve as approval of the president's excuses about torture.[13] On one occasion he personally left the president a note that spoke of the "importance of locating a group of prisoners that has disappeared." The resolution of the case would "prove the government's intentions to respect human rights" (Gaspari 1997b).

During the Geisel presidency, Dom Eugênio extended his defense of human rights to political refugees from Argentina, Chile, and Uruguay. Among these were guerrillas such as the Argentine Montoneros. Dom Eugênio received the refugees in the official episcopal residence. In early 1976, as the numbers seeking asylum rose, the cardinal organized an underground railroad to funnel individuals into exile in the United States and Europe. The archdiocese rented sixty-two apartments— mainly in Rio's middle-class Zona Sul neighborhoods of Flamengo, Botafogo, and Copacabana—to house the refugees temporarily. At first each exile was given an alias, later a number. Soon after the start of the program the United Nations lent financial support. By the end of the decade, some six thousand persons left the continent through these efforts.[14]

In one incident, Dom Eugênio negotiated with a group of political refugees who had invaded the Swiss embassy seeking asylum and requesting Dom Paulo and Dom Hélder as intermediaries. Dom Eugênio promised the refugees safety and took them in his official car to Sumaré, the cardinal's home in the hills overlooking Rio. There they stayed for several months until Dom Eugênio personally escorted them to Galeão for a flight to Switzerland (Dom Eugênio interview).

By aiding refugees Dom Eugênio knew he was violating the laws of the regime. He had disrupted the fight against subversion in the backyard of the First Army, Brazil's most important military group, and amid a swarm of intelligence operations run by police agencies, the SNI, and the three branches of the armed forces.

*Muricy (left),
Dona Virgínia,
and Paraguayan
dictator General
Alfredo Stroessner,
August 1970.
Muricy and
Stroessner shared
concerns about
subversion, and
Brazil provided the
Paraguayan with
military assistance.*

The situation was further complicated because Brazil had refused to sign a 1967 U.N. protocol on refugees. Dom Eugênio personally informed the First Army commander of the refugee operation, however, and he used his enormous prestige with the generals to cause the government to "close its eyes" to the escape of subversives (Dom Eugênio interview). This tolerance contradicted the military's efforts to cooperate with neighboring countries in the hunt for subversives.

General Muricy helped orchestrate international cooperation. Starting in the 1960s, the dictatorship of Paraguayan president Alfredo Stroessner collaborated with the Brazilian authorities. Stroessner had trained with the Brazilian military in the late 1930s under General Orlando Geisel. As Army chief of staff, Muricy visited Stroessner in order to strengthen ties between the two countries' armed forces. Brazil backed Stroessner with military equipment (Muricy 1993:657–58), and

Stroessner supported Muricy's warnings about the infiltration of subversives among youths.[15] One of the victims of the Paraguayan sweep against the left was Henrique Mariani Bittencourt, detained for two weeks in 1973 for carrying subversive literature. Bittencourt was the son of Clemente Mariani, the president of the Banco da Bahia and finance minister in the Quadros government.[16] In 1975, Brazil and Paraguay joined Argentina, Bolivia, Chile, and Uruguay to form Operation Condor, a cooperative police effort to capture subversives.[17]

The Brazilian regime never officially accepted the refugees, however. The Brazilian Polícia Federal, Interpol (the international police organization), and the Argentine embassy all knew of Dom Eugênio's operation and tried to obtain information from the archdiocese about wanted persons. The police even followed one of Dom Eugênio's assistants home because they incorrectly believed the man was harboring refugees. Sometimes they sent lists of names to the chancery offices. But the archdiocese refused to cooperate. For instance, when contacted about an individual being protected, Dom Eugênio denied the information and immediately had the person sent away so as to avoid his arrest (Ponte Neto interview).

The Brazilian Peace and Justice Commission

The third leading Church group in Rio was the CJP-BR, created in 1968 as a result of Vatican II's focus on issues of justice and peace. In order to avoid reprisals, the commission took the name "Pontifical—Brazilian Section" to associate itself with the Pontifical Peace and Justice Commission in Rome and therefore the Vatican's prestige.[18] Brazil's first representative on the Roman body was Alceu Amoroso Lima, succeeded in the early 1970s by Candido Mendes. Dom Eugênio also became a member. According to Vatican criteria, the CJP-BR was to dedicate itself exclusively to the study of social ills and other matters broadly related to peace and justice. It quickly became involved in the defense of political prisoners.

Although Paul VI had made his first public comments against torture in Brazil in early 1970 (Della Cava 1970:135), Vatican approval of the CJP-BR's activist approach came only in 1971. In March and April of that year, Rio hosted the Fourth Latin American Justice and Peace Conference and the First Brazilian Peace and Justice Seminar. In line with the academic orientation desired by Rome, leading center-left intellectuals such as Hélio Jaguaribe and Paul Singer joined with Candido Mendes, prominent clergymen, and others to study social and political issues. Rural workers, proletarians, and other grassroots representatives also spoke of their experiences (CJP-BR 1971). Outside the meeting hall, however, a more dramatic testimony of Brazilians' suffering convinced the Vatican's envoy of the need for an energetic defense of human rights. As people called CJP-BR member Marina Bandeira outside the room to seek help for their imprisoned relatives, she invited Dom Joseph Grémillion, the Roman commission's secretary general, to hear their stories of the repression (Marina Bandeira interview). This contact led Dom Grémillion to authorize the CJP-BR to offer assistance to the victims and their families. He further approved the Brazilians' proposal to establish additional, regional CJPs in order to cover more effectively the country's immense territory (CNBB 1983:18–19).

The last day of the meeting, a kind of expanded version of the Bipartite took place at which the government worked to counter negative images of Brazil. Dom Grémillion, Dom Mozzoni, Dom Eugênio, Dom Aloísio, and Dom Ivo attended a luncheon with General Muricy, officers from the Situação, Guanabara governor Antônio de Padua Chagas Freitas, and two of Médici's cabinet members, Minister of Planning João Paulo dos Reis Veloso and Minister of Mines and Energy Antônio Dias Leite. They discussed Brazil's social and economic problems, national security, Church-state relations, and the publicity given torture. General Muricy believed that the meeting gave Dom Grémillion a positive impression of the military regime, for the bishop expressed a desire to continue Church-military dialogue and pledged to inform Pope Paul VI about the growth of "the social conscience of the Brazilian military man."[19]

Nevertheless, the CJP-BR worked intensively to defend human rights. It received and evaluated denunciations of abuses from across Brazil. In all, it accumulated files on some two thousand individuals (Bandeira 1994:76). CJP-BR secretary general Candido Mendes took a number of these allegations to the Bipartite. In other instances, the CJP-BR worked with the bishops to locate political prisoners and in some cases help them leave Brazil, and it provided families with legal assistance. Led by attorney Heleno Fragoso, a national network of twenty-five lawyers handled the CJP-BR's cases. The CJP-BR's work was not only religious but political. It wanted to denounce human rights violations to the rest of the Church and to demonstrate that the victims were not forgotten. This approach eventually served as a model for similar commissions in other countries.[20]

The CJP-BR helped stimulate the creation of the regional commissions. Members of these groups belonged to the CJP-BR, which coordinated activities at the national level and conciliated differences of approach. The most prominent was the São Paulo Commission (CJP-SP), founded by Dom Paulo. Because it operated in the city with the heaviest repression, the CJP-SP came to overshadow the work of the others, including the CJP-BR. The CJP-SP's staff of top lawyers aided the families of hundreds of prisoners, while the cardinal himself frequently visited the jails and demanded to see prisoners. Dom Paulo emphasized public denunciation of human rights violations, and in the mid- to late 1970s, the CJP-SP led the national campaign against repression and for redemocratization.[21] In contrast, the CJP-BR took a low-profile approach inspired by Dom Eugênio's diplomacy and Candido Mendes's emphasis on dialogue. The two commissions clearly disagreed over style and occasionally engaged in power struggles, but they cooperated in the defense of human rights.[22]

Candido Mendes's key role in defending human rights extended beyond the termination of the Bipartite in August 1974. As the Muricy link declined in importance, the secretary general of the CJP-BR carried complaints to General Golbery, who had returned to the government as the head of Geisel's civilian presidential staff. Candido Mendes had opened this channel by arranging for a long private meeting between Golbery and Dom Paulo shortly before Geisel's inauguration.[23] The meeting temporarily raised hopes of improved Church-state relations and led to further contact between Golbery and the episcopal leadership. In mid-1974, for instance, Candido Mendes went with Dom Paulo and others to Brasília to protest against human rights violations by presenting Golbery with a list of twenty-two recent desaparecidos. One of the missing was Paulo Stuart Wright, a state representative removed from office by the military in the 1960s and later executed and "disappeared" by the DOI-CODI antisubversive unit in São Paulo because of his membership in Ação Popular Marxista-Leninista (Marxist-Leninist Popular Action), a revolutionary organization with roots in Catholic Action. The victim was the brother of Protestant minister Jaime Wright, a close collaborator of Dom Paulo in the human rights struggle and a suspected subversive.[24] According to Jaime Wright, Golbery was moved by the documentation presented by Dom Paulo (Skidmore 1988:169, and n. 28). The general promised to locate thirteen individuals missing in São Paulo. When a CJP-BR delegation returned a month later, however, Golbery had not found a single person. He admitted that the intermediate levels of the Army, where abuses were occurring, were out of control. The general stated to Candido Mendes that in order to stop the repression he would cut the military budget and therefore reduce the amount of funds going to the repressive sectors.[25] The pressure from the Church led Golbery, an architect of the abertura, to try to influence Geisel to end torture by the armed forces.[26]

The Bipartite and Human Rights

Because campaigns for human rights rallied the opposition and sullied Brazil's international image, the government classified them as a tactic of revolutionary warfare. The religious champions of human rights stood with the left and therefore the international Communist movement. Ipso facto, the Church was subversive. Through the Bipartite, the Grupo da Situação tried to convince the bishops to tone down their human rights message. On the other side, the Grupo Religioso demanded that the Situação explain and resolve cases of human rights violations. This position reflected the CNBB's desire for immediate accountability on human rights as violence and Church skepticism about the regime increased.

The Military Critique of Human Rights

The Situação upheld its position by attacking the bishops' statements on human rights. An outstanding example was General Adolpho João de Paula Couto's analysis of the CNBB's 1973 document commemorating the twenty-fifth anniversary of the U.N. Universal Declaration of Human Rights. Schooled in national security doctrine, Paula Couto feared the episcopal document would inspire the opposition and create further Church-state tension. After consulting the conservative Dom Vicente Scherer, who was disgruntled with the CNBB,[27] the general concluded that a small group of progressives had misled the uninformed majority of the CNBB's General Assembly into adopting the "Communist technique" for defending human rights. The bishops misunderstood the government's antisubversive methods. "The degree of repression has to be proportional to the nature of the crimes," Paula Couto wrote. "If these are violent, such as those practiced by terrorists, mild repression does not make sense." The prelates' critique of capitalism encouraged the subversion of liberal democracy, staunchly defended by the Church. The CNBB's support for unions, theological training courses, measures for the poor, and lay activism all encouraged "class struggle" and threatened to return Brazil to the political instability of the pre-1964 period. The human rights document reinforced the Church's leftward shift by protecting liberation theologians' right to express "new ideas." Abandoning its religious mission, the CNBB verged on becoming a political movement that both opposed and competed with the government.[28]

Paula Couto recommended that the regime neutralize the "monstrous" document by persuading moderate bishops to reconsider their support for progressives. If unsuccessful, the regime should then "put the Church on the defensive" by publishing critiques of CNBB pronouncements and by pressuring the Vatican to disavow the bishops' human rights declaration.[29] In the end the government opted for banning the document from the media, but the Church skirted the prohibition by circulating more than one million copies of a pamphlet on the U.N. Declaration in parishes and base communities (CEBs) (Della Cava and Montero 1991:40–41).

In May 1973, the Grupo da Situação harshly criticized another key document, the northeastern bishops' "I Heard the Cry of My People." Its distribution blocked, this manifesto denounced the extreme poverty of the Northeast, the government's failure to decrease social inequality, and the manipulative and abusive tactics of the regime (Câmara et al. 1973). The members of the Situação described the statement as "tendentious" and "aggressive" and condemned its use of such terms as "official terrorism." The Situação's written report on the pronouncement concluded that the radical bishops had penned the document to rally the Brazilian Catholic left and international opinion around Dom Hélder in their antigovernment struggle. At the next meeting General Muricy pointed out that the document had received press coverage in Cuba, Chile, and Europe.[30]

The Situação worked to blunt other efforts of the Grupo Religioso. For instance it denied a request by Candido Mendes to admit a bishop to the Ministry of Justice's National Council for the Rights of Man. With U.S. support the council actually obstructed the investigation of human rights violations. General Muricy instead recommended that the Church enroll priests in the ESG and take part in ADESG seminars on national problems.[31] The Situação later opposed efforts by Dom Cândido Padim to create a "tribunal" of bishops to judge acts of the Brazilian government. The Situação believed the panel would model itself on the Vietnam war crimes tribunal started by British philosopher and pacifist Bertrand Russell.[32] In fact, a second Russell tribunal convened in 1974. It criticized human rights violations in Brazil.[33]

In another example, General Muricy expressed fear that the work of the Pontifical Peace and Justice Commission in Rome could generate friction between Church and state. Rather than taking positions, it should concentrate on "conciliation." In his eyes it had made progress by establishing a protocol that required local denunciations in Brazil to be channeled through—and substantiated by—the CNBB before being sent to Rome. Candido Mendes hinted that informal contacts between the Grupo da Situação and Dom Grémillion had contributed to the creation of this mechanism. (Dom Eugênio pushed the measure in Rome.) It was already having an effect. A parish priest had written to Rome about "irregularities" on sugar plantations in Pernambuco, but Maurice Cardinal Roy, the president of the papal commission, referred the matter to the CNBB for evaluation.[34]

Church Demands for an Accounting of Atrocities

The most serious disputes involved specific complaints of abuse raised by the Grupo Religioso. Cross-referencing General Muricy's papers with data from the Brasil: Nunca Mais project and other sources, table 4 describes the circumstances of the cases discussed at the Bipartite. Most of the examples took place after 1972, when the Bipartite had made a definite shift away from ideological debate to resolving concrete conflicts. As repression deepened and hopes of collaboration faded, the emphasis on human rights became greater. Although Candido Mendes and the bishops frequently sought to aid clergymen and lay workers, they also defended the rights of members of the secular opposition. For instance, Dom Ivo brought up the case of Joaquim Pires Cerveira, a former Army major turned revolutionary. Mentioning him raised the specter of the tirelessly hunted Captain Carlos Lamarca, considered a traitor for turning against the regime. Cerveira was later confirmed dead, though his body was not recovered. The bishops pressed the Situação most in the case of Alexandre Vannucchi Leme, a member of the ALN and a popular student leader (his case is discussed in chapter 10). The Grupo Religioso broadened the concept of human rights by including concerns about victims' relatives and the situation of ordinary people caught up in typical conflicts of the day, such as peasants battling land development firms.

One of the most prominent cases of the Bipartite centered on the center-left political leader Rubens Paiva, purged from Congress after the coup. In 1971 he was captured by the DOI-CODI and tortured. After Paiva's disappearance, the regime claimed he had been kidnapped from the Army security forces, but few believed the outrageous assertion. When Candido Mendes relayed Dom Grémillion's concern about Paiva, General Muricy stated that nothing could be done because the case was in the hands of the courts. In its confidential Bipartite report, the Situação noted that the matter lay outside the Church's area of competence.[35] Paiva, in fact, had been murdered in the Casa de Petrópolis, an Army death center near Rio de Janeiro. His body was cut into pieces and disposed of in different places (Expedito Filho 1992:29).

In mid-1974 the two groups locked horns over the Movimento Popular de Libertação (MPL; Popular Liberation Movement), a Christian-Marxist group founded by Brazilian exiles. Like dozens of other revolutionary organizations, in the late 1960s the MPL fought to overthrow the regime. By the early 1970s, however, it lost its original impetus and may even have dissolved. Nevertheless, the military believed it still active, and in January 1974, the security forces carried out a

The Struggle Against Abuses

Table 4. Human Rights Cases Examined by the Bipartite

Date Case Discussed	Victim(s)	Activities	Comments
July 1, 1971	Employees of sugar plantations	None mentioned.	Candido Mendes asked General Muricy to help solve problem.
July 1, 1971	Rubens Paiva	Former congressman "disappeared" by security forces.	Candido Mendes informed Situação of Dom Grémillion's concern about the case.
July 1, 1971	Fr. Fernando Bastos de Ávila	Director, IBRADES.	Quarters violated during invasion of IBRADES. Later dropped from military investigation.
Jan. 24, 1972	Geomar Ribeiro da Silva, Juarez Monção Virote, Roberto Vicente da Silva, Wanderley de Oliveira	Soldiers at military barracks in Barra Mansa.	Killed by torturers during internal investigation ostensibly aimed against marijuana trafficking in barracks. Case denounced by Dom Waldyr and Dom Ivo (see chapter 9).
May 30, July 25, Aug. 29, 1973	Alexandre Vannucchi Leme	Student leader at USP, member of the ALN.	Died after torture by security forces (see chapter 10).
July 25, 1973	Dom Pedro Casaldáliga, clergymen, lay pastoral agents, and numerous peasants and Amerindians	Accused of subversion for involvement in Church activities and land conflicts.	Dom Ivo denounced human rights violations.
Aug. 29, 1973	Antônio Vieira dos Santos, Benedito Pereira da Silva	Worked for Operação Esperança, a Church social program in Recife.	Arrested and held incommunicado for several months. Located through Bipartite and released along with other pastoral workers being held prisoner.
Sept. 26, 1973	Numerous peasants in Maranhão	Difficulties with land development companies.	Dom Ivo brought problem before Situação.
Sept. 26, 1973	Numerous	None mentioned.	Dom Aloísio proposes pastoral care for jailed subversives. General Muricy promises to study request.
Nov. 5, 1973	Fr. Virgílio Leite Uchôa	CNBB aide and human rights activist, cleared of charges along with thirty-one other clerics for protesting death of student Edson Luís in 1968.	Dom Ivo informed that DOPS/GB blocked issuance of priest's passport.
Nov. 5, 1973	Unnamed prisoners held in Northeast	None given.	General Muricy confirmed that individuals were in prison but in good health.

(Table 4 continued)

Date Case Discussed	Victim(s)	Activities	Comments
Nov. 5, 1973	All prisoners	None given.	Candido Mendes cited focus on human rights as fundamental for improving Bipartite.
March 24, 1974	Cristina Schroeter Simeão	Former nun.	Arrested during sweep against MPL and interrogated in Petrópolis. Badly treated after transfer to DOPS/SP.
March 24, May 29, 1974	Waldemar Rossi	Labor leader, member of CJP-SP.	Arrested in São Paulo for alleged involvement with MPL. Eventually released.
March 24, 1974	Maria Nilde Mascelani	Pastoral agent and teacher removed from public job.	Arrested in São Paulo during sweep against MPL. Accused of authoring subversive literature. Tortured. Ultimately absolved and freed.
March 24, 1974	Relatives seeking information about prisoners through the CNBB	None mentioned.	Candido Mendes obtained consent from General Muricy to tell families that relatives were jailed.
March 24, 1974	Joaquim Pires Cerveira	Former Brazilian Army major turned guerrilla for the Frente de Libertação Nacional (National Liberation Front), linked to ALN and other groups.	Exiled, then captured in Argentina by Brazilian police and jailed in Rio. Dom Ivo pointed out that case had negative repercussion in Argentina. Witnesses stated that Cerveira was tortured. Desaparecido, later confirmed dead.
March 24, 1974	João Batista Pereda, a.k.a. João Batista Rita	None given.	Along with Cerveira, captured in Argentina and brought to Brazil. Desaparecido.
May 29, 1974	Fernando Augusto de Santa Cruz Oliveira, Eduardo Collier Filho	None given at Bipartite. Both belonged to Acão Popular Marxista-Leninista, originally a Catholic group.	Candido Mendes inquired about their whereabouts. Arrested by DOI-CODI in Rio in Feb. 1974. Regime claimed Oliveira was still clandestine. Both desaparecidos.

(table continues)

(Table 4 continued)

Date Case Discussed	Victim(s)	Activities	Comments
May 29, 1974	Father François Jentel	French missionary, defended peasants in land conflict with large company in São Félix do Araguaia.	Tried and convicted for violating the National Security Law. Absolved after retrial. Left Brazil after Candido Mendes negotiated with General Golbery. After return, expelled from Brazil in 1975 (see chapter 6 for details).
Aug. 26, 1974	Twenty-two unnamed cases	None given.	Candido Mendes stated that Dom Eugênio and Dom Paulo had encountered "good receptivity" with respect to "pending cases," of which twenty-two remained. Reference to earlier meeting with Golbery.
Aug. 26, 1974	Sérgio Rubens de Araujo Torres	None given. Member of MR-8 (Movimento Revolucionário 8 de Outubro).	Candido Mendes asked about whereabouts of Torres, feared captured by agents in São Paulo in a sweep against MR-8. Torres had participated in 1969 kidnapping of U.S. ambassador. Torres was freed, but other MR-8 members were detained.
Aug. 26, 1974	Unspecified cases	None given.	Dom Ivo complained about "certain mysteries" involving the "strange form" of imprisonment and disappearance of individuals in São Paulo.
Aug. 26, 1974	Theodomiro Romeiro dos Santos	None given.	Dom Avelar requested that life sentence of the seventeen-year-old prisoner, originally sentenced to death for shooting a policeman, be reduced.
Numerous	Dom Hélder Câmara	Human rights leader.	Defended by fellow bishops.

Sources: FGV/CPDOC/ACM; Archdiocese of São Paulo 1988; Comissão de Familiares 1996; Dom Waldyr interview.

sweep against it. In Rio, São Paulo, and elsewhere they arrested and tortured members of the Workers' Pastoral and other Catholic groups linked to the MPL.[36] The attacks were clearly aimed at undermining the Church's grassroots political activity and its defense of human rights. At least twenty Church workers were involved. Both Dom Lucas and Dom Paulo issued letters to the clergy denouncing the arrests. Along with Church lawyers, the clergymen managed to locate and obtain the release of most of the prisoners.[37] The case ultimately proved yet another example of military stonewalling.

At the March 1974 Bipartite meeting, the Grupo Religioso vigorously protested the arrests, showing particular concern for the safety of Waldemar Rossi, a leader of the Workers' Pastoral and a founding member of the CJP-SP. Rossi's case was handled by Sérgio Paranhos Fleury, the infamous police detective who killed Carlos Marighella and linked the Dominicans to subversion in 1969. Fleury was one of the regime's most brutal torturers and ran a death squad in São Paulo. Candido Mendes believed Fleury's assignment to Rossi was more than coincidence, and Dom Lucas feared that Rossi's declarations to the police "could have been obtained under [the] climate of fear and compulsion." The Situação denied the charges. In May 1974, Candido Mendes and the bishops again prodded the Situação for information on Rossi and other imprisoned MPL suspects.[38]

Rossi was ultimately released, but others caught in the dragnet disappeared. At the May 1974 encounter, Candido Mendes sought to learn the whereabouts of Fernando Augusto de Santa Cruz Oliveira and Eduardo Collier Filho, militants for Ação Popular Marxista-Leninista. Neither had been seen since their arrest in February 1974. It was Collier Filho's second brush with the regime, for, as a student in Salvador, he had been jailed in 1969 for subversive activities. Candido Mendes handed General Muricy a copy of a petition made by the victims' families to General Golbery. In a typical response, Muricy stated that he had requested information on the missing men from police and security organizations and that no record existed of their imprisonment. He asserted that Oliveira and Collier Filho likely had gone into hiding after hearing of the operation against the MPL. Both were never found.[39]

The military's intransigence on human rights meant that most cases were not resolved. Even the Church's public campaign for human rights in São Paulo freed few prisoners, though it probably prevented abuses (Pope 1985:437). Through the Bipartite, however, the Grupo Religioso located two pastoral workers who had disappeared from Recife in July 1973. The relatives and colleagues of Antônio Vieira dos Santos and Benedito José Pereira searched for them without success at the local police, the military police, the public hospitals, and the morgue. Dom Hélder contacted a local judge, who reported several days later that the federal police had no information. After Dom Hélder notified the CNBB in Rio, the Grupo Religioso twice raised the matter at the Bipartite. At first, the Situação had no knowledge of the matter, but later General Muricy, whose past in Recife gave him certain authority there, revealed that the men were being held in the city's Army barracks. Dom Hélder used Muricy's response to pressure the local commandant, General Walter Menezes Paes, to provide more details about the men's situation.[40] They were later released, as were other pastoral workers being held at the same installation (Piletti and Praxedes 1997:397–98). Muricy had achieved no small task, given Brazil's vast size, the insubordination among the numerous security units, the shifting of prisoners and their identities, and the central government's own lack of immediate access to prisoners (Barboza 1992:168, 174).

Censorship: The Attempt to Stop the "Voice of the Voiceless"

The Médici administration increased control over the media as part of national security policy and propaganda efforts in favor of the economic miracle. On one level the state invested massively in telecommunications infrastructure and helped stimulate the growth of the media, in particular television. Powerful media interests supported the regime. On another level the state fought against subversion with a number of tactics: the planting of false news; financial pressure on uncooperative publishers; the harassment and arrest of journalists; invasions, bombings, and other forms of violence against both mainstream and opposition newspapers. The tool most widely used was censorship. The authorities issued hundreds of written and oral orders to cut material from Brazil's papers and news programs. The theater, cinema, plastic arts, music, and literature were also affected. Censors seized entire editions of newspapers and closed radio stations. Faced with government orders, practically all newspapers agreed to some form of self-censorship. In extreme cases, the military and later federal police officers occupied the newsrooms and printing shops of papers. Among the most frequently censored topics were the security forces, the guerrilla war, intramilitary politics, peaceful dissent against the regime, human rights abuses, Church-state relations, and individual opposition leaders such as Dom Hélder.[41]

Fighting censorship was new for Catholicism. As a combatant of modernity, the Church had a centuries-long history of opposing heresies and ideas that threatened the intellectual monopoly of the clergy. In the nineteenth century, Pope Pius IX's famous *Syllabus* pointed out the errors of the modern world, among them freedom of thought and expression. Not until after World War II did the Church declare in favor of freedom of the press and the importance of public opinion as a guarantor of democracy. And only in 1953 did Pope Pius XII renounce papal or state censorship of the press. Even then the Church still tried to exert moral control over the emerging forms of mass media. In 1971 Paul VI's pastoral instruction *Communio et Progressio* marked a sea change in Catholic thinking on the media. For the first time the Church saw modern communications as a force to be understood—and, more important, used—in the process of evangelization. In Brazil this realization stimulated the expansion and professionalization of the Church's media efforts. Thus in 1971 the CNBB added a communications department as one of its major pastoral activities. Furthermore, because it coincided with the worst years of the repression, the new attitude fostered the proliferation of grassroots publications and informal news networks (Della Cava and Montero 1991, esp. 136–38).

The Brazilian Church was a major target of censorship. The regime closed a number of radio stations, blocked the publication and distribution of episcopal documents, and used the Bipartite to pressure the bishops to avoid, tone down, or retract their statements. The anti-Church campaign become most intense as the clergy assumed its role as the "voice of the voiceless." A prime example was the weekly archdiocesan newspaper *O São Paulo,* subject to prior censorship from 1971 to 1978. Under the aegis of Dom Paulo, the paper printed political commentaries and news of the Church's activities. Every week an aide from the Second Army command was one of the first individuals to buy a copy (Dom Amaury interview). The censors first telephoned the editors with orders prohibiting the mention of numerous topics (São Félix and JOC, for example). Later, acting on orders from Justice Minister Buzaid, the Federal Police stationed an officer in the printing plant. The agency blocked dozens of articles from the pages of *O São Paulo.* These actions impacted the highest levels of the Church, for the cuts included official CNBB communiqués. Dom Aloísio and Dom Ivo protested to Buzaid, and Dom Aloísio threatened to report incidents directly to the foreign press.[42] In 1977 *O São Paulo* unsuccessfully sued to strike down censorship as unconstitutional.

The Grupo Religioso confronted the Situação over control of the news. During the May 1973 Bipartite debate over the episcopal document "I Heard the Cry of My People," Major Lee attacked Dom Lucas for not heeding his warnings about *O São Paulo.* The paper insisted on "vehement criticisms of the government" and was the only one to disobey the ban on "I Heard the Cry." The paper could no longer continue in this manner, the major stated. Dom Lucas headed communications for the archdiocese of São Paulo as well as the CNBB and therefore spoke for the entire episcopate on matters of the press. He rejected Lee's "ultimatum" and preferred to see *O São Paulo* "closed rather than gagged."[43]

At the July 1973 Bipartite, Dom Ivo tendered examples of censors' written orders as specific proof of prohibitions against reporting on bishops and the CNBB. General Muricy stated that he agreed with some of the censors' decisions, although he professed ignorance about the motives for silencing the CNBB. The general countered the bishops' complaints by affirming that the government censored films, plays, and pornographic publications that threatened the Church. "Anything that disorganizes the family should be censored," he said.[44] At a subsequent meeting Muricy distributed copies of guidelines for movie censors as further evidence of the regime's "respect for moral norms and the Church." These statements reflected Muricy's religious convictions but also the way in which the conservative military used traditional morality as a way to shape the Church-state conflict.[45] They weakened the bishops' arguments against censorship because some such as Dom Eugênio indeed did believe that immoral materials should be banned (Soares, D'Araujo, and Castro 1995:60). The implication was that if the Church wanted the state's help against depravity, it should also accept the campaign against subversion.

The incisive Dom Ivo did not fall prey to such argumentation. In August 1973 he complained again about censorship of the CNBB. General Muricy explained that the "federal authorities" in Brasília denied the existence of "any order or recommendation" to proscribe its statements. The general promised to contact General Antônio Bandeira, the hard-line chief of the federal police, to halt the practice. But Muricy repeated his warning against "tendentious articles." Dom Ivo threatened that if the censorship of the CNBB did not stop, he would divulge the name of the officer in Rio directly responsible and cause problems for him *("ver a caveira" desse cidadão)*.[46]

Debate over censorship erupted again in September 1973. General Muricy criticized *O São Paulo* for its unfavorable commentary on the 1974 federal budget. "Security first, then man," the headline read. "The Army will receive more money than the Ministry of Education," the text stated. "We are overvaluing military spending to the detriment of social outlays."[47] General Muricy argued that funds for the military went not only for arms, but for developing Brazil economically. The *O São Paulo* piece should be reconsidered, he added. Dom Lucas revealed that he had disapproved of the article and had told the author so. Dom Lucas followed up this timid response, however, with a protest against the restrictions on *O São Paulo* as well as on the commercial *O Estado de São Paulo,* prohibited from printing controversial items on the Church. He asked General Muricy to intercede with General Bandeira on behalf of the Church or to arrange a meeting.[48]

Major Lee defended the regime. He told the bishops that they should criticize the harsher censorship of the Soviet Union, which permitted no negative news about that country; in Brazil the censors had actually permitted the publication of criticisms such as those leveled by *O São Paulo.* Lee further reminded the Grupo Religioso that political censorship at times benefited the Church. He cited the example of a Recife Catholic who wrote a letter to the press reproaching the local clergy for refusing to bury the man's dead father. The censors kept the letter out of the papers to "preserve the image of the Church." Dom Lucas and Dom Fernando Gomes disagreed and affirmed that the letter should have appeared so that Dom Hélder could have acted on the matter. Lee noted that the archbishop already had a copy.[49]

The military's heavy-handed approach against *O São Paulo* extended to the archdiocese's Rádio 9 de Julho, named in commemoration of São Paulo state's unsuccessful 1932 rebellion against the central government. In 1973 the bureaucracy in Brasília had practically approved a standard renewal of the station's license for ten years (Dom Amaury interview). On October 3, 1973, the day before Dom Paulo's third anniversary as archbishop, President Médici ordered the station closed, however. Broadcasting since 1955, the Rádio 9 de Julho had the second-most-powerful transmitter of Brazil's Catholic radio stations. Its significance was magnified by the fact that most of the other 117 stations had very weak signals and therefore little geographical coverage. The Church expected Rádio 9 de Julho's international shortwave rights to be cut under the regime's new rules, but the cancellation of the domestic frequency came as a complete surprise. Médici's order offered no explanation. Colonel Hygino Caetano Corsetti, the Minister of Communications, first cited "technical" reasons and then made the absurd accusation that the station, approved by government regulations, had been transmitting "clandestinely." A clearer answer came from congressman Clóvis Stenzel, a nemesis of the Church. He cited "political motives" caused by the station's broadcast of criticisms against the government instead of shows for "the salvation of souls."[50] Protests from loyal listeners, including ads published in *O São Paulo,* were useless. Dom Paulo had to sell the station's equipment in order to pay severance benefits to the employees who had lost their jobs (Dom Amaury interview). This incident further harmed relations between the government and the Vatican.[51]

At the Bipartite meeting on November 5, 1973, the station's last day of operation, Dom Lucas protested. Dom Aloísio added that rumors circulated about a potential closing of his archdiocesan station in Fortaleza. Dom Ivo and Dom Lucas both reminded the Situação that Catholic broadcasters helped foster Brazil's national integration.[52] Later, in a letter to the São Paulo faithful, Dom Lucas scathingly attacked the regime's reasoning. He recalled that Rádio 9 de Julho had aired a number of government programs, including free advertising for the armed forces' recruitment campaign, propaganda spots written by Médici's public relations office, and the officially produced "Voice of Brazil."[53]

The Church insisted but got no official accounting of the closing. The regime had clearly aimed to punish the archdiocese for Dom Paulo's outspokenness. Yet the Grupo da Situação was more flexible and actually hoped to turn the episode into further advantage for the government. Meeting privately the morning of their May 1974 encounter with bishops, the Situação learned from General Muricy that he was trying to obtain permission for the archdiocese to open another radio station. The other members of the Situação agreed, but with the proviso that the station's power be limited. They reasoned that such a solution could tip the upcoming CNBB elections in favor of "more conservative" candidates.[54] If achieved, this outcome could cause the bishops' conference to return to the policy of acquiescence of the period from 1964 to 1968. Progressives such as Dom Ivo would lose their platform for denouncing the regime, thus muting the "voice of the voiceless."

Muricy, however, was unsuccessful. The archdiocese of São Paulo remained without a radio station throughout the remainder of the dictatorship. Three months later, the Bipartite held its last meeting. With the worst of the repression over, the opposition began to gain strength. Ultimately, in 1978 the government lifted censorship, giving rise to a plethora of publications by the opposition and newly restored freedom for *O São Paulo* and other newspapers.

Conclusion

The Bipartite's struggle over human rights and censorship complemented the larger public struggles between Church and state. While fear and antisubversive warfare plagued Brazil from 1970 to 1974, the Church increasingly raised its voice against abuses. Because repression and censorship often muffled that voice, it remained for the Grupo Religioso to stand up to the military behind the scenes by demanding information about political prisoners and victims of torture. With the hard-liners in power, the Grupo da Situação did not yield. But the Grupo Religioso kept up the pressure on the regime. The bishops revealed the generals' policy of deceit on human rights. One of the most telling phrases of the Situação's post-meeting reports can be found in its very last entry after the final Bipartite encounter on August 26, 1974: "It has become evident that the intention of the Grupo Religioso, in this case led by Prof. Candido Mendes, is to persist in the search for the whereabouts of elements noted as 'pending cases,' that is, persons that they considered to be desaparecidos or fugitives."[55] As one of Candido Mendes's collaborators remembered years later, the bishops' participation at the Bipartite prevented the military from affirming that it had no knowledge of human rights violations (Bandeira 1994:77). As Candido Mendes himself recalled, the circulation of information about abuses caused an increased "awareness" about human rights. The accumulation of denunciations by the Grupo Religioso and other Church groups helped demonstrate that violence had reached its "saturation point," causing Geisel to react against it.[56] Divisive for the military, the autonomy of the security forces helped provoke Geisel to start political liberalization. The Grupo Religioso both confirmed and reinforced the Church's commitment to human rights, which would become a cornerstone of the return to civilian rule over the next ten years.

As the military correctly perceived, human rights were a profoundly political question. Both sides were biased. The Church, however, faced limits to the frequency and manner of its protests. Again and again the Situação tried to dampen criticisms of all forms, whether symbols, voices, or the printed word. The Church selected its cases well, capitalizing on the security forces' blundered choices of victims and implausible explanations of jailings, disappearances, and deaths. General Muricy demonstrated some attempts at goodwill. But just as the Church was constrained, so was the general. If his commission gave concessions or appeared to be too friendly to the Church, the hard line could easily justify its abolition.

Chapter 9

Death in Barra Mansa

The Admission and Punishment of Torture

The Bipartite and other channels of secret dialogue played a significant role in denouncing one of the most horrific incidents of the regime and, indeed, in the entire history of the Brazilian armed forces—the death by torture of four soldiers in the barracks at Barra Mansa. Ostensibly probing into illegal drug usage, in January 1972, intelligence officers at the First Armored Infantry Battalion (1st AIB) detained privates Geomar Ribeiro da Silva, Juarez Monção Virote, Roberto Vicente da Silva, and Wanderley de Oliveira. All four died from a variety of torments. The killers punched their nineteen-year-old victims with gloved hands, whipped them with belts and wires, pierced their fingernails, burned their fingers, beat them with an iron pipe and a *palmatória* (a large, perforated spatula once used to punish slaves and students), applied electric shocks, and used a vise to crush the soldiers' feet and the heads of Vicente and Geomar. To cover up the crime they staged an escape scene, claiming that Wanderley and Monção had deserted after killing the other two men. In reality, the criminals had decapitated Wanderley's body and thrown it into a dam; they dumped and burned Monção's body miles away in the state of São Paulo. Eleven other soldiers were also tortured.[1] A vigorous Army investigation of the atrocities led to the court-martial of eight soldiers, the conviction of two police officers, and the forced retirement of the battalion commander.

This chapter examines the history of abuses in the Barra Mansa battalion and the denunciations of the local bishop, Dom Waldyr Calheiros de Novaes. Violence and torture within the armed forces were not unique to this period (see Smallman 1997). Because torture

Geomar Ribeiro da Silva was crushed to death by his superiors.

For weeks a military cover-up prevented Pedro Paulo Virote from learning about the death of his son Juarez Monção Virote (pictured here).

First accused of using marijuana, Private Roberto Vicente da Silva was later buried with full military honors. He lived long enough to tell Dom Waldyr and Colonel Sampaio of the horrors of torture in the barracks. Like the other victims, he was poor; his mother, Maria Aparecida de Jesus Silva, washed clothes for a living.

by the security forces was so widespread during the Médici years, however, this incident provides special insight on how the security forces' torture of subversives began to undermine the military institution. The presentation of Dom Waldyr's accusations at the Bipartite prevented a cover-up of the deaths and helped force the military to investigate, reveal, and punish the practice of torture—the only time it did so during the twenty-one years of its rule. The chapter will close with a discussion of the significance of the Barra Mansa episode—an episode that is unknown to most Brazilians and largely absent from the historiography of the regime.[2]

Torture in the Barracks

The 1st AIB was located near Volta Redonda, the site of the large National Steel Company about 130 kilometers from Rio de Janeiro. Like military units across Brazil at this time, the 1st AIB hunted Communists and other alleged subversives. This mission, the economic importance of the Barra Mansa–Volta Redonda region, and the area's relatively small population gave the battalion prestige and immense power in local affairs. In 1969, for example, Barra Mansa councilmen visited the barracks and lunched with the commander.[3] Local residents were invited to parties at the installation, and the military assumed a kind of police power—mediating local quarrels, collecting promissory notes, and disconnecting electricity on delinquent accounts (Pedro Virote interview). On one occasion, the battalion assumed the unusual responsibility of jailing an individual accused of drug trafficking.[4] As one person recalled, the Army was "the law" in Barra Mansa and Volta Redonda (Geralsélia interview). In addition, involvement of soldiers in contraband came to light during the torture investigation (Sampaio interview). Their activities formed part of a larger pattern in which repressive units used their national security mandate to engage in highly profitable illegal activities. In Rio de Janeiro, for instance, the First Army uncovered a massive operation of contraband and robbery involving DOI-CODI members, military police, maritime police, customs officials, and civilians.[5]

By 1972, Church-Army tensions and suspicions of torture were old themes at the 1st AIB. Dom Waldyr first entered into conflict with its officers in 1967 after soldiers entered his home and detained priests and members of a Church group on charges of subversion. The investigation was headed by Lieutenant Colonel Gladstone Pernasetti Teixeira. Dom Waldyr criticized the commander for concentrating on subversion while the regime's policies kept Volta Redonda salaries and working

The author standing at the entrance to the 1st AIB, where "discipline" became torture.

conditions inadequate. In early 1969 Dom Waldyr declared himself a prisoner at the 1st AIB in protest against the jailing of two teachers. Later he and sixteen priests denounced the practice of torture at the battalion. The Army launched an investigation, but military judge Helmo de Azevedo Sussekind, a civilian, dismissed the case for lack of evidence. In retaliation against Dom Waldyr, the Army started the first of several inquests designed to intimidate him and his clergy. On one occasion Dom Waldyr was interrogated for twenty-five hours. Judge Sussekind denied a request from the military's own prosecutor to dismiss the first of these inquests and praised the 1st AIB's restraint in avoiding a Brazilian "Belfast." In November 1970 the 1st AIB struck again, arresting some thirty Jocistas, including two priests, in connection with the assault on JOC and IBRADES in Rio de Janeiro. Dom Waldyr officially reported the torture of several of these individuals to nuncio Dom Mozzoni in Rio de Janeiro. Lieutenant Colonel Gladstone denied the accusations.[6] These clashes galvanized national episcopal support for Dom Waldyr and raised the political stakes in Volta Redonda, but they also made Dom Waldyr one of the bishops most hated by the military, alongside Dom Hélder and Dom Paulo. In 1976 the kidnappers and torturers of Nova Iguaçu Bishop Dom Adriano Hypólito informed him that their next victim would be Dom Waldyr. Dom Waldyr subsequently received frequent threats from right-wing terrorists.[7]

In December 1971, the 1st AIB's intelligence and internal security section, the S2, began an inquiry into the battalion's own barracks. According to the Army's public statement on the Barra Mansa deaths, the S2 suspected a group of draftees of using and trafficking in marijuana.[8] The sentence against the torturers, all members of the S2, did not question the unit's motives,[9] probably because the investigating officer's instructions led him to focus exclusively on the accusations of torture, not on the activities of the victims (Sampaio interview). At least two of the victims had confided to their families that unusual activities were occurring in the barracks. For instance, Private Geomar told his parents that he had witnessed colleagues kill a man while on patrol early one morning in Volta Redonda. The driver of the patrol truck, Geomar recounted the scene in which the other soldiers dragged the victim into the vehicle and beat him. They attacked this man, a slum-dweller, because he was painting an advertisement for a local store—apparently mistaken for a subversive political slogan—on a hillside. Others in the barracks warned Geomar, who had a reputation for being a big man but "soft" of heart, to stop acting "cowardly" and to forget the incident.[10] Geomar also knew about contraband drugs, arms, and whiskey (Geralsélia and Evangelina interviews). At about this time, the 1st AIB once again undertook the unusual responsibility of housing a civilian criminal suspect, Expedito Botelho, identified as a "trafficker in marijuana." The local judge requested the transfer ostensibly because Botelho had been mistreated by the police, but this reason is difficult to believe given the already bad reputation for violence at the 1st AIB and the subsequent wave of torture. At the end of December 1971, the S2 began arresting and beating soldiers in the alleged marijuana investigation.[11] Geomar was detained on New Year's Eve 1971, kept incommunicado, and forced to write notes to his mother stating that he was in no danger. She saw him only briefly on January 1, 1972, and already noticed marks on his arms (Evangelina interview). When she took food for her son, the soldiers stole it and ate it as she watched. Geomar's twenty-one-year-old sister Geralsélia visited the barracks daily in an attempt to see him, but only once did she have success, on

January 2 (Geralsélia interview). Geomar vowed that he had not smoked marijuana and would refuse to confess to a crime he had not committed.[12]

Eleven days later, Geomar's family was suddenly called to the barracks to claim their son's body. Although signs of torture covered his body—bruises, broken teeth, burned fingers, damaged fingernails, exposed bones, detached skin, cigarette burns on the face, parts of the body smashed by the vise, the feet and head crushed by the vise—the coroner's report listed heart, liver, and kidney problems as the cause of death. Geomar's father asked for another report, but the battalion commander refused.[13]

A climate of fear and anger overtook Volta Redonda as news of Geomar's death quickly spread. When Dom Waldyr visited Geomar's family, the father reported that soldiers had threatened him with the loss of his job at the National Steel Company if he spoke to the bishop. The next day they returned to intimidate the family again. Other families began to fear the same deadly outcome for their detained sons (Dom Waldyr interview). The incident shocked the families even more because in the small-town milieu of Volta Redonda, soldiers' families were practically neighbors. For example, S2 leader Captain Dálgio Miranda Niebus lived near Private Monção's family, and the two men frequently drove together to the barracks. Monção had proudly entered the service, and his mother doted on his sharp-looking uniform (Efigênia Virote interview). Vicente's mother washed clothing for the Niebus family, and his sister worked there as a nanny (Maria Aparecida interview). The murders broke local trust in the military as an institution. Geomar's father tore the Brazilian flag from Geomar's casket and threw it into a gully, and later Monção's uncle, a Methodist pastor, had the national anthem omitted from his nephew's funeral. In the packed church Dom Waldyr refused to stand alongside military officers (Efigênia Virote interview).

On January 14, 1972, the day of Geomar's burial, Private Vicente's family was informed that he had been transferred to the Central Army Hospital in Rio de Janeiro. This news came only two days after they had learned of his confinement at the 1st AIB. With difficulty Vicente's relatives gained access to his room. Dom Waldyr also visited him. Vicente's head and much of his body were wrapped in gauze. He had lost much of his skin because of burnings and electric shocks.[14] As the military inquest later revealed, the S2 torturers had also put Vicente's head in the vise.[15] Before he died on January 24, 1972, Vicente revealed details of the atrocities (Geralsélia interview). In military eyes, Vicente was no longer a suspected marijuana smoker but now a victim of violence. He was buried with full military honors, including a twenty-one-gun salute and the covering of his body with the

Brazilian flag. Meanwhile, the two other victims, Monção and Wanderley, were considered deserters by the Army. As part of the cover-up, the 1st AIB broadcast radio reports and published announcements calling for the return of the two soldiers.

Dom Waldyr's Denunciations

There was little hope of justice for the victim's families. They were all of humble origin. Vicente's, for example, lived in a poor area on the outskirts of Volta Redonda. He and his family were also black—a huge disadvantage in Brazil. The climate of repression and military chauvinism made it unlikely that the working-class relatives of mere draftees would see their legal rights respected.

Dom Waldyr anguished over whether to take on the military again. He went to a chapel and prayed. He thought about the Church's offer of a promotion to archbishop of Teresina, Piauí. The military wanted him out of Barra Mansa. If he accepted, he would rid both the Church and the military of a prickly situation. But he knew that departing would eliminate the chance of justice for the soldiers' families.[16]

Dom Waldyr was determined not to let yet another violation of human rights in the Barra Mansa barracks be forgotten. He now had enough evidence to make a strong case: two brutalized soldiers and indignant members of the community. On January 16, 1972, Dom Waldyr visited the 1st AIB commander, Colonel Arioswaldo Tavares Gomes da Silva. During the Costa e Silva administration Colonel Arioswaldo had close ties to the presidency because of his friendship with first lady Dona Iolanda (Sampaio interview). He was on vacation during the atrocities in his barracks, having turned over command to Lieutenant Colonel Gladstone. Rosary in hand, Colonel Arioswaldo insisted desperately on the theory of men fleeing after attacking their fellow soldiers, but he accepted Dom Waldyr's version after the bishop discredited the commander's story and accused him of lying.[17] During this meeting Colonel Arioswaldo informed Dom Waldyr that the Army had officially set up an investigation into the incident.[18] However, this inquest was led by Lieutenant Colonel Gladstone, the bishop's old nemesis and a participant in the killings.

To foil the cover-up, Dom Waldyr tried other avenues of protest. Deeply angered, Geomar's sister Geralsélia was determined to obtain justice. Dom Waldyr took her to a private meeting with Dom Mozzoni at the nunciature in Rio and also put her in touch with Sobral Pinto, the devout human rights lawyer.[19] The cautious Dom Mozzoni contacted the government. He feared pushing the military too hard

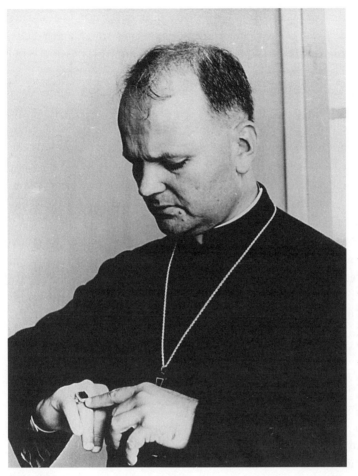

Dom Waldyr Calheiros de Novaes and others in his diocese experienced constant harassment by the 1st AIB. He put an end to the abuses by denouncing to the Bipartite the deaths of the four Barra Mansa privates.

and tried to dissuade Dom Waldyr from pressing ahead with the case (Dom Waldyr interview). The nuncio believed the bishop could be "used" for political purposes. Moreover, Dom Mozzoni had learned that the case would probably go to the government's National Council for the Rights of Man, which he believed to be the correct venue.[20] This commission was a sham, however (see chapter 8). Nevertheless, Dom Waldyr's contact with the nuncio opened a channel of protest to the highest levels of the government and created pressure for a more serious investigation of the crimes.

With evidence against the S2 mounting, on January 21, 1972, General Walter Pires de Carvalho e Albuquerque closed down Lieutenant Colonel Gladstone's cover-up investigation and ordered a new inquest under Colonel Mário Orlando

Ribeiro Sampaio. Commander of the Armored Infantry Division, General Pires headed General Muricy's staff during the coup and became Army Minister during the Figueiredo administration. Pires's superior, First Army head General Sílvio Frota, also followed the case assiduously, telephoning Sampaio nightly.[21] A hard-liner, Frota was Army Minister under Geisel until forced out in 1977. Sampaio later became a member of the Bipartite (see chapter 5). At the request of General Golbery, he had helped found the SNI in 1964 and spent a large part of his career in intelligence, becoming head of the CIE as a general in the early 1980s. He ulti-mately obtained four-star status. In 1972, he commanded the mechanized cavalry regiment headquartered in Rio de Janeiro. As one of his first actions Sampaio visit-ed Private Vicente the day before he died and saw unmistakable signs of torture (Sampaio interview).

At this point, however, the Barra Mansa deaths were still an internal Army mat-ter, known to only a few members of the leadership. The possibility of a cover-up still existed. Dom Waldyr kept pressing for an explanation. Dissatisfied with the nuncio's response, on January 24, 1972, he took Geomar's sister and a written report of the incident to the CNBB. The bishop and Geralsélia spoke with Dom Ivo. The Bipartite was to meet later that day, and Dom Ivo invited Dom Waldyr to give a report about Barra Mansa to the commission. Dom Waldyr declined. He feared that his acrimonious relationship with 1st AIB officers would compromise his testi-mony. Instead of Dom Waldyr, Dom Ivo gave the report. His presentation had the added advantage of coming from a leader of the CNBB and a member of the Grupo Religioso. General Muricy doubted the denunciation, especially because it had originated with the mistrusted Dom Waldyr. But Dom Ivo challenged Muricy to prove Dom Waldyr wrong (Dom Waldyr interview).[22] At this point Colonel Sampaio's investigation was still in the dark; on January 30, for instance, Private Monção's father still did not know the whereabouts of his supposedly deserter son and traveled to Rio de Janeiro to see if he might find him at the morgue.[23]

On February 1, 1972, General Muricy traveled to Brasília to meet with President Médici. The press reported that they discussed the mundane matter of reorganiz-ing the ADESG.[24] The real purpose was to discuss the crisis emerging in Barra Mansa. Within days Dom Mozzoni met with Médici (Dom Waldyr interview). On February 4, the nuncio then wrote Dom Waldyr that "severe measures" were now being taken.[25] Back in Rio, Muricy reversed his earlier skepticism and admitted to Dom Ivo that the atrocities at Barra Mansa were indeed true. For the first time in its history the Army would publish a note critical of itself, Muricy added (Dom Waldyr interview).

On February 6, 1972, Brazil's major newspapers printed on their inside pages a press release from the Army Public Relations Center. In it the Army admitted that the (unnamed) officers looking into drug trafficking in the Barra Mansa barracks had

> acted in a reprehensible manner, causing the death of the soldiers. . . . Completely contrary to the laws and determinations in force in the Army, such procedure is totally repudiated by the institution and repulses its members. Maximum rigor has been determined for the investigation, for facts of this nature, resulting from individual perversion, will never receive the complaisance of the Army.[26]

The Army had made an extraordinary admission of the existence of torture and abuse in its ranks precisely at the moment that it sought to deny the avalanche of accusations, at home and abroad, of human rights violations against the left. Through the Bipartite Dom Waldyr had forced the regime's hand, practically eliminated any further possibility of a cover-up, and elevated the incident from a local, internal military affair to one scrutinized by the top Army leadership and the press. In a letter to Minister Orlando Geisel he praised the generals for removing any hint of Army complicity in the deaths.[27]

The Army Investigates

Colonel Sampaio's investigation became one of the longest and most difficult inquests in nearly two centuries of Brazilian military justice. An inquest normally took less than a month, but in this instance he requested two postponements. He filed a final report after 108 days of investigation. During the early stages of the inquest the suspected S2 torturers tried to intimidate Sampaio, his assistants, and 1st AIB soldiers called as witnesses. He received telephone threats against his family. To avoid these pressures, the colonel took the witnesses to his own barracks in Rio, where he guaranteed their safety until the arrest of the accused officers. The colonel received the assistance of military prosecutor José Manes Leitão, known for his prosecution of suspected subversives. Sampaio kept the 1st AIB men and his own troops abreast of the case, and he used it to illustrate the wrongness of torture. The bodies of Privates Wanderley and Monção were soon discovered, providing crucial evidence against the S2. Colonel Sampaio listened to the aggrieved father of Wanderley note the irony of having given a son to serve his country and receiving a mutilated corpse in return (Sampaio interview).[28] Although as brutal as any other intelligence unit (with fifteen victims and four dead in only nineteen days), the S2 torturers lacked the professionalism of the Rio de Janeiro and São Paulo security agents, who left fewer marks on their victims, kept them alive longer, and more efficiently "disappeared" the dead. Sampaio quickly arrested the primary suspects: S2 head Niebus, reserve Lieutenant Paulo Reynaud Miranda da Silva, and Sergeants Ivan Etel de Oliveira, Rubens Martins de Souza, and Sideni Guedes. Corporals José Augusto Cruz and Celso Gomes de Freitas Filho soon joined them. Colonel Sampaio also found evidence of trafficking in contraband at the 1st AIB (Sampaio interview).[29] Sampaio completed the inquest on May 8, 1972.

Horrified by the violence, General Frota and other members of the military hierarchy supported the subsequent court-martial proceedings. Judge Sussekind and four colonels formed a "special council" or jury to hear the evidence against the fourteen men charged in the case. Initially the jury lottery had resulted in the selection of three Army physicians, but they refused to take part because they found the crimes too gruesome (Sussekind interview).[30] The proceedings were cloaked in secrecy because of censorship, military justice regulations, and the insistence of the defense lawyers. Overriding the judge and approving a motion by Niebus's attorney, the four colonels also voted to hold the actual trial in secret. The motion came from Augusto Sussekind de Moraes Rêgo, the judge's cousin and a defender of political prisoners.[31]

Two dozen people testified in the pretrial proceedings, including survivors of the torture and eyewitnesses to the abuses against the dead men. Testimony revealed that Captain Niebus had ordered the battalion carpenter to make two *palmatórias*. In order to escape further torture the imprisoned soldiers confessed to drug usage and named fellow draftees. The battalion medic did not treat any of the victims, in part because Niebus barred him from doing so. The S2 threatened other 1st AIB members who had seen the victims or wanted to help them. Niebus and Lieutenant Miranda accused each other of cutting up Private Wanderley's body; each claimed he had merely held up a lamp to illuminate the task. Niebus attempted an insanity defense but was found fit by examiners to face judgment. On July 10, 1972, Sussekind, the colonels, and the lawyers examined the Barra Mansa barracks. In the torture chamber known as the "archive" they viewed the *palmatória*, metal pipes, the battery for giving shocks, and other instruments.[32]

At the trial, attorney Moraes Rêgo argued that Captain Niebus and his men were engaged in a "Holy War" in which they were simply following the orders of their superiors. "These men were trained for war. They are not common men. Their specialty is to confront revolutionary warfare," Moraes Rêgo stated. Referring to the allegations of drug trafficking, Moraes Rêgo pointed out that Chinese leader Mao Tse Tung had ended drug usage by ordering that accused users be summarily

Colonel Mário Ribeiro Orlando Sampaio (center) reviewing his soldiers. Despite threats to his family, Sampaio investigated the Barra Mansa torturers. He later joined the Bipartite.

decapitated in public. The lawyer then likened Niebus to Lieutenant William L. Calley, the U.S. officer found responsible for an Army unit's massacre of unarmed civilians at the Vietnamese village of My Lai in 1971. Moraes Rêgo concluded about the S2 men that "either they are all responsible, or no one is." The defense lawyers further argued that the deaths were unintentional.[33]

The overwhelming evidence led to the defendants' conviction on January 22, 1973. To the noisy applause of victims' relatives allowed into the courtroom on the final day, Niebus received a sentence of eighty-four years for homicide and lost his officer's commission. Lieutenant Colonel Gladstone, who had ordered Niebus and Miranda to mutilate and hide the bodies of Wanderley and Monção, was also convicted along with six other officers and two civilian policemen. Lieutenant Miranda received seventy-seven years, Sergeants Souza and Oliveira and Corporal Cruz sixty-two years, and Sergeant Guedes and Corporal Freitas Filho fifty-eight years. The council further recommended further prosecution of Gladstone, a medic, a nurse, Colonel Arioswaldo, and another officer for additional crimes. In particular, the court found "vehement indications" that Arioswaldo had learned of the crimes from Niebus and had "deliberately" avoided taking any action.[34] The sentences were among the highest in Brazilian military history, though they were reduced on appeal. Niebus and others served prison terms, and Arioswaldo was forced to retire early.

The exemplary convictions countered the regime's poor image on human rights. According to Judge Sussekind, the crimes were "unique" in the history of Brazilian military justice and caused "negative repercussions" for the Army and a "democratic society." Thus they had received the "unanimous" abhorrence of the Army's highest commanders.[35] Despite the secrecy of the proceedings, the regime allowed the press to publish news of the convictions and, as a result, reaped favorable editorial comments. The *O Estado de São Paulo* and the *Jornal do Brasil*, for instance, echoed Sussekind, stating that the judgment demonstrated Army opposition to torture and vigorous punishment of those who practiced it.[36]

Conclusion

Notwithstanding the brave work of Colonel Sampaio and the court, the Barra Mansa episode was an isolated, narrowly investigated, almost surreal exception to the rule of impunity during the Médici years. The prosecution was indeed vigorous, but it was the *only* trial and conviction of torturers between 1964 and the announcement of the 1979 amnesty (which blocked prosecution of human rights violations).[37] The Army drew no connection whatsoever with the earlier denunciations of torture made by Dom Waldyr. Moreover, at least one and probably several of the convicted men had participated in previous abuses at Barra Mansa.[38] Nobody asked how, when, or why the "archive" was built and on whose orders. Nobody examined the origins and consequences of torture in the Army. Nobody appeared interested in weaving the lessons of the incident into military ethics and history.[39]

In addition, the Army did not investigate the numerous other allegations of torture made by the Church and human rights activists around Brazil. The Army did not question the original assumption of drug trafficking as the motive for the torture, even though at least two of the families believed their sons had died because they knew too much about illicit activities in the barracks. Aside from the insistent Geralsélia, no relatives of the dead or tortured men were called to testify or take part in the investigation. They received partial justice. Only two families collected their sons' pensions, and only one obtained a paltry compensation judgment a decade later (Melo 1997b).

While the defense's appeal to national security failed as an excuse for the crimes, it was clear that the S2's role in this area had given it immense power—to the point where its members bordered on insubordination.[40] As the trial ended, Lieutenant Miranda publicly threatened revenge against Geralsélia for her testimony (Geralsélia interview). With reduced sentences, after a few years in jail the torturers went free, and the additional allegations against Colonel Arioswaldo and others were dropped. Niebus, in fact, started a job at the Rio de Janeiro public telephone company in 1981. Documentation from the DOPS archives reveals that the phone company, the Ministry of Communications, and the Ministry of Mines and Energy had knowledge of his conviction.[41] The regime's security forces protected their torturer colleagues.

In the final analysis, the military punished Niebus and the others because the torture practiced against the regime's enemies had now turned its ugly face against the Army itself, with the incident providing irrefutable, horrible evidence that could not be ignored by the hierarchy. The Army was officially against torture. When it came to violations of human rights against its political enemies, however, it simply looked the other way.[42] (In 1975 the Army covered up the infamous death by torture of journalist Vladimir Herzog, but in 1995 former President Geisel affirmed that it was "murder" [Couto 1998:181–82].) On the same page as the Barra Mansa convictions *O Estado de São Paulo* published the news of the "suicide" by hanging of revolutionary Anatália de Souza Alves de Melo, who in reality had been found burned to death in her cell at the Recife DOPS.[43] There was no investigation.

Dom Waldyr's denunciations through the Bipartite were crucial in bringing the Barra Mansa incident into the public light and avoiding a cover-up. As Judge Sussekind observed in retrospect, the Barra Mansa case did not have the "political" overtones of the inquests involving accusations of subversion (Sussekind interview). The military investigated in a vigorous but highly legalistic and restricted way, losing the chance to extend the investigation to other intelligence units and to shut down the torture machine. The left ignored the incident because no one from its ranks was involved, and it failed to understand the potential for converting the case into a banner for human rights.[44] The Church alone realized the significance of the deaths of four youths who were mere draftees but also symbols of the powerless masses most often forgotten in the political struggles of Brazilian history.

For the Army, which held immense power at this juncture, winning the war against both the left and the Church was paramount. The death of yet another youth debated at the Bipartite revealed the extremes to which the military was willing to go.

Chapter 10 **Anatomy of a Death**

The Case of Alexandre Vannucchi Leme

I n mid-1973 the Church carried out a months-long protest against the killing of Alexandre Vannucchi Leme, a twenty-two-year-old University of São Paulo (USP) student who died in jail hours after his arrest and torture by security agents. One of the most shocking episodes of the Médici years, Leme's death on March 17, 1973, led students and Roman Catholic clergymen to defy riot troops and gather three thousand people to hear Dom Paulo criticize the government at a memorial service. When public and legal protest failed to force the regime to investigate, the Grupo Religioso pressed the matter at three consecutive meetings of the Bipartite.

This case is generally forgotten in discussions of military Brazil.[1] Most writings on the military dictatorship pinpoint a similar momentous religious protest against the murder by torture of journalist Vladimir Herzog in 1975 as the opposition's great awakening in the fight for human rights and democracy. In the words of fellow journalist and torture victim Paulo Markun, "The death of Vladimir Herzog changed Brazil. It provoked the first great popular reaction against torture, arbitrary imprisonment, [and] disrespect for human rights."[2] This incident occurred *after* President Geisel had already moved to liberalize the regime and restrict the repressive forces. The Herzog case marked the virtual end of killings in the cells of the security forces. Leme's death came in the midst of the worst repression. It sparked the *first* large-scale antiregime demonstration of the 1970s and set a precedent for the Herzog protest. The routine detention of a student activist escalated into a serious political problem for the regime and became the most important human rights case debated

Geology student and ALN militant Alexandre Vannucchi Leme was tortured to death at the São Paulo DOI-CODI. Three thousand people attended a memorial service for Leme, which launched the Church's public campaign for human rights.

at the Bipartite. It marked a turning point of the Médici period as the opposition began to reassert itself under Church leadership.

This chapter will examine three facets of the episode. The first section seeks to resolve controversial questions about Leme's political activities and the circumstances of his death. While most people at USP and in the Church viewed Leme primarily as a student and doubted the regime's version of events, the security forces had nevertheless accurately identified him as an important ALN militant. When he died unexpectedly, they resorted to a dual cover-up of their botched torture. The second section analyzes reactions to the incident and its role in building the opposition. Protest caused the police and the military to justify their actions and preserve the regime's image by falsely magnifying Leme's crimes to present him as a dangerous terrorist. On the other hand, clerics and students sought to clarify the death and raised Leme up as a symbol of heroic resistance. The Church walked a tightrope between the desire for justice and the need to avoid further violence. It faced high risks in taking up the Leme cause—reprisal by the military for becoming too close to the revolutionary left, the principal enemy of the regime, for instance. Yet it also gained political strength by firmly defending human rights. The third section delves into the debate over the case at the Bipartite, providing a detailed example of how Church and regime attempted dialogue to resolve their deepest differences.

From Arrest to Cover-Up: Setting the Record Straight

Leme's death shook the University of São Paulo campus and the São Paulo Church. Considered a model student, he had scored highest on the USP geology entrance exam. As a popular campus leader, he defended the university system against government interference and opposed efforts to end free tuition. He helped organize political street theater and spoke out on national issues, criticizing the drain on Brazil's resources through the export of mineral wealth and the construction of the Transamazon Highway, a symbol of Médici's economic miracle. Leme came from a leading Catholic family from the nearby traditional town of Sorocaba. Three of his aunts were nuns; his uncle Aldo Vannucchi was a prominent priest in Sorocaba. Father Vannucchi had frequent contact with the clergy of the archdiocese of São Paulo, Brazil's largest, and knew Dom Paulo. Leme expressed enthusiasm for Dom Hélder and other progressive bishops.[3]

The government saw Leme as a "terrorist" of the armed branch of the ALN, active mainly in São Paulo. Students and other youths made up most of the recruits of the ALN, a nationalist offshoot of the Brazilian Communist Party and the major urban guerrilla threat. The police accused Leme of armed robbery, thefts, and helping to plan the execution of Manoel Henrique de Oliveira, a Portuguese restaurateur targeted by the ALN for informing on three militants who were subsequently killed.[4]

Similar disagreement existed over Leme's death. The authorities said a truck hit Leme as he was fleeing his captors at a busy intersection. The Church asserted he was murdered by torture. Students, lawyers for the family, and clergymen pointed out faults in the police version and obtained decisive evidence of death by torture. How they did so is told below. Suffice it to say here that the police version immediately raised suspicions. It was not the first time nor the last that they used stories of accidents, suicide, or gunfights to explain the death of political prisoners. The best example was Herzog's clumsily forged hanging after a few hours in jail. Furthermore, the police had prevented examination of Leme's body for signs of abuse by quickly burying it in a pauper's cemetery and covering it with lime to speed its decomposition (Comissão de Familiares 1996:174). The security forces used this cemetery, located on the outskirts in Perus, to hide the bodies of other political prisoners.[5] After days of frantic searching for his son at police stations, the army, and the morgue, José de Oliveira Leme learned of Alexandre's interment from detective Fleury, the notorious torturer (José Leme interview).[6] Egle Maria

Vannucchi Leme, Alexandre's mother, went to Perus, where a grounds keeper showed her the plot.

The police evidence provides some clues about unexplained aspects of Leme's death. As in many cases, the investigators relied heavily on depositions taken under torture and in the absence of legal counsel. Mainly USP students and friends of Leme, these witnesses later retracted their statements before a military tribunal, where lawyers were present. Police lies and abuse do not preclude all of their evidence, however (Gorender 1998:261). A major question involves Leme's participation in the ALN. According to the police, Leme was the ALN's "brain" at USP. He politicized students, distributed newspapers, and recruited sympathizers. Leme hailed Church denunciations of regime abuses and allegedly contacted "priests ready for engagement in the ALN."[7]

Leme was indeed an ALN political coordinator. As the police claimed, he had close contact with Ronaldo Queiroz, a geology student who went into the ALN guerrilla underground. Mainly from the interior, most geology students were from a lower social station than other USP students. They were willing to dirty themselves on field trips and to live in rugged conditions. They also tended to be more politically outspoken because of their study of problems related to the exploitation of Brazil's natural resources. Queiroz praised Leme's political skills, and Leme eventually took over Queiroz's spot on the USP student council.[8]

In mid-1972 Leme had a key meeting with a top leader of the armed wing, Carlos Eugênio Sarmento Coelho da Paz, a tough, Army-trained gunman who eluded the security forces. Leme and Paz discussed ALN political strategy as they sat in a getaway car. Leme was a crucial tie to the outside world for the increasingly isolated revolutionaries. After the ALN's devastating defeats, Paz looked to him to raise badly needed student recruits, and membership rose. Leme reported to Paz that disgust with the regime was growing on campus and in the Church. Marighella had included the Church in his plan to unite a variety of social groups in the fight for national liberation against the military and U.S. imperialism. With its nationwide presence the Church could provide an excellent support network. After the Dominican debacle, the ALN counted on Leme to renew ties to Catholic progressives.[9]

Leme perceived the need to break the increasing isolation of the student movement and the decimated resistance by forging links with other movements, communities, and the Church. As part of this plan, he and others distributed antiregime pamphlets at churches in poor neighborhoods (Adriano Diogo and Arlete

Diogo interviews). Although Leme supported the ALN through legal activities, he endorsed armed struggle and saw it as consistent with his deep beliefs about Christian liberation (Arlete Diogo interview). His death dealt a serious blow to the organization (Carlos Eugênio Paz interview). A flyer of the revolutionary Movimento de Libertação Popular (MOLIPO; Movement for Popular Liberation) eulogized Leme as a "popular combatant."[10]

Except for one brief and vague statement by a tortured student, however, the police had no proof linking Leme to violence. First, their report did not mention him in a description of robberies and thefts allegedly carried out by Queiroz and others.[11] Second, the lead DEOPS-SP interrogator in the case, detective Edsel Magnotti, cited documents found on Oliveira's ALN assassins linking Leme to the crime, but these documents are nowhere to be found in the DEOPS-SP papers or in the investigation.[12] Moreover, it was unlikely for a guerrilla to carry information that could endanger a comrade. Third, Paz, who ordered the execution of Oliveira, gave the task of shadowing the restaurateur not to Leme but to Francisco Penteado. The ALN could not afford to expose a valuable student organizer to violence (Carlos Eugênio Paz interview). Penteado allegedly participated in the assassination in February 1973 and was murdered along with two other militants by the police days before Leme's arrest.[13] Most significant, the DEOPS-SP archive contains nothing on Leme *prior* to his death. The vast documentation of the political police testifies to their careful surveillance even of unthreatening groups and individuals. Leme was apparently too unimportant, or too unnoticeable in his peaceful ALN work, to attract police attention.[14]

Exactly how the security forces learned of Leme and arrested him remains a mystery. One possibility was through a former ALN militant who became an informant (Expedito Filho 1992:29). They most likely caught word of him in a furious sweep against the ALN for its February 25, 1973, assassination of Octávio Gonçalves Moreira Júnior, a DOI-CODI torturer with links to the ultraright Comando de Caça aos Comunistas (Communist-Hunting Command) and the extremist Catholic group Tradição, Família e Propriedade (Tradition, Family, and Property), which accused progressive clergymen of Communism.[15] The DOI-CODI needed to assert itself because its future had clouded with the coming presidency of Geisel, an advocate of liberalization. About a week before his detention, Leme noticed he was being trailed (Lisete interview; Lázaro interview 1). The only other clue came in an ALN intelligence report carried to Paz, who was in Cuba undergoing further guerrilla training. It stated that Leme and other ALN militants had fallen because of an unknown security breach in the student movement (Carlos

Eugênio Paz interview).[16] Leme was undoubtedly picked up by the DOI-CODI.[17] There two interrogation squads successively brutalized him on March 16 and 17. As the cell keeper went to get Leme for yet another session, he was surprised to find him dead (Comissão de Familiares 1996:173).

When only a few hundred of the tens of thousands of people arrested in military Brazil perished, why did Leme die? The torturers alone know the intimate details of his calvary. The only named perpetrator in Leme's death (the others are known only by code names), DOI-CODI commander Major Carlos Alberto Brilhante Ustra, made no comment on Leme in his 1986 book on the repression. He denied engaging in torture, although a former militant later elected to the Congress accused him of being her tormentor (Ustra 1986).[18] Ustra was one of the most infamous persecutors of the left (Gorender 1998:272; also Wright 1993).

Presumably Ustra and his agents did not intend Leme's death—at least not on the seventeenth. Although the sadistic traditions of Brazilian police work certainly thrived in the 1970s, the security forces basically used torture to gather intelligence. Torturers became professional at testing the physical and psychological limits of their victims, sometimes with the assistance of physicians and psychologists.[19] There is no evidence of such help at Leme's interrogation.[20]

Or perhaps Leme's executioners applied wrathful force because of his relatives' political activities. Father Vannucchi, who treated Leme as a son, had worked with JOC and was jailed briefly by the Sorocaba police in 1964 on suspicion of Communism.[21] The security forces had also tortured two of Leme's cousins, student revolutionaries José Ivo and Paulo de Tarso Vannuchi. Paulo belonged to the ALN. Leme visited him in prison and discussed political issues. Deeply worried about his safety, Leme's relatives tried to convince him to reduce his political activity.

Another factor might be the proud defiance of youth. Leme did not give up easily in a fight (Paulo Vannuchi interview). Days before his death he told a fellow student that he would resist arrest.[22] At the DOI-CODI he entered a maximum security cell. While many prisoners gave up information, Leme refused. According to witnesses, Leme, carried by jail keepers back to his cell after a torture session, cried out, "My name is Alexandre Vannucchi Leme. I am a geology student. They accuse me of belonging to the ALN. I only gave my name" (Comissão de Familiares 1996:175). One DOI-CODI agent referred to Leme as "crazy" (Pereira 1986:6). A friend, Arlete Diogo, who was also imprisoned and tortured stated the following:

> The torturers were very impressed because he didn't say anything. . . . They would become enraged when we said that he was a Christian. They wanted to talk about Alexandre. . . . Their concern was always to incriminate Alexandre, to create the image

of an atheist, a sectarian, a violent person. But that image didn't fit with the one that
we had of him. (Pereira 1986)

Whatever the reason, the DOI-CODI agents were unprepared for Leme's death.
They rushed to forge two stories. The first was for those who knew that Leme died
at DOI-CODI—prisoners, agents uninvolved in the interrogation, coroners who
signed false reports, and other police authorities. In this version Leme had committed suicide by cutting his throat with a razor blade in the infirmary. To authen-
ticate this story the interrogators and their commanders slit the neck from ear to
ear while the body still lay in the cell. Other prisoners saw the body covered with
blood as the agents dragged it away.[23] The jailers then faked a search for blades in
other cells (Archdiocese of São Paulo 1985:256).

The second version, the truck accident, went to the press. It became imperative
after a USP student phoned the family about the arrest, leading José Leme to search
for his son. The security agents could not keep the stories straight. Fleury gave
Leme's father the accident version; moments later, Magnotti insisted it was suicide
(Pereira 1986). In a letter to a top prosecutor DEOPS-SP Director Lúcio Vieira
mixed the two versions by referring to the truck accident as a "suicide."[24] After the
press belatedly reported the "accident" on March 23, 1973, a DOI-CODI man
bragged to prisoners: "We give out any version we want" (*Meu filho Alexandre
Vannucchi*, 5). Cover-up and false accusations allowed the regime to focus attention
on Leme as a dangerous "terrorist."

The incident's political implications led the police to substantiate Leme's death
by investigating him posthumously. They arrested other USP students to justify
their claim of the existence of a large ALN network on the campus (Lázaro interview 2). Only after the family's lawyers petitioned the courts for aid did the police
include Leme in the Oliveira murder case. In his case summary, Magnotti revealed
the underlying concern of the regime: students and the Church were protesting
Leme's death.[25] The official public statement extended the lie by accusing Leme of
crimes not even alleged by the police. The public statement also referred to Leme's
revelation of the names of other subversives—but no such deposition exists in the
police report.[26]

The Reaction to Leme's Death: Moving to the Brink, Building Opposition

Leme posed a bigger challenge to the regime in death than in life. His murder
tested the bishops' new commitment to human rights. In February 1973, they had

commemorated the twenty-fifth anniversary of the U.N. Declaration of Human Rights and adopted an unprecedented educational campaign by distributing hundreds of thousands of copies of the declaration.[27] Theory became action.

The Church and the students protested the incident not just because Leme was a popular campus leader. His was the only death of a USP activist who had not gone underground to join the guerrillas (Lázaro interview 2; Adriano Diogo and Arlete Diogo interviews). There was no link between Leme and violence. So the opposition was all the more adamant about learning the circumstances of his demise. Leme's death also contributed to the growing perception among the students and in the Church that the repression had reached its limits. Leme became a symbol against the repression.

The first outcry came from the bishop of Sorocaba. Dom José Melhado Campos (a neighbor of the Lemes) and the local council of priests issued a scathing criticism of the police. It was read at masses and published in the Sorocaba press, Church bulletins, and *O São Paulo,* the weekly newspaper of the archdiocese of São Paulo:

> Why wasn't the family notified of the "accident"? Why wasn't the body turned over to them? Who in the family carried out the proper identification of the cadaver before it was buried? Why did the family only learn about the occurrence in the newspapers, on Friday the 23rd, when, according to police, Alexandre had died the previous Saturday, the 17th? . . . It does not lie within our competence to refute the accusations imputed against this young university student. God knows the truth and judges. But it is evident that, torturing and killing the victim, the police authorities barbarically eliminated someone who could have recognized his acts and defended himself through the legal process.[28]

Several days later Dom José and the priests' council published another protest in the local paper. They based their action on the CNBB's February 1973 document. They also asked President Médici to improve the protection of human rights.[29]

Meanwhile, students at USP and other universities protested Leme's death. In late March and April 1973, USP buzzed with activity—with meetings, pamphleteering, discussion at information tables, and class stoppages. Students wore black arm bands and draped black banners around the campus.[30] Leme's geology colleagues organized a joint student-faculty committee to investigate the circumstances of his death and to establish proof of his innocence (Simas 1986:233).[31] Students from USP and other schools then issued a statement citing Leme's "excellent reputation among students and professors" and his qualities as a leader.[32] The geology students declared a state of mourning and proposed a memorial mass for Leme. The police monitored the students through an infiltrator and obtained copies of their manifestos.[33] The clergy also planned masses. On March 29, 1973, Dom José held a mass in Sorocaba. Another was set for March 30 in São Paulo.

How to carry it out was a delicate matter. São Paulo was the explosive center of the guerrilla movement and the repression. Second Army head General Humberto de Souza Mello, the city's top military authority, fully backed the security forces, while Dom Paulo built a campaign for human rights. Dom Paulo visited prisoners (including the imprisoned Dominicans), exposed torture, and formed the CJP-SP to investigate abuses. In 1972 he had led the bishops of the state of São Paulo in a vigorous denunciation of torture ("Testemunho de paz" 1972). Days before Leme's death, Pope Paul VI lent prestige to Dom Paulo's efforts by naming him a cardinal. Through the Bipartite, the military had managed to tone down some of the São Paulo Church's protest and even tried to co-opt Dom Paulo (see chapter 7). Seeking dialogue, he had by mid-1972 visited Second Army headquarters three times, but Souza Mello refused to see him.[34] President Médici also expelled Dom Paulo from his office after a meeting of only a few moments (Médici 1995:84). Emotions rising, the Leme issue threatened to burst into a major crisis.

Dom Paulo had to work carefully. He was archbishop of South America's largest city and an honorary vice president of Brazil. To celebrate mass for a suspected subversive could only anger the authorities. But Dom Paulo was also a pastor to students. Twenty-two of their leaders went to Dom Paulo's home. They informed him that the police had surrounded the USP. The leaders demanded that he say mass there for ten thousand students expected to appear. If not, they would start a riot. However, going to USP could only provoke the generals. Dom Paulo sought a nonviolent alternative. He convinced the students that a mass at the Sé Cathedral in downtown São Paulo would be an act for all Brazil to witness (Dom Paulo interview).[35]

It was the eve of the ninth anniversary of the coup. Despite the censors' ban on publicity, attempts to block traffic, and the presence of riot troops near the Sé and at USP, three thousand people attended the service. Upon entering the cathedral, each received a prayer sheet that also served to cover the face from police cameras (Dom Paulo interview).[36] The police distributed a falsified version of the student leadership's manifesto.[37] With police sirens blaring outside, Dom Paulo, Dom José, and twenty-four priests led the people in prayer and singing, including a prohibited protest song by exiled composer Geraldo Vandré.[38] Using biblical passages, Dom Paulo rebuked the authorities:

> Only God owns life. He is its origin, and only He can decide its end. . . . When he was born, Christ himself wanted to feel the tenderness of his mother and the warmth of the

Pope Paul VI conferred the status of cardinal on Dom Paulo, in Rome, on March 5, 1973, just days before Leme's death. Dom Paulo used his ecclesiastical prestige to oppose the repression.

family. And even after he died, his corpse was returned to his mother, friends, and relatives. This justice was done to Christ by a representative of the Roman government who was totally against His mission as the Messiah. . . . "Where is your brother? The voice of your brother's blood is crying out to Me from the ground!" . . . Who has done justice—the Supreme Judge asks—who has seen to it that the truth is said and that love has been given a chance? . . . Men are being imprisoned! Has anybody been able to visit them and free them?[39]

After the mass the people sang and calmly left the cathedral as security forces stood by in a one-hundred-block area ready to repress any attempt at political demonstration.

Not all students and clergy supported Dom Paulo. Dom Vicente Marchetti Zioni, the conservative archbishop whose arrival in Botucatu led to the exit of many clergymen, refused a request by students to say mass. The police were pleased.[40] In São Paulo right-wing organizations distributed flyers against the mass. A group at the highly conservative USP law school, for instance, called Leme a "terrorist" and the memorial "ridiculous." The group concluded: "Heads are going to roll, and you can be sure that they won't be ours."[41]

"Where is your brother? The voice of your brother's blood is crying out to Me from the ground!"
(Dom Paulo).

An exchange of private letters between Dom Paulo and Minister of Education Jarbas Passarinho revealed the extremes to which each side believed the other had gone. Dom Paulo complained that the security forces took "justice into their own hands" and were ignorant of "the most elemental principles of human rights." Dom Paulo added, "A crime—if it occurred—is not punished with an even larger crime." He continued:

> Your Excellency, Senhor Minister, knows as well as I do what Brazil expects from its youth . . . to whom lessons of this ilk, especially coming from where they do, are not the most apt for making this generation believe in the future or be ready to take charge of it. Whatever its source, violence is the most fertile seed from whose bosom hate will be born many times over and whose brutality and stupidity prepare the ruin of any nation. Violence is even more serious, incomprehensible, and unpardonable if it begins precisely with those whose highest mission is to safeguard the peace, protect families, and show tolerance and understanding towards those on whom age has not yet conferred maturity and who often confuse healthy ideals with the impetuous generosity of their young years. . . . There once was a time when having a son in the university was reason for just pride and serene tranquillity for parents. Today with ever greater frequency it is motive for fear and anxiety.

Dom Paulo asked Passarinho to use his prestige within the government to clarify the many doubts about the case.[42]

Passarinho's response was severe. He claimed that the episode did not concern the Ministry of Education (although DEOPS documentation shows that the ministry's spy service watched the situation at the USP).[43] Leme died because he was trying to overthrow the regime. "Alexandre was a student terrorist. . . . He belonged to the Armed Tactical Group of the ALN, whose mission, as is known, is armed combat. He was not affected as a student, but as a terrorist." Passarinho then attacked the Church's human rights campaign:

> Eminence, I cannot fathom a justice (I prefer to call it a pretense of justice) which consists only of invoking . . . defense of the prerogatives of human persons when they are guerrillas. I do not understand why nothing is said about the right to life of people like the Portuguese merchant, machine-gunned thanks to information from Alexandre and others.

Passarinho praised Dom Paulo's denunciation of violence and urged him to defend his position publicly, but he criticized the cardinal for holding the memorial:

> That mass, celebrated . . . when the day's activities are coming to an end and crowds become inevitable in downtown São Paulo; a mass awaited with intense expectation because of activists' publicity spread as a challenge to the temporal Power; a mass marked by a homily extremely harsh towards those responsible for state security (and therefore judging them in absentia); that mass, Senhor Cardinal, could have caused a river of blood, and yes, this time, the blood of the innocent and the pious! Fortunately, thanks to the Mercy of God and the prudence of the authorities, this did not happen. But the probability was extremely high. I believe that Your Excellency considered that possibility but preferred to run the risk for reasons surely ponderable but beyond me.[44]

The government reacted strongly. Censors blocked news of Dom Paulo's sermon (Silva 1973), although some reports did slip through, resulting in the punishment of a São Paulo television station under the LSN and prior censorship of the Rio opposition paper *Opinião*.[45] In the Chamber of Deputies, MDB congressman Lysâneas Maciel berated the government, but no newspaper printed his speech or the demand of a colleague that the Congress investigate human rights violations.[46] The security forces arrested dozens in a search for the campus organizers of the event. Students were also detained in Rio de Janeiro.[47]

At the DOI-CODI, Major Ustra and his torturers beat their prisoners in a fit of rage and fear over the mass (Adriano Diogo and Arlete Diogo interviews). The episode reverberated across the state of São Paulo, keeping the DEOPS and intelligence units on alert for months. In an unusual development, President Médici's public relations office received a notice about the case. Like Communism, mention of Leme's name immediately raised suspicions and led to the opening of intelligence files on individuals. As one report put it, the regime now had an "Alexandre Vannucc[h]i Leme problem."[48]

The government feared and the campuses hoped for one thing: the revival of the student movement. The mass was the first large political gathering of students since 1969 ("A marca da cruz" 1978). One flyer stated that it showed the "force of mobilization and unity, which leave the repressors with their hands tied" against the masses.[49] The spy services in Rio de Janeiro and across São Paulo analyzed the "fresh outbreak of leftist activities" at colleges and schools, some experiencing agitation for the first time. Activists were organizing meetings, strikes, marches, and murals; distributing literature; and seeking ties to the progressive clergy.[50] Fearing the spread of Communist influence, the federal police saw the need for all spy agencies to "conduct a general investigation of the entire student movement."[51]

The Bipartite: Pressure Behind the Scenes

In the weeks after Leme's death, the opposition continued to pressure the government to resolve the case. Responding to faculty and student demands, USP president Miguel Reale sent a laconic, formal request for an explanation to Brigadier General Sérvulo Mota Lima, the secretary of public security for the state of São Paulo.[52]

General Lima had taken part in the investigation of the Barra Mansa deaths (Sampaio interview) and was therefore no stranger to the horrors of torture. Yet in a public reply to Reale, the general attempted to erase all suspicion of wrongdoing in the Leme case. The statement appeared widely in the press. Lima reaffirmed the accusations as well as the accident story. He added that Leme had revealed names of other ALN members and *confessed* to participating in two robberies and the Oliveira murder. However, Leme had refused to state his occupation or his address, where he kept subversive documents. Lima asserted that the security forces delayed public notification because they needed secrecy to break up a "terrorist cell" at the USP. Lima claimed he had witnesses to prove that Leme died from an accident. The burial took place quickly to prevent what had happened in Recife, where "terrorists" tried to steal a comrade's cadaver from the morgue to exploit his death politically.[53] As the secret Bipartite meetings subsequently revealed, the military feared that Leme would become another Edson Luís, a student victim of the repression whose publicly displayed corpse inspired nationwide protests in 1968.[54]

After Lima's statement, the Leme family and the Church opened another front with the help of two lawyers from the CJP-SP—Mário Simas, who had defended the Dominicans, and José Carlos Dias. They petitioned the police, the courts, and the military to turn over the body and to investigate the incident thoroughly. The requests went up the chain of command to General Souza Mello (Simas 1986, ch. 16). His failure to respond or to send the case to the civilian authorities signified implicit recognition that the death had occurred in a military installation such as DOI-CODI (Mário Simas interview).

The episode gained international dimensions when Leme's mother wrote a letter to Pope Paul VI on Good Friday, the day of Christ's death. "My son Alexandre, who was a person of ideals and self-giving, was summarily assassinated by the organs of repression exactly because he was struggling for the protection of human rights in Brazil and defending justice and liberty," she wrote. She asked the pontiff to help bring "peace and justice" to Brazil *(Meu filho Alexandre Vannucchi)*. The foreign press also reported on the case.

When all else failed, the bishops took the Leme case to the Bipartite Commission. The Grupo Religioso persistently pressed the Situação for an accounting of Leme's death. At the May 30, 1973, meeting Candido Mendes described the moment as an important "test" of the Bipartite's dialogue.[55] The day before, he had been in São Paulo. He presented the petitions from the Leme family drafted by Dias and Simas. The attorneys enumerated inconsistencies in the official version, including the claim that Leme was buried as an anonymous indigent because nothing was known of him. The death certificate carried full information. The petitioners requested an exhumation and a detailed autopsy in the presence of the family's doctor, dentist, and lawyers. They explained that their motive was not political but to "discover the truth."[56]

General Muricy declared that the government wanted to clarify the incident. He read the depositions of the alleged witnesses who had seen Alexandre run over. Then Major Lee attempted to rebut the petition point by point using the same argumentation as General Lima. Working at CIE, Lee knew more about the repression than perhaps any other member of the Situação (Moraes Rego interview). He denied that the security forces knew that either Leme or those he allegedly denounced were students. The police wanted to know about subversive activities, not the men's professions. Moreover, there was "nothing strange" in the fact that General Lima's statement placed Leme's death at 11 A.M., while the death certificate stated 5 P.M. Most significant, Lee said that the time, place, and circumstances of Leme's arrest were unimportant.[57] Candido Mendes insisted that the government order the judiciary to approve the petition, but Professor Padilha refused the idea as a violation of the separation of powers. The Situação's postmeeting report stated that the Leme case "polarized" the two sides. Yet the military was confident that its version would eventually be proved correct, thus forcing Dom José and other clergymen to retract their criticisms.[58]

The Grupo Religioso came well prepared to counterargue the military's points at the July 25, 1973, Bipartite. Dom Lucas presented documents verifying Leme's appendectomy in late January and his recuperation in Sorocaba during part of February. This evidence contradicted the security forces' mention of an "old incision" on the corpse and the assertion that Leme was engaged in subversive activity in São Paulo in February. Thus an exhumation might show the cadaver to be of another person. (As Dom Ivo observed, the security forces switched the identities of prisoners to prevent their location by friends or family. Dom José had raised this possibility during the Sorocaba mass.) If so, cases of other missing prisoners might be resolved. The bishop made reference to the DOI-CODI, thus indicating that the Grupo Religioso had good information as to who was carrying out the repression. Dom Lucas also claimed that Leme's family was receiving threatening phone calls. Candido Mendes added that the petition was valid not only for the civilian justice system but also for the military courts that judged cases of alleged subversion. General Muricy tried to deflect these arguments. The family had not approached the Army with its petition, he stated. The case was "practically closed," but Candido Mendes was "pressuring" the Lemes to continue. The bishops forced the issue yet further, with Dom Ivo defending Candido Mendes's role in the case as representative of the CNBB and the Peace and Justice Commission. Even the more conciliatory Dom Avelar entered the debate, affirming that "this case should be carried to its ultimate consequences . . . because it involved the probity of the CNBB and the bishop of Sorocaba." If Dom José were wrong, the CNBB would recognize that he had been used. If he were right, the police would have to correct their ways.[59]

Dom Lucas then dropped a bombshell: at least one other prisoner would testify that Leme had died differently from the military version. Candido Mendes suggested that attorney Simas be brought to the Bipartite. General Muricy refused, stating that Simas was "against the government." He preferred a member of the Leme family. Padilha added that the family had given up on their petition.[60] (In fact, they had not.) But the evidence continued to mount against the Situação. At the August Bipartite, Dom Ivo showed the commission the depositions of five witnesses stating in a military court that Leme had died in his cell after torture by DOI-CODI agents.[61]

Dom Ivo's words were the last recorded by the Bipartite on the Leme death. As the military predicted, it had won a battle against the Grupo Religioso because the official version stood. No body was exhumed, no satisfaction or further explanation given the family and the public. Wittingly or unwittingly, the Situação took part in the cover-up. Yet in the Situação's estimation, the bishops had persisted because the case was "polemical" and thus gave them "certain triumphs."[62]

The ultimate moral victory came for the Church in 1985, when it published testimony about Leme's death in *Brasil: nunca mais*. One eyewitness at the DOI-CODI spoke of seeing "many people being tortured." "The worst case took place with a young man named Alexandre Vannucchi. For two or three days I heard his cries and, in the end, . . . I saw his cadaver taken out of the maximum security cell, with blood spreading all over the floor" (Archdiocese of São Paulo 1985:256).

Conclusion

As his death produced repercussions throughout the 1970s, Leme's name became a symbol of resistance for the opposition but also a signal alerting the police to new acts of subversion. In 1974 Amnesty International included a description of Leme's death in its human rights report on Brazil.[63] USP's Diretório Central dos Estudantes (DCE; Central Student Directorate) was renamed the "DCE Alexandre Vannucchi Leme." In March 1978 students across Brazil organized a day of protest to commemorate the fifth anniversary of Leme's death and the tenth anniversary of the Edson Luís incident. They used the occasion to demonstrate against President Geisel and the visit of U.S. President Jimmy Carter.[64] Leme's parents became rallying points in the broad-based amnesty movement for exiles and political prisoners. With the political opening, a number of opposition candidates tried to recruit the couple to support their campaigns.[65] Leme's case also appeared in denunciations of physicians accused of signing false death certificates to hide torture.[66] Many of these and other recollections of Leme caught the attention of DEOPS officers. Thus different interpretations of his importance contributed to the creation of the historical memory of the incident. The opposition cast Leme as a martyr, while the police saw him as a dangerous individual who, when remembered, led to further subversion.

Justice came slowly. In late 1978 the Superior Military Tribunal, which heard all appeals cases involving political prisoners, reviewed testimony of six witnesses to Leme's torture in the DOI-CODI. One of the judges, General Rodrigo Octávio Jordão, proposed an investigation but was outvoted (13–1). Encouraged by Jordão's initiative, attorney Simas once again petitioned the military justice system. He too was denied (Simas 1986:237–39). In 1983, with Brazil headed for civilian rule, the Leme family finally received permission to remove their son's bones from the Perus cemetery. With the help of a dental mold taken in early 1973 two dentists confirmed that the bones were Leme's (José Prestes interview). They were buried in the family plot in Sorocaba after a ceremony in São Paulo that also welcomed home the remains of Frei Tito, the brutally tortured Dominican who committed suicide in France. In December 1995, President Fernando Henrique Cardoso signed into law a bill making government compensation possible for families of victims of the dictatorship. Leme's name was approved as a government commission began reviewing cases in 1996 (see Miranda 1996b). The family received compensation payment in 1997.

The swell of outrage against Leme's death led the Church to exercise its new policies in defense of human rights. It became the "voice of the voiceless" for the family and the thousands of mourners prohibited from protesting. The notion of human rights passed from abstraction to concrete action. Dom José's and Dom Paulo's gestures did not represent individual positions but the national consensus of the bishops. The Church's position was fraught with risks. The potential for violence was great, and the Leme mass identified the Church with subversion and endangered its historically nonpartisan stance. Had the Church known fully Leme's ALN ties, it might have trod more cautiously.[67]

Paradoxically, the Church's position increased its political strength. The Leme incident forged a tighter bond between the Church and the students. The growing confluence between the Church and the left laid the basis for a strategic alliance that would help knit together the opposition during the transition to democracy.[68] Leme was dead, but his vision of a coalition of forces was becoming reality.

Dom Paulo's actions demonstrated the complexities and tensions involved in building the opposition. He walked a thin line between violence and demands for justice. He went with the students to the brink of confrontation with the government, but, unbeknownst to the regime, he also played a moderating role by staying away from the political hotbed of the USP campus and insisting on nonviolent protest. Dom Paulo understood well how to test the limits of the generals' patience. He was prudent but firm in his opposition to the repression. The Leme protest removed any doubt that he might be co-opted. It was a defining moment for Dom Paulo and the Church. Keeping the institution intact, he skillfully maneuvered it into opposition. Dom Paulo helped to define the options and limits of public protest against the regime.

The Leme mass served as a key rehearsal for Dom Paulo's important ecumenical memorial service for well-known Jewish journalist Herzog in 1975. This protest presented an even greater challenge to the regime because it united the opposition—not only students and Catholic clergymen, but Jews, media professionals, intellectuals, and other members of the elite. Thirty thousand students at USP went on strike, and forty-two bishops signed a statement denouncing the regime's violence. Two rabbis and a Protestant minister helped preside over the memorial at the cathedral, which drew eight thousand people despite the authorities' attempts to prevent the event. Dom Hélder, a pariah of the regime, also attended. The Herzog death came after Geisel had created new expectations about the end of the repression. Indeed, by then, the regime had begun to use repression more selectively, a result of Médici's effective stifling of the opposition. Violence diminished even further after the Herzog incident and further pressure by Geisel against the hard-liners. The debate over the case took place in public. The censors, for instance, did not stop a thousand journalists from publishing a petition in newspapers demanding an investigation. Herzog's status as a member of the media elite magnified the indignation about his death.[69] The protest against his death marked a turning point in the struggle for democracy.

Two and a half years earlier, however, the Leme mass had served as a key precedent by drawing three thousand people in protest during one of the bloodiest moments of the regime and *before* the Geisel administration's attempts to reduce human rights abuses. The opening of Dom Paulo's Herzog sermon echoed his earlier commentary: "God owns life."[70] The Leme case did not have greater impact because the regime imposed a big lie about his death. Herzog colleague Fernando Jordão observed that Dom Paulo had regularly denounced human rights violations throughout the Médici years, but "we journalists, because of pressure from our bosses, selfishness, professional incompetence, or lack of political awareness, often did not cover or make [the denunciations] public" (Jordão 1984:37).

Another tension resulted from the Church's confluence with the left. Dom Paulo's embrace of the Leme case and other similar actions by the Church marked a certain bias resulting from the sharp polarization of Brazilian society. Defenders of the regime complained that human rights often meant defense of the left but not of the right's victims. Minister Passarinho expressed this theme to Dom Paulo, and it was also an important subtext of the police investigation of Leme. Officer Magnotti wrote that "elements of the left in the Catholic Church . . . who knew how to protest, although without justification, the death of Alexandre Vannucchi Leme, . . . did not mention a single word in the pulpits of the Church in protest of the barbarous murder carried out by the subversive agents of the ALN against a . . . simple and humble merchant."[71] The right, too, suffered losses and held its memorial ceremonies (Ustra 1986, Giordani 1986).

The Bipartite Commission's treatment of the Leme case displayed a class bias. A crucial point was whether the security agents knew Leme was a student. Another fundamental factor was Leme's connection to the Church through relatives. These considerations implied that high social status and institutional ties somehow made the violation more serious—more heinous for the Church, more politically troublesome for the military. As in the Herzog case, indignation corresponded to a person's fame and importance. Both the military and the Church thus reflected the highly stratified Brazilian class system. Not everybody had the same human rights.

The Bipartite demonstrated that, while the Church struggled to develop a public stance on human rights, it also resorted to behind-the-scenes dialogue. Candido Mendes's intermediary role meant dialogue did not have to halt after General Muricy's refusal to speak to CJP-SP attorney Simas. More important, when public efforts failed and repression and censorship muffled the Church's public voice, the Grupo Religioso kept pressure on the regime by demanding information about political prisoners and victims of torture. The denunciations were also a sign that the opposition had begun to stir. This development struck fear in the security forces, leading them to lash out at the Church and the human rights movement.[72]

The Leme case underscored the political importance of human rights. The regime worked to present Leme as a terrorist. The Church used the case to denounce human rights abuses. Although threatened with violence, the Church took advantage of the opening provided by the incident to challenge the repression.

Chapter 11 **Conclusion**

As the regime finished off the urban guerrillas in 1973, a group of Castellistas successfully maneuvered within the armed forces to name Ernesto Geisel as Médici's successor. Geisel wanted to return Brazil to civilian rule and immediately embarked on a campaign of distensão, or liberalization of the political system. He reined in the torturers and the hard-liners, revoked AI-5, restored civil liberties, and relaxed press censorship. By the time Figueiredo assumed power in 1979, the abertura was well underway. But, as Geisel had determined, it was a gradual, slow, and secure abertura—secure especially for the armed forces. In August 1979 the Figueiredo government granted amnesty to political prisoners and exiles—but also to torturers. After a decade of careful control of the political process by the military, in 1985 a civilian again occupied the Palácio do Planalto.

Geisel began his term hoping to improve relations with the Church. A Lutheran of Germanic lineage, he was Brazil's first Protestant president to serve a full term.[1] But he recognized the political importance of the Catholic hierarchy. Brazil's cardinals took a prominent spot at his inauguration on March 15, 1974 (in fact, they did not all appear at the inauguration of any of the other four [Catholic] military presidents). General Golbery, Geisel's principal adviser on distensão, met with Candido Mendes, Dom Paulo, and other Church leaders. In January 1976, Geisel fired Second Army Commander General Ednardo D'Ávila Mello for failing to prevent the deaths of Herzog and Manoel Fiel Filho, a Catholic union activist murdered at the São Paulo DOI-CODI. In an apparent display of sympathy, Geisel visited Dom Geraldo Maria de Morais Penido, the cousin of the murdered Jesuit Father João Bosco Penido Burnier.[2]

Conclusion

A significant part of Geisel's Church strategy was to phase out the Bipartite. General Muricy wanted to continue, however (Piletti and Praxedes 1997:414). He appealed to his friend Geisel. Muricy was one of the very few officers who could call the president "Ernesto" or "Alemão" (German), a nickname. Around the time of the inauguration, Muricy approached Geisel to discuss the Bipartite. He also met with Golbery, Minister of Justice Armando Falcão, and the Navy and Army ministers. Muricy volunteered to remain at the commission's head.[3] Golbery also favored its continuation (Piletti and Praxedes 1997:414). The president ordered the Bipartite to proceed "until it was necessary to establish modifications." General Muricy informed the bishops of this decision, and both sides were eager to proceed. When the Grupo Religioso pressed for collaboration with the government, however, Muricy became noncommittal, stating that he needed to await further orientation.[4] Clearly, Muricy had not been given the same kind of authority by Geisel as he had enjoyed under Médici. Geisel was applying the brakes to the Bipartite. The commission met in March, May, and August 1974. Then Geisel decided that area Army commanders should establish contact with the bishops in order to improve relations at the local level (Muricy 1993:662–63). Dialogue continued, but hiding it was no longer necessary because the press was freer and the government somewhat more open.[5] After August 26, 1974, the Bipartite ceased to exist, leaving the political scene as secretly as it had entered it in November 1970.

Three days later, General Muricy entered into the U.S. Army Command and General Staff College Allied Officer Hall of Fame. The ceremony took place in Rio and was attended by Brazilian and North American officials, including U.S. ambassador John Crimmins. Muricy joined Castello Branco, Orlando Geisel, Oswaldo Cordeiro de Farias, and other prominent Brazilian generals honored in the hall, located at Fort Leavenworth, where Muricy had trained during World War II.[6] The unofficial extension of Muricy's military career had come to a fitting end.

It was now Geisel's turn to deal with the bishops. He viewed relations with the Church as a question of two states, Brazil and the Vatican. Therefore, he considered the papal nuncio the proper representative of the Church. Furthermore, Geisel recognized the authority of the pope within the Church and believed that the CNBB, which took the strongest positions at the Bipartite, was questioning that authority.[7] After the nuncio, Geisel preferred to deal first with the cardinals and then with the bishops. Geisel delegated to General Golbery some of these contacts. With the Bipartite gone, the CNBB now spoke directly with the government.[8] Because the abertura brought about a gradual end to censorship and the repression, a secret commission was no longer essential for Church-state communication.

Yet Church-state relations remained difficult. Geisel cracked down on both the hard-line military and its civilian opponents in order to control the abertura. He was as dictatorial as any of his predecessors. In addition to the Burnier killing, numerous violent attacks on the Church took place, including the 1976 kidnapping and torture of Dom Adriano Hypólito, the bishop of Nova Iguaçu. Conflict raged especially in the countryside, where the clergy defended the poor against powerful interests and the authorities. Generals and conservative politicians still accused the Church of subversion and of embracing Communism, while the bishops' growing criticism helped turn sentiment against the regime. Relations improved somewhat under Figueiredo, but strife continued in the countryside (Mainwaring 1986:154–64).

The Achievements of the Bipartite: Reducing Church-State Conflict

After four years of secret dialogue, what had the Bipartite achieved? What was its significance for the Catholic Church, the military, and the Médici era? And what does it suggest for the study of recent Brazilian history?

In the twentieth century the Church and the Army, two of Brazil's leading institutions, cooperated and clashed as they sought to modernize and influence the development of society. The military increased its political prominence, culminating in the regime of 1964–1985. The Church too became deeply involved in politics by rebuilding itself and restoring its influence on the state. Although culturally and ideologically quite different, in the period from 1930 to 1964 the Church and the armed forces built a working relationship based largely on their mutual anti-Communism. Some of the military leadership that matured in this era strongly embraced traditional Catholicism as a basis of Brazilian identity and patriotism. General Muricy exemplified this attitude. Muricy surely suffered a crisis of guilt while seeing his Church attacked by comrades in arms. Similarly, bishops such as Dom Jaime Câmara held the armed forces in high respect. This relationship is essential for understanding modern Brazil.

Cross and sword entered into conflict after the "dual revolution" that began in 1964. The Church increasingly stressed social justice, while the military fought Communism and subversion in the name of Western Christian civilization. The worst Church-state crisis in Brazilian history ensued. The security forces increasingly targeted the Church, while members of the clergy developed a network of political resistance to the regime. Catholic activism, attacks on the Church, and torture became central issues that spilled into the diplomatic arena in Rome and other parts of Europe. General Muricy and Dom Eugênio worked to salvage Brazil's deteriorating image. The crisis involved ideological struggle, but also the competition for the right to shape the future of Brazilian society. The crisis further highlighted the differences between the Church and the military and how little they understood each other's motives, institutional culture, and efforts at modernization. The conflict was exacerbated by the political polarization of the cold war, which affected all of the Americas. Within this context existed a vast area of theological and political ambiguity captured in Dom Avelar's conundrum: "Where does social justice end and subversion begin?"

The Brazilian solution was the Bipartite. The repression and rapid deterioration of Church-state relations under Médici ostensibly ruled out dialogue. The crucial papers of General Muricy have revealed, however, that the Bipartite institutionalized dialogue precisely as the Church and the military entered the worst period in their history. The talks were systematic and encompassed religion, ideology, the moral order, socioeconomic and political development, and human rights. Both harsh debate and conciliation marked the meetings. Dialogue was a precious last resort to avoid a Church-state rift. The Bipartite served as a bridge between an era of episcopal support for the regime and the distensão. It was a political solution to an increasingly violent crisis. Rather than rupture, the Bipartite represented a great deal of continuity—and innovation—in the Church-state relationship that had evolved over the previous half century. The Bipartite was a central episode in the history of authoritarian Brazil.

The Grupo Religioso and the Grupo da Situação met in the shadows of a regime that ruled by economic braggadocio, fear, and violence. The Bipartite involved military intelligence-gathering such as the taping of the bishops without their knowledge. The Bipartite was a secret—a formal dialogue kept as informal as possible, a way to conduct politics in times of strict censorship. It was not a Church-state summit. General Muricy prevailed over foes of the Bipartite within the regime, but Médici kept the commission at a distance. In Médici's nebulous administration it was never quite clear whom Muricy and the Grupo da Situação represented or how much power they wielded.

The military overwhelmingly held power in Brazil, but the Church freely entered the dialogue. In fact, it had insisted for years on dialogue. The Bipartite became a political tool that each side employed to its own advantage. It was a forum for understanding differences and negotiating concessions in the larger context of the struggle for control over Brazil's future.

The Bipartite was a remarkable revelation of the Church's willingness to collaborate with the regime. Candido Mendes launched the Bipartite with his bold proposal to establish Church-state cooperation on development. Overly optimistic, this plan stalled because of the deepening repression, opposition from hard-liners, and disagreement over what kind of democracy was best for Brazil. Yet it demonstrated the Church's intentions and its perception of itself as a moral guide for the Brazilian political economy. Candido Mendes hoped to fuse the military's technocratic drive for development with radical Catholic notions of social justice. This proposal was quite consistent with the history of Brazilian Church-state cooperation and the Church's desire for influence. Candido Mendes had formulated a new, more modern version of the moral concordat—an alliance in which the Church would be linked to the most powerful and dynamic sectors of the new socioeconomic order projected by the military. This was striking but not new in Brazilian history. The Church frequently sought to associate itself with power. The plan was nationalistic and state-driven. Once more the Church was promoting a "third way" to development between Communism and capitalism. The plan also attested to the degree of mutual confidence that, despite the repression, still existed between the Church and a portion of the military. In sum, the bishops flirted with dictatorship as a way to develop Brazil. Had such an alliance come about, the history of Church-state relations and, indeed, of the regime itself would have taken a quite different path.

The bishops and the officers turned instead to the practical resolution of specific conflicts. Some of these involved repression of alleged subversion at the base of the Church. The bishops accepted the Grupo da Situação's request to control activism at this level. The most important cases concerned the bishops, however. Pressured by the Situação, they toned down or eliminated some of their statements about the regime. The Bipartite avoided incidents such as the potential clash at the sesquicentennial celebrations in São Paulo. The result was a lessening of Church-state tensions.

The views of some of the participants provide a measure of the Bipartite's effectiveness in reducing conflict. Dom Eugênio, the champion of private contacts, was ultimately skeptical. Reflecting on the commission two decades later, he stated that it only partially alleviated tensions because it lacked a greater number of high-ranking generals. Other participants believed that the Bipartite clearly avoided a deeper crisis. General Muricy, General Sampaio, and Candido Mendes stated that the commission created a political understanding between the bishops and the generals. Candido Mendes observed that the Bipartite fostered this result by removing the regime's control of intelligence about the Church from local military commanders and centralizing it at the national level. Professor Padilha asserted that the

Bipartite averted open Church-state clashes and, therefore, eliminated pretexts for hard-liners to attack the Church. Dom Paulo described the Bipartite as "highly important" because "people from both sides were listened to."[9]

From the standpoint of the regime the Bipartite contributed to political stability and the protection of Brazil's international image. The Situação projected the notion of a state interested in conciliation and the welfare of all Brazilians. Dialogue allowed the generals, privately and persuasively, to present their views on national security to the bishops. The generals urged the bishops to distance themselves from radical interpretations of the Medellín document and to control grassroots militants. At the Bipartite, the regime acquired some of the religious legitimacy it so ardently sought from the Church.

By opening a secret channel with the Church, Médici expanded his political options beyond direct, physical repression. Without compromising the regime publicly, Muricy held out to the bishops the possibility of collaboration. He also pressured the bishops to soften criticism and to leash in the activists. In this sense the Bipartite led to what might be termed negotiated censorship and repression (see Smith 1997). In addition, the Bipartite provided a military listening post for understanding the bishops' positions and motivations.

The Church apparently gained less. But it saw advantages in dialogue. The Bipartite gave the Church time to regroup from the regime's attacks. The bishops were also interested in preserving the moral concordat and Catholicism's privileges as Brazil's semi-official religion. Their agenda included such issues as divorce, birth control, state financial assistance, and competition from other religions. They also pressured the generals on human rights.

Conflict resolution did not extend beyond Church-state relations. The Bipartite did not, for instance, affect the structural problems of Brazilian society such as the heavily skewed concentration of wealth and land. Such issues required far more than a secret commission. Likewise, the Bipartite had no effect on the political liberalization engineered by Geisel. The commission did not discuss the distensão, which (as most analysts have pointed out) was a purely military initiative, made possible by the end of the armed opposition and then made necessary because the security forces had become a cancer within the armed forces.

The Bipartite did display some liberalizing tendencies, however. It attempted a Church-military consensus on development, debated ideology, and furnished an excellent example of decompression between the regime and a main opposition group. Moreover, some participants wanted liberalization and would support it during the Geisel administration. Candido Mendes was one of the earliest advocates of liberalization. He and Dom Eugênio raised the need for Church-state decompression at the first meeting in 1970, and Candido Mendes helped introduce the concept into the larger political arena by convincing Leitão de Abreu, Médici's civilian chief of staff, to ponder liberalization in 1972. Golbery, the intellectual architect of abertura, supported the Bipartite. In early 1974 Candido Mendes brought Dom Paulo and Golbery together in an important meeting for Church-state relations and the start of the distensão.

A New View of the Church

The Bipartite demonstrates that the Brazilian Church during the Médici era involved far more than opposition to the regime and pastoral innovations. Historical continuities, institutional needs, and intramilitary politics also affected the Church's development. The concept of the "voice of the voiceless" that guided the Church in the early 1970s had public *and* private modes. Traditions of opposition *and* accommodation were both operative. The Church clearly became more popular, but at the Bipartite it also focused on influence and power. The bishops were more pragmatic than the religious idealism of the period indicated. Catholic progressivism did not stop the bishops from seeing themselves as intermediaries between the people and the state. They sought to free Brazil's poor from socioeconomic exploitation but also to preserve the institution. Expressed in the Bipartite, this latter objective contradicted the most radical wing of the Popular Church, which criticized traditional institutional interests (see, for example, Boff 1985) and focused primarily on grassroots political organization. As seen in the examples of JOC and Dom Pedro Casaldáliga, this group was at best extremely skeptical of the Bipartite. Dom Ivo, both a progressive and a key leader of the institution, also had doubts. Yet he participated. Thus the Bipartite refutes the notion that Catholic officials who publicly opposed authoritarian regimes did not make conciliatory gestures or seek preferential treatment. Whereas some see a tendency toward church-state cooperation only in the absence of serious conflict (see, for example, Gill 1998:183), the Bipartite demonstrates that a search for common ground can occur even during the tensest moments.

The Bipartite furnished an especially good illustration of how the bishops tempered the CNBB's critical public pronouncements with private understandings. A progressive who doubted civilians' ability to rule, Dom Fernando Gomes was the best example. The bishops were particularly concerned about negating accusations of Communism and subversion directed at the Church. The CNBB and the Popular

Church challenged the social order sustained by the generals, but the institution still needed to avoid the appearance of subversion because this would contradict Catholic notions of inclusiveness, corporatism, and of course anti-Communism. Also, political activism perhaps appeared as too deep an involvement in the temporal realm and therefore would entail a loss of the Church's identity as a transcendent institution.[10] Inconsistency resulted from the need for maximum political flexibility (see also Gill 1998:13–14). As the Bipartite demonstrated, dialogue is possible even during opponents' worst moments. Depending on circumstances, public and private stances could contradict or reinforce each other. The public/private dichotomy helped the Church and the military negotiate the ambiguous frontier between social justice and subversion.

But why did the bishops jeopardize their commitment to social justice by talking with a government that tortured people? Dialogue brought the Church benefits and allowed it to coexist with the regime. Attempting to influence the regime through the promotion of the Church's values and human rights was better than ignoring the generals. The Church was a prestigious, influential, and transnational, but also native, institution that necessarily saw itself as pastor to all Brazilians. It alone had the moral authority—and the obligation—to enter into what some critics might have called a dialogue with the devil (see also Gill 1998:4–5).

The Bipartite and Human Rights

The Bipartite had little direct effect on the repression. The bishops met with envoys from the security forces, but they had no influence over units given carte blanche by a military dictator. One close observer of the Bipartite has asserted that the bishops "saved many lives" by talking with the generals (Bandeira 1994:77). The Bipartite did save at least some people from torture and perhaps even death, but the available evidence does little to support anything more along these lines. It is impossible to know whether repression would have increased if the Bipartite had not existed.

The Bipartite did have an indirect effect on the repression, however. The commission secured the release of some political prisoners (see chapter 8). Given the immense power of the security forces, this achievement was extraordinary. The Bipartite also avoided potentially explosive incidents. And it was a key conduit for denouncing abuses to the regime. While censorship and repression made it impossible for Brazilians to protest these abuses, behind the scenes the Grupo Religioso defended human rights as vigorously as the Grupo da Situação leveled accusations of subversion. The cases of the Barra Mansa soldiers and Alexandre Vannucchi Leme are prime examples. Each of these incidents acquired strong but limited public dimensions. The ultimate channel for resolving them was the Bipartite.

The Bipartite obliged the military to hear and to respond to the bishops' accusations. The generals paid a high price: in hoping to influence the Church, they opened themselves to criticism. The agreement to discuss human rights was an implicit—and at times an explicit—admission that the regime was not respecting them. The bishops' accusations discredited the repressive hard-liners and helped demonstrate to the regime that the violence had reached a saturation point. This was a victory for the Church. Although they were manipulated, the bishops had managed to turn the Bipartite on the regime.

The Barra Mansa case illuminates how the military dealt internally with the question of torture. The case proved irrevocably that torture existed and that the military leadership knew of it. Because this case involved a court-martial and detailed testimony by military personnel, it provided the most compelling evidence of atrocities in authoritarian Brazil, including the Brasil: Nunca Mais project. In the entire history of the regime, this was the only instance of prosecution and punishment of torturers. The publication of the sentences in the press amounted to an exercise of self-criticism by the Army. Colonel Sampaio's investigation was risky and exemplary. He unraveled one of the most violent cases of the Médici years. His presence at the Bipartite demonstrated the seriousness of General Muricy and the regime in choosing accomplished and respected officers to dialogue with the bishops.

The Barra Mansa trial was the exception that proved the rule. The torturers had gone out of control. Dom Waldyr and the Bipartite made this point crystal clear to the military. Institutional discipline, the very heart of martial life, had fallen apart. Torture boomeranged against the Army, leaving the generals no choice but to punish the Barra Mansa perpetrators. But the overwhelming majority of abuses were targeted against members of the opposition. The military leadership purposely ignored these atrocities. By not extending the Barra Mansa inquiry to all of Brazil's barracks, the Army lost the chance to construct a more positive image. Torture cost the armed forces the trust of much of the nation (see, for example, Soares, D'Araujo, and Castro 1995:139–41).

The Bipartite played an important role in the human rights movement in Brazil. First, it made human rights an eminently political question, albeit within the framework of private, elite political conciliation. The bishops achieved this goal by transforming incidents into a subject of Church-military debate. The bishops chose their battles wisely, and they skillfully used human rights against the Situação. Second, the Bipartite helped build the Church's commitment to human rights. This commitment increased throughout the 1970s, blossomed into other political initiatives, and translated into leadership of the opposition. The human rights campaigns of today's Brazil are in part a legacy of the Church's struggle against torture during the authoritarian era. Directly or indirectly, the Church's discourse informs the debate about the continuing problem of police brutality and corruption, the structure of the justice system, and ultimately the foundations of Brazilian democracy.[11]

The story of the Bipartite also demonstrates the political, social, and historical constraints on the human rights movement. The Church worked to educate the populace about human rights, but a series of factors—repression, the regime's propaganda machine, censorship and manipulation of the media, and ideological polarization—blocked or twisted the truth about this effort and the abuses it denounced. The media transformed murdered opponents such as Leme into "terrorists." Family, friends, and lawyers had no chance of rebuttal in print or over the airwaves. Political bias shaped perception of human rights. It was partly rooted in Alceu Amoroso Lima's proposal to "exaggerate" regime atrocities—a necessary response to censorship and the unchecked power of the military. But exaggeration was also a symptom of polarization. Competing visions of patriotism and the struggle over Brazil's foreign image caused yet further distortion. The defense of patriotism required that perception override fact. As a result, it was easy for misunderstanding about human rights to develop. The impact of the Médici era is still present. Brazilians have still not reached a consensus on this issue, and some, including elements of the media, still see human rights as subversive (Zirker 1988; Caldeira 1991).

Another limitation was the reinforcement of unequal treatment before the law. The establishment of universal respect for human rights would have meant a significant transformation in the way Brazilians understood the general concepts of individual rights and citizenship and would have required major changes in such institutions as the police and the courts.[12] The regime worked in the opposite direction, by suspending the legal and political rights of thousands of individuals and by using the police, the courts, and the law for political and repressive purposes. It is ironic that Leme's killers remain hidden or protected by the 1979 amnesty law, which prevented the prosecution of torturers. Because of the supposedly apolitical character of their actions, the killers in Barra Mansa were practically the only individuals punished for human rights abuses.

Class bias was a major obstacle to equal treatment. In 1996 a government commission approved compensation for the Leme family, while the four soldiers of humble origin who were tortured to death in Barra Mansa have not been considered victims of the regime. Left-wing militants pleading the case of the poor and the victims of torture failed to grasp the significance of the Barra Mansa episode for their own cause. Similarly, the defense of political prisoners overshadowed the more common human rights violations that have long occurred in Brazil's jail cells. USP students called attention to such everyday abuses, as did a prominent member of the São Paulo Peace and Justice Commission (Bicudo 1976). While political torture of middle-class militants disappeared, mistreatment of the poor remains a serious structural problem. By defending human rights in both the Leme and the Barra Mansa cases, the Church began to break down some of the social prejudice inherent in Brazilian notions of justice.

In sum, the story of the Bipartite illustrates the gradual, difficult, and complex history of the human rights movement in the Brazilian and international contexts. It also demonstrates the challenges faced by religious institutions in their attempt to influence societies on moral questions. As a transnational institution the Church was uniquely positioned to advance the human rights movement in Brazil, but it was also subject to the peculiarities of the Brazilian situation and also to its own substantial secular interests as a large and old institution. The debate over human rights at the Bipartite revealed how the struggle for human rights is constantly fraught with political, historical, and cultural considerations.

Rethinking Factionalism

The Bipartite demonstrated a multiplicity of sometimes contradictory voices and strategies in both the Church and the regime. In the same setting, the Grupo Religioso touched on issues ranging from social justice and torture to collaboration with the regime. General Muricy defended the Revolution he had helped to carry out but also spoke of dialogue and resolving human rights disputes. Publicly expressed, these dichotomous sets of positions would have threatened internal splits in the Church and the military. The regime especially rejected any public discussion of human rights. But privately, the Church and the military acknowledged each other's complexities and internal factionalism. They also discussed institutional and political concerns.

Among observers of the Brazilian and Latin American Church there has been a tendency to ignore multiplicity and instead to divide the episcopate into progres-

sive and conservative factions based on political attitudes and theological orientation. These are powerful, helpful, and to a certain extent unavoidable categories.
But they do not fully explain the bishops' actions. Historical specificity and a bishop's personal evolution and social habitat are also important ingredients. The
Bipartite confirms this complexity.

Dom Eugênio provides an interesting example. He defies easy categorization.
For decades he has been one of the most controversial figures in the Brazilian
Church. He has frequently been portrayed as a promilitary conservative. Yet in the
1950s he worked for social and ecclesial reform. In 1964 he was called a Communist.
Thereafter he maintained a critical attitude toward the government. Himself an
anti-Communist, Dom Eugênio chided the generals for exaggerating anti-
Communism to the detriment of Brazil. Dom Eugênio could make such a comment
because military leaders respected him more than they did any other bishop. He
cultivated public and private relations with them not for ideological reasons but
out of a sense of service to the Church, Brazil, and human rights. He recognized the
value of access to power, especially in a dictatorship. (Not by accident did he
become one of the Church's most influential cardinals.) Dom Eugênio proceeded
this way knowing that it would make him unpopular in the Popular Church (see
also Gaspari 1997b). Political polarization made it difficult for anybody perceived
as a moderate or middleman. Although he later opposed some liberation theologians, the root of Dom Eugênio's differences with progressives lay not in theological outlook (Dom Eugênio was an enthusiast of Medellín) but in their perceptions
of patriotism and Church hierarchy (see also Peritore 1989). The progressives
denounced injustice in public and abroad, while Dom Eugênio worked behind the
scenes and within Brazil. By quitting the Bipartite, Dom Eugênio both displayed his
skepticism about the regime and admitted the limits of his style.

Which strategy was more effective? It is hard to tell. Together they embodied
the perennial dilemma of the Church's need for both prudent pastors and daring
prophets to lead a majority that may be neither or a mixture of the two.
Polarization made it hard to strike a balance between them. Both Dom Eugênio and
progressive leader Dom Paulo helped numerous prisoners. A similar contrast existed between Dom Eugênio and Alceu Amoroso Lima in the diplomatic sphere. The
cardinal wanted to safeguard Brazil's image, while the intellectual wanted to exaggerate the regime's atrocities. Perhaps the better question is to ask how the
approaches of different sectors of the Church complemented one another as the
institution came to oppose the regime. Dom Paulo and Alceu dwelled in the public
realm, Dom Eugênio in the private.[13] The progressive-conservative dichotomy is

perhaps necessary but certainly insufficient for understanding them and the peri-od. The positions of other progressives at the Bipartite reinforce the point: Candido Mendes advocated Church-state dialogue and cooperation; Dom Fernando wanted a strong government and doubted the ability of civilians to achieve it. These are contradictions of progressivism only if rigid classification is demanded.[14]

If factionalism is overemphasized for the Church, it is not sufficiently appreci-ated in the case of the armed forces under Médici. While Castellistas and hard-lin-ers struggled for control of the regime, they always coexisted in power and publicly presented a united front (Couto 1998:219). Hard-liners dominated the Médici gov-ernment—but not completely, as is commonly assumed. The Bipartite further undermines this assumption. General Muricy belonged to the Castellista bloc, which came to recognize that the security forces had gone out of control. Members of this group had a more moderate view of the Church than other sectors of the regime, for example, hard-liners who saw the clergy as an enemy or irrelevant. These Castellistas were loyal to the traditional Church and wanted it as a partner in stability, not as a nemesis. The Bipartite involved political machination, and its mil-itary leader, General Muricy, clearly favored the repression of the revolutionary left and radical Catholic militants. But the Bipartite was nonviolent. There the military revealed its more conciliatory bloc in dialogue with the opposition. Muricy's pro-posal to create the Bipartite won out over the objections of opponents within the leadership of the Médici administration. Faction but also function mattered. Muricy permitted human rights to come onto the military's agenda. He even extri-cated some disappeared political prisoners from the security apparatus. This approach to Church-state relations defied the typical heavy-handed methods of the Médici-era hard-liners.

The Bipartite, the Médici Years, and Brazilian History

The Bipartite is a key chapter in the historical narrative of the Médici years and also underscores some important points about modern Brazil. Most writings focus on two conspicuous developments of the Médici period: spectacular economic growth and the high level of political and military repression. Other trends such as dialogue and conciliation have been overlooked and should be added as subtle hues to the portrait of this era.

Not so subtle were the Barra Mansa and Leme cases. They were major violent events that confirmed the importance of secret dialogue. Furthermore, the public and private protests against Leme's death spotlighted the Church as a rallying point for the opposition, whose resurgence occurred long before the moment identified by most observers. A periodization of the opposition should begin with 1973 rather than with 1975 and the Herzog case. This outlook challenges the rather traditional, mechanical, and top-down division of the regime according to presidential terms. It suggests instead that trends be seen as processes, which cross over inauguration dates. The Médici period is rich in trends and events to be more fully explored as new documentary evidence is uncovered.

The Bipartite emphasized that Brazil's Church-state conflict was primarily a question of Church-*military* relations. Changes in these institutions' internal lives explained the difficulty of resolving the conflict. Although Brazil has generally been a society of weak institutions, the study of these two key organizations, and especially the relations between them, sheds much light on the modern social and political history of Brazil. As the regime further weakened the political system by eliminating political and civil liberties, the Church and the armed forces' importance became proportionately magnified. During the Médici years they were transformed into the major political arbiters. Their meeting place was the Bipartite.

The Bipartite reveals a complex image of both and builds appreciation for the seriousness with which they viewed themselves and their missions in Brazilian society. The bishops were pastors, but also politicians concerned with socioeconomic development, human rights, and their influence on Brazilian society. The root of these concerns lay in the bishops' religious convictions and the long history of the Brazilian Church, and of the Church as a worldwide organization with a two-thousand-year history. The Bipartite further underlined the importance of religion in Brazilian politics. The military is harder to understand and sympathize with because of its use of violence and torture. For many Brazilians and at least some authors, the generals were little better than "gorillas," as Brizola described General Muricy. Yet the armed forces were just as confident of their convictions as the Church. Since the mid–nineteenth century and especially between 1964 and 1974, the Brazilian officer corps believed that it was more competent to govern than the civilians. This is a belief traditionally shared by the militaries of many other Latin American countries and, indeed, of many nations in history. In the Brazilian case the generals were interested in power, but also in developing the country and establishing what they considered the best model for politics and government. General Muricy and other members of the Situação were convinced that they could sway the bishops toward their way of thinking. They were the military intelligentsia in action, the cordial and professorial faces of authoritarianism.

The debate over social justice and subversion flushed out the similarities and differences between the Church and the Army. They admired each other's hierarchy and emphasis on discipline, but in the end they could not agree on a common vision for Brazilian society. The bishops wanted a more just, democratic, and egalitarian system in which they would nevertheless continue to have an important role as moral judges. The generals envisioned a limited authoritarian democracy that they would continue to safeguard by rooting out subversion.

Despite its risks and failures, dialogue made sense in light of Brazil's tradition of elite accommodation. The military not only failed to achieve its goal of purging Brazil of traditional politics; it embraced them, reinforcing the elitist nature of the society (Hagopian 1996). The Bipartite exemplified elite conciliation and the highly personalistic nature of Brazilian politics. The participants—bishops, generals, intellectuals—represented the upper strata of society. They were all men, light-skinned, and from middle-aged to old. Most of them lived privileged lives because of family background or professional success. Many were devout Catholics. Women, Protestants, peasants, workers, victims of the repression and their families, and politicians had no access to the Bipartite. Insofar as it was an "elite settlement," the Bipartite excluded the people from its deliberations.[15] The military takeover had damaged elite consensus in Brazil, pitting two of the main pillars of society against each other. The Bipartite was an attempt to restore consensus and establish new rules of conciliation. It was made possible by the personal ties of Professor Padilha, a leading intellectual and son of a governor. He brought together Candido Mendes and General Muricy. The commission mirrored the decision-making process of Brazilian politics and government, with debate and decisions taking place behind closed doors (and away from the press), over meals and at informal appointments, on the telephone, or through private correspondence such as the exchanges between General Muricy and Dom Eugênio or Dom Lucas's letter to President Médici. At issue were Church-state relations, but also questions of honor among gentlemen as in the government's humiliation of Dom Avelar. In Muricy the military had found a general tough enough—but also highly cultured and affable enough—to deal with the bishops. Candido Mendes became the glue of the Bipartite by means of his noblesse oblige, ability to network, and the realization that the Church needed the state and the elite to forge a new version of the moral concordat.

Good Church-state relations were customary in modern Brazil. From Dom Leme's understandings with Vargas in the 1930s to the Bipartite in the 1970s, the moral concordat was but another form of elite conciliation. Church-state conflict

and cooperation were rooted deeply in Latin American history. In Brazil, cooperation took on a unique form. Lieutenant Colonel Pacífico's notion of the Bipartite as
a sui generis Brazilian solution can be applied to the entirety of modern Brazil's
Church-state relations. In the 1950s the Catholic leadership believed that "before
the world Brazil is accomplishing a singular experience with respect to relations
between Church and state." Official ties did not exist, but harmony and collaboration did (*XXXVI Congresso Eucarístico* 1955:119). The dictatorship represented an
interlude during which a Church in transition faced the destruction of this relationship. The Bipartite appeared as a way for the Church to maintain its moral and
religious dominance and to address its institutional concerns. Exclusively Catholic
in an era of ecumenism, the Grupo Religioso preserved the Brazilian tradition of
the Church's privileged part in elite decision-making. As the regime faded, the
Church began to withdraw from opposition politics and to focus again on cooperation with the state. Throughout the modern period, the Church maintained its
self-image as creator and protector of Brazil's Catholic identity and as the country's
moral guardian.

The uniqueness of this solution stands out in comparative perspective. In
authoritarian Argentina some leaders of the Church collaborated with the repression, whereas in Chile it stood up for human rights but did not have any secret
understandings with the dictatorship. In Brazil the Bipartite worked to tone down
or explain alleged Catholic subversion, maintain Church influence, *and* to
denounce human rights violations. The Bipartite was a remarkable development in
the history of dictatorial regimes in contemporary Latin America.

In the post–cold war order, East-West tensions have diminished as former
Communist regimes have become capitalist. Ethnic strife and other social contradictions have come to the forefront, however, and new variations of authoritarianism have emerged. The struggle for social justice will remain a central theme of history. New forms of subversion will rise up and undoubtedly be met by demands for
repression. The historical pattern certainly suggests that militarism is far from
dead in Latin America. Institutions such as the transnationally influential Catholic
Church and powerful national military forces will see it as their duty to influence
conflicts. As they did during the cold war, religious as well as military leaders will
need to rethink their roles in society. The Brazilian bishops and officers of the
Bipartite testified to the fact that, in highly charged situations clouded by both
polarization and ambiguity, the solution begins with dialogue.

Notes

Chapter 1

1. On the public and the prophetic, see Casanova 1994, esp. ch. 5 on Brazil; on Catholic political change see Bruneau 1974b.

2. The analyst is Mainwaring 1986:74–75, 149, 181. Even observers skeptical of religious motives for its anti-authoritarianism recognize the Church's contribution to democratic stabilization. See the work of rational choice theorist Gill 1998:6.

3. My analysis here is echoed in part by de Groot 1996:148–49; also see Gill 1998:48, 201. Previous scholars used little archival documentation, either because it did not fit with their methodologies or because they were writing on the heel of events and did not have access to primary sources; see the discussion of documentation below. One partial exception to these trends was McDonough 1981. Conducting research at the height of the repression, he examined relations within the Brazilian elite and revealed the multidimensional nature of its ideology. However, he was unable to obtain data on the military, and he does not name any of his 250 interviewees. For examples of major writings on Church-state conflict during the military regime, see Bruneau 1974b, 1982; Mainwaring 1986; Mainwaring and Wilde 1989; Casanova 1994; Alves 1979; Salem 1981; Alves 1985; Della Cava 1989; Couto 1998; Skidmore 1988; Flynn 1978; R. Schneider 1991. Similarly, the subject of secret dialogue is virtually absent from the research on redemocratization; for an exception, see Higley and Gunther 1992. For a good discussion of dialogue in the Chilean and Peruvian cases, see Fleet and Smith 1997:119–29, 277.

4. National security doctrine was more a rationale for than a cause of the military regimes that ruled Brazil and other Latin American countries; see Loveman 1999.

5. In the 1920s and 1930s, the Church had concordats with countries such as Italy, Germany, Portugal, Poland, and Ecuador. These agreements provided for legislation protecting Catholic norms in the family and education, and they guaranteed the Church's institutional freedom. They also included special benefits; see Beozzo 1986:338–40.

6. See chapter 5 of the present work for further discussion.

7. On ecumenical relations, see Wright 1989:57, 68–70; Berryman 1996.

8. On Kissinger, see Gaddis 1994, Golan 1976, Burr 1998. For other examples of back-channel diplomacy, see Miner 1994.

9. Dietz 1992:242; Sanchez 1992:318. In the 1990s the Chilean military resorted to informal political contacts in an attempt to preserve its influence; see Weeks forthcoming.

10. A similar point is made in Crahan 1989:12 and Crahan 1999.

11. Lowden 1996:14–19; also see Gill 1998. For Gill (1998), the level of competition from other religions was the single most important factor in leading the Catholic Church to oppose dictatorship in Latin American countries during the 1960s and 1970s.

12. Hanson 1987:42–45; also see Lewy 1964:293–94; Cornwell 1999.

13. Blancarte 1992:72–85; Loaeza-Lajous 1990:283–87; Knight 1992.

14. Lowden 1996; Smith 1982; Fleet and Smith 1997.

15. On recent developments in religion and politics, see Serbin 2000, 1993a. For the Latin American context see Sigmund 1999. There are many interpretations of the Church's roll-back from its radical positions in Brazil and elsewhere; see for example, Della Cava 1989; Mainwaring 1986, ch. 11; Libânio 1983; Lernoux 1989; Ghio 1992; Beozzo 1994, ch. 4.

16. Grudin 1996:12–13; also see the theoretical considerations about Church-state bargaining in Gill 1998:49.

17. In Chile Cardinal Raúl Silva Henríquez took a similar stance toward the Pinochet dictatorship; see Lowden 1996:35–36. As Fleet and Smith (1997:119–29) point out, the public nature of the dialogue in Chile reduced its effectiveness.

18. A similar situation occurred in Chile, where Catholic radicals opposed attempts by Church leaders to negotiate with the government; see Fleet and Smith 1997:119.

19. Alves 1973:156, 1979:120. This view is echoed in Lernoux 1982:276, 301; Weschler 1998.

20. An alternative interpretation views the progressive movement as a populist strategy; see Paiva 1985a.

21. D'Araujo, Soares, and Castro 1994a:13–31; also Dassin 1992:167; Loveman 1999, ch. 8.

22. One of the most celebrated examples is Gabeira 1979, which recounts ventures of the revolutionary left, including the kidnapping of U.S. ambassador Burke Elbrick in September 1969. "O que é isso companheiro," a controversial movie based on the book, was released in May 1997. For critiques of the film, see Reis Filho et al. 1997. For a discussion of memoirs by leftists, see Ridenti 1997, esp. note 10; Dassin 1992.

23. Archdiocese of São Paulo 1985; for the English version see Dassin 1986. On the research for the book see Weschler 1998; Wright 1989:70–71. The Brasil: Nunca Mais project was unique. In most other Latin American countries this kind of documentation has not been available, let alone compiled by human rights organizations. One exception is the extraordinary Centro de Documentación y Archivo para la Defensa de los Derechos Humanos, the so-called Archive of Terror, of Paraguayan dictator Alfredo Stroessner's political police, discovered in Asunción in 1992. See chapter 8 for discussion of the relevance of this archive for Brazil. In the tradition of the Nuremberg trials and other postwar judgments, the end of military rule and civil wars in the 1980s and 1990s brought the creation of so-called truth commissions. The commissions accounted for human rights abuses but did not have the power to judge perpetrators. The exception was Argentina, where generals went to jail for their role in the country's "dirty war." Brazil did not get a truth commission until 1996, and then only a very limited one, eleven years after the return to civilian rule and seventeen years after the amnesty law that protected human rights violators from prosecution. Before then, Brasil: Nunca Mais and groups such as Tortura Nunca Mais (Torture never again) served as surrogate truth commissions. For a study of the Church's secret gathering of

human rights information in Chile, see Lowden 1996:38–43, 75–84. On human rights violations in that country also see *Report of the Chilean National Commission* 1993. In 1998 General Pinochet was detained in England, after a Spanish judge filed extradition proceedings in an attempt to prosecute him for human rights violations.

24. For example, Abreu 1979; Mello 1979; Passarinho 1996. For officer accounts, see the interviews in D'Araujo, Soares, and Castro 1994a, 1994b; Soares, D'Araujo and Castro 1995; D'Araujo and Castro 1997.

25. The only exclusive treatments of the Médici era are in McDonough 1981; Silva and Carneiro 1983; also see Fico 1997. A journalistic account is Drosdoff 1986. A very brief oral history of Médici's term is in Médici 1995. There are no biographies of Médici or works dealing specifically with his administration. This is in contrast with General Humberto de Alencar Castello Branco, the first military president; see Viana Filho 1976; Dulles 1978, 1980. On the administrations of Castello Branco and General Artur da Costa e Silva, the second military president, see Mello 1979; Martins Filho 1995:29–30. For brief overviews of the Médici period, see Skidmore 1988, Flynn 1978, Schneider 1991, Silva and Carneiro 1975.

26. For examples of this genre in U.S. history, see Branch 1988, Goodwin 1988. Lack of good narrative has become an important item of discussion in the historical profession. For an analysis of this problem, see Limerick 1993. The topic was most recently the subject of debate at a panel titled "Journalists, Scholars, and Historical Writing" at the American Historical Association's 114th Annual Meeting, Chicago, Jan. 8, 2000. The importance of narrative is a key question for a new generation of scholars that seeks to interpret the history of the recent authoritarian period in Latin American history and its impact on current political developments. For examples of this emerging literature, see, Wilde 1999; Bickford 1998.

27. The "soft-line Castellistas were virtually silenced, but still present," states Alfred Stepan (1988:40). On the Latin American military and patriotism, see Loveman 1999.

28. I have in mind Guillermo O'Donnell's influential description of the Brazilian and other South American military regimes as "bureaucratic-authoritarian." Their guiding principles were rationalization of the economy in favor of the elite and exclusion of the rest of the populace from decision-making; see O'Donnell 1988:31–32. I think that O'Donnell's analysis is accurate as far as it goes. More recently, however, O'Donnell and others have been criticized for emphasizing bureaucracy and ignoring the military character and intramilitary distinctions within this system; see Martins Filho 1995:18–28. McDonough (1981:xxvi) emphasizes the "internal heterogeneity" of Brazilian elite sectors. In addition, the regime was not completely "bureaucratic" in the sense that it did not achieve the depoliticalization of the society and the state (Hagopian 1996:107–08; also B. Schneider 1991).

29. Médici considered starting the *abertura* at the end of his administration but opted not to because of the continued activity of rural guerrillas; see, for example, Soares, D'Araujo, and Castro 1995:47, 177, 260–61; Médici 1995:31–32, 49; also the discussion in chapter 5 of the present work.

30. See, for example, Couto 1998:218. Likewise, as Loveman states, "The armed forces are both part of society and apart from it" (1999:xiii).

31. This view is echoed by Loveman (1999:228): "Militarylore and doctrine shape and justify missions for . . . officers just as revolutionary ideology does for guerrillas, and religious and humanist values do for human rights organizations. Obviously, taking these values seriously does not require sharing them." See also S. Davis 1996.

32. The classic study of the Brazilian military is Stepan 1971. Stepan's research is

unequaled. It makes many of the points raised here, but it is a sociological and rather schematic political analysis of the military, not a historical narrative, which is the aim here. Written before the Médici years, Stepan's work does not address many of the themes treated here such as Church-military relations. On Latin American militaries' beliefs about democracy, see Loveman 1999; for an approach that emphasizes the functionality of the military electoral system, see B. Schneider 1991, esp. 238–42.

33. Fleet and Smith similarly discuss a search for common ground during the difficult Church-led negotiations toward the National Accord in Chile. See Fleet and Smith 1997:122–23, 137, 156.

34. The best example is the Nicaraguan Revolution, which had the support of many in the progressive Church, including Brazilian clerics such as Dom Pedro Casaldáliga. The overall history of the Latin American churches and the cold war can be found in Antoine 1999. For a fine overview of the secondary literature, see Klaiber 1997.

35. Hess and DaMatta 1995, Lewin 1987, Page 1995, Hagopian 1996.

36. Rodrigues 1982; Schmitter 1971, ch. 14; Cohen 1989; B. Schneider:245–47; Conniff and McCann 1989a. Historically, Latin American societies have been extremely elitist, largely because of their former colonial status. In the twentieth century, most Latin American countries have struggled to implant some form of democratic government. Yet the importance of elites has continued. For an overview of Brazil's elites, see Conniff and McCann 1989b. Elites and elite conciliation have been an important theme in other parts of Latin America; see, for example, P. Smith 1979, Wilde 1982.

37. The power of the technocrats declined after the Médici administration because the regime's need to maintain a democratic facade and to obtain political legitimacy caused it to turn once again to conservative politicians who could deliver votes from the traditional system of Brazilian pork-barreling; see Hagopian 1996.

38. Like Knight (1992), I employ this concept of "elite settlement" very narrowly and avoid the broad generalizations sought by political scientists.

39. On elite political expression, see McDonough 1981:15, 37, 175; also Almeida 1977:43–44, 86–87, 97.

40. I attended this ceremony in October 1996. Academies of letters were the traditional bastion of the Brazilian cultural elite, though they seem to have declined in importance; see Conniff 1989:27. On the origins of the academy, see Needell 1987:192–96.

41. Many might hope to find here yet another contemporary view of Brazil's vibrant popular religiosity and the religious transformations occurring at the base of Brazilian society. Political scientists, anthropologists, sociologists, and others have produced a growing body of literature from this perspective. See, among many examples, Ireland 1991; Sanchis 1992a, 1992b, 1992c; Burdick 1993; Mariz 1994; Chesnut 1997; Drogus 1997; Vásquez 1998; Nagle 1998. The present work does not negate this approach; in fact, it studies the elite in light of struggles taking place at the grass roots. Nevertheless, the present work is distinctly historical and concerned with other, neglected facets of Brazilian religious life, especially mediation among elites.

42. Cited in "Relatório do XVII encontro bipartite," Arquivo Antônio Carlos Muricy, Fundação Getúlio Vargas, Centro de Pesquisa e Documentação de História Contemporânea do Brasil (hereafter FGV/CPDOC/ACM), roll 2, doc. no. 43, p. 2 (microfilm).

43. The notion of cordiality originates in the classic work by Holanda 1948.

44. The most explicit reference to the Bipartite is in Gomes 1982:240–50. This work has been overlooked by scholars. A very brief reference is also in Piletti and Praxedes 1997:397–

98, 413–14. Almeida and Bandeira (1996:60–62, 74–75) incorrectly identify General Golbery do Couto e Silva as the military leader of the Bipartite. See also Bandeira 1994:76–77; "Murici, Antônio Carlos" 1984; Prandini, Petrucci, and Dale 1986–1987:5:15–16; also indirect references in Romano 1979:186–87; Arns 1978:127; and Bittencourt and Markum 1979:63–64. The most recent major English-language work on the Brazilian Church does not mention the Bipartite; see Mainwaring 1986. In the Portuguese version of his book Bruneau (1974a:346) alludes to attempts at dialogue but does not elaborate in detail or discuss the Bipartite.

45. I twice pressed the general on the whereabouts of these other minutes. He stated that they were in military archives and could not be accessed. Author's interviews with Antônio Carlos da Silva Muricy, Rio de Janeiro, June 17, 1993, and July 14, 1995 (hereafter cited as Muricy interview 1 and Muricy interview 2; full citations of all interviews are in the bibliography). In 1997 I made other attempts to obtain the minutes, including contact with a former highly placed intelligence official, but I was unsuccessful. Padilha stated that he had once kept copies of the minutes but lost them in a move to a new apartment (Padilha interview 1). General Pacífico, the longtime secretary of the Bipartite, also stated that he kept no copies (Pacífico interview). We can only speculate as to the content of the gap in Muricy's Bipartite papers. The missing papers perhaps included highly sensitive issues such as the Barra Mansa deaths (see chapter 9 for a detailed discussion of this case). There is an ongoing controversy between human rights activists and the military over whether the security forces' archives actually exist (see, for example, Couto 1998:29–30, 113 n. 5). One former commander of the CIE assured me that its archive is in Brasília (Sampaio interview). The Tortura Nunca Mais group also believes that such archives exist and has pressured the government to open them. In addition, military officers have private archives of regime materials (Togo Meirelles Netto interview).

46. In addition (as discussed in chapter 5), secret recordings were made of two Bipartite meetings. The whereabouts of the tapes is a mystery. General Pacífico stated that he did not make any transcripts of tapes in preparing the Bipartite minutes. He prepared synopses of the meetings based on notes (Pacífico interview).

47. In early 1999 the RioCentro case was reopened after military officials admitted Army responsibility for the explosion, first attributed to left-wing terrorists.

48. For background on this archive, see APERJ 1996a, 1996b; D. Davis 1996. The DOPS-GB is held at the Arquivo Público do Estado do Rio de Janeiro (APERJ). The DOPS material is hereafter cited as APERJ/DOPS-GB. The former federal capital of Rio de Janeiro became the state of Guanabara in 1960 and remained so until its absorption by the state of Rio de Janeiro in 1975. For background on the political police in Rio, see Cancelli 1993.

49. For background on this archive, see Pimenta 1995. The DEOPS-SP is housed in the Arquivo do Estado de São Paulo (AESP). Hereafter the DEOPS holdings are cited as AESP/DEOPS-SP.

50. In reality, the DOI units carried out the repression. The CODI was a meeting of security chiefs from the police and the armed forces to plan missions; see Lagôa 1983:70–71. However, the term "DOI-CODI" is used widely by Brazilians and in the literature on the regime to indicate the torture centers and will be employed throughout this work. (Ironically, in Portuguese *dói* means "it hurts.")

51. The Arquivo Ana Lagôa is located at the Universidade Federal de São Carlos. The Brasil: Nunca Mais (BNM) collection is held at the Centro de Pesquisa e Documentação Social, Associação Cultural Arquivo Edgard Leuenroth (AEL), Instituto de Filosofia e Ciências Humanas, Universidade Estadual de Campinas, Campinas, São Paulo. Hereafter

these materials are cited as AEL/BNM. BNM is also available on microfilm through the Center for Research Libraries in Chicago. However, because there is no index to the more than five hundred rolls of film, it is difficult to locate specific cases. CEDIC (Center for Documentation and Scientific Information) is housed at the Pontifícia Universidade Católica de São Paulo. It is subsequently cited as PUC-SP/CEDIC. For background on this archive, see Khoury 1995. The Alceu Amoroso Lima center is in Petrópolis. Located in Rome, the private archive of the Argentine Embassy contains secret Argentine diplomatic reports on the Brazilian Church-state conflict; I am grateful to Loris Zanatta of the Instituto per le Scienze Religiose, Bologna, for copies. I thank Dom Waldyr Calheiros de Novaes for copies of documents from his diocese's archive in Volta Redonda. The Van der Weid papers are at APERJ. The Branca Alves documents are at the Biblioteca Cardeal Câmara of the Archdiocese of Rio de Janeiro. For background on Branca Alves, see chapter 4. The Instituto Nacional do Pastoral is at the CNBB headquarters in Brasília. The Arquivo do Itamaraty is located in Brasília. I am grateful to James Green for copies of documents fom this collection.

Chapter 2

1. The terms "military" and "Army" are used synonymously in this book because of the greater role exercised by the Army in politics in comparison with the Air Force and the Navy. References to all the military branches are designated as "armed forces" or "armed services."

2. Priests control the Church despite being far outnumbered by nuns. In the early 1970s, Brazil had thirteen thousand clergymen and thirty-eight thousand sisters.

3. Octávio Costa interview 1. Costa was a first lieutenant in the FEB infantry.

4. On the "pious 1950s," see Della Cava 1976:11–12, 36, inc. note 51.

5. Serbin 1996. Dom Jaime Câmara and Dom Hélder Câmara were not related.

6. On the intelligence community, see Lagôa 1983. Ernesto Geisel noted that the DOI-CODI units often had better intelligence than the SNI (D'Araujo and Castro 1997:369). The CENIMAR had existed since the 1940s. CISA and CIE were created at the end of the 1960s. In São Paulo, DOI-CODI was commonly known during the Médici years by the name of its predecessor, the OBAN, or Operação Bandeirantes (Amelinha interview). The *bandeirantes* were the rugged, mestizo backwoodsmen of the colonial era who explored the interior, searched for gold, and enslaved the natives for sale.

7. On right-wing terror, see Argolo, Ribeiro, and Fortunato 1996. Ridenti (1993:61–63) dispels the myth that the revolutionary left planned guerrilla action only after the military repression began.

8. The four "armies" refer to the geographical breakdown of Brazil's Army commands. The First was headquartered in Rio de Janeiro, the Second in São Paulo, the Third in Porto Alegre, the Fourth in Recife.

9. "Brazil Program Analysis," National Security Study Memorandum no. 67 (1969–1970), National Security Archive, Washington, D.C. The memorandum, which resulted from a presidential national security directive, was declassified in July 1997. For background on such directives, see Richelson 1994.

10. "Civil war" is how at least some in the military leadership have called the conflict; see, for example, D'Araujo and Castro 1997:223.

11. Those alone who testified to military tribunals about having been tortured numbered

nearly two thousand. The total was probably far higher; see Archdiocese of São Paulo 1985:34–42, 87; also Amnesty International 1973.

12. Fico 1997; for additional background on Costa, see D'Araujo, Soares, and Castro 1994a:259–81.

13. Overall economic performance from 1964 to 1985 was actually below that of the democratic period (1945–1964), thus nullifying the effects of the miracle years. For a critical overview of the economy under the military, see Cysne 1994; also Baer 1995:73–88. For descriptions of exploitation of the Amazon and growth in São Paulo, see Page 1995, chaps. 11–12. For the view of one of Castello Branco's economic ministers, see Campos 1994, esp. ch. 12. On the arms industry, see Stepan 1988:82–87.

14. Couto 1998:39, 99, 116–17. On regime popularity, see Silva and Carneiro 1983:55; McDonough 1981:237 n. 8; Cohen 1989:46–49; also Perlman 1976:175–79.

15. Serbin 1993b. On Brazilian Catholicism in the post-conciliar era, see Sanchis 1992a, 1992b, 1992c; on the clergy crisis, also see Casanova 1994:125.

16. CNBB, "Reunião extraordinária dos metropolitas," CNBB/INP, doc. no. 4019.

17. Antoine 1970:29–31 (quotation); Bruneau 1974b:120–21; Mainwaring 1986:80–81.

18. Piletti and Praxedes 1997:296–97, 302–03, 306, 319–20, 329, 342; also "Dom Helder: país livre com comunistas de fora," Diário de Notícias, May 26, 1964.

19. See, for example, Almeida 1994:67; Kehl and Vannuchi 1997:168. This affirmation also came in Candido Mendes interview 2; a similar affirmation came in the Pretto and Marcos Noronha interviews. See also Freire, Almada, and Ponce 1997:257; Mainwaring 1986:83–84, 110; "Brazil Program Analysis," National Security Study Memorandum no. 67 (1969–1970), National Security Archive; B. Smith 1979:182.

20. This point and further confirmation of the bishops' hesitancy to admit torture came in the Dom Amaury interview.

21. While the bishops stood farther from military interests than any other elite group, the MDB was overall the most leftist in its political outlook; see McDonough 1981:127, 160, 176–78, 180–81.

22. Primeira Região Militar, "Boletim Reservado No. 6," Dec. 2, 1967, FGV/CPDOC/ ACM, roll 1, doc. no. 782, p. 2, doc. no. 783, p. 1.

23. Calliari 1996:639; Comissão de Familiares 1996:98–100. For Dom Hélder, see Cirano 1983; Ferrarini 1992. On the denial of the prize, see Piletti and Praxedes 1997:378, 381–84, 388, 392.

24. For sources on this case and discussion of it at the Bipartite, see chapter 6.

25. Centro Ecumênico 1979. The most detailed presentation of Church-regime conflict is Prandini, Petrucci, and Dale 1986–1987. On censorship of the Church, see also Smith 1997.

26. "Dossier PCB," c. 1949, APERJ/DOPS-GB, setor "Político," pasta 3B, p. 610.

27. Heitor Corrêa Maurano was a career DOPS-GB officer and headed its information division during the Médici government.

28. See, for example, "Boletim Reservado," no. 6, March 11, 1974, APERJ/DOPS-GB, setor "Boletim Reservado," pasta 1, p. 1; also APERJ/DOPS-GB, setor "DGIE," pasta 247; Piletti and Praxedes 1997, ch. 37.

29. See, for example, Francisco Eugênio Santiago, "São Paulo por dentro," Relatório no. 1.374, Feb. 16, 1971, APERJ/DOPS-GB, setor 34, pasta 1, p. 405. The DOPS-GB file on Dom Paulo includes tapes of a speech given by the archbishop in Volta Redonda; see APERJ/DOPS-GB, setor "Municípios," pasta 152, p. 2766B.

30. "Dom Hélder Câmara," Feb. 15, 1969, APERJ/DOPS-GB, setor "Secreto," pasta 39, pp. 197–99. This report inaccurately charged that Dom Hélder did not give an accounting of public funds spent at the 1955 Eucharistic Congress. In fact, the Church published a financial report (see *XXXVI Congresso* 1955). The exact origins of the document are unclear. According to *O Estado de São Paulo (OESP)*, it was written by the conservative Father Álvaro Negromonte and was discovered among his belongings after his death in 1964. There is also evidence, however, that the police had produced the document by consulting with Dom Hélder's clerical enemies, held it for years, and then leaked it. For instance, one marginal note indicates that the police intended to submit it for "evaluation by Father Negromonte." In another, the initials "D.J." suggest that Dom Jaime may also have been consulted. In general, however, DOPS-GB agents received little help from conservatives in the repression against progressives. For discussion of the *OESP* usage, see Piletti and Praxedes 1997, ch. 38; Cirano, 1983:245.

31. See, for example, Ministério de Exército, I Exército, Pedido de Busca no. 129/74-E, March 11, 1974, "Assunto: Dom Eugênio de Araújo Sales, Arcebispo do Rio de Janeiro," APERJ/DOPS-GB, setor "DOPS," pasta 200, p. 295.

32. "Boletim Reservado," no. 5, March 8, 1974, APERJ/DOPS-GB, setor "Boletim Reservado," pasta 1, p. 26; Protocolo 6550/71-DI, APERJ/DOPS-GB, Nov. 12, 1971, setor "DOPS," pasta 183, p. 430 (quotation).

33. See, for example, Divisão de Operações, Seção de Buscas Especiais, Informação no. 063, Aug. 24, 1971, APERJ/DOPS-GB, setor "DOPS," pasta 153, pp. 144–51. One priest who traveled frequently from his base in Rio Grande do Sul to points throughout Brazil was always followed by DOPS officers (Orestes Stragliotto interview).

34. See the discussion of the Movimento Popular de Libertação in chapter 8.

35. Ministério da Guerra, Io. Exército, 1a. Região Militar, Estado Maior da 2a. Seção, Pedido de Busca no. 215/66, Oct. 27, 1966, APERJ/DOPS-GB, setor "Secreto," pasta 10, pp. 238–42.

36. Ministério do Exército, I Exército, 2a. Seção, Informação no. 1022 CH/69, "Assunto: situação do IPM sobre atividades subversivas na Igreja Católica," APERJ/DOPS-GB, setor "Secreto," pasta 48, p. 90.

37. Secretaria de Estado de Segurança Pública, "Informação No. 114/77/DPPS/RJ/Interior," May 4, 1977, APERJ/DOPS-GB, setor "DGIE," pasta 247, pp. 296E–L.

38. Prandini, Petrucci, and Dale 1986–1987:2:144; on rings see also Piletti and Praxedes 1997:325.

39. Ministério da Justiça, DPF-DR/GB, "Assunto: Francisco Rocha Guimarães (Padre)," Sept. 27, 1973, APERJ/DOPS-GB, setor "Secreto," pasta 123, pp. 23–25.

40. Protocolo 6550/71-DI, APERJ/DOPS-GB, Nov. 12, 1971, setor "DOPS," pasta 183, pp. 429–36 (quotation). Secretaria de Estado de Segurança Pública, DPPS/RJ/Interior, Informação no. 114/77/DPPS/RJ/Interior, April 5, 1977, APERJ/DOPS-GB, setor "DGIE," pasta 247, pp. 296E–L (quotation). In the 1980s DOPS agents spied on the CEBS; see APERJ/DOPS-GB, setor "DGIE," pasta 247B. CIE, "Assunto: Missa Leiga," 1972, APERJ/DOPS-GB, setor 25, pasta 177, pp. 243–44 ("brothel").

41. DOPS-GB, Divisão de Operações, Serviço de Buscas, Seções de Buscas Especiais, Informe no. 0145-05, "Guerra Revolucionária," "Assunto: A Igreja e o estado," APERJ/DOPS-GB, setor "Secreto," pasta 86, pp. 269–73. Tupi-Guarani was an amalgam of native languages created by the Jesuits to facilitate communication with and among the indigenous peoples of colonial Brazil.

42. For Umbanda, see Brown 1994:128, 162–64, 186–87; also Della Cava 1985:168–69. For the Pentecostals, see Chesnut 1995, ch. 9. For the Presbyterian Church, see Cavalcanti 1992. For a discussion of similar tactics in Chile, see Lowden 1996:45.

43. Ministério do Exército, Io. Exército, 2a. Seção, "Assunto: infiltração de comunistas em seminários católicos," April 13, 1971, APERJ/DOPS-GB, setor "Secreto," pasta 86, p. 275. The regime also tried to blackmail bishops believed to be homosexual (Evilásio de Jesus interview).

44. Pretto interview. As discussed in chapter 8, nonprogressive clergy also aided refugees. For another example, see Kehl and Vannuchi 1997.

45. Dom Waldyr interview. For details on Father Nathanael's imprisonment, see Prandini, Petrucci, and Dale 1986–1987:2:148–62.

46. Ernanne Pinheiro interview. Prostitutes provided the Church accurate information in other areas of Brazil as well (Luiz Viegas interview 2).

47. Dom Paulo interview. The ultimate act of counterintelligence was the BNM project's acquisition of documents from the military courts proving the existence of torture (see chapter 1).

48. Queiroz 1994:41; Barros 1994a:170; information also from Virgílio Leite Uchôa interview 2.

49. Luiz Viegas interviews 1 and 2. On the Church and human rights, see chapters 8, 9, and 10.

50. Luiz Viegas interview 2. Dom Hélder was criticized by the right, which unsuccessfully attempted to link his sources to a Communist conspiracy; see, for example, Prandini, Petrucci, and Dale 1986–1987:3:35.

51. Cardoso et al. 1975; on opposition intellectuals and their cooperation with the Church, see Leoni 1997, ch. 9.

Chapter 3

1. "Centenário do General José Cândido da Silva Muricy," *Diário do Paraná,* Aug. 11, 1963.

2. Côrtes de Lacerda was Dom Hélder's archivist in the 1940s; see Bandeira 1994:80.

3. Muricy 1993:7, 65, 304 (quotation), 593. On Catholic teachings on sex and procreation, see Pierucci 1978. Information about the confessor role from Padilha interview 1.

4. No title, FGV/CPDOC/ACM, roll 2, doc. no. 581, p. 2; doc. nos. 582–83.

5. Muricy interview 1; and see Ministério do Exército, Estado-Maior do Exército, 2a. Subchefia—2a. Seção, "Assunto: terrorismo," Nov. 4, 1970, FGV/CPDOC/ACM, roll 1, doc. no. 652, p. 1.

6. The assault and the police search for the suspects, finally caught, made headlines for weeks in Rio's newspapers. See, for example, "General Muricy é baleado no coração por assaltante," *Jornal do Brasil (JB),* Feb. 18, 1979, sec. 1. According to this report, the bullet had become lodged in the pericardium, the sack surrounding the heart. General Muricy died in March 2000 at the age of 93.

7. "Centenário do General José Cândido da Silva Muricy," *Diário do Paraná,* Aug. 11, 1963.

8. This paragraph and the remainder of this section are based on Muricy 1993 and "Murici, Antônio Carlos" 1984.

9. For Muricy's pay receipts, see FGV/CPDOC/ACM, roll 1, docs. nos. 78–84.

10. Dom Vicente Scherer to Antônio Carlos da Silva Muricy, Porto Alegre, Oct. 12, 1961, FGV/CPDOC/ACM, roll 1, doc. 300, p. 2.

11. The texts of Muricy's speeches are in Muricy 1971; on this incident see also Dulles 1978:281–83.

12. Muricy 1993:460–503, 540; information on Muricy's good relations within the Army also from Moraes Rego interview.

13. Muricy 1993:509–46; also Muricy, "O Destacamento Tiradentes e o 31 de março de 1964," *O Globo*, March 25, 1979, p. 6.

14. Muricy 1993:344–48; information on Catholic Action came from Virgínia Ramos da Silva Muricy interview.

15. Muricy 1993:441; IV Exército, 7a. Região Militar, "Instrução teórica de oficiais sobre guerra insurrecional," FGV/CPDOC/ACM, roll 1, doc. nos. 323–48. A similar situation existed in the United States until the Kennedy administration; see Huggins 1998:102.

16. Muricy, "A guerra revolucionária e a ação decisiva dos civis," in Muricy 1971:158, 181, 182, 183–84 (quotations).

17. "Movimento de Cultura Popular do Recife (considerações do Gen. . . . Muricy)," FGV/CPDOC/ACM, roll 1, docs. 362A, 363.

18. According to Dom Waldyr, at the time President Castello Branco considered Dom Eugênio to be Brazil's most dangerous bishop (Dom Waldyr interview). On drought, see also Callado 1964:21.

19. The comment was made by Rosita Teixeira de Mendonça, a psychiatrist who investigated human rights abuses in Recife, cited in Alves 1967:93. For a description of incidents of violence and torture in the Northeast, see also Alves 1968, 1973.

20. "Murici, Antônio Carlos," 1984:2352; Muricy 1993:553–54, 557, 559–60.

21. FGV/CPDOC/ACM, roll 1, doc. no. 800, p. 4. In this document the phrase "por ofício do General Muricy" (by order of General Muricy) is discernible beneath an inked-out phrase that suggests someone, perhaps the general himself, tried to cover up his involvement in the Meneses arrest.

22. Muricy 1993:548–53, 564–65; on Muricy's opposition to torture, see Alves 1967:57, 61–63.

23. Virgínia Ramos da Silva Muricy interview; for a former Communist's testimony to the aid offered by the Muricys, see Pomar and Melleiro 1997:363–64. Dom Hélder further confirmed Muricy's assistance; see Piletti and Praxedes 1997:306.

24. Alves 1967; also Paulo Rehder, "General Ernesto Geisel não ouviu todos os presos políticos do Recife," *JB*, Sept. 20, 1964. For Muricy's version of the Geisel visit, see Muricy 1993:564–65. See also "O General Murici contesta as notícias sobre violências e prêsos no Nordeste," *O Globo*, Sept. 21, 1964, p. 11; "Murici pára tortura de presos no Nordeste," *Tribuna da Imprensa*, Sept. 23, 1964; "Murici assume 1a. RM e diz que há paz no Nordeste graças à atuação da 7a. RM," *JB*, Sept. 30, 1966, p. 7.

25. See, for example, Frei Luiz Gonzaga da Silva to Muricy, Nova Iguaçu, May 21, 1966, FGV/CPDOC/ACM, roll 1, doc. no. 777.

26. In his autobiography Castello Branco's Minister of Planning and Economic Coordination Roberto Campos states that he had tried to convince the president to name Dom Hélder as Minister of Agrarian Reform in order to "discipline his radicalism" by exposing him to "reality." Castello Branco declined, stating that Dom Hélder had "no affinity with the Revolution" (Campos 1994:694–95). There is no mention of this offer, however, in the

most complete biographical work on Dom Hélder to date; see Piletti and Praxedes 1997. It is also absent from Viana Filho 1976.

27. General Muricy claimed that Dom Hélder had promised to say the mass, but Dom Hélder's biographers demonstrate that there was no such promise. Muricy further asserted that the two men did not speak again. In referring to press reports in which Dom Hélder stated that the two men did speak, Muricy called Dom Hélder a "liar." For Muricy's account of this incident, see Muricy 1993:551, 553, 559–60, 581, 587–88, 591–95; for Dom Hélder's perspective, see Piletti and Praxedes 1997:330–33, 335–37, 340–41. In interviews 1 and 3 Muricy in 1993 and 1997 admitted that he still felt the hurt of his rupture with Dom Hélder and expressed a desire for reconciliation.

28. For a discussion of Muricy's promotion, see Flynn 1978:381.

Chapter 4

1. Mello 1979:869; also Schneider 1971:375; Muricy 1993:638–41.

2. Barboza 1992:161–62; Mello 1979:865; also see subsequent statements by Muricy in "Guerra revolucionária," *O Jornal*, Aug. 17, 1969; "Murici chama atenção para guerrilha," *JB*, Aug. 26, 1969; "A voz do Exército," *Veja*, Aug. 5, 1970. Muricy's positions gave rise to a popular rhyme: "É a lei do Muricy/Cada um cuida de si" (The law of Muricy:/Every man for himself). This saying was later recorded in a song performed by the Brazilian rock group Blitz.

3. "Muricy: plenitude democrática não é sinônimo de democracia liberal," *O Globo*, Dec. 9, 1970, p. 14.

4. Dom Eugênio interview. This point is developed in greater detail below and in chapter 8.

5. Dom Eugênio de Araújo Sales to General Muricy, Salvador, Jan. 5, 1967, FGV/CPDOC/ACM, roll 1, doc. no. 783, p.1.

6. Bruneau 1974b:172–73, 218–19. For a discussion of the subsequent theological tenor of the archdiocese of Rio de Janeiro under Dom Eugênio, see Peritore 1989. This study concludes that liberation theology was accepted in the archdiocese, with the exception of its deemphasis on Church hierarchy.

7. Piletti and Praxedes 1997:296; also "Bispos fazem apêlo para que os presos sejam tratados com humanidade," *O Jornal*, April 15, 1964.

8. Prandini, Petrucci, and Dale 1986–1987:2:106–09; Mello 1979:598–99.

9. Dom Eugênio interview. For subsequent examples of Dom Eugênio's resistance, see chapter 8.

10. Quotations in this and the following paragraphs are from Dom Eugênio to Muricy, Salvador, Dec. 25, 1968, FGV/CPDOC/ACM, roll 1, doc. no. 784, p. 2.

11. Quotations in this and the following paragraphs are from Muricy to Dom Eugênio, Rio de Janeiro, Dec. 27, 1968, FGV/CPDOC/ACM, roll 1, doc. nos. 784, 785.

12. Dom Eugênio to Muricy, Salvador, April 7, 1969, FGV/CPDOC/ACM, roll 1, doc. no. 789, pp. 1–2. The background on Sulik and his jailing also comes from Tibor Sulik interview 1; for the police file on Sulik, see Ministério do Exército, Io. Exército, Pedido de Busca no. 34/74-SCh, Jan. 18, 1974, APERJ/DOPS-GB, setor "DOPS," pasta 200, pp. 183–91.

13. "Entrevista do Cardeal D. Agnelo Rossi," *Serviço de Documentação (SEDOC)*, 3 (July 1970):105.

14. Ambassador Pedro J. Frías to Juan B. Martín, Minister of Foreign Relations and Religion, Rome, April 4, 1970, Archivo de la Embajada de la República Argentina ante la Santa Sede (Archive of the Argentine Embassy to the Holy See, hereafter cited as AEAASS), Santa Sede 84.

15. Dom Benelli quoted in Frías to Nicanor Costa Méndez, Minister of Foreign Relations and Religion, Rome, May 19, 1969, AEAASS, MREC 154; also see Frías to Méndez, Rome, May 12, 1969, AEAASS, MREC 154.

16. Osvaldo M. Brana to Alberto J. Vignes, Minister of Foreign Relations and Religion, Rome, Aug. 31, 1973, AEAASS, Santa Sede 366.

17. Frías to Martín, Rome, Jan. 29, 1970, AEAASS, Santa Sede 344.

18. For José Jobim, see Frías to Martín, Rome, April 4, 1970, AEAASS, Santa Sede 84; Ambassador Santiago de Estrada to Luís María de Pablo Pardo, Minister of Foreign Relations and Religion, Rome, Feb. 18, 1971, AEAASS, Santa Sede 43. For Paul VI, see Estrada to Pardo, Rome, Oct. 23, 1970, AEAASS, Santa Sede 268.

19. Estrada to Pardo, Rome, Oct. 23, 1970, AEAASS, Santa Sede 268; on Dom Agnelo's attempts to change Brazil's image, see also chapter 7.

20. Estrada to Pardo, Oct. 30, 1970, Rome, AEAASS, Santa Sede 273; Estrada to Pardo, Rome, Nov. 6, 1970, AEAASS, Santa Sede 281 and appendix; Estrada to Pardo, Rome, Aug. 21, 1971, AEAASS, Santa Sede 220 and appendix.

21. Frías to Martín, Rome, Jan. 29, 1970, AEAASS, Santa Sede 27.

22. Frías to Martín, Rome, July 25, 1969, AEAASS, Santa Sede 234.

23. Unedited transcript of interview with Mário Gibson Barboza, 1981, FGV/CPDOC, tape 58, side 1.

24. Prandini, Petrucci, and Dale 1986–1987:3:35; Estrada to Pardo, Rome, Oct. 30, 1970, AEAASS, Santa Sede 275.

25. Frías to Martín, Rome, Jan. 29, 1970, AEAASS, Santa Sede 27.

26. Frías to Martín, Rome, July 25, 1969, AEAASS, Santa Sede 234; also Piletti and Praxedes 1997, ch. 36; Della Cava 1985:118; Estrada to Pardo, Rome, Aug. 20, 1971, AEAASS, Santa Sede 220 (one observer).

27. Untitled document discussing Branca Alves's appointment, n.d. (probably 1968), Biblioteca Cardeal Câmara, Branca de Mello Franco Alves Collection (hereafter cited as BMFA), pasta "Correspondência s/nomeação para o conselho de leigos." See also "Consilium de Laicis. Plenary Session XII. October 1–8, 1973. Group on Women in Society and the Church," BMFA, pasta "Promoção da mulher—XIa. S—outubro 1972–1973," doc. no. AG/XII/687I. For further background on Branca Alves, see "O sepultamento de Branca Alves" 1978; "Branca Alves levanta a situação do laicato no Brasil para o Vaticano," *JB*, July 30, 1973. On the Council, see BMFA, pasta "Regulamento do Conselho de Leigos."

28. Untitled document, Nov. 25, 1971, BMFA, pasta "IXa. sessão—março 1971."

29. "Rapport du voyage en Amérique Latine de Mgr Uylenbroeck (du 14 mai au 1er juin 1970)," BMFA, pasta "8a. sessão—outubro 1970." See also Frías to Martín, Rome, March 26, 1970, AEAASS, Santa Sede 72.

30. "Consilium de Laicis. VIIIème Session Plénière. 1–10 octobre 1970," BMFA, pasta "8a. sessão—outubro 1970." For other examples of Branca Alves's reports to the council, see "Tour d'horizon," BMFA, pasta "XIIa. Sessão"; "Travail des laics. Brésil," BMFA, pasta "Conselho—Ama. Lata. 1974."

31. Letter (author's name illegible) to Branca de Mello Franco Alves, Rome, Feb. 4, 1969, BMFA, pasta "Consilium," doc. no. 250/69/M14.

32. Branca Alves to Cardinal Jean Villot, Vatican secretary of state, Rome [?], March 11, 1970, BMFA, pasta "Consilium de Laicis—VII sessão—março 1970."

33. Dom Waldyr interview; and see Della Cava 1985:45, 57; Prandini, Petrucci, and Dale 1986–1987:2:142–43; Calliari 1996:613–14. Later, however, Baggio gave an interview in which he alluded to Dom Hélder's positions as "extremist"; see Estrada to Pardo, Rome, Aug. 20, 1971, AEAASS, Santa Sede 220 and appendix.

34. Frías to Nicanor Costa Méndez, Minister of Foreign Relations and Religion, Rome, April 22, 1969, AEAASS, MREC 122.

35. On Alceu, see Almeida et al. 1993; Almeida 1996a, ch. 1; Ferreira and Soares 1984; "Alceu: 85 anos" 1978; Lima 1973; Vilaça 1983; for the vast bibliography by and about Alceu, see *Alceu Amoroso Lima* 1987.

36. For Alceu's columns, see Lima 1964 (which contains the piece titled "Terrorismo cultural," 232–33), 1965, 1968, 1969, 1974, 1977.

37. Alceu Amoroso Lima to Dom Aloísio Lorscheider, Fazenda de São Lourenço, June 26, 1969, Centro Alceu Amoroso Lima para a Liberdade (hereafter cited as CAALL), pasta no. 46 (Lo a Lz).

38. Frías to Martín, Rome, Jan. 29, 1970, AEAASS, Santa Sede 27.

39. Estrada to Pardo, Rome, Oct. 30, 1970, AEAASS, Santa Sede 275; Estrada to Pardo, Rome, Dec. 11, 1970, AEAASS, Santa Sede 320; also Frías to Martín, Rome, Jan. 29, 1970, AEAASS, Santa Sede 27. For Alceu's views on the commission at the time, see Lima 1974:169–72; 1973:316–22.

40. Dom Eugênio to Branca Alves, Salvador, June 19, 1970, CAALL, pasta no. 26 E/2.

41. Dom Vicente Scherer to Alceu, Porto Alegre, July 7, 1970, CAALL, pasta no. 39.

42. Alceu to Dom Eugênio, Rio de Janeiro, Sept. 10, 1970, CAALL, pasta no. 26 E/2.

43. See, for example, Silva and Carneiro 1983:35–36; Della Cava 1985.

44. On Dom Eugênio's prestige in the military, see chapter 5. Because he preferred behind-the-scenes contacts, the cardinal shrugged off requests to become an official mediator between Church and state.

45. Information on Sobral Pinto from Dom Eugênio interview. Ministério do Exército, Gabinete do Ministro, Centro de Informações do Exército, Informação no. 2260S/102-S3-CIE, "Assunto: 'A Cruz,'" APERJ/DOPS-GB, setor "DOPS," pasta 181, p. 185 (quotation). Alceu to Dom Eugênio, Rio de Janeiro, Sept. 10, 1970, CAALL, pasta no. 26 E/2. For further examples of Dom Eugênio's support for human rights, see chapter 8; also Gaspari 1997b. On private contacts between the Chilean bishops and the military, see Lowden 1996:35–36.

46. "Muricy aponta aliciamento de jovens para o terror," *JB*, July 20, 1970, p. 5; "Muricy: a juventude é vítima de complô," *OESP*, Nov. 12, 1971, p. 4; "Muricy analisa pesquisa com subversivos presos," *JB*, Nov. 12, 1971; "Muricy: recuperar jovens que se desviaram é a grande tarefa," *O Globo*, Nov. 12, 1971. For a critical overview of the studies commissioned by Muricy, see Coimbra 1995:196–204.

47. Coimbra 1995:202; Eurípides Cardoso de Menezes, "Psicoterapia para os subversivos," speech in the Câmara dos Deputados (1970), FGV/CPDOC/ACM, roll 1, doc. no. 692.

48. "Relatório do 40. encontro bipartite," FGV/CPDOC/ACM, roll 1, doc. no. 975, p. 1.

49. The allegations of torture came from former political prisoners interviewed by Coimbra 1995:202–03; Coimbra does not name these interviewees. Muricy vehemently denied Coimbra's assertions in Muricy interview 3. Before the publication of her book, Coimbra gave a newspaper interview in which she referred to Muricy's request for research

on prisoners; see Cezimbra 1992. See chapter 3 of the present work for a discussion of Muricy's attempts to free political prisoners in 1964.

50. Muricy, "O Brasil e seu Exército," Portuguese draft of article, FGV/CPDOC/ACM, roll 1, doc. nos. 199–207; Muricy 1972.

51. Dom Eugênio to Muricy, Salvador, May 8, 1970, FGV/CPDOC/ACM, roll 1, doc. no. 798, pp. 1–2; Father Eugênio Alberto Collard to Dom Eugênio, Salvador, April 28, 1970, FGV/CPDOC/ACM, roll 1, doc. no. 799, p. 1, and newspaper clippings and radio transcript, pp. 2–3.

52. Dom Eugênio to Muricy, Salvador, May 8, 1970, FGV/CPDOC/ACM, roll 1, doc. no. 798, pp. 1–2. On foreign missionaries, see also Dom Eugênio to Foreign Minister Mario Gibson Barboza, Salvador, May 4, 1970, FGV/CPDOC/ACM, roll 1, doc. no. 798, p. 3.

53. For details of the May 1970 assembly, see Alves 1979:189–91. Alves states that it was Dom Aloísio who charged Candido Mendes with the investigation of torture, but Candido Mendes (interview 2) affirmed that it was Dom Eugênio. The fact that Dom Eugênio had earlier proposed a "private investigation" of torture to General Muricy further suggests that he was behind the inquiry, although it is not clear whether the private probe was one and the same with the Candido Mendes action. There is another discrepancy: Alves maintains that Dom Eugênio determined the withdrawal of Candido Mendes's documentation from the assembly to avoid a leak to the press, whereas Candido Mendes (interview 2) asserted that the decision was made not by Dom Eugênio but by the assembly. Candido Mendes's work also made its way to the Vatican; see Antoine 1970:259 n. 10.

54. Mainwaring 1986:111; for a skeptical interpretation, see Alves 1979:189–90.

55. Dom Eugênio to Muricy, Salvador, July 15, 1970, FGV/CPDOC/ACM, roll 1, doc. no. 800, p. 2; see pp. 1, 3, 4, for the Army Ministry documents. The documentation does not indicate how or if Dom Eugênio used this information.

56. On Medici, the Eucharistic Congress meetings, and their impact, see Prandini, Petrucci, and Dale 1986–1987:3:22–26. Dom Eugênio to Muricy, Salvador, July 15, 1970, FGV/CPDOC/ACM, roll 1, doc. no. 800, p. 2.

57. "Declaraciones de Monseñor Arístides Pirovano publicadas en 'Avvenire' del 21.3.1971," appendix to letter from Estrada to Pardo, Rome, April 2, 1971, AEAASS, Santa Sede 87.

58. Estrada to Pardo, Rome, Oct. 27, 1971, AEAASS, Santa Sede 307. Concerned with protecting Brazil's image abroad, Dom Mozzoni also discouraged Dom Pedro Casaldáliga from publishing a letter on the oppression of the poor of Brazil's countryside (Tierra 1997:381).

Chapter 5

1. See also "Médici lembra o seu pai ao ser recebido na Santa Casa," *JB*, Oct. 1, 1970, sec. 1, p. 3.

2. Prandini, Petrucci, and Dale 1986–1987:2:43–47; also see Bruneau 1974a:346.

3. Frías to Martín, Rome, April 4, 1970, AEAASS, Santa Sede 84 (Jobim); Estrada to Pardo, Rome, Aug. 20, 1971, AEAASS, Santa Sede 220 and appendix (Baggio).

4. FGV/CPDOC/ACM, roll 1, doc. no. 788, pp. 1–2; doc. no. 898, p. 2; doc. no. 899, p. 1. "Encontro tripartite," *Renovação* (Porto Alegre) 22 (May 1969): 16–17. Information on the Tripartite comes also from the Octávio Costa interview 1; Pereira 1996.

5. Prandini, Petrucci, and Dale 1986–1987:3:39–40 (quotation). On technocrats and the military versus the Church, see McDonough 1981:103–04, 241.

6. Dom Hélder continued to embrace the idea of economic development through Church-state cooperation until the early 1970s, when he and other bishops adopted the concept of liberation as the solution to poverty. On this point and Dom Hélder's emphasis on dialogue, see Piletti and Praxedes 1997:319–20, 353–54 (quotes), 410; also "Comandante do Quarto Exército visitou D. Hélder," *Jornal do Comércio*, Aug. 25, 1966, p. 2.

7. "Brazil Program Analysis," National Security Study Memorandum no. 67 (1969–1970), National Security Archive, annex D, p. 31; also see Silva 1984:463.

8. The weekly CNBB bulletin, *Notícias* (Rio de Janeiro) Oct. 16, 1970; information on priests' activities from Pretto and Prigol interviews.

9. Passarinho 1996:341, 382–83. For background on IBRADES, see Doimo 1995:163, 171.

10. This assessment is shared by Muraro 1985:75–76.

11. Dom Agnelo Rossi, Dom Carlos Carmelo de Vasconcelos Motta, Dom Vicente Scherer, Dom Eugênio Sales, and Dom Jaime de Barros Câmara to General Emílio Garrastazu Médici, São Paulo, Oct. 8, 1970, FGV/CPDOC/ACM, roll 1, doc. no. 845, p. 1. For CNBB leadership, see "Bispos encerram no Zacarias reunião extraordinária da Comissão Central da CNBB," *JB*, sec. 1, p. 4 (quotation); also *Notícias*, Oct. 9, 16, 1970; "Projeto de declaração dos bispos," *SEDOC* 3 (Feb. 1971): 985–86.

12. "Papa condena terror e violência mundial," *JB*, Oct. 22, 1970, sec. 1, p. 2 (Pope Paul VI); "Médici acusa os exilados pela imagem do Brasil," *JB*, Oct. 21, 1970, sec. 1, p. 3; "Incidentes com o clero irritam o Presidente," *JB*, Oct. 16, 1970, sec. 1, p. 6.

13. Dom Lucas Moreira Neves to the Brazilian bishops, Rio de Janeiro, Sept. 30, 1970, PUC-SP/CEDIC, JOC, roll 9. See also "CNBB faz gestões por religiosos," *JB*, Oct. 24, 1970, sec. 1, p. 7; "CNBB dá apoio total a Fragoso," *JB*, Nov. 12, 1970, sec. 1, p. 4; "Dom Alberto ainda não viu presos," *JB*, Nov. 13, 1970, sec. 1, p. 13. Trevisan contacts noted in Dom Mário interview.

14. Father Celso José Pinto da Silva, assistant secretary, CNBB National Secretariat for the Lay Apostolate, to Colonel Vieira Ferreira, CODI commander, Rio de Janeiro, Sept. 14, 1970, PUC-SP/CEDIC, JOC, roll 9; "Dom Jaime confirma prisão pelo DOPS de três padres e teve encontro com Siseno," *JB*, Oct. 1, 1970, sec. 1, p. 4. While the combat of subversion was the main reason for the First Army's attacks on JOC and IBRADES, an additional explanation circulated among Church militants: General Sizeno Sarmento wanted to create difficulties for the Médici government in revenge for his having lost the 1969 internal military race for president. This version given in Prigol interview.

15. Silva to Monsignor Marcel Uylenbroeck, secretary, Pontifical Council for the Laity, Rio de Janeiro, Sept. 24, 1970, PUC-SP/CEDIC, JOC, roll 9; Dom Lucas to the Brazilian bishops, Rio de Janeiro, Sept. 30, 1970, PUC-SP/CEDIC, JOC, roll 9.

16. "Dom Jaime confirma prisão pelo DOPS de três padres e teve encontro com Siseno," *JB*, Oct. 1, 1970, sec. 1, p. 4 (quotation). Dom Lucas to the Brazilian bishops, Rio de Janeiro, Oct. 23, 1970, PUC-SP/CEDIC, JOC, roll 9; "Relato de fatos da vida jocista (1970)," PUC-SP/CEDIC, JOC, roll 21; also Calliari 1996:633.

17. Dom Lucas Moreira Neves to General Emílio Garrastazu Médici, Rio de Janeiro, Oct. 2, 1970, PUC-SP/CEDIC, JOC, roll 9.

18. *OESP* cited in Prandini, Petrucci, and Dale 1986–1987:3:37. See also "Bispos vão reunir-se na quinta-feira," *JB*, Oct. 11–12, 1970, sec. 1, p. 4; "Bispos instalam amanhã reunião extraordinária no Colégio Maria Zacarias," *JB*, Oct. 14, 1970, sec. 1, p. 4.

19. "Emissário revela deseja do governo," *JB*, Oct. 17, 1970, sec. 1, p. 4; "Dom Avelar revela apreensão entre bispos," *JB*, Oct. 16, 1970, sec. 1, p. 4.

20. "Relato de fatos da vida jocista (1970)," PUC-SP/CEDIC, JOC, roll 21; Dom Lucas to the Brazilian bishops, Rio de Janeiro, Oct. 23, 1970, PUC-SP/CEDIC, JOC, roll 9.

21. "Relato de fatos da vida jocista (1970)," PUC-SP/CEDIC, JOC, roll 21; Father Celso José Pinto da Silva to Enrique del Rio, JOC International official, Rio de Janeiro, Nov. 12, 1970, PUC-SP/CEDIC, JOC, roll 9.

22. Pretto interview. Incidents of torture were also confirmed in the Cecília Coimbra interview.

23. "Relato de fatos da vida jocista (1970)," PUC-SP/CEDIC, JOC, roll 21. For examples of ambivalent views of JOC, see Dom Lucas to Jocistas at Morro São Carlos, Rio de Janeiro, Jan. 30, 1971, roll 9; Dom Lucas to Father Agostinho Pretto, Rio de Janeiro, Jan. 31, 1971, roll 9; Dom Lucas to Father Pretto, Rio de Janeiro, Feb. 11, 1971, roll 9.

24. "Dom Avelar crê no diálogo após o pleito," *JB*, Oct. 21, 1970, sec. 1, p. 3.

25. Also note that the bishops were pressuring Dom Eugênio to serve as an intermediary between Church and government, although the archbishop was reluctant to accept such a role; "Dom Eugênio Sales vai falar com o presidente," *JB*, Oct. 10, 1970, sec. 1, p. 12. See also "Bispos renovarão apelos a Dom Eugênio para que seja mediador junto ao govêrno," *JB*, Oct. 13, 1970, sec. 1, p. 14.

26. Padilha interviews 1 and 2; and see Padilha 1971:71–82; Padilha 1975. Additional data on Padilha available in his curriculum vitae. See also "Padilha (Tarcísio)" 1990; Lippmann et al. 1984. On Padilha's ESG activities, see António de Arruda, Tarcísio Meirelles Padilha, and Danton Pinheiro de Andrade Figueira, "Regimes políticos contemporâneos—soluções democráticas," ESG, Departamento de Estudos, C9-123–72, speech given on March 24, 1972, Arquivo Ana Lagôa.

27. Candido Mendes interview 3. For background on the senator, see Vilaça 1981. According to Candido Mendes, his is the only title of nobility in Brazil that has allowed inheritance by the eldest son, thus bringing the title into the present.

28. "Cândido Mendes: primeiro tema Justiça," *O Globo*, Nov. 12, 1971, p. 11. Biographical data on Candido Mendes came from his curriculum vitae and also from Candido Mendes interviews 1 and 3 and Marina Bandeira interview.

29. "Informes. D.O.," Oct. 15, 1968, APERJ/DOPS-GB, setor 33, pasta 23, pp. 73–74. Candido Mendes is mentioned in more than twenty other military and police reports on file at the DOPS-GB. See, for example, Ministério da Marinha, CENIMAR, "Informe," Jan. 8, 1969, APERJ/DOPS-GB, setor 29, pasta 59, pp. 266–67; Ministério do Exército, DOI-CODI/I Ex, "Interrogatório No. 107/74," Sept. 9, 1974, APERJ/DOPS-GB, setor 10, pasta 128, pp. 554–55.

30. On Leitão de Abreu, Candido Mendes, and liberalization, see Skidmore 1988:108, 151, 164–66, including nn. 9–18. Information on Candido Mendes's suggestion to Leitão de Abreu and the links to Merquior and Huntington is from Candido Mendes interview 2. Candido Mendes also brought Professor Karl Deutsch and Professor Georges Lavau to speak with Brazilian leaders about political liberalization.

31. Muricy 1993:660. Muricy incorrectly identifies the director of IBRADES as Father Leonel Franca, who was deceased.

32. Brian Burke and Enrique del Rio, JOC International officials, to Father Celso José Pinto da Silva, Rio de Janeiro, Oct. 19, 1970, PUC-SP/CEDIC, JOC, roll 9.

33. "Relatório sobre o 10. encontro 'bipartite,'" FGV/CPDOC/ACM, roll 1, doc. no. 906, p. 1 (quotes); doc. no. 907, p. 1 *(descompressão)*.

34. Ibid., doc. no. 906, p. 2.

35. "Relatório do 40. encontro bipartite," FGV/CPDOC/ACM, roll 1, doc. no. 977, p. 1. See chapter 6 for a detailed discussion of the second Bipartite encounter.

36. "Relatório sobre o 10. encontro 'bipartite,'" FGV/CPDOC/ACM, roll 1, doc. no. 907.

37. Muricy first contacted Army Minister Orlando Geisel, who took the idea to Médici. The president gave his approval (Muricy interview 1). On Médici as a conciliator, see Muricy 1993:749; also on this point and Médici's delegative governing style, see Skidmore 1988:105, 108.

38. "Muricy passa à reserva e é alvo de homenagens," *JB*, Nov. 26, 1970; "Murici, Antônio Carlos" 1984:2352. Muricy went to work as president of two companies, Noralage and Companhia Docas de Imbituba.

39. General Adolpho João de Paula Couto, "Bipartite. Resultado do encontro do Gen. Paula Couto com o Gen. Figueiredo," Dec. 29, 1970, FGV/CPDOC/ACM, roll 1, doc. no. 916, p. 2; doc. no. 917, p. 1. Candido Mendes recalled that the military debated whether even the SNI should be present at the Bipartite (Candido Mendes interview 3).

40. On Muricy's relations with Médici and Orlando Geisel, see Muricy 1993:123–25, 252, 724. Ernesto Geisel also considered himself Muricy's friend; see D'Araujo and Castro 1997:214.

41. "Muricy bate recorde na eleição da ADESG," O Globo, Dec. 11, 1970; "Médici assiste à posse de Murici na direção da ADESG," O Globo, Jan. 8, 1971. On newspaper interviews, see chapter 4; on ADESG's activities, see Stepan 1988:47. A member of the ADESG, Padilha pushed the Muricy candidacy. Padilha believed that a leader of Muricy's stature could revive the organization, which one general refused to participate in any further because it had become a sort of vaudeville act ("respirava 'o clima do Chacrinha'"); see Tarcísio Meirelles Padilha to Muricy, Rio de Janeiro, June 16, 1970, FGV/CPDOC/ACM, roll 1, doc. 276, p. 2.

42. "Reunião com a CNBB," FGV/CPDOC/ACM, roll 1, doc. no. 916, p. 1. In his 1981 interview General Muricy stated that he met with Médici before the first Bipartite encounter (see Muricy 1993:660). However, documents such as the one cited here, as well as Paula Couto's report ("Bipartite. Resultado do encontro do Gen. Paula Couto com o Gen. Figueiredo," Dec. 29, 1970, FGV/CPDOC/ACM, roll 1, doc. no. 916, p. 2; doc. no. 917, p. 1), indicate that contact with Médici came *after* the start of the commission. Also see note 37 of this chapter.

43. Muricy 1993:662 (quote), 749; Muricy elaborated on these points in Muricy interview 1. Muricy stated emphatically that the hard-liners did not interfere in the Bipartite. Muricy believed he had the respect of the hard line and influence over it ("eu atuava ela"). Confirmation of Muricy's authority also from Pacífico interview.

44. "Relatório da reunião preparatória p/o 30. encontro bipartite," FGV/CPDOC/ACM, roll 1, doc. no. 940, p. 1.

45. Muricy 1993:661 (quotation); Fontoura interview; Padilha interview 1; Candido Mendes interview 1; Dom Eugênio interview.

46. "Relatório do XXIo. encontro bipartite," FGV/CPDOC/ACM, roll 2, doc. no. 116, p. 2 (Dom Aloísio), and doc. no. 117, p. 1 (Padhilha). See the conclusion to the present work for a more detailed discussion of the end of the Bipartite.

47. Wagley 1963:100–104. On the Brazilian elite, see also Needell 1987.

48. "Relatório do 40. encontro bipartite," FGV/CPDOC/ACM, roll 1, doc. no. 974.

49. The theoretical point about the expression of elite opinion is made by McDonough 1981:15, 37, 175.

50. Virgílio Rosa Netto interview. A top CNBB assistant, Netto came into frequent contact with Dom Ivo, Candido Mendes, and other important Church officials in the 1970s.

51. Virgílio Rosa Netto interview; also see the discussion of Candido Mendes's Bipartite texts in the next chapter.

52. This analysis from Candido Mendes interview 2.

53. "Relatório especial do grupo bipartite, sobre problemas surgidos na área Igreja X governo, referentes à participação do clero nas comemorações do sesquicentenário da independência do Brasil," FGV/CPDOC/ACM, roll 1, doc. no. 986, p. 1.

54. "30. encontro bipartite," FGV/CPDOC/ACM, roll 1, doc. no. 943, p. 2.

55. Muricy stated that he had not been concerned about Air Force representation at the Bipartite (interview 2). A likely factor was the strength of the hard-liners within the Air Force.

56. Muricy interview 1. See also "Relatório do XXIIo. encontro bipartite," FGV/CPDOC/ACM, roll 2, doc. no. 122, p. 3; doc. no. 123, p. 1.

57. "Dom Avelar crê no diálogo após o pleito," *JB*, Oct. 21, 1970, sec. 1, p. 3; Castello Branco 1979:3:693–94; "Igreja admite que relações com Estado encontraram o caminho de uma solução," *JB*, Oct. 20, 1970, sec. 1, p. 7.

58. "Relatório do XX encontro bipartite," FGV/CPDOC/ACM, roll 2, doc. no. 107, p. 2; doc. no. 108, p. 1. "Arcebispo de Goiânia esclarece autoridades militares sobre sua exata posição," Centro de Informações Ecclesia, *Boletim Informativo* 253 (1973), in FGV/CPDOC/ACM, roll 1, doc. nos. 903–04; "Brasil: choques y diálogo entre Iglesia y gobierno," *La Nación*, Sept. 3, 1973, in FGV/CPDOC/ACM, roll 2, doc. no. 113, p. 2. The *Boletim* also contained all of the articles that had been excised by government censors from *O São Paulo*, yet the *Boletim* itself, which had a circulation of only three hundred or so, usually escaped censorship (Dom Amaury interview). "Relatório do XXIIo. encontro bipartite," FGV/CPDOC/ACM, roll 2, doc. no. 122, p. 1 (Major Lee).

59. Marina Bandeira interview; on the importance of social networks for human rights, see Loveman 1998.

60. Nevertheless, the Bipartite remained a strictly Brazilian initiative. For instance, the Vatican secretary of state did not interfere in the talks (Candido Mendes interview 2). The lack of any official Vatican link to the Bipartite further demonstrated the CNBB's rising importance and autonomy.

61. Virgílio Rosa Netto interview; interviews with several priests and former priests; "Relatório do XX encontro bipartite," FGV/CPDOC/ACM, roll 2, doc. no. 110, p. 2.

62. For an example of the distribution of the military reports, see "Relatório do 20. encontro 'bipartite,'" FGV/CPDOC/ACM, roll 1, doc. no. 915, p. 3.

63. "Relatório da reunião preparatória p/o 30. encontro bipartite," FGV/CPDOC/ACM, roll 1, doc. no. 941.

64. Candido Mendes interview 1. The bishops were not defenseless, however, because they had their own communications network (see chapter 2).

65. "Relatório do 20. encontro 'bipartite,'" FGV/CPDOC/ACM, roll 1, doc. no. 912. This report states that Colonel Omar established the authenticity of the tape but does not explain how. For the transcript of the recording, see "Infiltração de comunistas na Igreja," FGV/CPDOC/ACM, roll 1, doc. nos. 931–33.

66. Roberval interview; Muricy interview 2. Neither officer could recall what subsequently happened with these tapes. It is ironic that, although quite gracious and frank in his interview, Admiral Roberval declined to be taped. Former CNBB assistant Netto stated that Dom Ivo also secretly recorded the Bipartite meetings. He recalled another occasion on which Dom Ivo wanted to record a meeting with General Figueiredo. The officer became angry and expelled the bishop from his office (Virgílio Rosa Netto interview). I was unable to confirm the Bipartite recording with Dom Ivo himself. Candido Mendes (interview 3) denied that Dom Ivo made tapes.

67. "Relatório do XVII encontro bipartite," FGV/CPDOC/ACM, roll 2, doc. no. 40, p. 2.

68. For Dom Fernando Gomes, "Relatório do XVIII encontro bipartite," FGV/CPDOC/ACM, roll 2, doc. no. 93, p. 1. For Dom Paulo, "Relatório especial do grupo bipartite, sobre problemas surgidos na área Igreja X governo, referentes à participação do clero nas comemorações do sesquicentenário da independência do Brasil," FGV/CPDOC/ACM, roll 1, doc. no. 933; untitled notes, FGV/CPDOC/ACM, roll 1, doc. no. 900, p. 2. For Dom Eugênio and Dom Ivo, see Muricy 1993:664; for Candido Mendes, "Relatório do 40. encontro bipartite," FGV/CPDOC/ACM, roll 1, doc. no. 977, p. 1; "Relatório do XXIIo. encontro bipartite," FGV/CPDOC/ACM, roll 2, doc. no. 124.

69. For Dom Luciano, "Relatório especial do grupo bipartite, sobre problemas surgidos na área Igreja X governo, referentes à participação do clero nas comemorações do sesquicentenário da independência do Brasil," FGV/CPDOC/ACM, roll 1, doc. no. 991, p. 1; doc. nos. 992–93. "Relatório do XXIV encontro bipartite," FGV/CPDOC/ACM, roll 2, doc. no. 132, p. 2; also FGV/CPDOC/ACM, roll 1, doc. no. 899, p. 1; doc. no. 900. For Dom Vicente Scherer, "Visita a D. Vicente Scherer," FGV/CPDOC/ACM, roll 1, doc. no. 870.

70. "Relatório do XXIIIo. encontro bipartite," FGV/CPDOC/ACM, roll 2, doc. no. 125; "Relatório do XXIV encontro bipartite," ibid., doc. no. 132, pp. 2–3.

71. For an earlier interpretation that lays stress on dialogue in the Geisel era, see Bruneau 1982:71–72.

Chapter 6

1. "Relatório sobre o 10. encontro 'bipartite,'" FGV/CPDOC/ACM, roll 1, doc. no. 907, p. 1; also see Dom Avelar's public comments in "Dom Avelar crê no diálogo após o pleito," *JB*, Oct. 21, 1970, sec. 1, p. 3. For the 1967 request, see Prandini, Petrucci, and Dale 1986–1987: 2:46.

2. For Barreto, "Relatório sobre o 10. encontro 'bipartite,'" FGV/CPDOC/ACM, roll 1, doc. no. 906, p. 2. For Mendes, see Almeida, "Perspectivas para o diálogo entre a Igreja e o estado no relance do desenvolvimento," FGV/CPDOC/ACM, roll 1, doc. no. 910, p. 4; doc. no. 911, p. 1.

3. LaRosa 1995:257–62. See also chapter 2 of the present work for background on the Church's evolution in the post–World War II era.

4. Data on Dom Eugênio's role at Medellín from Tibor Sulik interview 2; Dom Waldyr interview; and LaRosa 1995:282.

5. Almeida, "Princípios fundamentais do documento de Medellín sobre o desenvolvimento," FGV/CPDOC/ACM, roll 1, doc. no. 908.

6. Almeida, "Perspectivas para o diálogo entre a Igreja e o estado no relance do desenvolvimento," FGV/CPDOC/ACM, roll 1, doc. nos. 909–10.

7. Ibid., doc. no. 910, pp. 2–3.

8. Ibid., pp. 2–4.

9. "Relatório sobre o 10. encontro 'bipartite,'" FGV/CPDOC/ACM, roll 1, doc. no. 905, p. 2; doc. no. 906.

10. See, for example, "A Igreja e a guerra revolucionária," FGV/CPDOC/ACM, roll 1, doc. no. 919, p. 2; doc. no. 920; doc. no. 921, p. 1.

11. "Relatório sobre o 10. encontro 'bipartite,'" FGV/CPDOC/ACM, roll 1, doc. no. 906.

12. General Adolpho João de Paula Couto, "A guerra revolucionária e a Igreja, à luz dos documentos de Medellín," FGV/CPDOC/ACM, roll 1, doc. no. 923, p. 2.

13. Paula Couto, "A guerra revolucionária e a Igreja," FGV/CPDOC/ACM, roll 1, doc. no. 923, p. 2; doc. nos. 924, 928.

14. Ibid., doc. no. 924; doc. no. 925, p. 1.

15. Ibid., doc. nos. 925, 926; doc. no. 927, p. 2; doc. no. 928, p. 1; doc. no. 930, p. 1.

16. Ibid., doc. no. 928, p. 2; doc. no. 929.

17. "Relatório do 20. encontro 'bipartite,'" FGV/CPDOC/ACM, roll 1, doc. no. 911, p. 3; doc. no. 912, p. 1.

18. Ibid., doc. no. 912, p. 1.

19. Ibid., doc. no. 913, p. 1.

20. Ibid., p. 2.

21. Dantas Barreto, "Simples reflexões a propósito do documento 'Perspectivas para o diálogo entre a Igreja e o estado, etc.,' apresentado ao governo em nome da CNBB," FGV/CPDOC/ACM, roll 1, doc. nos. 934–38; doc. no. 939, pp. 1–2. For government document see Presidência da República 1970.

22. "Relatório do 20. encontro 'bipartite,'" FGV/CPDOC/ACM, roll 1, doc. no. 914, pp. 2–3; doc. no. 915, pp. 1–2.

23. "Relatório da reunião preparatória p/o 30. encontro bipartite," FGV/CPDOC/ACM, roll 1, doc. no. 941, p. 1.

24. Paula Couto, "Observações para a 3a. bipartite," FGV/CPDOC/ACM, roll 1, doc. no. 944, p. 2; doc. no. 945, p. 1.

25. "Apreciação sobre pontos do documento apresentado na 1a. reunião pelo Prof. Candido Mendes," FGV/CPDOC/ACM, roll 1, doc. no. 951, p. 1.

26. Ibid., p. 2; doc. no. 952; doc. no. 953, p. 1.

27. On Lopes, see Prandini, Petrucci, and Dale 1986–1987:1:24–26.

28. Golbery do Couto e Silva, José Murta Ribeiro, Francisco Leme Lopes, José Garrido Tôrres, and Geraldo Eulálio do Nascimento e Silva, "Doutrina social da Igreja e diretrizes do govêrno do Brasil," FGV/CPDOC/ACM, roll 1, doc. no. 953, p. 2; doc. nos. 954–65.

29. Paula Couto, "Observações para a 3a. bipartite," FGV/CPDOC/ACM, roll 1, doc. no. 945, p. 1; "Relatório da reunião preparatória p/o 30. encontro bipartite," FGV/CPDOC/ACM, roll 1, doc. no. 942, p. 1.

30. "Relatório do 40. encontro bipartite," FGV/CPDOC/ACM, roll 1, doc. no. 968.

31. "Conclusiones de la reunión de presidentes de Comisiones Episcopales de Acción Social del CELAM," FGV/CPDOC/ACM, roll 1, doc. no. 978, p. 2; doc. nos. 979–80. On Dom Eugênio's presentation of this document, see "Relatório do 40. encontro bipartite," FGV/CPDOC/ACM, roll 1, doc. no. 968, p. 2; doc. no. 969.

32. "Relatório do 20. encontro 'bipartite,'" FGV/CPDOC/ACM, roll 1, doc. no. 914, p. 2.

33. "Igreja admite que relações com Estado encontraram o caminho de uma solução," *JB*, Oct. 20, 1970, sec. 1, p. 7 (emphasis in the original).

34. "Relatório sobre o 10. encontro 'bipartite,'" FGV/CPDOC/ACM, roll 1, doc. no. 905, p. 2; doc. no. 907, p. 1.

35. Ibid., doc. no. 906, p. 1.

36. Ibid., doc. no. 907, p. 2.

37. "Relatório do 20. encontro 'bipartite,'" FGV/CPDOC/ACM, roll 1, doc. no. 915, p. 1 (responsibility); "Relatório sobre o 10. encontro 'bipartite,'" FGV/CPDOC/ACM, roll 1, doc. no. 906, p. 1 (corrections). See also Dom Aloísio Lorscheider to General Luís de França Oliveira, secretary of security of the State of Guanabara, Rio de Janeiro, Dec. 6, 1968, APERJ/DOPS-GB, setor "Secreto," pasta 36, p. 30.

38. "Arcebispo de Goiânia esclarece autoridades militares sobre sua exata posição," Centro de Informações Ecclesia, *Boletim Informativo* 253, in FGV/CPDOC/ACM, roll 1, doc. no. 904, p. 1.

39. "Relatório do 20. encontro 'bipartite,'" FGV/CPDOC/ACM, roll 1, doc. no. 913, p. 3; doc. no. 915, p. 2.

40. "30. encontro bipartite," FGV/CPDOC/ACM, roll 1, doc. no. 943, p. 1; "Relatório da reunião preparatória p/o 30. encontro bipartite," FGV/CPDOC/ACM, roll 1, doc. no. 942, p. 2. General Fontoura relayed his response to Dom Ivo's request in a telephone call to General Paula Couto.

41. "Relatório da reunião preparatória p/o 30. encontro bipartite," FGV/CPDOC/ACM, roll 1, doc. no. 941, p. 2.

42. Alves 1968:213–19. Artola was regularly investigated by the DOPS-GB (anonymous interview with former DOPS-GB officer).

43. "Relatório do 40. encontro bipartite," FGV/CPDOC/ACM, roll 1, doc. no. 973, p. 2; doc. no. 974, p. 1.

44. Ibid., doc. no. 973, p. 2; doc. no. 974, p. 2; doc. no. 975, p. 1.

45. Prandini, Petrucci, and Dale 1986–1987:3:214–19. For a transcript of the sentence and the dissenting opinion, see Auditoria da 9a. Circunscrição Judiciária Militar, "Sentença," May 28, 1973, FGV/CPDOC/ACM, roll 1, doc. nos. 877–79; on Dom Pedro, see the present work, chapters 5 and 8.

46. "Relatório do XXIIIo. encontro bipartite," FGV/CPDOC/ACM, roll 2, doc. no. 127, p. 3; doc. no. 128, pp. 1–2; doc. no. 129, p. 3. *Le Monde* reported Jentel's release but did not publish an interview with him; see Della Cava 1985:195.

47. For police suspicions of Father Daniel, see Ministério do Exército, I Exército, Informe no. 17/72-H, Jan. 12, 1972, "Assunto: Grupo de Amigos de Oswaldo Cruz," APERJ/DOPS-GB, setor "Secreto," pasta 98, p. 245. For the incident concerning the woman, "Professora enlouquece no DOPS," *Denúncia* 6 (Feb. 1972): 4, in APERJ/DOPS-GB/Jean Marc van Der Weid Collection, series 1, doc. P1, doc. no. 41. See also Prandini, Petrucci, and Dale 1986–1987:3:68; "Prisão do Padre Daniel de Castro," *SEDOC* 4 (April 1972): 1196–97.

48. Paula Couto, "Relatório 'bipartite.' Assunto: posição do Cardeal D. Eugênio Sales face à prisão do Padre Daniel," FGV/CPDOC/ACM, roll 1, doc. no. 860.

49. For accounts of the Dominicans' involvement in the Marighella incident, see José 1997; Frei Betto 1987; Simas 1986; Mata 1992; Gorender 1998, ch. 25; Mir 1994:435–74; Freire, Almada, and Ponce 1997; also Prandini, Petrucci, and Dale 1986–1987:3:203–13; Antoine 1970; Della Cava 1985. Additional background from Ivo Lesbaupin interview and Dom Amaury interview. On the lack of clergy involvement in revolutionary groups, see Ridenti 1993.

50. Frei Tito and sixty-nine other political prisoners were freed in exchange for the freedom of the Swiss ambassador, kidnapped by revolutionaries.

51. General Pacífico stated that the matter was "ultrapassado" (concluded) by the start of the Bipartite (Pacífico interview).

52. Freire, Almada, and Ponce 1997:258; also Frei Betto 1987:236–37.

53. "Relatório do XVIII encontro bipartite," FGV/CPDOC/ACM, roll 2, doc. no. 86, p. 2 (Muricy); "Relatório sobre o 10. encontro 'bipartite,'" FGV/CPDOC/ACM, roll 1, doc. no. 907, p. 2 (Grupo da Situação). Dom Avelar, one of the leading proponents of Church-state dialogue, also pressed for broadening dialogue to include leaders from all social and cultural categories. He made this proposal in September 1971 in a speech before the ESG that was published in the press. Dom Avelar also criticized extremists in both the repressive forces and the opposition (see Prandini, Petrucci, and Dale 1986–1987:3:59–62). The ESG commander, General Rodrigo Octávio Jordão, was immediately fired. The kind of dialogue proposed by Dom Avelar did not occur until the so-called Missão Portella in 1977.

54. "Relatório do 40. encontro bipartite," FGV/CPDOC/ACM, roll 1, doc. no. 969, p. 1 (Dom Eugênio); doc. no. 975, p. 1. "Muricy aponta aliciamento de jovens para o terror," *JB*, July 20, 1970, p. 5.

Chapter 7

1. On the regime's use of Independence Day, see Fico 1997:126–27, 142–43.

2. "Atas de reunião do Alto Comando do Exército. 43a. reunião," Sept. 5, 1969, FGV/CPDOC/ACM, roll 2, doc. no. 197, p. 2.

3. For January, "A Igreja e o sesquicentenário da independência," *Comunicado Mensal (CM)* 232 (Jan. 1972): 11–12. For April, see Prandini, Petrucci, and Dale 1986–1987:3:102; "Comemorações religiosas do sesquicentenário," *O São Paulo*, Aug. 19, 1972, p. 1. For the official announcement, see "O sesquicentenário da independência do Brasil," *CM* 235 (April 1972): 24.

4. "Centenário de D. Vital," *SEDOC* 5 (Aug. 1972): 241–50. On the Religious Question, see chapter 2 of the present work.

5. Fabrício Conceição, "50 anos de independência: a nossa e a deles," *Voz Operária* (May 1972), in BNM microfilm collection, role no. 20, case no. 21, p. 30.

6. "3 de setembro," *O São Paulo*, Aug. 12, 1972, p. 3. In the same edition, see also "A Igreja nos festejos do sesquicentenário da independência." The CNBB had announced the September 3 date in a January press release; see "A Igreja e o sesquicentenário da independência," *CM* 232 (Jan. 1972): 11.

7. "Atas da II reunião da Comissão Representativa," *CM* 239 (Aug. 1972): 19.

8. "Relatório especial do grupo bipartite, sobre problemas surgidos na área Igreja X governo, referentes à participação do clero nas comemorações do sesquicentenário do Brasil" (hereafter cited as "Relatório especial"), FGV/CPDOC/ACM, roll 1, doc. no. 984, p. 2; doc. no. 985, p. 1; doc. no. 986. On the Church's preparations, see also Prandini, Petrucci, and Dale 1986–1987:3:102.

9. "Terminam as obras no Parque," *OESP*, Aug. 29, 1972, p. 56; "Em Roma, 'Te Deum' pelo sesquicentenário," *OESP*, Aug. 23, 1972, p. 46.

10. CNBB, Comissão Representativa, "1a. redação," rough draft of sesquicentennial statement, Aug. 1972, INP, doc. no. 757.

11. Alfredo Buzaid, "No sesquicentenário da independência," *O Globo*, Sept. 6, 1972, p. 2.

12. "Relatório especial," FGV/CPDOC/ACM, roll 1, doc. no. 984, p. 2; doc. no. 985, p. 1.

13. "Documentos sobre a Independência," *Imprensa Popular* 2, n.d., in BNM, role no. 20, case no. 21, pp. 181–91, and "Igreja combate a ditadura," *Voz Operária* (Aug. 1972), in ibid., p. 206; also "Le Brésil commémore son Indépendence . . . sans le peuple!" *Solidarité Brésil* 2.3, pp. 3–7, APERJ/JeanMarc van Der Weid Collection, series 1, dossier 2, doc. JM, P2, D40.

14. "Entrevista: Tristão de Athayde," *Libertas* 11.4 (Aug.–Sept. 1972): 4–5, in APERJ/DOPS-GB, setor "Comunismo," pasta 116, p. 87.

15. "Testemunho de paz," *SEDOC* 5 (July 1972): 107–09 (quotation); Ministério do Exército, 10. Exército, "Informação No. 1345/72-Sch. Assunto: CNBB," June 29, 1972, APERJ/DOPS-GB, setor "DOPS," pasta 175, pp. 198–202F.

16. "Missa grandiosa, prevê o arcebispo," *OESP*, Aug. 29, 1972, p. 22; "D. Paulo lembra omissão de 1922," *OESP*, Aug. 30, 1972, p. 30. Notwithstanding Dom Paulo's comments, the Church *did* mark a strong presence in 1922 by holding its first national Eucharistic congress in Rio de Janeiro and inaugurating the construction of the famed Cristo Redentor (Christ the Redeemer) statue atop the city's Corcovado peak (see Serbin 1996).

17. "Relatório especial," FGV/CPDOC/ACM, roll 1, doc. no. 985. The press also commented briefly on the content of *Celebrações;* see "Médici não irá à missa," *OESP*, Aug. 29, 1972, p. 56.

18. "Relatório especial," FGV/CPDOC/ACM, roll 1, doc. nos. 985–87.

19. Ibid., doc. no. 987, p. 2; doc. no. 988, p. 1.

20. Ibid., doc. nos. 985, 988; doc. no. 989, p. 1. See also "Celebração litúrgica por ocasião do sesquicentenário da independência do Brasil," *O São Paulo*, Sept. 3, 1972, pp. 8–11, which contains the truncated version of *Celebrações*. For the copy of the CNBB statement provided by Dom Avelar, see FGV/CPDOC/ACM, roll 1, doc. no. 996, p. 2; doc. no. 997.

21. "Igreja não lança o seu documento," *OESP*, Sept. 1, 1972; "Transcendente e imanente na missão atual da Igreja," *OESP*, Sept. 3, 1972, p. 44.

22. "Atas da II reunião da Comissão Representativa," *CM* 239 (Aug. 1972): 17–26.

23. "Relatório especial," FGV/CPDOC/ACM, roll 1, doc. no. 991, p. 2; doc. no. 992; doc. no. 993, p. 1. For the published text of the bishops' sesquicentennial statement, see "Mensagem da CNBB," *SEDOC* 5 (Oct. 1972): 477. Press reports on the meeting did not mention Church-state friction over the sesquicentennial; see, for example, "CNBB prepara mini-assembléia." On the question of torture, see the allusion made by Dom Valfredo Tepe in "Bispos devem denunciar a injustiça," *OESP*, Aug. 27, 1972, p. 28.

24. "Relatório especial," FGV/CPDOC/ACM, roll 1, doc. no. 993.

25. "Atas da II reunião da Comissão Representativa," *CM* 239 (Aug. 1972): 24–25.

26. "Relatório especial," FGV/CPDOC/ACM, roll 1, doc. nos. 989–90.

27. Ibid., doc. nos. 989–90; doc. no. 993, p. 1.

28. Ibid., doc. no. 990, p. 1; doc. no. 993, p. 1.

29. The minutes do not record the words of Dom Ivo nor of Dom Aloísio, who appeared at the end of the exchange. Ibid., doc. no. 989, p. 2; doc. no. 993, p. 1.

30. Ibid., doc. no. 990.

31. McDonough (1981:37) also noted a gap between the public opinions and the confidential views of other members of the elite during the Médici years.

32. "Alguns destaques das comemorações religiosas do sesquicentenário da independência," *O São Paulo*, Sept. 9, 1972, p. 3; "Nesta missa, o sermão é do papa," *OESP*, Sept. 3, 1972, p. 48. The biblical texts were Exodus 34:10–27; Romans 6:1–4; and Matthew 13:31–33. *O Estado de São Paulo* estimated the crowd at only twenty thousand; see "Paulo VI aponta o dever de todos," *OESP*, Sept. 5, 1972, p. 50.

33. "Armas e povo encerram a festa," *OESP,* Sept. 8, 1972, p. 1; "Congresso lembra a independência," *OESP,* Sept. 2, 1972, p. 13; Prandini, Petrucci, and Dale 1986–1987:3:103. While the sesquicentennial dispute mainly took place at the federal level, local government representatives did attend the CNBB's September 3 Te Deum, and the CNBB thanked the municipality and the state for their cooperation; see "Ao arcebispo de São Paulo felicitando pela preparação e celebração do 'Dia de Orações pela Pátria,'" *CM* 240 (Sept. 1972): 26. "Arcebispo diz que vai tudo bem com govêrno," *OESP,* Sept. 3, 1972, p. 50 (quotation).

34. Brandão 1992:13. An ally of Brizola in the 1961 succession crisis, Goiás Governor Mauro Borges had also opposed the coup and was deposed in November 1964.

35. For Dom Fernando in 1968, Prandini, Petrucci, and Dale 1986–1987:2:66–68. For further background, see Gomes 1982, Duarte 1996.

36. For a detailed analysis of these documents, see Bernal 1989:94–117; on the origins of the documents and Dom Fernando's role, see also Lopes 1994:132.

37. Dom Fernando Gomes dos Santos, "Indústria de calúnia?" *O São Paulo,* Aug. 19, 1972, p. 6; "Declaração da comissão episcopal regional," *CM* 238 (July 1972):71–74.

38. For background on Dom Pedro and São Félix, see Salem 1981:190–200; on the death of Father Burnier, see Prandini, Petrucci, and Dale 1986–1987:4:270–311. It is ironic that Fr. Burnier was the cousin of hard-line General João Paulo Moreira Burnier, head of CISA (the Air Force intelligence service that ran a torture center) and then Air Force base commander in Rio. On Fr. Burnier, see Tierra 1997:385.

39. "Opressão cai sobre Igreja do Araguaia," *Libertação,* 6.43, July 31, 1973, pp. 3–5, FGV/CPDOC/ACM, roll 1, doc. no. 681, p. 2; doc. no. 682.

40. On the Araguaia war, see Richopo 1987, Portela 1979, Cabral 1993; for attacks on the Church, see Prandini, Petrucci, and Dale 1986–1987:3:88–94.

41. Salem 1981:190–200; Prandini, Petrucci, and Dale 1986–1987:3:142–44.

42. FGV/CPDOC/ACM, roll 2, doc. nos. 45–82.

43. "Relatório do XVII encontro bipartite," FGV/CPDOC/ACM, roll 2, doc. nos. 40–42; Dom Pedro's document was "Do posseiro," FGV/CPDOC/ACM, roll 2, doc. no. 67, p. 2; doc. no. 68, p. 1.

44. FGV/CPDOC/ACM, roll 2, doc. no. 82.

45. "Relatório do XVII encontro bipartite," FGV/CPDOC/ACM, roll 2, doc. no. 42, p. 1.

46. Ibid., doc. no. 40, p. 2; doc. no. 41; doc. no. 42, p. 1.

47. Dom Fernando Gomes [dos Santos], "Carta pastoral sobre como vemos a situação da Igreja em face do atual regime" (Goiânia, 1973), CNBB/INP. The Grupo da Situação quickly obtained a draft of the pastoral and a June 27, 1973, letter from Dom Fernando to other bishops asking for comments; see "Relatório do XVII encontro bipartite," FGV/CPDOC/ACM, roll 2, doc. nos. 82–84 ("Anexo E"), doc. no. 92.

48. Clóvis Stenzel, "De D. Hélder a D. Fernando," *Diário de Notícias,* July 20, 1973.

49. "Relatório do XVII encontro bipartite," FGV/CPDOC/ACM, roll 2, doc. no. 40, p. 2; doc. no. 42, p. 2 (Muricy and Lee); doc. no. 43, p. 1. On Lee's acquisition of the letter, see Gomes 1982:229.

50. "Relatório do XVIII encontro bipartite (reunião extraordinária)," FGV/CPDOC/ACM, roll 2, doc. no. 87, p. 1 ("God" and "Our Lady"); doc. no. 88, p. 1; doc. 89, p. 1; doc. no. 94, p. 2 (nation) and doc. no. 95. I rely here on the military's detailed report of the meeting. For Dom Fernando's less detailed but consistent report, see "Arcebispo de Goiânia esclarece autoridades militares sobre sua exata posição," Centro de Informações Ecclesia, *Boletim*

Informativo 253, in FGV/CPDOC/ACM, roll 1, doc. no. 903, p. 2; doc. no. 904; also Gomes 1982:240–47.

51. "Relatório do XVIII encontro bipartite (reunião extraordinária)," FGV/CPDOC/ACM, roll 2, doc. no. 89, pp. 1–2.

52. Ibid., doc. nos. 90–92; doc. no. 92, p. 1 (quotation).

53. Ibid., doc. nos. 94–95 ("Anexos").

54. Ibid., doc. no. 92.

55. Ibid., doc. nos. 87–90, 92.

56. Ibid, doc. no. 93, p. 2. On the repercussions of Dom Fernando's publication for the Bipartite, see chapter 5.

57. "Relatório do XVIII encontro bipartite (reunião extaordinária)," FGV/CPDOC/ACM, roll 2, doc. no. 93.

58. Ibid., doc. no. 93.

59. "Encontro c/D. Aloísio e D. Ivo," FGV/CPDOC/ACM, role 1, doc. no. 851, p. 2; "Pontifício Colégio Pio Brasileiro," FGV/CPDOC/ACM, doc. no. 852, p. 1.

60. Dom Ivo Lorscheiter, "Pontifício Colégio Pio Brasileiro," FGV/CPDOC/ACM, doc. no. 852, p. 2.

61. José Jobim to Secretaria de Estado, Rome, Nov. 9, 1970, Arquivo do Itamaraty, Secretaria de Estado das Relações Exteriores, Correspondência Especial 4429; "Pontifício Colégio Pio Brasileiro," FGV/CPDOC/ACM, role 1, doc. no. 852, p. 1.

62. Ibid.; also doc. nos. 853–58; "Resumo do relatório anual do Pontifício Colégio Pio Brasileiro," *CM* 223 (April 1971): 25–29; Laufer interview.

63. "D. Agnelo diz que lutará em Roma pela boa imagem do país," *JB*, Nov. 10, 1970, sec. 1, p. 4; also "D. Agnelo fará centro informativo do Brasil em Roma," *JB*, Oct. 24, 1970, sec. 1, p. 3.

64. Colonel Fernando Cerqueira Lima to Muricy, Rome, Dec. 4, 1972, FGV/CPDOC/ACM, roll 1, doc. no. 864, p. 2; Lima to Muricy, Rome, Feb. 21, 1973, ibid., doc. no. 866, pp. 1–2. See also Dom Agnelo's proregime discourse at the Pio, "'Dia Nacional de Ação de Graças' em 23.XI.72 no Pontifício Colégio Pio Brasileiro de Roma," in ibid., doc. no. 864, p. 3; doc. no. 865, pp. 1–3. Lima was a friend of the owner of *O Estado de São Paulo*. Under Geisel he became a four-star general and headed up the investigation that ruled the suspicious death of journalist Vladimir Herzog a suicide (see Soares, D'Araujo, and Castro 1995:65, 229). On the Herzog case, see chapter 10 of the present work.

65. Gervásio Queiroga interview; "Pontifício Colégio Pio Brasileiro. Relatório anual," *CM* 271 (April 1975): 388.

66. "Encontro c/D. Aloísio e D. Ivo," FGV/CPDOC/ACM, roll 1, doc. no. 851, p. 2; Frederico Laufer to Muricy, Rome, Nov. 24, 1971, FGV/CPDOC/ACM, roll 2, doc. no. 516 (quotation); "Pontifício Colégio Pio Brasileiro," *CM* 278 (Nov. 1975): 1152–55. See also "Colégio Pio Brasileiro," *CM* 226 (July 1971): 63–64; "Colégio Pio Brasileiro," *CM* 246 (March 1973): 475; on support from the German Church, see Serbin 1995:165–67.

67. "Relatório do XXIV encontro bipartite," FGV/CPDOC/ACM, roll 2, doc. no. 133, pp. 1, 4; doc. no. 134, pp. 1, 4. On the China decision, including the hard-liners' opposition, see Couto 1998:158, 229–30; also D'Araujo and Castro 1997:363–64. A number of Brazilian businessmen supported the China initiative as a way to open new markets for Brazilian exports (see Médici 1995:86).

68. Ribeiro and Ribeiro 1994:111, 114, 117 (Costa e Silva), 118–19, 121, 123 ; for background

on the Church and population questions, see Pierucci 1978. "Relatório do XXIV encontro bipartite," FGV/CPDOC/ACM, roll 2, doc. no. 134, p. 2 (Candido Mendes).

69. Ribeiro and Ribeiro 1994:115–18, 129; on the bishops, see Prandini, Petrucci, and Dale 1986–1987:4:47–48.

70. "Geisel em resumo," *JB*, March 20, 1974, sec. 1, p. 5.

71. "Relatório do XXII encontro bipartite," FGV/CPDOC/ACM, roll 2, doc. no. 123, p. 3; doc. no. 124, p. 1. "Relatório do XXIII encontro bipartite," ibid., doc. no. 125, p. 1; doc. no. 128, p. 3; doc. no. 129, p. 1.

72. "Relatório do XXIV encontro bipartite," FGV/CPDOC/ACM, role 2, doc. no. 133, pp. 1–3; also "A respeito da BEMFAM," *CM* 228 (Sept. 1971): 51; "A Igreja, a questão demográfica e a pastoral familiar," *CM* 263 (Aug. 1974): 673–81.

73. "A Sociedade Bem-Estar Familiar (BEMFAM) diante da doutrina católica," *CM* 260 (May 1974): 416.

74. "De vários bispos ao presidente da CNBB," *CM* 261 (June 1974): 429.

75. "Relatório do XXIV encontro bipartite," FGV/CPDOC/ACM, roll 2, doc. no. 133, pp. 2–3.

76. Ibid., pp. 3–4.

77. "Relatório do XIX encontro bipartite," FGV/CPDOC/ACM, roll 2, doc. no. 97, p. 2; doc. no. 98, p. 1. On Protestantism and spiritism, also see Padilha 1975:83–86.

78. Octávio Costa interview 1. General Costa further speculated that Orlando Geisel's initiative may have been a deliberate effort to irritate the Church.

79. "Relatório do XXII encontro bipartite," FGV/CPDOC/ACM, roll 2, doc. no. 120, pp. 1–2; doc. no. 121, p. 1.

80. Octávio Costa interview 1. As the general recalled, Dom Newton later convinced the transit authority to put up traffic signs in Brasília indicating the way to the "chapel" rather than to the oratory. Fearful of the reaction of Orlando Geisel, Costa had the signs changed. Nevertheless, the Church later asserted control over the oratory; indeed, according to Costa, no Protestant activities were ever held there. See also Muricy 1993:663.

81. Octávio Costa interview 1; for the text of one of Dom Aloísio's requests, see "Ao sr. presidente da república sobre veiculação da CF-73 nas emissoras de rádio e TV," *CM* 239 (Aug. 1972): 130–31.

82. Gervásio Queiroga interview (quotation); on Senator Vilela, also see Skidmore 1988:241.

83. For a general narrative of these incidents, see Prandini, Petrucci, and Dale 1986–1987:3:163–69; also "À opinião pública," *A Arquidiocese em notícias*, in FGV/CPDOC /ACM, roll 1, doc. no. 880A, p. 4; "Dom Avelar espera uma explicação," *JB*, Sept. 4, 1973; Dom Avelar, "'Eu ouvi os clamores de meu povo': parecer sucinto sobre o documento," FGV/CPDOC/ACM, roll 1, doc. no. 900, p. 3; "Relatório do XX encontro bipartite," FGV/CPDOC/ACM, roll 2, doc. no. 108, p. 2; doc. no. 110, p. 1.

84. In order, Dom Avelar to Muricy, Salvador, Sept. 2, 1972 [1973], FGV/CPDOC/ACM, roll 1, doc. no. 861, p. 1; Muricy to Dom Avelar, Rio de Janeiro, Sept. 12, 1973, doc. no. 880, p. 2; Dom Avelar to Muricy, Salvador, Sept. 17, 1973, doc. no. 880A, p. 3; Dom Avelar to Muricy, Sept. 29, 1973, doc. no. 881, pp. 2–3.

85. "Relatório do XXIIo. encontro bipartite," FGV/CPDOC/ACM, roll 2, doc. no. 120, p. 2; "Relatório do XXIV encontro bipartite," FGV/CPDOC/ACM, roll 2, doc. no. 133, p. 1.

Chapter 8

1. In March and April 1997, Brazilian television networks offered stark evidence of continuing torture when they aired secretly recorded videos of policemen abusing favela-dwellers in São Paulo and Rio.

2. Barboza 1992:193–94 (quotation); Médici 1995:43–45, 47, 60–62, 73; Gazzotti 1998:79–83.

3. In addition to the Church, the Associação Brasileira de Imprensa (Brazilian Press Association) and elements of the Ordem dos Advogados do Brasil (Brazilian Bar Association) and the MDB took up the cause of human rights in the 1970s.

4. See chapter 2 for a description of the network. My analysis here differs from most studies of the CNBB, which stress the organization's ideological evolution as expressed in official pronouncements while giving little emphasis to concrete actions in defense of human rights.

5. Marina Bandeira interview; see also her comments in Lopes 1994:132–33.

6. "Une partie du clergé de Rio conteste les 'méthodes autoritaires' de Rome," Le Monde, April 16, 1971, p. 10. On "remaking" Brazil's image, see chapter 4.

7. "Eleição do nôvo arcebispo do Rio de Janeiro," SEDOC 3 (May 1971): 1393–404; "Une partie du clergé de Rio conteste les 'méthodes autoritaires' de Rome," Le Monde, April 16, 1971, p. 10.

8. Ministério do Exército, Gabinete do Ministro, CIE, Informação no. 2260/S/102-S3-CIE, Sept. 5, 1972, "Assunto: 'A Cruz,'" APERJ/DOPS-GB, setor "DOPS," pasta 181, p. 185.

9. Secretaria de Segurança Pública, Departamento Geral de Investigações Especiais, Informação no. 029-J. Santos/75, Oct. 13, 1975, APERJ/DOPS-GB, setor "DGIE," pasta 247, pp. 125–26.

10. Virgílio Rosa Netto interview. The organization was FASE (Federação de Órgãos de Assistência Social e Educacional); see Prandini, Petrucci, and Dale 1986–1987:3:63–64.

11. Tibor Sulik interview 1. According to Sulik, before Dom Eugênio's arrival in Rio, the nunciature was used as a hiding place for clergy sought by the repressive forces.

12. Candido Mendes interview 2. Dom Eugênio himself also confirmed contacts with Dom Paulo, though Dom Eugênio could not recall the content of the conversations (Dom Eugênio interview).

13. Dom Eugênio interview; on Médici and human rights violations, see Médici 1995:43–45, 47, 73.

14. Dom Eugênio interview; Ponte Neto interview. Ponte Neto was the archdiocesan administrator of Caritas, the Catholic relief organization. As such he handled the day-to-day operation of the underground railroad. These efforts occurred in cooperation with a similar program in the archdioceses of São Paulo and Santiago, Chile. See Wright 1989:60; Lowden 1996:31–32.

15. Alfredo Stroessner to Muricy, Asunción, Sept. 18, 1970, FGV/CPDOC/ACM, roll 1, doc. no. 651.

16. See CDADDH, police file no. 1931, Feb. 22, 1973; CDADDH, "Declaración informativa formulada por el detenido Pedro Enrique [sic] Mariani Bittencourt," bibliorato "L 53–54"; also Gregorio López Moreira to General Francisco A. Brítez, Asunción, Aug. 12, 1967, CDADDH, bibliorato "C.2. Notas J.I. IV-67 a I-68"; "IV Conferencia Bilateral de inteligencia entre los ejércitos de Paraguay y Brasil," CDADDH, bibliorato 1008, pp. 436–48.

17. On Operation Condor, see Sannemann 1993, 1994; Paz, González, and Aguilar 1994, ch. 6; "Paraguay: les archives" 1993.

18. For an overview of the CJP-BR's history, see Almeida and Bandeira 1996; CNBB 1983; Doimo 1995:81 n. 5, 191–92.

19. "Relatório da reunião preparatória p/o 30. encontro bipartite," FGV/CPDOC/ACM, roll 1, doc. no. 940, pp. 1 and 2 (quotation); doc. no. 941, p. 1.

20. Candido Mendes interview 2; and see CNBB 1983.

21. For an overview of the CJP-SP, see Pope 1985; also Wright 1989. The actions of both the CJP-BR and the CJP-SP contradict Lowden's assertion that the Vicariate of Solidarity in Chile, founded years later, "was an entirely new structure" in the Catholic Church; see Lowden 1996:54, 76.

22. Candido Mendes interview 2. On cooperation, see chapter 10; also Wright 1989:60. Additional information on cooperation, frictions, and differences in style comes from Dalmo Dallari interview and Margarida Genevois interview (both Dallari and Genevois belonged to the CJP-SP). For an alternative interpretation that, I believe, incorrectly overemphasizes friction between the CJP-BR and the CJP-SP, see Pope 1985:430–31, 434–35.

23. Arruda 1996; also *Boletim Reservado*, no. 4, May 3, 1974, APERJ/DOPS-GB, setor 38, p. 19; additional information and perceptions of the meeting from Candido Mendes interview 3.

24. Candido Mendes interview 2. On Paulo Wright, see Wright 1993; Archdiocese of São Paulo 1988:37, 256–57.

25. Tibor Sulik interview 1. On lack of control in the security forces, see Couto 1998:174–94, 253–54; also D'Araujo and Castro 1997:227–28, 377–79.

26. Candido Mendes interview 2; also Huggins 1998:177, 179.

27. "Visita a d. Vicente Scherer," FGV/CPDOC/ACM, roll 1, doc. no. 870. Among General Muricy's papers there is also a copy of a letter from Dom Vicente Scherer to Dom Aloísio harshly criticizing the CNBB human rights statement; see FGV/CPDOC/ACM, roll 2, doc. no. 6; also Dom Vicente Scherer, "Cardeal analisa decisões da última reunião da CNBB," *Correio do Povo* (Porto Alegre), April 24, 1973.

28. Adolpho João de Paula Couto, "Proposições aprovadas pela XIII Assembléia Geral da CNBB. Análise sumária das *proposições aprovadas* consideradas como sendo as mais graves," FGV/CPDOC/ACM, roll 1, doc. nos. 871–76. See also the Situação's marginal notes on a CNBB press release on the human rights document in FGV/CPDOC/ACM, roll 2, doc. no. 1, p. 2; doc. nos. 2–5. Air Force Intelligence produced a harshly critical analysis of this document; see Costa 1979:4–5. For the CNBB text, see CNBB 1973. The Bipartite debated the statement at its April 1973 meeting. However, the minutes are not in Muricy's archive.

29. Paula Couto, "Análise sumária das *proposições aprovadas* consideradas como sendo as mais graves," FGV/CPDOC/ACM, roll 1, doc. no. 876.

30. "Relatório do XVI encontro bipartite," FGV/CPDOC/ACM, roll 2, doc. nos. 12–13; doc. no. 16, pp. 2–3; also "Relatório do XVII encontro bipartite," FGV/CPDOC/ACM, roll 2, doc. no. 42.

31. "Relatório sobre o 10. encontro 'Bipartite,'" FGV/CPDOC/ACM, roll 1, doc. no. 907, pp. 1–2; "Relatório do 20. encontro 'Bipartite,'" ibid., p. 3. On the ineffectiveness of the National Commission, see Huggins 1998:175–76; Silva 1984:475–76; Silva and Carneiro 1983:25, 103–11, 118–26; Della Cava 1985:181; "La dictadura militar de Medici a Geisel," *Campanha*, no. 15/16, April 15, 1974, pp. 19–23, APERJ/Jean Marc van Der Weid Collection, series 1, dossier 2, doc. JM, P2, D25; Lima 1974:179–81; further confirmation from Candido Mendes interview 3.

32. "Relatório do XVII encontro bipartite," FGV/CPDOC/ACM, roll 2, doc. no. 43, p. 1; doc. no. 44, p. 1. The tribunal was suggested in the CNBB's 1973 human rights statement (CNBB 1973:14). See also Russell 1967.

33. *Actes* 1974:46–50. On preparation for the tribunal, see letter from Committee Against Repression in Brazil to friends, Hyattsville, Maryland, Aug. 30, 1972, APERJ/Jean Marc van Der Weid Collection, series 1, dossier 2, doc. JM, P2, D-12, D-13, D-16.

34. "Relatório do 40. encontro bipartite," FGV/CPDOC/ACM, roll 1, doc. no. 972; doc. no. 973, p. 1. For the text of the protocol, see "Anexo E (ao relatório do IV enc. bip.)," ibid., doc. no. 981, p. 2; doc. no. 982, p. 1; Jobim to Secretaria do Estado, Rome, June 7, 1971, Arquivo do Itamaraty, Secretaria de Estado das Relações Exteriores, Correspondência Especial 2497.

35. "Relatório do 40. encontro bipartite," FGV/CPDOC/ACM, roll 2, doc. nos. 12–13; doc. no. 973, p. 1; doc. no. 977, p. 1.

36. Archdiocese of São Paulo 1988:116. In a stark documentary revelation of torture, a DOI-CODI interrogator noted that Joaquim Arnaldo Albuquerque, suspected of ties to the MPL, could not continue under questioning "because of his state of health"; Ministério do Exército, Io. Exército, Informação no. 405/74-H, Feb. 19, 1974, "Assunto: depoimentos prestados no DOI/IEX," APERJ/DOPS-GB, setor "Comunismo," pasta 126, p. 194.

37. "Cartas sobre presos," *SEDOC* 6 (June 1974): 1412–14.

38. "Relatório do XXIIo. encontro bipartite," FGV/CPDOC/ACM, roll 2, doc. no. 121, p. 2; doc. no. 122 (quotation). For May 1974, see doc. no. 126, pp. 2–3; doc. no. 127, pp. 1–2. On Rossi, see Pope, "Human Rights," 433, 437.

39. "Relatório do XXIIo. encontro bipartite," FGV/CPDOC/ACM, roll 2, doc. no. 127, p. 2. On Collier Filho, see Archdiocese of São Paulo 1988:189–90; on Oliveira, see Archdiocese of São Paulo 1985:292.

40. Dom Hélder to General Walter Menezes Paes, Recife, Oct. 4, 1973, FGV/CPDOC/ACM, roll 1, doc. no. 882. On the Bipartite discussions of the prisoners, see "Relatório do XIX encontro bipartite," ibid., role 2, doc. no. 96, p. 2.

41. For an overview of press censorship, see Smith 1997, Gazzotti 1998, Aquino 1995, also Cotta 1997. On censorship of other media and the arts, see Couto 1998:168–69; for a defense of censorship, see Médici 1995:52–54.

42. Prandini, Petrucci, and Dale 1986–1987:3:83–86. Information on censorship also from Dom Amaury interview (Dom Amaury edited *O São Paulo* during the Médici years). For a detailed analysis of the censorship of *O São Paulo*, see Pereira 1982. The *Boletim de Informações Ecclesia*, a Church circular that printed news censored from *O São Paulo*, usually escaped censorship, but on at least one occasion it did receive an order not to publish an article; see "Governo censura editorial católico," *Denúncia* 2.9 (May 1972): 4, APERJ/Jean Marc van Der Weid Collection, series 1, doc. P1, 40.

43. "Relatório do XVI encontro bipartite," FGV/CPDOC/ACM, roll 2, doc. no. 12, p. 2; doc. no. 13, p. 1; also "Os clamores do povo," *O São Paulo*, May 19–25, 1973, p. 3.

44. "Relatório do XVII encontro bipartite," FGV/CPDOC/ACM, roll 2, doc. no. 42.

45. "Relatório do XX encontro bipartite," FGV/CPDOC/ACM, roll 2, doc. no. 106, p. 1.

46. "Relatório do XIX encontro bipartite," FGV/CPDOC/ACM, roll 2, doc. no. 96.

47. "Orçamento federal para 74: segurança primeiro, depois o homem," *O São Paulo*, xeroxed copy in FGV/CPDOC/ACM, roll 2, doc. no. 112, p. 2.

48. "Relatório do XX encontro bipartite," FGV/CPDOC/ACM, roll 2, doc. no. 105; doc.

no. 106, p. 2; doc. no. 107, p. 1. I have found no record of a meeting between Dom Lucas and General Bandeira.

49. "Relatório do XX encontro bipartite," FGV/CPDOC/ACM, roll 2, doc. no. 106, p. 1; doc. no. 107 (quotation). Lee cited a newspaper report on Soviet censorship; see "Moscou censura a imprensa," *OESP*, July 17, 1973, in FGV/CPDOC/ACM, roll 2, doc. no. 113, p. 1. On one occasion the Church itself exercised censorship of *O São Paulo*. One series of articles that was particularly critical of the regime came to a halt upon orders from nuncio Dom Mozzoni (Dom Amaury interview).

50. "A Rádio Nove de Julho," *SEDOC* 6 (April 1974): 1115–22; Prandini, Petrucci, and Dale 1986–1987:3:220–22. On Brazil's Catholic radio stations, see Della Cava and Montero 1991:223–34.

51. Consejero Osvaldo M. Brana to D. Alberto J. Vignes, Minister of Foreign Relations and Religion, Rome, Feb. 22, 1974, AEAASS, Santa Sede 82.

52. "Relatório do XXIo. encontro bipartite," FGV/CPDOC/ACM, roll 2, doc. no. 116, p. 2.

53. "A Rádio Nove de Julho," *SEDOC* 6 (April 1974): 1119–22.

54. "Relatório do XXIIIo. encontro bipartite," FGV/CPDOC/ACM, roll 2, doc. no. 125; doc. no. 127, pp. 2–3. (Dom Avelar lost the race for the CNBB presidency to Dom Aloísio.)

55. "Relatório do XXIV encontro bipartite," FGV/CPDOC/ACM, roll 2, doc. no. 134, p. 4.

56. Candido Mendes interview 2. Stepan (1988:13) states that "liberalization began within the state apparatus owing to the contradictions generated by the increasing autonomy of the security apparatus." At the start of his term, Geisel called in General Milton Tavares, the head of the CIE under Médici, for a complete report on the repression (Octávio Costa interview 3). Thereafter he requested a monthly report on the jailing and release of political prisoners (see Couto 1998:174, 220–21).

Chapter 9

1. Details of the atrocities and the subsequent Army investigation come from "Sentença," Processo 17/72, Justiça Militar, 1a. Circunscrição Judiciária Militar, 2a. Auditoria do Exército, Jan. 22, 1973. I am grateful to retired military judge Helmo de Azevedo Sussekind for access to the only known existing copy of this valuable document. It contains the judge's summary of the proceedings, which were apparently destroyed (or at the very least are being kept under lock in military archives). In April 1997, the president of the superior military tribunal General Antonio Joaquim Soares Moreira granted me permission to examine the documentation on the Barra Mansa incident. However, the permission was quickly revoked following newspaper articles on the case sparked by my discovery of the sentence (see Gaspari 1997a, Melo 1997a). Additional details on the atrocities are available in Dom Waldyr Calheiros de Novaes, "Relatório geral sobre a morte e o desaparecimento de soldados no 10. BIB, sediado em Barra Mansa–RJ" (hereafter cited as "Relatório geral sobre a morte e o desaparecimento de soldados"), Arquivo da Diocese de Barra do Piraí–Volta Redonda (hereafter cited as ADBPVR); also see José Manes Leitão, Procurador da Justiça Militar, to Exmo. Sr. Dr. Auditor da 2a. Auditoria do Exército da 1a. CJM (Helmo de Azevedo Sussekind), official filing of charges, Rio de Janeiro, March 24, 1972, ADBPVR.

2. There are brief references to the case in Gorender 1998:260, and D'Araujo, Soares, and Castro 1994a:274, but no work has investigated the episode in detail.

3. "Vereadores foram almoçar no BIB," *Folha Mercantil* (Barra Mansa), Aug. 15, 1969, p. 1.

4. "Despacho," Justiça Militar, 1a. Circunscrição Judiciária Militar, 2a. Auditoria do Exército, July 29, 1971, APERJ/DOPS-GB, setor "Prontuário," pasta 3338-RJ, p. 3. The irregular nature of this action was commented on in the Sampaio interview. General Sampaio was the colonel charged with investigating the torture deaths.

5. "Ref.: Contrabando. Inquérito Policial Militar, instaurado no I Exército," APERJ/DOPS-GB, setor "Secreto," pasta 155, pp. 180–363.

6. Prandini, Petrucci, and Dale 1986–1987:2:137–62; Bruneau 1974b:188–96. See also the extensive material in the files on Dom Waldyr in the DOPS-GB archive, for example, "Relação nominal e respectiva qualificação de indivíduos envolvidos em movimento subversivo," Jan. 22, 1971, APERJ/DOPS-GB, setor 1, pasta 50481, pp. 5–6. On Sussekind's rulings, see also "Despacho," Justiça Militar, 1a. Circunscrição Judiciária Militar, 2a. Auditoria do Exército, July 29, 1971, APERJ/DOPS-GB, setor "Prontuário," pasta 3338-RJ. On the torture investigation, see "Bispo prestou ontem depoimento no IPM," *Folha Mercantil*, Aug. 8, 1969, p. 1; "Comandante do BIB diz que bispo é extremista," *Diário de Notícias* (Rio de Janeiro), Aug. 16, 1969. For additional background on Dom Waldyr, see chapter 2.

7. Dom Waldyr interview. On military involvement in the kidnapping of Dom Adriano, see Argolo, Ribeiro, and Fortunato 1996:218, 234. For a description of the kidnapping, see Prandini, Petrucci, and Dale 1986–1987:4:240–69. According to one general, the armed forces cultivated negative sexual innuendo about Dom Waldyr as a way to further denigrate his image (Octávio Costa interviews 2 and 3).

8. "Investigação mata soldados," *OESP*, Feb. 6, 1972, p. 30.

9. "Sentença," Processo 17/72, Justiça Militar, 1a. Circunscrição Judiciária Militar, 2a. Auditoria do Exército, Jan. 22, 1973, p. 1.

10. Dom Waldyr interview. The comment on "soft" came in the Geralsélia interview (she was Geomar's sister). Geomar's mother recalled that it was the death of another man within the barracks that upset him (Evangelina interview). Private Monção also confided to his family that he had witnessed a tumultuous situation at the barracks (Pedro Virote and Efigênia Virote interviews).

11. "Sentença," Processo 17/72, Justiça Militar, 1a. Circunscrição Judiciária Militar, 2a. Auditoria do Exército, Jan. 22, 1973, pp. 1, 4–5. On Botelho's transfer, see Manes Leitão to Exmo. Sr. Dr. Auditor, Rio de Janeiro, March 24, 1972, ADBPVR. One explanation for the transfer informally suggested to me by one of Private Geomar's relatives was that Botelho's presence was a pretext to investigate drug trafficking in the barracks, in order to attack those soldiers who did not agree with the illicit activities occurring there. Lending credence to this version is the fact that Botelho's brother Hélio was a soldier at the 1st AIB. According to the documents cited in this note, Expedito Botelho denounced his own brother for involvement in drug trafficking in the barracks. Hélio was then tortured but survived and escaped. His flight provided the torturers with the idea for the false deserter story, used to explain the death of Privates Wanderley and Monção.

12. Dom Waldyr, "Relatório geral sobre a morte e o desaparecimento de soldados," ADBPVR; denial of marijuana confirmed in Geralsélia interview.

13. Dom Waldyr, "Relatório geral sobre a morte e o desaparecimento de soldados," ADBPVR; information on signs of alleged causes of death and additional details on signs of torture also from Geralsélia interview.

14. Dom Waldyr interview; Dom Waldyr, "Relatório geral sobre a morte e o desaparecimento de soldados," ADBPVR.

15. "Sentença," Processo 17/72, Justiça Militar, 1a. Circunscrição Judiciária Militar, 2a. Auditoria do Exército, Jan. 22, 1973, pp. 16–17.

16. Interview of Dom Waldyr by Célia Costa and Dulce Chaves Pandolfi, Volta Redonda, Nov. 19, 1998.

17. Dom Waldyr interview. Colonel Arioswaldo refused to be interviewed for this book, claiming that it would deeply upset his family to reopen discussion of the incident (author's telephone conversation with retired Colonel Arioswaldo, Rio de Janeiro, May 7, 1997).

18. Dom Waldyr, "Relatório geral sobre a morte e o desaparecimento de soldados," ADBPVR.

19. Dom Waldyr and Geralsélia interviews. Because of military distrust and hatred of Dom Waldyr and the ongoing investigations against the bishop, Geralsélia had to swear during the subsequent proceedings against the Barra Mansa torturers that she did not know him.

20. Dom Humberto Mozzoni to Dom Waldyr, Rio de Janeiro, Jan. 21, 1972, ADBPVR.

21. Sampaio interview; and see Sergio de Ary Pires, "Perfil de um soldado" (advertisement), *JB*, Nov. 12, 1990, p. 2. For background on Pires, see this article and also Albuquerque 1985. The judge in the case attributed Sampaio's selection to Frota (Sussekind interview). Frota's importance over Pires was also expressed by General Octávio Costa; see D'Araujo, Soares, and Castro 1994a:274; Octávio Costa interviews 2 and 3.

22. For a copy of Dom Waldyr's report, see Dom Waldyr, "Fatos que recentemente impressionaram a população de Volta Redonda," Jan. 24, 1972, ADBPVR. The January 24, 1972, meeting at the CNBB is confirmed in Dom Waldyr's private letter to the Brazilian bishops, Volta Redonda, Feb. 11, 1972, ADBPVR. Additional confirmation of the conversation of Dom Waldyr, Geralsélia, and Dom Ivo from Geralsélia interview.

23. "Relatório geral sobre a morte e o desaparecimento de soldados," ADBPVR. Early on, officials from the military justice system asked Private Geomar's sister Geralsélia, the only relative of the victims to become involved in the investigation, not to inform Private Monção's family of their son's death. Only in March did the family learn of Monção's true fate (Geralsélia interview).

24. "Médici recebe Murici," *JB*, Feb. 1, 1972, sec. 1, p. 3; "Muricy trata da ADESG com Médici," *JB*, Feb. 2, 1972, sec. 1, p. 3. According to the latter article, Bipartite member Padilha also took part in the ADESG discussion. However, Padilha did not recall meeting Médici on this occasion and doubted that Muricy would have gone to Brasília to discuss a matter so insignificant as the internal organization of the ADESG (Padilha interview 2). Another ADESG leader reported to have attended the meeting also had no recollection of it (Araken Faissol interview).

25. Dom Mozzoni to Dom Waldyr, Rio de Janeiro, Feb. 4, 1972, ADBPVR.

26. See, for example, "Investigação mata soldados," *OESP*, Feb. 6, 1972, p. 30.

27. Dom Waldyr to General Orlando Geisel, Volta Redonda, Feb. 21, 1972, ADBPVR.

28. The description of Manes Leitão from Sussekind interview.

29. The charges against the men included infractions under the following articles of the Brazilian Military Penal Code: 53 (accomplice to a crime), 205 (murder, including the use of torture), 209 (assault), 264 (damage to military installations), and 352 (destruction of evidence); see Oliveira 1996. General Pires assigned prosecution of the contraband to another colonel. I was unable to discover any documentation on this inquest.

30. Another version states that General Frota chose the jury; written response to the

author's questions to General Augusto César da Fonseca Lessa, Rio de Janeiro, April 22, 1997.

31. "Ata No. 01—sessão de Conselho Especial de Justiça," Jan. 17–22, 1973, ADBPVR.; also see "Sentença," Processo 17/72, Justiça Militar, 1a. Circunscrição Judiciária Militar, 2a. Auditoria do Exército, Jan. 22, 1973; "Oito militares são punidos com rigor," OESP, Jan. 23, 1973, p. 21.

32. "Sentença," Processo 17/72, Justiça Militar, 1a. Circunscrição Judiciária Militar, 2a. Auditoria do Exército, Jan. 22, 1973; details on the visit also from Sussekind interview.

33. "Ata No. 01—sessão de Conselho Especial de Justiça," Jan. 17–22, 1973, ADBPVR.; also see "Sentença," Processo 17/72, Justiça Militar, 1a. Circunscrição Judiciária Militar, 2a. Auditoria do Exército, Jan. 22, 1973.

34. "Sentença," Processo 17/72, Justiça Militar, 1a. Circunscrição Judiciária Militar, 2a. Auditoria do Exército, Jan. 22, 1973.

35. Ibid.

36. "Justiça exemplar," JB, Jan. 24, 1973, p. 22; "Um julgamento que honra o Exército," OESP, Jan. 24, 1973, p. 3. For other coverage of the sentencing, see "Auditoria condena a 473 anos réus do I BIB, de Barra Mansa," O Globo, Jan. 23, 1973, p. 10; "Oito militares são punidos com rigor," OESP, Jan. 23, 1973; "Mais longo julgamento da Justiça Militar condena 10 acusados a 291 anos," JB, Jan. 23, 1973; "Militares do BIB e agentes policiais condenados pela auditoria," Zero Hora (Porto Alegre), Jan. 27–Feb. 3, 1973; "Oficiais punidos," Veja, Jan. 31, 1973, p. 25.

37. In 1971 Médici fired his Air Force Minister for failing to control an officer who abused political prisoners; in 1976 Geisel removed the Second Army commander for similar reasons. However, no trials or punishments of torturers resulted from these episodes. See D'Araujo, Soares, and Castro 1994a:210–28.

38. Lieutenant Miranda had been earlier denounced by Dom Waldyr; see Prandini, Petrucci, and Dale 1986–1987:2:153–54; also Melo 1997b. One former political prisoner asserted that Lieutenant Colonel Gladstone coordinated torture sessions at the 1st AIB; see Melo and Noel 1997. While he was jailed at the 1st AIB in 1971, during which time he was tortured, Father Nathanael de Moraes Campos saw that several of the accused in the Barra Mansa case had witnessed earlier atrocities (Father Nathanael interview).

39. On the Brazilian armed forces' historic tendency to create a kind of "collective amnesia" about violence against its own members, see Smallman 1997.

40. According to General Sampaio, the S2 saw themselves as the "owners" of security questions at the 1st AIB (Sampaio interview). There is no evidence to support Niebus's defense lawyer's implication, repeated more explicitly years later in General Ary Pires's eulogy of Walter Pires, that the S2 was involved in an antisubversive operation at the time of the atrocities; for Ary Pires's assertions, see his "Perfil de um soldado" (advertisement), JB, Nov. 12, 1990, p. 2.

41. P[edido de] B[usca] no. 1039/81/ASI/TELERJ (DI/9369/81), DSI/Ministério das Comunicações, APERJ/DOPS-GB, setor "Informação," pasta 167, pp. 316–17; P[edido de] B[usca] no. 1039/81/ASI/TELERJ (Prot. DI-9369/81), DSI/M. Minas e Energia, APERJ/DOPS-GB, setor "Informação," pasta 167, p. 153; also see "Sem punição," Veja, Sept. 2, 1987. This article incorrectly states that Niebus spent eleven years in prison. The period from his initial jailing in 1972 to the start of his telephone company job in 1981 is approximately nine years, assuming that he moved directly from prison to work. Niebus refused an interview.

42. In the words of Judge Sussekind, the Army had "vista grossa" with respect to human rights violations against alleged subversives (Sussekind interview). A similar opinion is expressed in Octávio Costa interview 2; also see Gazzotti 1998:80–81. Other interpretations claim that some in the Army did try to stop torture. See, for instance, the discussion of General Frota in D'Araujo, Soares, and Castro 1994a:62, 67–73, 105, 175–76; D'Araujo and Castro 1997:224, 362; Couto 1998:219.

43. Comissão de Familiares 1996:178; "Anatália Alves se suicida no Recife," *OESP,* Jan. 23, 1973, p. 21.

44. In an egregious omission, human rights groups that defend the left failed to view the four dead soldiers and their eleven tortured comrades as victims of the dictatorship. These victims' stories are absent, for instance, from one of the most recent and comprehensive studies of regime violence, Comissão de Familiares 1996.

Chapter 10

1. For instance, the Leme case receives no mention in Skidmore 1988 or Couto 1998 and only a scant reference in Mainwaring 1986:106.

2. Markun 1988:10; also Stepan 1989.

3. Background on Leme from Egle and José Leme interviews and from *Meu filho Alexandre Vannucchi* n.d.

4. On the ALN, see chapters 2 and 6; also Paz 1996, 1997; Archdiocese of São Paulo 1988; Ridenti 1993; Mir 1994. On the student movement, see Martins Filho 1987; for a military view, Ustra 1986; for police accusations, "Terrorista morre atropelado no Brás," *Folha de São Paulo,* March 23, 1973.

5. Prado 1990; Prado and Fragelli 1990. See also the documentary film "Vala Comum," directed by João Godoy (1994), and José 1997:101–02.

6. For a basic outline of the publicly known events surrounding the Leme case, see "Síntese cronológica" 1973; *Meu filho Alexandre Vannucchi* n.d.

7. Superior Tribunal Militar, Apelação 40.425, AEL/BNM, case no. 670, vol. 1, pp. 1A, 1E, 1H, 94–95; vol. 3, pp. 300, 348, 350, 352.

8. Information on Queiroz's evaluation from Paulo Vannuchi interview. Information on the contact from Lázaro interviews. The police killed Queiroz shortly after the death of Leme; see Comissão de Familiares 1996:202.

9. Carlos Eugênio Paz interview. Paz was the only ALN guerrilla leader to survive the repression. For a description of his activities, see Paz 1996, 1997. Gorender (1998:228) estimates that on average urban guerrillas lived only a year. On ALN strategy shifts in 1972 and 1973, see Archdiocese of São Paulo 1988:48; Mir 1994:658–59.

10. Ministério da Educação e Cultura, Divisão de Segurança e Informações, Encaminhamento no. 1.034/AESI/USP/73, April 11, 1973, "Assunto: panfletagem na Universidade de São Paulo," AESP/DEOPS-SP, series "Dossiês," doc. no. 50E/30/159.

11. The student was Alberto Alonso Lázaro; in interview 1 Lázaro denied the information attributed to him. On his testimony and the other crimes, see Superior Tribunal Militar, Apelação 40.425, AEL/BNM, case no. 670, vol. 1, pp. 1B, 1C, 1D; vol. 3, pp. 348, 452–53.

12. Magnotti to Lúcio Vieira, director of the DEOPS, São Paulo, April 12, 1973, AESP/DEOPS-SP, series "Dossiês," doc. no. 30Z/165/38.

13. Paz recalled that Penteado, who ate regularly in the restaurant to watch Oliveira,

heard the merchant brag that he had telephoned the DOI-CODI to inform on the presence of ALN members in the establishment (Carlos Eugênio Paz interview).

14. See note 16 for discussion of other possible sources.

15. DOI-CODI agents expressed anger about this incident to political prisoners (Lázaro interview 1). For a detailed description of the assassination, see Ustra 1986:212–18. On Moreira Júnior as torturer and right-wing militant, see Archdiocese of São Paulo 1988:48; also Mir 1994:659.

16. A key leader of the security forces, General Adyr Fiúza de Castro recalled that "it was very easy to infiltrate the student movement, because they were very amateurish" (D'Araujo, Soares, and Castro 1994a:40). For an example of infiltration, see the discussion below of the students' reaction to Leme's death. DEOPS-SP and DOPS-GB documentation maintains the anonymity of infiltrators. Information from as yet unopened DOI-CODI archives might provide the key to infiltrators' identities and modus operandi and/or to the depositions of prisoners who may have revealed information about Leme. Copies of DOI-CODI depositions from other cases do exist in the DOPS and DEOPS-SP archives, but they do not reveal the names of interrogators or informants. See, for example, Ministério do Exército, I Exército, Informação no. 404/74-C, "Assunto: depoimentos prestados no DOI/I Ex," APERJ/DOPS-GB, setor "Comunismo," pasta 128, pp. 1–26. On infiltrators and militants turned informants, see Expedito Filho 1992.

17. Edsel Magnotti to Lúcio Vieira, director of the DEOPS-SP, São Paulo, April 12, 1973, AESP/DEOPS-SP, series "Dossiês," doc. no. 30Z/165/38.

18. Ustra refused requests for an interview. Several former political prisoners interviewed for this book affirmed that they had been beaten or tortured by Ustra; confirmation also in Marival Chaves interview.

19. See, for example, Coimbra 1995:99–107, 194–206; Expedito Filho 1992; Comissão de Familiares 1996:33; Archdiocese of São Paulo 1985. For a physician's confession of collaboration, see Lobo 1989.

20. Perhaps the torturers did not know that Leme had undergone an appendectomy in late January; one source stated that the body "was bleeding profusely in the abdominal region" (Comissão de Familiares 1996:174). However, this explanation for the presence of blood is unlikely, because sufficient postoperation scar tissue would have formed by the time of the torture. An alternative explanation is given below.

21. Father Vannucchi was quickly released under pressure from local leaders. The police also had a file on him (Aldo Vannucchi interview). Information on the anti-Communist climate in Sorocaba from João Luiz Peçanha interview.

22. Lázaro interview 1; and see Superior Tribunal Militar, Apelação 40.425, AEL/BNM, case no. 670, vol. 3, p. 189.

23. Fax communication to author from Marival Chaves Dias do Canto (Vila Velha, Espírito Santo), Rio de Janeiro, Jan. 28, 1997. A sergeant in the São Paulo DOI-CODI, in 1992 Canto became the first (and to date only) member of a repressive organization to reveal in detail his knowledge of abuses. Canto analyzed interrogation reports. See Expedito Filho, 1992; also see "Ex-sargento" 1996; also see *Atenção* 2.8 (1996).

24. Vieira to Oscar Xavier de Freitas, Procurador Geral da Justiça, São Paulo, April 12, 1973, AESP/DEOPS-SP, series "Dossiês," doc. no. 30Z/165/39.

25. Superior Tribunal Militar, Apelação 40.425, AEL/BNM, case no. 670, vol. 3, p. 362.

26. "Ofício esclarece morte de subversivo," *SEDOC* 6 (July 1973): 103–05.

27. On the declaration, see *Declaração Universal* 1978; also see Castanho 1973.

28. "Comunicado do bispo de Sorocaba," *SEDOC* 6 (July 1973): 105.

29. "Síntese cronológica" 1973:109; "Nota do conselho de presbíteros," *SEDOC* 6 (July 1973): 106–07.

30. *Boletim Informativo* (São Paulo) 6, March 26, 1973, AESP/DEOPS-SP, series "Dossiês," doc. 50K/104/326; "A marca da cruz" 1978.

31. For details of student discussions, see "Resoluções da assembléia de geologia," *Boletim Informativo* 6, March 26, 1973, p. 4, AESP/DEOPS-SP, series "Dossiês," doc. 50K/104/326.

32. "Comunicado dos centros acadêmicos," *SEDOC* 6 (July 1973): 107.

33. For the infiltrator's information, see unsigned report titled "Observações realizadas na USP," March 29, 1973, AESP/DEOPS-SP, series "Dossiês," doc. no. 50K/104/324.

34. On Dom Paulo's attempts to contact Souza Mello, see "Relatório especial do grupo bipartite, sobre problemas surgidos na área Igreja X governo, referentes à participação do clero nas comemorações do sesquicentenário do Brasil," FGV/CPDOC/ACM, roll 1, doc. nos. 989–90; doc. no. 993, p. 1. On his relations with São Paulo generals, see Arruda 1996.

35. See also Mayrink 1998. A DEOPS infiltrator was aware of the students' intention to contact Dom Paulo; see "Observações realizadas na USP," March 29, 1973, AESP/DEOPS-SP, series "Dossiês," doc. no. 50K/104/324. According to another version, Dom Paulo at first wanted to use a smaller church, but the students convinced him they would fill the cathedral (Egle interview). Yet another version states that the students were at most bluffing and did not really want a riot, but that Dom Paulo in any case feared that violence could occur (Geraldo Siqueira interview).

36. For the text of the sheet, see "Celebração da esperança," AESP/DEOPS-SP, series "Dossiês," doc. no. 50C/22/9325; on press censorship, see "Comunicado do bispo de Sorocaba," 105.

37. This charge was made by MOLIPO in its document titled "Glória aos que tombaram lutando por seu povo!" See Ministério da Educação e Cultura, Divisão de Segurança e Informações, Encaminhamento No. 1.034/AESI/USP/73, April 11, 1973, "Assunto: panfletagem na Universidade de São Paulo," AESP, DEOPS-SP, series "Dossiês," doc. no. 50E/30/159.

38. For details on the mass, see Silva 1973; "A marca da cruz" 1978; "Brasil: Deus será o juiz," the military's translation of an article published in *Latin America* 3.16, April 29, 1973, FGV/CPDOC/ACM, roll 1, doc. nos. 867–69; "Missa para um estudante morto," *Opinião*, (Rio de Janeiro), April 2–9, 1973; "Estudiantes protestan por compañero asesinado," *Campanha* (Santiago, Chile), May 1, 1973, AESP/DEOPS-SP, series "Dossiês," doc. no. 50F/4/107.

39. Dom Paulo Evaristo Arns, "Palavras de fé sobre a vida, a dignidade e a missão do homem," *O São Paulo*, April 7, 1973. Dom Paulo's citation is from the story of Cain and Abel in the Book of Genesis, ch. 4.

40. Secretaria de Segurança Pública, Delegacia Seccional de Polícia–Botucatu, "Relatório," AESP/DEOPS-SP, series "Dossiês," doc. no. 50H/63/1428.

41. Comitê de Advertência aos Que Estão em Perigo, "A morte de um terrorista," AESP/DEOPS-SP, series "Dossiês," doc. no. 50Z/13/845.

42. Dom Paulo Evaristo Arns to Jarbas Passarinho, São Paulo, April 4, 1973, AESP/DEOPS-SP, series "Ordem Política," pasta 14, doc. no. 64.

43. Ministério da Educação e Cultura, Divisão de Segurança e Informações, Informação no. 1.049/AESI/USP/73, May 10, 1973, "Assunto: Marcos Alberto Castelhano Bruno," AESP/DEOPS-SP, series "Dossiês," doc. no. 50E/30/212.

44. Passarinho to Dom Paulo, Brasília, June 1973, AESP/DEOPS-SP, series "Ordem Política," pasta 14, doc. no. 64. Parts of this letter were first published in 1979; see Costa, "Investigação no clero," 3–4. Passarinho (1996) does not comment on the Leme case in his memoirs, which have two substantial chapters on education and the universities and on the Médici government.

45. "Brasil: Deus será o juiz," the military's translation of an article published in *Latin America* 3.16, April 29, 1973, FGV/CPDOC/ACM, roll 1, doc. no. 868, p. 2.

46. For the text of one of the censored articles, see AESP/DEOPS-SP, series "Dossiês," doc. no. 50Z/9/31631; for the text of the congressional debate, see Lysâneas Maciel, "Um assassinato político," pamphlet distributed at the Pontifical Catholic University of Rio de Janeiro (1974), APERJ/DOPS-GB setor "DOPS," pasta 217, docs. 126–37.

47. On the search for organizers, see, for example, Ministério da Educação e Cultura, Divisão de Segurança e Informações, Informação no. 1.049/AESI/USP/73, May 10, 1973, "Assunto: Marcos Alberto Castelhano Bruno," AESP/DEOPS-SP, series "Dossiês," doc. no. 50E/30/212; for interrogations of alleged organizers carried out by Edsel Magnotti, see AESP/DEOPS-SP, series "Dossiês," doc. nos. 50C/22/7202, 7206, 7207.

48. Companhia Paulista de Força e Luz, Assessoria de Segurança e Informações, Informe no. 26/ASSI/10/CS/73, April 30, 1973, "Assunto: recrudescimento de atividades esquerdistas," AESP/DEOPS-SP, series "Dossiês," doc. no. 50J/0/2984.

49. Ministério da Educação e Cultura, Divisão de Segurança e Informações, Encaminhamento no. 1.033/AESI/USP/73, April 10, 1973, "Assunto: panfletagem na Universidade de São Paulo," AESP/DEOPS-SP, series "Dossiês," doc. no. 50E/30/158.

50. For Rio, see "Atuação das esquerdas no movimento estudantil," APERJ/DOPS-GB, setor "DOPS," pasta 193, doc. nos. 477–92; for São Paulo, see Companhia Paulista de Força e Luz, Assessoria de Segurança e Informações, Informe no. 26/ASSI/10/CS/73, April 30, 1973, "Assunto: recrudescimento de atividades esquerdistas," AESP/DEOPS-SP, series "Dossiês," doc. no. 50J/0/2984.

51. Ministério da Justiça, Departamento de Polícia Federal, Centro de Informações, Informação no. 1512, "Assunto: movimento estudantil," May 18, 1973, AESP/DEOPS-SP, series "Dossiês," doc. no. 50Z/9/33962.

52. Miguel Reale to General Sérvulo Mota Lima, São Paulo, March 27, 1973, AESP/DEOPS-SP, series "Dossiês"; Ministério da Aeronáutica, Gabinete do Ministro, CISA, Documento de Informações no. 13/CISA-ESC RCD, "Assunto: movimento estudantil," May 8, 1973, AESP/DEOPS-SP, series "Dossiês," doc. no. 50D/26/4388.

53. "Ofício esclarece morte de subversivo," *SEDOC* 6 (July 1973): 103–05. General Lima's statement appeared in the *Folha da Tarde* (São Paulo), *OESP, O Dia*, and other papers. In *O Dia*, for example, the headline read "Terrorista atropelado aliciava universitários" (Run-over terrorist lured university students); see FGV/CPDOC/ACM, roll 2, doc. no. 37, p. 2. As stated above, no record of any deposition by Leme has been found in the archives.

54. "Relatório do XVI encontro bipartite," FGV/CPDOC/ACM, roll 2, doc. no. 14, p. 2.

55. Ibid., doc. no. 13, p. 2; doc. no. 14, p. 1.

56. Mário de Passos Simas and José Carlos Dias to Judge Tácito Morbach de Goes Nobre, São Paulo, April 10, 1973, FGV/CPDOC/ACM, roll 2, doc. no. 13, p. 2; doc. no. 34, p. 2; doc. no. 35; doc. no. 36, p. 1. "Petição do advogado da família do Alexandre Vannucchi," FGV/CPDOC/ACM, roll 2, doc. no. 13, p. 2; doc. no. 36, p. 2; doc. no. 37, p. 1.

57. "Relatório do XVI encontro bipartite," FGV/CPDOC/ACM, roll 2, doc. no. 14; doc. no. 15, p. 1. Compare Lee's comments with "Petição do advogado da família do Alexandre

Vannucchi," FGV/CPDOC/ACM, roll 2, doc. no. 13, p. 2; doc. no. 36, p. 2; doc. no. 37, p. 1.

58. "Relatório do XVI encontro bipartite," FGV/CPDOC/ACM, roll 2, doc. no. 15.

59. "Relatório do XVII encontro bipartite," FGV/CPDOC/ACM, roll 2, doc. no. 39.

60. Ibid., doc. no. 40, p. 1.

61. "Relatório do XIX encontro bipartite," FGV/CPDOC/ACM, roll 2, doc. no. 96, p. 2.

62. Ibid., doc. no. 98, p. 2.

63. Amnesty International, "Deaths in Custody in Brazil" (Jan. 1974), in AESP/ DEOPS-SP, series "Dossiês."

64. "Foi calmo o 'Dia do Protesto,'" *Diário da Noite*, March 29, 1978; "Manifesto dos estudantes paulistas," AESP/DEOPS-SP, series "Dossiês," doc. no. 43C/1/27; "Manifesto," AESP/DEOPS-SP, series "Dossiês," doc. no. 50Z/300/2509; Divisão de Informações, setor "Estudantil," DOPS, RE 482/78, "Assunto: sessão de abertura do congresso nacional pela anistia no Tuca, PUC-SP," Nov. 2, 1978, AESP/DEOPS-SP, series "Dossiês," doc. no. 50Z/130/5116–22.

65. Egle and José Leme interviews; Congresso Nacional pela Anistia, "Resoluções," AESP/DEOPS-SP, series "Dossiês," doc. no. 50J/0/6204; Direito USP, "Avançar na luta pela anistia," AESP/DEOPS-SP, series "Dossiês," doc. no. 50Z/130/5285.

66. 3a. Delegacia da Divisão de Informações, DOPS, RE/326–79, "Assunto: encontro de profissionais de saúde," Aug. 24, 1979, AESP/DEOPS-SP, series "Dossiês," doc. no. 50Z/130/2504–05; "O falso laudo de Alexandre Vannucchi," *Jornal da República*, Aug. 27, 1979.

67. For comparison with the Chilean case, see Lowden 1996:6, 33.

68. Della Cava 1989; Mainwaring 1986, part 3; Doimo 1992.

69. On Herzog, see Markun 1988; Almeida Filho 1978; Jordão 1984; Landau 1986; Skidmore 1988:176–77; Skidmore 1989:11–12; Della Cava 1989:148; Prandini, Petrucci, and Dale 1986–1987:4:89–91; Wright 1989:72–73. Major U.S. newspapers and newsmagazines published articles on the case. For differing military perspectives of the incident, see Soares, D'Araujo, and Castro 1995:11, 33, 65, 86, 173–74, 214, 228–29. On the impact of the memorial service, see Pope 1985:437–38. On selective use of violence, see Gorender 1998:232.

70. Prandini, Petrucci, and Dale 1986–1987:4:90. Dom Paulo has also recalled the Leme incident as the most startling of the 1970s (see Mayrink 1998).

71. Superior Tribunal Militar, Apelação 40.425, AEL/BNM, case no. 670, vol. 3, p. 362.

72. DOI-CODI II EX, Informação no. 569-SSA/DOI-73, Oct. 12, 1973, "Assunto: estratégia para a tomada do poder," APERJ/DOPS-GB, setor "Comunismo," pasta 126, pp. 94–99.

Chapter 11

1. President João Café Filho (1954) was also Protestant. He was elected vice president in 1950 and served out only part of the remainder of Vargas's term after the latter committed suicide in August 1954.

2. Prandini, Petrucci, and Dale 1986–1987:4:148–50. For Burnier, see chapter 7 in the present work.

3. Muricy 1993:662–63; "Relatório do XXIIo. encontro bipartite," FGV/CPDOC/ACM, roll 2, doc. no. 119, p. 2; doc. no. 120, p. 1; doc. no. 123.

4. "Relatório do XXIIo. encontro bipartite," FGV/CPDOC/ACM, roll 2, doc. no. 119, p. 2; doc. no. 120, p. 1 (quotation); doc. no. 123.

5. See examples of Church-state dialogue under Geisel in Prandini, Petrucci, and Dale 1986–1987:vols. 4, 5. In 1977, for instance, the so-called Missão Portela, coordinated by Senator Petrônio Portela, opened contacts between the government and the opposition, including the Church.

6. Maurice W. Kendall to Muricy, Rio de Janeiro, Aug. 27, 1974, FGV/CPDOC/ACM, roll 2, doc. no. 668, pp. 1–2; "Brief paper. Presentation of USAC&GSC Allied Officer Hall of Fame Certificate to General de Exército Antônio Carlos da Silva Muricy," FGV/CPDOC/ACM, roll 2, doc. no. 668, p. 3, doc. no. 669, p. 1; "Press release. Allied Officer Hall of Fame," FGV/CPDOC/ACM, roll 2, doc. no. 671, p. 3, doc. no. 672, p. 1.

7. Moraes Rego interview; and see Soares, D'Araujo, and Castro 1995:59–60.

8. See, for example, the comments of Dom Ivo in Prandini, Petrucci, and Dale 1986–1987:5:15–16.

9. Dom Eugênio interview; Muricy interview 1; Sampaio interview; Candido Mendes interview 2; Padilha interview 1; Dom Paulo interview (quotation). The attempt by the Church and opposition forces in Chile to cultivate better relations with the military reinforced martial support for democracy in the twilight of the Pinochet regime (see Fleet and Smith 1997:135, 137, 156).

10. Similarly, in the 1930s Dom Leme allowed the clergy to participate in the Integralista movement but did not give it official Church blessing. After its proscription, the Church quickly disengaged from Integralismo. I am grateful to Lúcia Lippi de Oliveira for calling this parallel to my attention. McDonough (1981:191) also noted that the dissidence of the bishops was tempered.

11. In 1997, for instance, the Church focused on the controversial theme of "Fraternity and the Imprisoned" for its annual Lenten campaign (see CNBB 1997). On human rights, also see Lowden 1996:75–91.

12. Of course, impediments to this goal predate the dictatorship (see Hess and DaMatta 1995). Nevertheless, the authoritarian era served to reinforce them.

13. In the Chilean case, Archbishop Juan Francisco Fresno most effectively contributed to regime-opposition dialogue "not as a public critic but as convener and interlocutor *among* critics," and the Chilean episcopate "was most influential when it was least prophetic, when it worked behind the scenes on behalf of compromise instead of denouncing evils and abuses publicly" (Fleet and Smith 1997:126, 272).

14. See also Gill 1998:175; and the discussion of the multidimensionality of elite ideologies in McDonough 1981.

15. On elite settlements and exclusion, see Burton, Gunther, and Higley 1992:18–19; Knight 1992:119.

References

Archives

Archivo de la Embajada de la República Argentina ante la Santa Sede (AEAASS), Rome.

Arquivo Ana Lagôa, Universidade Federal de São Carlos, São Carlos, São Paulo.

Arquivo Antônio Carlos [da Silva] Muricy, Fundação Getúlio Vargas, Centro de Pesquisa e Documentação de História Contemporânea do Brasil, Rio de Janeiro (FGV/CPDOC/ACM), Rio de Janeiro.

Arquivo da Diocese de Barra do Piraí–Volta Redonda (ADBPVR), Volta Redonda.

Arquivo do Itamaraty, Brasília.

Branca de Mello Franco Alves Collection, Biblioteca Cardeal Câmara, Arquidiocese do Rio de Janeiro (BMFA), Rio de Janeiro.

Brasil: Nunca Mais, Centro de Pesquisa e Documentação Social, Associação Cultural Arquivo Edgard Leuenroth, Instituto de Filosofia e Ciências Humanas, Universidade Estadual de Campinas (AEL/BNM), Campinas, São Paulo.

Central de Documentação e Informação Científica "Prof. Casemiro dos Reis Filho," Pontifícia Universidade Católica de São Paulo (PUC-SP/CEDIC), São Paulo.

Centro Alceu Amoroso Lima para a Liberdade (CAALL), Petrópolis.

Centro de Documentación y Archivo para la Defensa de los Derechos Humanos ("Archivo del Terror") (CDADDH), Asunción, Paraguay.

Coleção Jean Marc van Der Weid, Arquivo Público do Estado do Rio de Janeiro (APERJ/Jean Marc van Der Weid Collection), Rio de Janeiro.

Departamento de Ordem Política e Social da Guanabara, Arquivo Público do Estado do Rio de Janeiro (APERJ/DOPS-GB), Rio de Janeiro.

Departamento Estadual de Ordem Política e Social, Arquivo do Estado de São Paulo (AESP/DEOPS-SP), São Paulo.

Instituto Nacional de Pastoral, Conferência Nacional dos Bispos do Brasil (INP), Brasília.

National Security Archive, Washington, D.C.

References

Interviews

Italicized portions of names indicate how the interview is referenced in the notes. Numbers in parentheses indicate multiple interviews with the same individual. All interview notes, tapes, and transcripts are in the possession of the author.

Candido [Antonio José Francisco] *Mendes* de Almeida, Rio de Janeiro, (1) Aug. 9, 1994; (2) July 5, 1995; (3) April 10, 1997.
Anonymous interview with former DOPS-GB officer, Rio de Janeiro, March 10, 1997.
Evilásio de Jesus Araújo, Brasília, June 11, 1993.
Dom Paulo Evaristo Arns, São Paulo, Sept. 10, 1996.
Father Fernando Bastos de *Ávila*, Rio de Janeiro, July 10, 1995.
Marina Bandeira, Rio de Janeiro, July 4, 1994.
General Roberto *Pacífico* Barbosa, Rio de Janeiro, Jan. 24, 1999.
Mário Gibson Barboza, Rio de Janeiro, April 3, 1997.
Raimundo *Caramuru* de Barros, Brasília, Feb. 7, 1990.
Father Nathanael de Moraes Campos (Belo Horizonte), Rio de Janeiro, telephone interview, May 13, 1997.
Marival Chaves Dias do Canto, Vila Velha, Espírito Santo, Jan. 20, 1999.
Dom Pedro Casaldáliga, Belo Horizonte, July 18, 1995.
Dom Amaury Castanho, Itu, Sept. 20, 1996.
Cecília Coimbra, Rio de Janeiro, Nov. 9, 1996.
General *Octávio* [Pereira da] *Costa*, Rio de Janeiro, (1) Aug. 12, 1994; (2) March 1, 1997; (3) March 17, 1997.
Dalmo Dallari, São Paulo, Sept. 11, 1996.
Adriano Diogo, São Paulo, May 19, 1997.
Arlete Diogo, São Paulo, May 19, 1997.
General Carlos Alberto *Fontoura*, Rio de Janeiro, Aug. 12, 1994.
Margarida Genevois, São Paulo, Sept. 11, 1996.
Dom Mário Teixeira Gurgel, Itabira, July 18, 1996.
Father Frederico Karl *Laufer*, Porto Alegre, Aug. 13, 1989.
Alberto Alonso *Lázaro* (São Paulo), Rio de Janeiro, (1) telephone interview, Jan. 14, 1997; (2) personal interview, São Paulo, May 18, 1997.
Egle Vannucchi Leme, Sorocaba, Sept. 19, 1996.
José de Oliveira *Leme*, Sorocaba, Sept. 19, 1996.
Ivo Lesbaupin, Rio de Janeiro, July 14, 1994.
General Augusto César da Fonseca *Lessa*, Rio de Janeiro, April 22, 1997.
Heitor Corrêa *Maurano*, Rio de Janeiro, Jan. 16, 1997.
General Antônio Carlos da Silva *Muricy*, Rio de Janeiro, (1) June 17, 1993; (2) July 14, 1995; (3) March 1, 1997.
Virgínia Ramos da Silva Muricy, Rio de Janeiro, March 1, 1997.
Togo Meirelles Netto, Rio de Janeiro, March 21, 1997.
Virgílio Rosa Netto, Rio de Janeiro, July 5, 1995.
Marcos Noronha, Belo Horizonte, July 20, 1996.
Dom Waldyr Calheiros de Novaes, Volta Redonda, Feb. 14, 1997.
Tarcísio Meirelles *Padilha*, Rio de Janeiro, (1) July 15, 1994; (2) May 10, 1997.
Carlos Eugênio Sarmento Coelho da *Paz*, Rio de Janeiro, Jan. 30, 1997.

João Luiz Gonzaga *Peçanha*, Sorocaba, Sept. 18, 1996.
Father *Ernanne Pinheiro*, São Paulo, July 27, 1995.
Araken Faissol Pinto, Rio de Janeiro, telephone interview, March 13, 1997.
José Prestes de Barros, Sorocaba, Sept. 17, 1996.
Father Agostinho *Pretto*, Nova Iguaçu, July 3, 1996.
Father Mário *Prigol*, Rio de Janeiro, July 10, 1996.
Cândido Feliciano da *Ponte Neto*, Rio de Janeiro, July 7, 1995.
Father *Gervásio Queiroga*, Belo Horizonte, July 17 and 18, 1995.
General Gustavo *Moraes Rego* Reis, Rio de Janeiro, Jan. 15, 1997.
Admiral *Roberval* Pizarro Marques, Rio de Janeiro, July 13, 1995.
Evangelina de Assis Ribeiro, Volta Redonda, Dec. 29, 1998.
Lisete Lídia de Sílvio Russo, São Paulo, Sept. 30, 1996.
Dom Eugênio de Araújo Sales, Rio de Janeiro, July 7, 1995.
General Mário Ribeiro Orlando *Sampaio*, Rio de Janeiro, April 8, 1997.
Geralsélia Ribeiro da Silva, Volta Redonda, April 12, 1997.
Maria Aparecida de Jesus da Silva, Volta Redonda, Dec. 29, 1998.
Mário dos Passos *Simas*, São Paulo, Sept. 30, 1996.
Geraldo Augusto de *Siqueira* Filho, São Paulo, March 15, 1998.
Father *Orestes* João *Stragliotto*, Belo Horizonte, July 19, 1995.
Tibor Sulik (1) Luziânia, Goiás, July 26, 1994; (2) Rio de Janeiro, July 6, 1995.
Helmo de Azevedo *Sussekind*, Rio de Janeiro, March 26, 1997.
Maria Amélia *(Amelinha)* de Almeida Teles, São Paulo, May 19, 1997.
Father *Virgílio Leite Uchôa* (1) Brasília, June 10, 1993; (2) Luziânia, July 26, 1994.
Aldo Vannucchi, Sorocaba, Sept. 19, 1996.
Paulo de Tarso *Vannuchi*, São Paulo, Sept. 11, 1996.
Luiz Viegas de Carvalho, Rio de Janeiro, (1) Aug. 27, 1996; (2) Aug. 29, 1996.
Efigênia Monção *Virote*, Volta Redonda, April 11, 1997.
Pedro Paulo *Virote*, Volta Redonda, April 11, 1997.

Newspapers and Periodicals Consulted (abbreviations in brackets)

Boletim do Clero (da Arquidiocese do Rio de Janeiro), Rio de Janeiro.
Comunicado Mensal (da CNBB) [*CM*], Rio de Janeiro.
O Estado de São Paulo [*OESP*], São Paulo.
Jornal do Brasil [*JB*], Rio de Janeiro.
Revista Eclesiástica Brasileira [*REB*], Petrópolis.
Serviço de Documentação [*SEDOC*], Petrópolis.

Books and Articles

Abramo, Bia, ed. 1997. *Um trabalhador da notícia: textos de Perseu Abramo.* São Paulo: Editora Fundação Perseu Abramo.
Abreu, Hugo. 1979. *O outro lado do poder.* Rio de Janeiro: Editora Nova Fronteira.
Actes do Tribunal Russell II. 1974. Rome.

References

Albuquerque, Walter Pires de Carvalho e. 1985. *Administração Gen. Ex. Walter Pires de Carvalho e Albuquerque.* Rio de Janeiro: Biblioteca do Exército.

"Alceu: 85 anos. Homenagem ao grande brasileiro." 1978. *Encontros com a Civilização Brasileira* 6 (Dec.), special issue.

Alceu Amoroso Lima (1893–1983): bibliografia e estudos críticos. 1987. Salvador: Centro de Documentação do Pensamento Brasileiro.

Almeida, Candido Antonio José Francisco Mendes de. 1943. *O senador do Império Candido Mendes de Almeida:* Rio de Janeiro: n.p.

———. 1959. *Perspectiva atual da América Latina.* Rio de Janeiro: ISEB.

———. 1963. *Nacionalismo e desenvolvimento.* Rio de Janeiro: Instituto Brasileiro de Estudos Afro-Asiáticos.

———. 1966a. *Memento dos vivos: a esquerda católica no Brasil.* Rio de Janeiro: Tempo Brasileiro.

———. 1966b. "Sistema político e modelos de poder no Brasil." *Dados,* 7–41.

———. 1969. "Elites de poder, democracia e desenvolvimento." *Dados,* 57–90.

———. 1972. "The Potential and the Promise: A Challenge to the Intelligentsia." In *One Spark from Holocaust: The Crisis in Latin America,* ed. Elaine H. Burnell, 168–75. New York: Center for the Study of Democratic Institutions.

———. 1977. *Beyond Populism.* Translated by L. Gray Cowan. Albany: State University of New York.

———. 1996. *O vinco do recado.* Rio de Janeiro: Editora Nova Fronteira.

Almeida, Candido Antonio José Francisco Mendes de, and Marina Bandeira. 1996. *Comissão Brasileira Justiça e Paz (1969–1995): empenho e memória.* Rio de Janeiro: Educam.

Almeida, Candido Antonio José Francisco Mendes de, et al. 1973. *O outro desenvolvimento.* Rio de Janeiro: Editora Artenova.

———. 1993. *Dr. Alceu e o laicato hoje no Brasil.* Rio de Janeiro: Editora Nova Fronteira.

Almeida, Luciano Mendes. 1994. "Igreja e regime militar de 64." In *Pastoral da Igreja no Brasil nos anos 70: caminhos, experiências e dimensões,* ed. Instituto Nacional de Pastoral, 15–21. Petrópolis: Vozes.

Almeida, Maria Hermínia Tavares de, and Luiz Weis. 1998. "Carro-zero e pau-de-arara: o cotidiano da oposição da classe média ao regime militar." In *História da vida privada no Brasil,* ed. Fernando A. Novais and Lilia Moritz Schwarcz, 4:320–409. São Paulo: Companhia das Letras.

Almeida Filho, Hamilton. 1978. *A sangue-quente: a morte do jornalista Vladimir Herzog.* São Paulo: Alfa-Omega.

Alves, Márcio Moreira. 1967. *Torturas e torturados.* 2nd edition. Rio de Janeiro: Empresa Jornalística.

———. 1968. *O Cristo do povo.* Rio de Janeiro: Editora Sabiá.

———. 1973. *A Grain of Mustard Seed.* Garden City, N.Y.: Anchor Books.

———. 1979. *A Igreja e a política no Brasil.* São Paulo: Brasiliense.

Alves, Maria Helena Moreira. 1985. *Estado e oposição no Brasil, 1964–1984.* Translated by Clóvis Marques. Petrópolis: Vozes.

"A marca da cruz para trás ficou." 1978. *Em Tempo.*

"Amérique Latine: les très discrètes conférences des armées américaines." 1995. *Diffusion de l'Information sur l'Amérique Latine* No. 1943 (Jan. 4).

Amnesty International. 1973. *Report on Allegations of Torture in Brazil.* Palo Alto, Calif.: Amnesty International.

278

_____. 1990. *Brazil: Torture and Extrajudicial Execution in Urban Brazil.* London: Amnesty International Publications.

Antoine, Charles. 1970. *Church and Power in Brazil.* Translated by Peter Nelson. Maryknoll, N.Y.: Orbis Books.

_____. 1980. *O integrismo brasileiro.* Translated by João Guilherme Linke. Rio de Janeiro: Civilização Brasileira.

_____. 1999. *Guerre froide et Eglise Catholique: l'Amerique latine.* Paris: Cerf.

APERJ. *See* Arquivo Público do Estado do Rio de Janeiro (APERJ).

Aquino, Maria Aparecida. 1995. "Caminhos cruzados: imprensa e estado autoritário no Brasil." Ph.D. thesis, Universidade de São Paulo.

Archdiocese of São Paulo. 1985. *Brasil: nunca mais.* Petrópolis: Vozes.

_____. 1988. *Perfil dos atingidos.* Petrópolis: Vozes.

Argolo, José A., Kátia Ribeiro, and Luiz Alberto M. Fortunato. 1996. *A direita explosiva no Brasil.* Rio de Janeiro: Mauad.

Arns, Paulo Evaristo. 1978. *Em defesa dos direitos humanos. Encontro com o repórter.* Rio de Janeiro: Civilização Brasileira.

Arquivo Público do Estado do Rio de Janeiro (APERJ). 1996a. *DOPS: a lógica da desconfiança.* Rio de Janeiro: Arquivo Público do Estado.

_____. 1996b. *Os arquivos das polícias políticas: reflexos de nossa história contemporânea.* Rio de Janeiro: Fundação de Amparo à Pesquisa do Estado do Rio de Janeiro.

Arruda, Roldão O. 1996. "D. Paulo relembra diálogo com generais." *OESP*, Sept. 8, p. A30.

Azevedo, Ricardo de, and Flamarion Maués, eds. 1997. *Rememória: entrevistas sobre o Brasil do século XX.* São Paulo: Editora Fundação Perseu Abramo.

Baer, Werner. 1995. *The Brazilian Economy: Growth and Development.* 4th edition. Westport, Conn.: Praeger.

Baffa, Ayrton. 1989. *Nos porões do SNI: o retrato do monstro de cabeça oca.* Rio de Janeiro: Editora Objetiva.

Bandeira, Marina. 1978. "D. Hélder Câmara e o Vaticano II." *Revista de Cultura Vozes*, year 72, vol. 82, no. 10 (Dec.): 73–76.

_____. 1994. "Alguns aspectos. Acentuações." In *Pastoral da Igreja no Brasil nos anos 70: caminhos, experiências e dimensões,* ed. INP, 73–82. Petrópolis: Vozes.

Barboza, Mário Gibson. 1992. *Na diplomacia, o traço todo da vida.* Rio de Janeiro: Record.

Barros, Raimundo Caramuru de. 1994a. "A tensão escatalógica e a pastoral." In *Pastoral da Igreja no Brasil nos anos 1970: caminhos, experiências e dimensões,* ed. INP, 161–85. Petrópolis: Vozes.

_____ (Servus Mariae). 1994b. *Para entender a Igreja no Brasil: a caminhada que culminou no Vaticano II, 1930–1968.* Petrópolis: Vozes.

Beloch, Israel, and Alzira Alves de Abreu, eds. 1984. *Dicionário histórico-biográfico brasileiro, 1930–1983.* 3 vols. Rio de Janeiro: FGV/CPDOC; Forense Universitário/FINEP.

Beozzo, José Oscar. 1986. "A Igreja entre a Revolução de 1930, o Estado Novo e a redemocratização." In *História geral da civilização brasileira,* ed. Boris Fausto, tomo 3, vol. 4, pp. 271–341. São Paulo: DIFEL.

_____. 1994. *A Igreja do Brasil.* Petrópolis: Vozes.

Bernal, Sergio. 1989. *CNBB—da Igreja da Cristandade à Igreja dos pobres.* São Paulo: Edições Loyola.

Bernstein, Carl, and Marco Politi. 1996. *His Holiness: John Paul II and the Hidden History of Our Time.* New York: Doubleday.

References

Berryman, Phillip. 1987. *Liberation Theology*. Philadelphia: Temple University Press.

_____. 1996. *Religion in the Megacity: Catholic and Protestant Portraits from Latin America.* Maryknoll, N.Y.: Orbis Books.

Bickford, Louis. 1998. "Human Rights Archives and Research on Historical Memory: Argentina, Chile, and Uruguay," consultant report, Ford Foundation, Santiago, Chile.

Bicudo, Hélio Pereira. 1976. *Meu depoimento sobre o esquadrão da morte*. São Paulo: Pontifícia Comissão de Justiça e Paz.

Bierrenbach, Julio de Sá. 1996. *1954–1964: uma década política*. Rio de Janeiro: Domínio Público.

Bittencourt, Getúlio, and Paulo Markun. 1979. *D. Paulo Evaristo Arns: o cardeal do povo*. São Paulo: Alfa-Omega.

Blancarte, Roberto. 1992. *Historia de la Iglesia católica en México*. Mexico City: Fondo de Cultura Económica.

Boff, Leonardo. 1978. *Jesus Christ Liberator*. Translated by Patrick Hughes. Maryknoll, N.Y.: Orbis Books.

_____. 1985. *Church: Charism and Power*. Translated by John W. Diercksmeier. New York: Crossroad.

Branch, Taylor. 1988. *Parting the Waters: America in the King Years, 1954–63*. New York: Simon and Schuster.

Brandão, Carlos Rodrigues. 1992. "Crença e identidade, campo religioso e mudança cultural." In *Catolicismo: unidade religiosa e pluralismo cultural*, ed. Pierre Sanchis, 7–74. São Paulo: Edições Loyola.

"Brazil: Government by Torture." 1970. *Look* 34.14, July 14, pp. 70–71.

Brown, Diana DeG. 1994. *Umbanda: Religion and Politics in Urban Brazil*. New York: Columbia University Press.

Bruneau, Thomas C. 1974a. *O catolicismo brasileiro em época de transição*. Translated by Margarida Oliva. São Paulo: Edições Loyola.

_____. 1974b. *The Political Transformation of the Brazilian Catholic Church*. London: Cambridge University Press.

_____. 1982. *The Church in Brazil: The Politics of Religion*. Austin: University of Texas Press.

Burdick, John. 1993. *Looking for God in Brazil*. Berkeley and Los Angeles: University of California Press.

Burnell, Elaine H., ed. 1972. *One Spark from Holocaust: The Crisis in Latin America*. New York: Center for the Study of Democratic Institutions.

Burr, William. 1998. *The Kissinger Transcripts: The Top-Secret Talks with Beijing and Moscow.* New York: New Press.

Burton, Michael, Richard Gunther, and John Higley. 1992. "Introduction: Elite Transformations and Democratic Regimes." In *Elites and Democratic Consolidation in Latin America and Southern Europe*, ed. John Higley and Richard Gunther, 1–37. Cambridge, England: Cambridge University Press.

Cabral, Pedro Corrêa. 1993. *Xambioá: guerrilha no Araguaia*. Rio de Janeiro: Record.

Caldeira, Teresa Pires do Rio. 1991. "Direitos humanos ou 'privilégios de bandidos'?" *Novos Estudos CEBRAP* (July): 162–74.

Callado, Antônio. 1964. *Tempo de Arraes: padres e comunistas na revolução sem violência*. Rio de Janeiro: José Alvaro.

Calliari, Ivo. 1996. *D. Jaime Câmara: diário do IV cardeal arcebispo do Rio de Janeiro*. Rio de Janeiro: Léo Christiano Editorial.

Câmara, Hélder. 1979. *The Conversions of a Bishop. An Interview with José de Broucker.* Translated by Hilary Davies. New York: Collins.

Câmara, Hélder, et al. 1973. *Eu ouvi os clamores do meu povo.* Salvador: Editora Beneditina.

Camargo, Cândido Procópio Ferreira de. 1971. *Igreja e desenvolvimento.* São Paulo: CEBRAP.

Campos, Roberto. 1994. *A lanterna na popa.* Rio de Janeiro: Topbooks.

Cancelli, Elizabeth. 1993. *O mundo da violência: a polícia da era Vargas.* Brasília: Editora Universidade de Brasília.

Cardoso, Fernando Henrique, et al. 1975. *São Paulo 1975: crescimento e pobreza.* São Paulo: Edições Loyola.

Carter, Miguel. 1991. *El papel da la Iglesia en la caída de Stroessner.* Asunción: RP Ediciones.

Carvalho, José Murilo de. 1982. "Armed Forces and Politics in Brazil, 1930–1945." *Hispanic American Historical Review* 62.2 (May): 193–223.

————. 1987. *Os bestializados: o Rio de Janeiro e a república que não foi.* Rio de Janeiro: Companhia das Letras.

Casanova, José. 1994. *Public Religions in the Modern World.* Chicago: University of Chicago Press.

Castanho, Amaury. 1973. *Direitos humanos: aspiração ou realidade?* São Paulo: Edições Loyola.

Castello Branco, Carlos. 1979. *Os militares no poder.* 4 vols. Rio de Janeiro: Nova Fronteira.

Castro, Celso. 1990. *O espírito militar.* Rio de Janeiro: Jorge Zahar Editor.

————. 1995. *Os militares e a república.* Rio de Janeiro: Jorge Zahar Editor.

Cavalcanti, H. B. 1992. "Political Cooperation and Religious Repression: Presbyterians Under Military Rule in Brazil, 1964–1974." *Review of Religious Research* 34.2 (Dec.): 97–116.

CELAM. *See* Conselho Episcopal Latino-Americano (CELAM).

Celebrações litúrgicas por ocasião do sesquicentenário da independência. 1972. São Paulo: Edições Paulinas.

Centro Ecumênico de Documentação e Informação. 1979. *Repression Against the Church in Brazil, 1968–1978.* English translation. Austin: n.p.

Cezimbra, Márcia. 1992. "Psicóloga defende tese sobre a violência difundida no país após a ditadura." *JB*, May 19, p. 6.

Chesnut, R. Andrew. 1995. "Assembly of the Anointed: Pentecostalism and the Pathogens of Poverty in an Amazonian City of Brazil, 1962–1993." Ph.D. dissertation, University of California, Los Angeles.

————. 1997. *Born Again in Brazil.* Philadelphia: Temple University Press.

Chevigny, Paul. 1995. *Edge of the Knife: Police Violence in the Americas.* New York: New Press.

Cirano, Marcos. 1983. *Os caminhos de Dom Hélder.* Recife: Editora Guararapes.

CJP-BR. *See* Comissão Pontifícia Justiça e Paz–Seção Brasileira (CJP-BR).

CNBB. *See* Conferência Nacional dos Bispos do Brasil (CNBB).

Cohen, Youssef. 1989. *The Manipulation of Consent: The State and Working-Class Consciousness in Brazil.* Pittsburgh: University of Pittsburgh Press.

Coimbra, Cecília. 1995. *Guardiães da ordem: uma viagem pelas práticas psi no Brasil do "Milagre".* Rio de Janeiro: Oficina do Autor.

Comblin, José. 1979. *The Church and the National Security State.* Maryknoll, N.Y.: Orbis Books.

————. 1984. "Dom Hélder e o novo modelo episcopal do Vaticano II." *Perspectivas Teológico-Pastorais* 3.4, pp. 23–45.

Comissão de Familiares de Mortos e Desaparecidos Políticos et al. 1996. *Dossiê dos mortos e desaparecidos políticos a partir de 1964.* São Paulo: Governo do Estado de São Paulo.

References

Comissão Pontifícia Justiça e Paz–Seção Brasileira (CJP-BR). 1971. *I Seminário Brasileiro de Justiça e Paz. IV Encontro regional latino-americano. Anais.* Rio de Janeiro.

Conferência Nacional dos Bispos do Brasil (CNBB). 1973. *Direitos humanos.* São Paulo: Edições Paulinas.

————. 1983. *Comissão Justiça e Paz. Documentos normativos.* Series "Estudos da CNBB," No. 38. São Paulo: Edições Paulinas.

————. 1984. *Membros da Conferência Nacional dos Bispos do Brasil.* São Paulo: Edições Paulinas.

————. 1997. *Cristo liberta de todas as prisões.* São Paulo: Editorial Salesiana Dom Bosco.

Conniff, Michael L. 1989. "The National Elite." In *Modern Brazil: Elites and Masses in Historical Perspective,* ed. Michael L. Conniff and Frank D. McCann, 23–46. Lincoln: University of Nebraska Press.

Conniff, Michael L., and Frank D. McCann. 1989a. "Introduction." In *Modern Brazil: Elites and Masses in Historical Perspective,* ed. Michael L. Conniff and Frank D. McCann, ix–xxiv. Lincoln: University of Nebraska Press.

————, eds. 1989b. *Modern Brazil: Elites and Masses in Historical Perspective.* Lincoln: University of Nebraska Press, 1989.

Conselho Episcopal Latino-Americano (CELAM). 1985. *A Igreja na atual transformação da América Latina à luz do Concílio.* 1969. Reprint, Petrópolis: Vozes.

Cornwell, John. 1999. *Hitler's Pope: The Secret History of Pius XII.* New York: Viking.

Costa, Raymundo de Souza. 1979. "Investigação no clero." *Veja,* April 11, pp. 3–6, 8.

Cotta, Pery. 1997. *Calandra: o sufoco da imprensa nos anos de chumbo.* Rio de Janeiro: Bertrand Brasil.

Couto, Ronaldo Costa. 1998. *História indiscreta da ditadura e da abertura: Brasil, 1965–1985.* Rio de Janeiro: Editora Record.

Crahan, Meg. 1989. "Catholicism and Human Rights in Latin America." Columbia University Papers on Latin America, No. 10. New York: Columbia University.

————. 1999. "Religion and Societal Change: The Struggle for Human Rights in Latin America." In *Religion and Human Rights: Competing Claims?* ed. Carrie Gustafson and Peter Juviler, 57–80. Armonk, N.Y.: M. E. Sharpe.

Craig, Gordon A., and Francis L. Loewenheim, eds. 1994. *The Diplomats, 1939–1979.* Princeton, N.J.: Princeton University Press.

Cruz, Sebastião C. Velasco e, and Carlos Estevam Williams. 1984. "De Castello a Figueiredo: uma incursão na pré-história da 'abertura'." In *Sociedade e política no Brasil pós-64,* ed. Bernardo Sorj and Maria Hermínia Tavares de Almeida, 13–61. São Paulo: Brasiliense.

Cysne, Rubens Penha. 1994. "A economia brasileira no período militar." In *21 anos de regime militar: balanços e perspectivas,* ed. Gláucio Ary Dillon Soares and Maria Celina D'Araujo, 232–70. Rio de Janeiro: Editora da Fundação Getúlio Vargas.

D'Araujo, Maria Celina, and Celso Castro, eds. 1997. *Ernesto Geisel.* Rio de Janeiro: Editora Fundação Getúlio Vargas.

D'Araujo, Maria Celina, Gláucio Ary Dillon Soares, and Celso Castro. 1994a. *Os anos de chumbo: a memória militar sobre a repressão.* Rio de Janeiro: Relume Dumará.

————. 1994b. *Visões do golpe: a memória militar sobre 1964.* Rio de Janeiro: Relume Dumará.

Dassin, Joan. 1992. "Testimonial Literature and the Armed Struggle in Brazil." In *Fear at the Edge: State Terror and Resistance in Latin America,* ed. Juan E. Corradi, Patricia Weiss Fagen, and Manuel Antonio Garretón, 161–83. Berkeley and Los Angeles: University of California Press.

Dassin, Joan, ed. 1986. *Torture in Brazil: A Report by the Archdiocese of São Paulo.* Translated by Jaime Wright. New York: Vintage Books.

Davis, Darién J. 1996. "The Arquivos das Policias Politicais [*sic*] of the State of Rio de Janeiro." *Latin American Research Review* 31.1, pp. 99–104.

Davis, Sonny B. 1996. *A Brotherhood of Arms: Brazil–United States Military Relations, 1945–1977.* Niwot: University Press of Colorado.

Declaração Universal dos Direitos Humanos. 1978. 1973. Reprint, São Paulo: Edições Paulinas.

de Groot, C. F. G. 1996. *Brazilian Catholicism and the Ultramontane Reform, 1850–1930.* Amsterdam: CEDLA.

Della Cava, Ralph. 1970. "Torture in Brazil." *Commonweal*, April 24, pp. 129, 135–41.

———. 1976. "Catholicism and Society in Twentieth-Century Brazil." *Latin American Research Review* 11, pp. 7–50.

———. 1985. *A Igreja em flagrante: catolicismo e sociedade na imprensa brasileira, 1964–1980.* Rio de Janeiro: Editora Marco Zero.

———. 1989. "The 'People's Church,' the Vatican, and Abertura." In *Democratizing Brazil*, ed. Alfred Stepan, 143–67. New York: Oxford University Press.

Della Cava, Ralph, and Paula Montero. 1991. *. . . E o Verbo se faz imagem: Igreja católica e os meios de comunicação no Brasil, 1962–1989.* Petrópolis: Vozes.

Dietz, Henry. 1992. "Elites in an Unconsolidated Democracy: Peru During the 1980s." In *Elites and Democratic Consolidation in Latin America and Southern Europe*, ed. John Higley and Richard Gunther, pp. 237–56. Cambridge, England: Cambridge University Press.

Doimo, Ana Maria. 1992. "Igreja e movimentos sociais pós-70 no Brasil." In *Catolicismo: cotidiano e movimentos*, ed. Pierre Sanchis, 275–308. São Paulo: Edições Paulinas.

———. 1995. *A vez e a voz do popular: movimentos sociais e participação política no Brásil pós-70.* Rio de Janeiro: Relume-Dumará.

"Dom Sebastião Leme. Príncipe da Igreja—soldado da pátria." 1930. *A Defesa Nacional*, year 18, nos. 202–04 (Dec.): 26.

Dória, Palmério, Sérgio Buarque, Vincent Carelli, and Jaime Sautchuk. 1978. *A guerrilha do Araguaia.* São Paulo: Alfa-Omega.

Dreifuss, René Armand. 1987. *1964: a conquista do estado.* Petrópolis: Vozes.

Drogus, Carol Ann. 1997. *Women, Religion, and Social Change in Brazil's Popular Church.* Notre Dame, Ind.: University of Notre Dame Press.

Drosdoff, Daniel. 1986. *Linha dura no Brasil: o governo Médici, 1969–1974.* São Paulo: Global.

Duarte, Teresinha Maria. 1996. "Se as paredes da catedral falassem: a Arquidiocese de Goiânia e o Regime Militar, 1968–1985." Masters thesis, Universidade Federal de Goiás.

———. 1998. "Entre a realidade e a utopia: Goiânia em 1968." In *1968 faz 30 anos*, ed. João Roberto Martins Filho, 129–44. Campinas: Mercado de Letras.

Dulles, John W. F. 1967. *Vargas of Brazil: A Political Biography.* Austin: University of Texas Press.

———. 1978. *Castello Branco: The Making of a Brazilian President.* College Station: Texas A&M University Press.

———. 1980. *President Castello Branco: Brazilian Reformer.* College Station: Texas A&M University Press.

———. 1991. *Carlos Lacerda, Brazilian Crusader.* 2 vols. Austin: University of Texas Press.

Eblak, Luís. 1998. "A Igreja reage." *Folha de São Paulo*, June 7, section "Mais," p. 4.

Expedito Filho. 1992. "Autópsia da sombra." *Veja*, Nov. 18, pp. 20–32.

References

"Ex-sargento revela local de ossadas." 1996. *JB*, July 12, p. 7.

Fagen, Richard. 1995. "Latin America and the Cold War: Oh for the Good Old Days?" *LASA Forum* 26 (fall): 5–11.

Farias, Ignez de Cordeiro de. 1994. "Um *troupier* na política: entrevista com o general Antônio Carlos Muricy." In *Entre-vistas: abordagens e usos da história oral*, ed. Marieta de Moraes Ferreira, 124–46. Rio de Janeiro: Editora da Fundação Getúlio Vargas.

Fausto, Boris, ed. 1985. *Historia geral da civilização brasileira.* tomo 2, *O Brasil republicano;* vol. 4, *Economia e cultura, 1930–1964.* São Paulo: DIFEL.

Ferrarini, Sebastião Antonio. 1992. *A imprensa e o arcebispo vermelho, 1964–1984.* São Paulo: Edições Paulinas.

Ferreira, Marieta de Moraes, and Leda Soares. 1984. "Lima, Alceu Amoroso." In *Dicionário histórico-biográfico brasileiro, 1930–1983*, ed. Israel Beloch and Alzira Alves de Abreu, 3:1828–31. 3 vols. Rio de Janeiro: FGV/CPDOC; Forense Universitário/FINEP.

Fico, Carlos. 1997. *Reinventando o otimismo: ditadura, propaganda e imaginário social no Brasil.* Rio de Janeiro: Editora Fundação Getúlio Vargas .

Figueiredo, Marcus Faria, and José Antônio Borges Cheibub. 1986–1987. "A abertura política de 1973 a 1981: quem disse o que e quando—inventário de um debate." In *O que se deve ler em ciências sociais no Brasil*, 2:243–85. São Paulo: Cortez; ANPOCS.

Fleet, Michael, and Brian H. Smith. 1997. *The Catholic Church and Democracy in Chile and Peru.* Notre Dame, Ind.: University of Notre Dame Press.

Flynn, Peter. 1978. *Brazil: A Political Analysis.* Boulder, Colo.: Westview Press.

Frei Betto [Carlos Alberto Libânio Christo]. 1987. *Batismo de sangue.* Rio de Janeiro: Bertrand Brasil.

Freire, Alípio, Izaías Almada, and J. A. de Granville Ponce. 1997. *Tiradentes, um presídio da ditadura: memórias de presos políticos.* São Paulo: Scipione Cultural.

Freire, Alípio, and Paulo de Tarso Venceslau. 1997. "Jacob Gorender." In *Rememória: entrevistas sobre o Brasil do século XX*, ed. Ricardo de Azevedo and Flamarion Maués, 173–203. São Paulo: Editora Fundação Perseu Abramo.

Furtado, Bernardino. 1996. "Laudo cadavérico indica que Lamarca foi executado." *O Globo*, July 7, p. 12.

Gabeira, Fernando. 1979. *O que é isso, companheiro?* Rio de Janeiro: Editora CODECRI.

Gaddis, John Lewis. 1994. "Rescuing Choice from Circumstance: The Statecraft of Henry Kissinger." In *The Diplomats, 1939–1979*, ed. Gordon A. Craig and Francis L. Loewenheim, 565–92. Princeton, N.J.: Princeton University Press.

Gaspari, Elio. 1997a. "O professor achou dois esqueletos da ditadura." *O Globo*, May 11, p. 12.

———. 1997b. "Um sacerdote de intransigência." *O Globo*, Oct. 3.

———. 1998. "Torturado não é delator." *O Globo*, April 11.

———. 1999. "A ABIN deve ser fechada." *O Globo*, June 1.

Gazzotti, Juliana. 1998. "Imprensa e ditadura: a revista Veja e os governos militares, 1968–1985." Masters thesis, Universidade Federal de São Carlos.

Ghio, José María. 1992. "The Latin American Church and the Papacy of Wojtyla." In *The Right and Democracy in Latin America*, ed. Douglas A. Chalmers, Maria do Carmo Campello de Souza, and Atilio A. Borón, 183–201. New York: Praeger.

Gill, Anthony. 1998. *Rendering unto Caesar: The Catholic Church and the State in Latin America.* Chicago: University of Chicago Press.

Giordani, Marco Pollo. 1986. *Brasil sempre.* Porto Alegre: Tche!

Golan, Matti. 1976. *The Secret Conversations of Henry Kissinger: Step-by-Step Diplomacy in the Middle East.* Translated by Ruth Geyra Stern and Sol Stern. New York: Quadrangle.

Gomes, Fernando. 1982. *Sem violência e sem medo: escritos, homilias e entrevistas.* Goiânia: Universidade Católica de Goiás.

Goodwin, Richard N. 1988. *Remembering America: A Voice from the Sixties.* Boston: Little, Brown.

Gorender, Jacob. 1998. *Combate nas trevas.* 2nd, revised edition. São Paulo: Editora Ática.

Grudin, Robert. 1996. *On Dialogue: An Essay in Free Thought.* New York: Houghton Mifflin.

Gutiérrez, Gustavo. 1973. *A Theology of Liberation.* Translated by Caridad Inda and John Eagleson. Maryknoll, N.Y.: Orbis Books.

Hagopian, Frances. 1996. *Traditional Politics and Regime Change in Brazil.* Cambridge, England: Cambridge University Press.

Hanson, Eric O. 1987. *The Catholic Church in World Politics.* Princeton, N.J.: Princeton University Press.

Hess, David J., and Roberto A. DaMatta, eds. 1995. *The Brazilian Puzzle: Culture on the Borderlands of the Western World.* New York: Columbia University Press.

Higley, John, and Richard Gunther, eds. 1992. *Elites and Democratic Consolidation in Latin America and Southern Europe.* Cambridge, England: Cambridge University Press.

Holanda, Sergio Buarque de. 1948. *Raizes do Brasil.* Rio de Janeiro: Editora José Olympio.

Huggins, Martha. 1998. *Political Policing: The United States and Latin America.* Durham, N.C.: Duke University Press.

Hunter, Wendy. 1997. *Eroding Military Influence in Brazil.* Chapel Hill: University of North Carolina Press.

Instituto Nacional de Pastoral, ed. 1994. *Pastoral da Igreja no Brasil nos anos 1970: caminhos, experiências e dimensões.* Petrópolis: Vozes.

Ireland, Rowan. 1991. *Kingdoms Come: Religion and Politics in Brazil.* Pittsburgh: University of Pittsburgh Press.

Irmandade da Santa Cruz dos Militares: resume histórico. 1981. N.p.

Jordão, Fernando. 1984. *Dossiê Herzog: prisão, tortura e morte no Brasil.* São Paulo: Global.

José, Emiliano. 1997. *Carlos Marighella: o inimigo número um da ditadura militar.* São Paulo: Sol e Chuva.

Kehl, Maria Rita, and Paulo Vannuchi. 1997. "Madre Cristina." In *Rememória: entrevistas sobre o Brasil do século XX*, ed. Ricardo de Azevedo and Flamarion Maués, 153–71. São Paulo: Editora Fundação Perseu Abramo.

Keogh, Dermot, ed. 1990. *Church and Politics in Latin America.* New York: St. Martin's Press.

Khoury, Yara Aun, ed. 1995. *Guia da Central de Documentação e Informação Científica "Prof. Casemiro dos Reis Filho".* São Paulo: EDUC.

Kinzo, Maria D'Alva G. 1988. *Legal Opposition Politics Under Authoritarian Rule in Brazil: The Case of the MDB.* New York: St. Martin's Press.

Kirk, John M. 1992. *Politics and the Catholic Church in Nicaragua.* Gainesville: University of Florida Press.

Klaiber, Jeffrey. 1997. *Iglesia, dictaduras y democracia en América Latina.* Lima: Fondo Editorial de la Pontificia Universidad Católica del Peru.

Knight, Alan. 1992. "Mexico's Elite Settlement: Conjuncture and Consequences." In *Elites and Democratic Consolidation in Latin America and Southern Europe*, ed. John Higley and Richard Gunther, 113–45. Cambridge, England: Cambridge University Press.

References

Lagôa, Ana. 1983. *SNI: como nasceu, como funciona*. São Paulo: Editora Brasiliense.

Landau, Trudi. 1986. *Vlado Herzog: o que faltava contar*. Petrópolis: Vozes.

Langguth, A. J. 1978. *Hidden Terrors*. New York: Pantheon Books.

LaRosa, Michael. 1995. "Cleavages of the Cross: The Catholic Church from Right to Left in Contemporary Colombia." Ph.D. dissertation, University of Miami.

Leoni, Brigitte Hersant. 1997. *Fernando Henrique Cardoso: o Brasil do possível*. Translated by Dora Rocha. Rio de Janeiro: Editora Nova Fronteira.

Lernoux, Penny. 1982. *Cry of the People*. New York: Penguin Books.

———. 1989. *People of God: The Struggle for World Catholicism*. New York: Viking.

Lesser, Jeffrey. 1995. *Welcoming the Undesirables: Brazil and the Jewish Question*. Berkeley and Los Angeles: University of California Press.

Lewin, Linda. 1987. *Politics and Parentela in Paraíba: A Case Study of Family-Based Oligarchy in Brazil*. Princeton, N.J.: Princeton University Press.

Lewy, Guenter. 1964. *The Catholic Church and Nazi Germany*. New York: McGraw-Hill.

Libânio, João Batista. 1983. *Volta à grande disciplina*. São Paulo: Edições Loyola.

———. 1987. *Teologia da libertação*. São Paulo: Edições Loyola.

Lima, Alceu Amoroso. 1964. *Revolução, reação ou reforma?* Rio de Janeiro: Tempo Brasileiro.

———. 1965. *Pelo humanismo ameaçado*. Rio de Janeiro: Tempo Brasileiro.

———. 1968. *A experiência reacionária*. Rio de Janeiro: Tempo Brasileiro.

———. 1969. *Violência ou não?* Petrópolis: Vozes.

———. 1974. *Em busca da liberdade*. Rio de Janeiro: Paz e Terra.

———. 1977. *Revolução suicida*. Rio de Janeiro: Editora Brasília/Rio.

Lima, Cláudio Medeiros. 1973. *Alceu Amoroso Lima: memórias improvisadas*. Petrópolis: Vozes.

Lima, Luiz Gonzaga de Souza. 1979. *Evolução política dos católicos e da Igreja no Brasil*. Petrópolis: Vozes.

Limerick, Patricia Nelson. 1993. "Dancing with Professors: The Trouble with Academic Prose." *New York Times Book Review* (Oct. 31), 3.

Lippmann, Hanns Ludwig, et al. 1984. *Pela filosofia: homenagem a Tarcísio Meirelles Padilha*. Rio de Janeiro: Pallas.

Loaeza-Lajous, Soledad. 1990. "Continuity and Change in the Mexican Catholic Church." In *Church and Politics in Latin America*, ed. Dermot Keogh, 272–98. New York: St. Martin's Press.

Lobo, Amilcar. 1989. *A hora do lobo, a hora do carneiro*. Petrópolis: Vozes.

Lopes, Eliseu. 1994. "A experiência de Goiás Velho." In *Pastoral da Igreja no Brasil nos anos 1970: caminhos, experiências e dimensões*, ed. Instituto Nacional de Pastoral, 125–33. Petrópolis: Vozes.

"Lorscheider, Aluísio." Forthcoming. *Dicionário histórico-biográfico brasileiro*. 2nd edition. Rio de Janeiro: FGV/CPDOC.

"Lorscheiter, Ivo." Forthcoming. *Dicionário histórico-biográfico brasileiro*. 2nd edition. Rio de Janeiro: FGV/CPDOC.

Loveman, Brian. 1999. *For la Patria: Politics and the Armed Forces in Latin America*. Wilmington, Del.: Scholarly Resources Books.

Loveman, Mara. 1998. "High-Risk Collective Action: Defending Human Rights in Chile, Uruguay, and Argentina." *American Journal of Sociology* 104.2 (Sept.): 477–525.

Lowden, Pamela. 1996. *Moral Opposition to Authoritarian Rule in Chile, 1973–1990*. Basingstoke, England: Macmillan.

Mainwaring, Scott. 1986. *The Catholic Church and Politics in Brazil, 1916–1985.* Stanford, Calif.: Stanford University Press.

Mainwaring, Scott, and Alexander Wilde, eds. 1989. *The Progressive Church in Latin America.* Notre Dame, Ind.: University of Notre Dame Press.

Marighella, Carlos. 1971. *For the Liberation of Brazil.* Translated by John Butt and Rosemary Sheed. Baltimore: Penguin Books.

Mariz, Cecília. 1994. *Coping with Poverty in Brazil.* Philadelphia: Temple University Press.

Markun, Paulo. 1988. "Introdução." In *Vlado: retrato da morte de um homem e de uma época,* ed. Paulo Markun, 9–11. São Paulo: Círculo do Livro.

Martins Filho, João Roberto. 1987. *Movimento estudantil e ditadura militar.* Campinas: Papirus.

_____. 1995. *O palácio e a caserna: a dinâmica militar das crises políticas na ditadura, 1964–1969.* São Carlos: Editora da Universidade Federal de São Carlos.

_____, ed. 1998a. *1968 faz 30 anos.* Campinas: Mercado de Letras.

_____. 1998b. "Os estudantes nas ruas, de Goulart a Collor." In *1968 faz 30 anos,* ed. João Roberto Martins Filho, 11–26. Campinas: Mercado de Letras.

Mata, Sérgio da. 1992. "Ex-dominicano reaparece e fala dos tempos da repressão no Brasil." *Sete Dias* (Sete Lagoas), March 23–April 2, pp. 10–11.

Mayrink, José Maria. 1998. "Dom Paulo, a memória da tortura." *JB,* April 26, p. 12.

McCann, Frank D. 1989. "The Military." In *Modern Brazil: Elites and Masses in Historical Perspective,* ed. Michael L. Conniff and Frank D. McCann, 47–80. Lincoln: University of Nebraska Press.

McDonough, Peter. 1981. *Power and Ideology in Brazil.* Princeton, N.J.: Princeton University Press.

Médici, Emílio Garrastazu. 1970. *Nova consciência de Brasil.* Departamento Nacional de Imprensa.

_____. 1971. *A verdadeira paz.* Departamento de Imprensa Nacional.

Médici, Roberto Nogueira. 1995. *Médici: o depoimento.* Rio de Janeiro: Mauad.

Mello, Jayme Portella de. 1979. *A revolução e o govêrno Costa e Silva.* Rio de Janeiro: Guavira Editores.

Melo, Murilo Fiúza. 1997a. "Ditadura condenou torturadores." *JB,* May 25, p. 8.

_____. 1997b. "Torturadores fizeram outras vítimas." *JB,* May 27, p. 6.

Melo, Murilo Fiúza, and Francisco Luiz Noel. 1997. "Batalhão era centro de torturas." *JB,* May 25, p. 9.

Meu filho Alexandre Vannucchi: depoimento de Egle e José Vannucchi a Teodomiro Braga e Paulo Barbosa. N.d. Edição S.A.

Miceli, Sergio. 1988. *A elite eclesiástica brasileira.* Rio de Janeiro: Editora Bertrand Brasil.

Mignone, Emilio. 1990. "Human Rights and the 'Dirty War' in Argentina." In *Church and Politics in Latin America,* ed. Dermot Keogh, 352–71. New York: St. Martin's Press.

Miner, Steven Merritt. 1994. "Soviet Ambassadors from Maiskii to Dobrynin." In *The Diplomats, 1939–1979,* ed. Gordon A. Craig and Francis L. Loewenheim, 609–28. Princeton, N.J.: Princeton University Press.

Mir, Luís. 1994. *A revolução impossível: a esquerda e a luta armada no Brasil.* São Paulo: Editora Best Seller.

Miranda, Ricardo. 1996a. "Exército reage à reabertura do caso." *O Globo,* July 9, p. 3.

_____. 1996b. "Famílias de 160 desaparecidos serão indenizados." *O Globo,* July 25, p. 12.

Muraro, Valmir Francisco. 1985. *Juventude Operária Católica.* São Paulo: Brasiliense.

References

"Murici, Antônio Carlos." 1984. *Dicionário histórico-biográfico brasileiro, 1930–1983*, ed. Israel Beloch and Alzira Alves de Abreu, 3:2350–52. 3 vols. Rio de Janeiro: FGV/CPDOC; Forense Universitário/FINEP.

Muricy, Antônio Carlos da Silva. 1971. *Palavras de um soldado*. Rio de Janeiro: Imprensa do Exército.

————. 1972. "Brasilien und sein Heer." *Wehrkunde* 21.3, pp. 123–29.

————. 1993. *Antônio Carlos Muricy (depoimento, 1986)*. Rio de Janeiro: FGV/CPDOC.

Nagle, Robin. 1998. *Claiming the Virgin: The Broken Promise of Liberation Theology in Brazil*. New York: Routledge.

Nassif, Luís. 1995. "Documento do Exército admitia a tortura." *Folha de São Paulo*, April 23, pp. 1–8.

Needell, Jeffrey D. 1987. *A Tropical Belle Epoque: Elite Culture and Society in Turn-of-the-Century Rio de Janeiro*. Cambridge, England: Cambridge University Press.

"Neves, Lucas Moreira." Forthcoming. *Dicionário histórico-biográfico brasileiro*. 2nd edition. Rio de Janeiro: FGV/CPDOC.

O'Donnell, Guillermo. 1988. *Bureaucratic Authoritarianism: Argentina, 1966–1973, in Comparative Perspective*. Translated by James McGuire. Berkeley and Los Angeles: University of California Press.

Oliveira, Juarez de, ed. 1996. *Código Penal Militar*. São Paulo: Editora Saraiva.

Oltramari, Alexandre. 1998. "Eu torturei." *Veja*, Dec. 9, pp. 44–53.

"O sepultamento de Branca Alves." 1978. *REB* 38 (June): 351.

"Padilha (Tarcísio)." 1990. *Enciclopédia luso-brasileiro de filosofia*, 3:1301–02. Lisbon: Verbo.

Padilha, Tarcísio Meirelles. 1971. *Filosofia, ideologia e realidade brasileira*. Rio de Janeiro: Companhia Editora Americana.

————. 1975. *Brasil em questão*. Rio de Janeiro: Livraria José Olympio Editora.

Page, Joseph. 1972. *The Revolution That Never Was: Northeast Brazil, 1955–1964*. New York: Grossman Publishers.

————. 1995. *The Brazilians*. Reading, Mass.: Addison-Wesley.

Paiva, Vanilda. 1985a. "A Igreja moderna no Brasil." In *Igreja e questão agrária*, ed. Vanilda Paiva, 52–67. São Paulo: Edições Loyola.

————, ed. 1985b. *Igreja e questão agrária*. São Paulo: Edições Loyola.

Palhares, Gentil. 1969. *Frei Orlando, o capelão que não voltou*. Belo Horizonte: Editoras Associadas do Brasil.

Paoli, Maria Célia, et al. 1982. *A violência brasileira*. São Paulo: Editora Brasiliense.

"Paraguay: la guerre froide des années 70 et 80." 1995. *Diffusion de l'Information sur l'Amérique Latine*, no. 1960, March 2.

"Paraguay: les archives secrètes de l'Opération Condor.'" 1993. *Diffusion de l'Information sur l'Amérique Latine*, no. 1767, April 15.

Passarinho, Jarbas. 1996. *Um híbrido fértil*. Rio de Janeiro: Expressão e Cultura.

Pattnayak, Satya. 1995. *Organized Religion in the Political Transformation of Latin America*. Lanham, Md.: University Press of America.

Paz, Alfredo Boccia, Myrian Angélica González, and Rosa Palau Aguilar. 1994. *Es mi informe. Los archivos secretos de la policía de Stroessner*. Asunción: Centro de Documentación y Estudios.

Paz, Carlos Eugênio [Sarmento Coelho da]. 1996. *Viagem à luta armada*. Rio de Janeiro: Civilização Brasileira.

————. 1997. *Nas trilhas da ALN*. Rio de Janeiro: Bertrand Brasil.

Pedreira, Fernando. 1975. *Brasil política, 1964–1975.* São Paulo: DIFEL.

Pereira, Anthony. 1998. "'Persecution and Farce': The Origins and Transformation of Brazil's Political Trials, 1964–1979." *Latin American Research Review* 33.1, pp. 43–66.

Pereira, Antônio Aparecido. 1982. "A Igreja e a censura à imprensa no Brasil, 1968–1978 (Com particular atenção à censura ao semanário arquidiocesano 'O São Paulo')." Rome: Tesi de diploma in Giornalismo, Centro Internazionale per gli Studi sull'Opinione Pubblica.

Pereira, Luís Estevam. 1986. "Alexandre Vannucchi Leme: verdades e mentiras." *Jornal do Campus* 31, p. 6.

Pereira, Pablo. 1996. "Diálogo Igreja-militares incluiu empresários." *OESP,* March 4, p. A-14.

Peritore, N. Patrick. 1989. "Liberation Theology in the Brazilian Catholic Church: A Q-Methodology Study of the Diocese of Rio de Janeiro in 1985." *Luso-Brazilian Review* 26.1 (summer): 59–92.

Perlman, Janice. 1976. *The Myth of Marginality: Urban Poverty and Politics in Rio de Janeiro.* Berkeley and Los Angeles: University of California Press.

Petry, André. 1998. "Porão iluminado." *Veja,* Dec. 9, pp. 42–43.

Pierucci, Antônio Flávio de Oliveira. 1978. *Igreja: contradições e acomodação. Ideologia do clero católico sobre a reprodução humana no Brasil.* Cadernos CEBRAP No. 30. São Paulo: Brasiliense.

Piletti, Nelson, and Walter Praxedes. 1997. *Dom Hélder Câmara: entre o poder e a profecia.* São Paulo: Editora Ática.

Pimenta, João Paulo Garrido. 1995. "Os arquivos do DEOPS-SP: nota preliminar." *Revista de História* 132, pp. 149–54.

Pinheiro, José Ernanne. 1994. "Uma visão a partir de Olinda e Recife—um depoimento pastoral." In *Pastoral da Igreja no Brasil nos anos 70: caminhos, experiências e dimensões,* ed. Instituto Nacional de Pastoral, 101–25. Petrópolis: Vozes.

Pinheiro, Paulo Sérgio. 1982. "Polícia e crise política: o caso das polícias militares." In Maria Célia Paoli, et al., *A violência brasileira,* 57–91. São Paulo: Editora Brasiliense.

Pinto, Bilac. 1964. *Guerra revolucionária.* Rio de Janeiro: Forense.

Pomar, Valter, and Waldeli Melleiro. 1997. "Maria Augusta Capistrano." In *Rememória: entrevistas sobre o Brasil do século XX,* ed. Ricardo de Azevedo and Flamarion Maués, 349–71. São Paulo: Editora Fundação Perseu Abramo.

Pope, Clara Amanda. 1985. "Human Rights and the Catholic Church in Brazil, 1970–1983." *Journal of Church and State* 27.3 (autumn): 429–52.

Portela, Fernando. 1979. *Guerra de guerrilhas no Brasil.* São Paulo: Editora Global.

Power, Timothy, and Peter Kingstone, eds. 2000. *Democratic Brazil: Actors, Institutions, and Processes.* Pittsburgh: University of Pittsburgh Press.

Prado, Antonio Carlos. 1990. "Um corpo da ditadura." *IstoÉ/Senhor,* Sept. 19, pp. 20–22.

Prado, Antonio Carlos, and Beatriz Fragelli. 1990. "Luz nas trevas." *IstoÉ/Senhor,* Oct. 3, p. 30.

Prandini, Fernando, Victor A. Petrucci, and Romeu Dale. 1986–1987. *As relações Igreja-estado no Brasil,* 6 vols. São Paulo: Edições Loyola.

Presidência da República. 1970. *Metas e bases para a ação de govêrno.* Presidência da República.

Queiroz, Celso. 1994. "O papel da Conferência Nacional dos Bispos do Brasil." In *Pastoral da Igreja no Brasil nos anos 70: caminhos, experiências e dimensões,* ed. Instituto Nacional de Pastoral, 40–45. Petrópolis: Vozes.

Rangel, Carlos. 1979. *1978: a hora de enterrar os ossos.* Rio de Janeiro: Tipo Editor.

References

Reich, Peter Lester. 1995. *Mexico's Hidden Revolution: The Catholic Church in Law and Politics in Mexico.* Notre Dame, Ind.: University of Notre Dame Press.

Reis Filho, Daniel Aarão, and Jair Ferreira de Sá, eds. 1985. *Imagens da revolução: documentos políticos das organizações clandestinas de esquerda dos anos 1961 a 1971.* Rio de Janeiro: Marco Zero.

Reis Filho, Daniel Aarão, et al. 1997. *Versões e ficções: o seqüestro da história.* 2nd edition. São Paulo: Editora Fundação Perseu Abramo.

Relatório do irmão provedor da Irmandade da Santa Cruz dos Militares. 1952. N.p.

Report of the Chilean National Commission on Truth and Reconciliation. 1993. Translated by Phillip E. Berryman. Notre Dame, Ind.: University of Notre Dame Press.

Retrato do Brasil. 1984. 4 vols. São Paulo: Editora Política.

Ribeiro, Helcion, ed. 1989. *Paulo Evaristo Arns, cardeal da esperança e pastor da Igreja de São Paulo.* São Paulo: Edições Paulinas.

Ribeiro, Ivete, and Ana Clara Torres Ribeiro. 1994. *Família e desafios na sociedade brasileira: valores como um ângulo de análise.* Rio de Janeiro: Centro João XXIII.

Richelson, Jeffrey T. 1994. "National Security Policy and Presidential Directives." In *Presidential Directives on National Security from Truman to Clinton,* consultant and project director Jeffrey T. Richelson, 17–30. Washington, D.C.: National Security Archive.

Richopo, Neide. 1987. "A esquerda no Brasil: um estudo de caso." Masters thesis, Universidade de São Paulo.

Ridenti, Marcelo. 1993. *O fantasma da revolução brasileira.* São Paulo: Editora da Universidade Estadual Paulista.

————. 1997. "Que história é essa." In Daniel Aarão Reis Filho, et al., *Versões e ficções: o seqüestro da história,* 11–30. 2nd edition. São Paulo: Editora Fundação Perseu Abramo.

Rodrigues, José Honório. 1982. *Conciliação e reforma no Brasil: um desafio histórico-cultural.* 2nd edition. Rio de Janeiro: Nova Fronteira.

Romano, Roberto. 1979. *Brasil: Igreja contra Estado.* São Paulo: Kairós.

"Rossi, Agnelo." Forthcoming. *Dicionário histórico-biográfico brasileiro.* 2nd edition. Rio de Janeiro: FGV/CPDOC.

Russell, Bertrand. 1967. *War Crimes in Vietnam.* New York: Monthly Review Press.

Salem, Tânia, ed. 1981. *A Igreja dos oprimidos.* São Paulo: Editora Brasil Debates.

Sanchez, Peter M. 1992. "The Dominican Case." In *Elites and Democratic Consolidation in Latin America and Southern Europe,* ed. John Higley and Richard Gunther, pp. 300–22. Cambridge, England: Cambridge University Press.

Sanchis, Pierre. 1980. "Padres, militares e o culto à pátria." *JB,* Nov. 23, "Especial," p. 2.

Sanchis, Pierre, ed. 1992a. *Catolicismo: cotidiano e movimentos.* São Paulo: Edições Loyola.

————. 1992b. *Catolicismo: modernidade e tradição.* São Paulo: Edições Loyola.

————. 1992c. *Catolicismo: unidade religioso e pluralismo cultural.* São Paulo: Edições Loyola.

Sannemann, Gladys Meilinger de. 1993. *Paraguay en el Operativo Cóndor: represión e intercambio de prisioneros políticos en el Cono Sur.* 3rd edition. Asunción: n.p.

————. 1994. *Paraguay y la "Operación Condor" en los "Archivos del Terror."* Asunción: n.p.

Schmitter, Philippe C. 1971. *Interest Conflict and Political Change in Brazil.* Stanford: Stanford University Press.

Schneider, Ben Ross. 1991. *Politics Within the State: Elite Bureaucrats and Industrial Policy in Authoritarian Brazil.* Pittsburgh: University of Pittsburgh Press.

Schneider, Ronald M. 1971. *The Political System of Brazil: Emergence of a "Modernizing" Authoritarian Regime, 1964–1970.* New York: Columbia University Press.

_____. 1991. *"Order and Progress": A Political History of Brazil*. Boulder, Colorado: Westview Press.

Schwartzman, Simon, Helena Maria Bousquet Bomeny, and Vanda Maria Ribeiro Costa. 1984. *Tempos de Capanema*. Rio de Janeiro: Paz e Terra; São Paulo: Editora da Universidade de São Paulo.

Serbin, Kenneth P. 1992. "Os seminários: crise, experiências, e síntese." In *Catolicismo: modernidade e tradição*, ed. Pierre Sanchis, 91–151. São Paulo: Edições Loyola.

_____. 1993a. "Latin America's Catholic Church: Religious Rivalries and the North-South Divide." *North-South Issues* 2.1.

_____. 1993b. "Priests, Celibacy, and Social Conflict: A History of Brazil's Clergy and Seminaries." Ph.D. dissertation, University of California, San Diego.

_____. 1995. "Brazil: State Subsidization and the Church Since 1930." In *Organized Religion in the Political Transformation of Latin America*, ed. Satya Pattnayak, 153–75. New York: University Press of America.

_____. 1996. "Church-State Reciprocity in Contemporary Brazil: The Convening of the International Eucharistic Congress of 1955 in Rio de Janeiro." *Hispanic American Historical Review* 76.4 (Nov.): 721–51.

_____. 1997. "Anatomia de um crime: repressão, direitos humanos e o caso do Alexandre Vannucchi Leme." *Teoria e Pesquisa* 20–23 [1998]: 1–23.

_____. 1998a. "The Anatomy of a Death: Repression, Human Rights and the Case of Alexandre Vannucchi Leme in Authoritarian Brazil." *Journal of Latin American Studies* 30, pp. 1–33.

_____. 1998b. "Rethinking Repression and Resistance During the Médici Years: The Cases of Barra Mansa and Alexandre Vannucchi Leme." Paper presented at the twenty-first Congress of the Latin American Studies Association, Chicago, Illinois, Sept. 24–27.

_____. 2000. "The Catholic Church, Religious Pluralism, and Democracy in Brazil." In *Democratic Brazil: Actors, Institutions, and Processes*, ed. Timothy Power and Peter Kingstone, 144–61. Pittsburgh: University of Pittsburgh Press.

Sigmund, Paul E. 1990. *Liberation Theology at the Crossroads*. New York: Oxford University Press.

Sigmund, Paul E., ed. 1999. *Religious Freedom and Evangelization in Latin America: The Challenge of Religious Pluralism*. Maryknoll, N.Y.: Orbis Books.

Silva, César. 1973. "La muerte de un estudiante en San Pablo actualiza el problema de las torturas." *La Opinión* (Argentina), April 7, p. 2.

Silva, Hélio. 1975. *1964, golpe ou contragolpe?* Rio de Janeiro: Civilização Brasileira.

_____. 1984. *O poder militar*. Porto Alegre: L&PM Editores.

_____. 1988. *A vez e a voz dos vencidos*. Petrópolis: Vozes.

Silva, Hélio, and Maria Cecília Ribas Carneiro. 1975. *Os governos militares*. São Paulo: Editora Três.

_____. 1983. *Emílio Médici: o combate às guerrilhas, 1969–1974*. São Paulo: Grupo de Comunicação Três.

Simas, Mário. 1986. *Gritos de justiça: Brasil, 1963–1979*. São Paulo: FTD.

Simões, Renato, and Sérgio Ferreira. 1997. "Herbert de Souza (Betinho)." In *Rememória: entrevistas sobre o Brasil do século XX*, ed. Ricardo de Azevedo and Flamarion Maués, 241–57. São Paulo: Editora Fundação Perseu Abramo.

"Síntese cronológica dos fatos." 1973. *SEDOC* 6 (July): 108–10.

References

Skidmore, Thomas E. 1988. *The Politics of Military Rule in Brazil, 1964–85.* New York: Oxford University Press.

———. 1989. "Brazil's Slow Road to Democratization." In *Democratizing Brazil: Problems of Transition and Consolidation,* ed. Alfred Stepan, 5–42. New York: Oxford University Press.

Smallman, Shawn C. 1997. "A Garland of Human Roses: The Origins of Military Terror in Brazil, 1910–1964." Paper presented at the twentieth International Congress of the Latin American Studies Association, Guadalajara, Mexico, April 17–19.

Smith, Anne-Marie. 1997. *A Forced Agreement: Press Acquiescence to Censorship in Brazil.* Pittsburgh: University of Pittsburgh Press.

Smith, Brian H. 1979. "Churches and Human Rights in Latin America: Recent Trends on the Subcontinent." In *Churches and Politics in Latin America,* ed. Daniel H. Levine, 155–93. Beverly Hills: Sage Publications.

———. 1982. *The Church and Politics in Chile.* Princeton, N.J.: Princeton University Press.

Smith, Gaddis. 1994. *The Last Years of the Monroe Doctrine, 1945–1993.* New York: Hill and Wang.

Smith, Peter H. 1979. *Labyrinths of Power: Political Recruitment in Twentieth-Century Mexico.* Princeton, N.J.: Princeton University Press.

Soares, Gláucio Ary Dillon, and Maria Celina D'Araujo, eds. 1994. *21 anos de regime militar: balanços e perspectivas.* Rio de Janeiro: Editora da Fundação Getúlio Vargas.

Soares, Gláucio Ary Dillon, Maria Celina D'Araujo, and Celso Castro. 1995. *A volta aos quartéis: a memória militar sobre 1964.* Rio de Janeiro: Relume Dumará.

Sodré, Nelson Werneck. 1992. *A ofensiva reacionária.* Rio de Janeiro: Editora Bertrand Brasil.

Souza, Luiz Alberto Gómez de. 1984. *A JUC: os estudantes católicos e a política.* Petrópolis: Vozes.

Stein, Andrew. 1999. "Nicaragua." In *Religious Freedom and Evangelization in Latin America: The Challenge of Religious Pluralism,* ed. Paul E. Sigmund, 175–86. Maryknoll, N.Y.: Orbis Books.

Stepan, Alfred. 1971. *The Military in Politics: Changing Patterns in Brazil.* Princeton, N.J.: Princeton University Press.

———, ed. 1973a. *Authoritarian Brazil: Origins, Policies, and Future.* New Haven: Yale University Press.

———. 1973b. "The New Professionalism of Internal Warfare and Military Role Expansion," in *Authoritarian Brazil: Origins, Policies, and Future,* ed. Alfred Stepan, 47–65. New Haven: Yale University Press.

———. 1988. *Rethinking Military Politics.* Princeton, N.J.: Princeton University Press.

———, ed. 1989. *Democratizing Brazil: Problems of Transition and Consolidation.* New York: Oxford University Press.

"Testemunho de paz." 1972. *SEDOC* 5 (July): 107–09.

"Texto aborda psicologia do prisioneiro." 1995. *Folha de São Paulo,* April 23, pp. 1–8.

Tierra, Pedro [Hamilton Pereira]. 1997. "D. Pedro Casaldáliga." In *Rememória: entrevistas sobre o Brasil do século XX,* ed. Ricardo de Azevedo and Flamarion Maués, 373–94. São Paulo: Editora Fundação Perseu Abramo.

Trindade, Hélgio. 1994. "O radicalismo militar em 64 e a nova tentação fascista." In *21 anos de regime militar,* ed. Gláucio Ary Dillon Soares and Maria Celina D'Araujo, 123–41. Rio de Janeiro: Editora da Fundação Getúlio Vargas.

Uchôa, Virgílio Leite. 1995. "Breves reflexões históricas: a caminhada da Conferência Nacional dos Bispos do Brasil (CNBB), 1952–1995." Paper presented at the second Conferência Geral, História da Igreja na América Latina e Caribe, 1945–1995, São Paulo, July.

Ustra, Carlos Alberto Brilhante. 1986. *Rompendo o silêncio*. Brasília: Editerra Editorial.

Vásquez, Manuel A. 1998. *The Brazilian Popular Church and the Crisis of Modernity*. Cambridge, England: Cambridge University Press.

Veiga, Sandra Mayrink, and Isaque Fonseca. 1990. *Volta Redonda: entre o aço e as armas*. Petrópolis: Vozes.

Ventura, Zuenir. 1988. *1968, o ano que não terminou*. Rio de Janeiro: Editora Nova Fronteira.

Verani, Sérgio. 1996. *Assassinatos em nome da lei*. Rio de Janeiro: Aldebará.

Viana Filho, Luís. 1976. *O Governo Castelo Branco*. Rio de Janeiro: Livrario José Olympio Editora.

Vilaça, Antônio Carlos. 1981. *O senador Candido Mendes*. Rio de Janeiro: EDUCAM.

_____. 1983. *O desafio da liberdade*. Rio de Janeiro: Agir.

Wagley, Charles. 1963. *An Introduction to Brazil*. New York: Columbia University Press.

Wanderley, Luiz Eduardo W. 1984. *Educar para transformar*. Petrópolis: Vozes.

Weeks, Gregory. Forthcoming. "The Long Road to Civilian Supremacy over the Military: Chile, 1990–1998." *Studies in Comparative International Development*.

Weis, W. Michael. 1993. *Cold Warriors and Coups d'Etat: Brazil-American Relations, 1945–1964*. Albuquerque: University of New Mexico Press.

Weschler, Lawrence. 1998. *A Miracle, a Universe: Settling Accounts with Torturers*. 2nd edition. Chicago: University of Chicago Press.

Wilde, Alexander. 1982. *Conversaciones de caballeros: la quiebra de la democracia en Colombia*. Bogotá: Ediciones Tercer Mundo.

_____. 1999. "Irruptions of Memory: Expressive Politics in Chile's Transition to Democracy." *Journal of Latin American Studies* 31, pp. 473–500.

Wright, Delora Jan. 1993. *O coronel tem um segredo: Paulo Wright não está em Cuba*. Petrópolis: Vozes.

Wright, Jaime. 1989. "D. Paulo e os direitos humanos—II." In *Paulo Evaristo Arns, cardeal da esperança e pastor da Igreja de São Paulo*, ed. Helcion Ribeiro, 56–78. São Paulo: Edições Paulinas.

_____. 1995. "Dez anos de 'Brasil: nunca mais'." Folha de São Paulo, July 14.

XXXVI Congresso Eucarístico Internacional. Relatório oficial. 1955. Rio de Janeiro: Secretariado Geral.

Zirker, Daniel. 1988. "Democracy and the Military in Brazil: Elite Accommodation in Cases of Torture." *Armed Forces and Society* 14 (summer): 587–606.

Index

Index

Index

Brazilian Expeditionary Force (FEB), 25, 53
Brazilian Federal Tourist Agency (EMBRATUR), 154
Brazilian General Staff College, 53
Brazilian Integralist Action (AIB), 25
Brazilian Labor Party, 55
Brazilian Military Commission, 54
Brazilian Society for Family Welfare (BEMFAM), 156–57
Brizola, Leonel, 55–56, 58, 232
Bruneau, Thomas, 12
Burnier, Father João Bosco Penido, 146–47, 219, 221
business, in Tripartite Encounters, 84
Buzaid, Alfredo, 72, 123, 128, 181; and bishops, 86–87, 138

Calderari, Arnaldo José, 89
Calley, William L., 197
Câmara, Dom Hélder, 36, 62, 91, 149; on Church-state relations, 5, 38, 84–85; dealings of, with military regime, 26–27, 66; friendship of, with Muricy, 49–50, 60; at mass for Herzog, 217; at Medellín CELAM conference, 116; Muricy's break with, 48, 60–63; organizational memberships of, 25, 35; as paragon of moral concordat, 26–27; and political prisoners, 60, 180; relations with military regime, 38; repression of, 39, 167; tactics of, against human rights abuses, 71–72, 76–78, 167
Câmara, Dom Jaime de Barros, 26–27, 39, 167; trying to locate imprisoned clergy, 86–87
Câmara, João Xavier da, 26
Câmara, Joel, 58–59
Campanha da Fraternidade, television public service spots for, 159
Campo Grande, 147
Campos, Dom José Melhado, 207–08, 214
Campos, Father Nathanael de Moraes, 44
Cândido Mendes, 24
Candido Mendes. *See* Almeida, Candido Antonio José Francisco de
Canudos massacre, 24
capitalism: and Church's third way proposal, 15, 115, 120, 223; criticized by bishops, 60, 145, 173
cardinals, 2, 17, 69; Dom Eugênio as, 66–68; and Geisel, 220
Cardoso, Fernando Henrique, 45, 46, 216
Carter, Jimmy, 215
Carvalho, Father Luiz Viegas de, 44

Carvalho, Omar Diógenes de, 93, 109, 121
Casa de Petróplis, torture at, 175
Casaldáliga, Dom Pedro, *146*, 176; accused of subversion, 110–11, 147; aiding posseiros, 129, 147–48, 163; and Bipartite Commission, 102, 108, 163, 225; and Dom Fernando, 145–47
cassação (suspension of rights), 67–68
Castanho, Father Amaury, 38
Castellistas, 30, 219, 231
Castello Branco, Carlos, 13, 108
Castello Branco, Humberto de Alencar, 56, 60, *61*, 220; bishops' influence with, 2–3; and Muricy, 53, 60, 63; presidency of, 29–30, 57; relations of, with Church, 38, 127, 156
Castro, Father Ormindo Viveiros de, 85
Castro Filho, Father João Daniel de, 130
Catholic Church, 33, 139; abroad, 2, 132; accused of subversion, 40–43, 58, 69, 101, 147, 223; activism of, 90, 124, 223; attacks on, 2, 3, 86–87; benefits of Bipartite Commission to, 5, 9–10, 224; and Bipartite Commission, 3; *Celebrações Litúrgicas* of, 139–40; and censorship, 139–40, 180–84; changes in, 35–37, 51; collaboration of, with regime, 40, 222–23; Communist/Marxist infiltration of, 51, 109, 119–21, 126; compared to military, 13–14, 51, 133–34; conservatives *vs.* progressives in, 11–12, 66, 77; dialogues of, with governments, 6–9; divisiveness in, 71, 90, 115–16, 125–26; and Dom Eugênio, 66, 77; and ecclesiastical honor, 159–61; factionalism in, 8, 10, 225–26, 229–31; and human rights abuses, 10–11, 76–78, 139, 164–65; human rights campaign of, 166–72, 211, 216, 228; influence of, 1–2, 5, 8–10, 192; intelligence gathered on, 40–43, 109–12, 222–24; lack of control by, over clergy, 126; and Leme murder, 200–201, 207, 215; looking for definition of subversion, 4, 114; media of, 159, 180–84; military's views of, 18–20, 100, 118–19, 231; Muricy's relations with, 48–51; networking with opposition groups, 203, 216; opposition of, to Communism, 2, 15, 28, 51, 150–51, 221; in opposition to regime, 1, 43–46, 139, 228; patriotism of, 77, 117; privileged role of, 1, 96, 155, 234; public *vs.* private positions by, 5–9, 76–78, 226; radicals in, 1, 9, 58, 122; relations of, with elite, 15–17; relations of, with military, 13–14, 16, 22–47, 48, 100; relations of, with state, 13, 219–20; repression of, 1–2, 41, 44, 102, 179, 221; role of, in national identity,

Index

Index

Index

Vilela, Dom Avelar Brandão, 57, 67, 155; on Bipartite Commission, 93, 100, 102, 122; call by, for dialogue with military, 88; on Church-state commission, 84; on definition of subversion, 114, 222; ecclesiastical honor of, 159–61; on errors in Vatican II, 126; government humiliation of, 233; on Leme killing, 214; at Medellín CELAM conference, 116; and priests' subversion, 69; and sesquicentennial celebration, 140–41

Villot, Cardinal Jean, 73

violence, 217; against Church, 221; Church stance on, 120–21, 167; failure to link clergy to, 131; failure to link Leme to, 204, 207. *See also* human rights abuses; murder; terrorism; torture

Virote, Juarez Monção, 176, 186, 187, 191–92, 195

voice of the voiceless: Church as, 38, 181–84, 216, 225; CNBB as, 1

voting, educating illiterates for, 57–58

wages, under Médici, 35

Washington Luís. *See* Sousa, Washington Luís Pereira de

workers. *See* labor movement

Workers' Pastoral, 179–80

World War II, 25, 53

Wright, Jaime, 172

Wright, Paulo Stuart, 172

youth groups, as targets of Communists, 120

Zioni, Dom Vicente Marchetti, 209

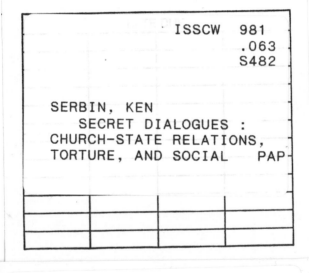